The Larger Life

Sister Devamata's
Life and Legacy

The Larger Life

LIVE in the eternity of God
Not in the fleeting course of hours and days,
Live in the immensity of God.
Not in the narrowness of smaller ways.
Live in the infinitude of God,
Not in the pettiness of finite things.
Rise to the farthest heights of God,
Stay not content to soar on lesser wings.

Sister Devamata
Open Portal

The Larger Life

Sister Devamata's Life and Legacy

Joan Elisabeth Shack
Author of the Biography

Rev. Mother Sudha Puri
Compiler and Editor of the Teachings

2023
Vedanta Centre Publishing
Cohasset, MA

Copyright © 2023
Vedanta Centre Publishers

ISBN: 978-0-911564-24-2
ISBN: 978-0-911564-38-9 (eBook)

All rights reserved. No part of this book may be used or reproduced in any manner whatsoever without permission in writing from the publisher, with the sole exception of brief quotations embodied in critical articles or reviews.

Library of Congress Control Number: 2023935198

Vedanta Centre Publishers
130 Beechwood Street
Cohasset, MA 02025
781-383-0940
centrevedanta@gmail.com
vedantacentre.org

Printed in the U.S.A.

In humble tribute to

Srimata Gayatri Devi

minister of the Cohasset Vedanta Center in Massachusetts
and the Ananda Ashrama in La Crescenta, California
from 1940 to 1995.

A life consecrated to the awareness of the One.

Publications by Sister Devamata

Books
Swami Paramananda and His Work, Vol. 1 & II (1926, 1941, current edition (2016) is titled *Swami Paramananda: Mystic, Poet & Teacher*)
Days in an Indian Monastery (1927, 1975, 2014)
Sri Ramakrishna and his Disciples (1928, 2005)
The Habit of Happiness (1930)
The Book of Daily Thoughts and Prayers (compiled and edited) (1926, 2016)
Sri Ramakrishna and Saint Francis of Assisi (1935)

Articles in *Message of the East* that became booklets
The Indian Mind and Indian Culture (1912)
Practice of Devotion (1913)
Eastern and Western Religious Ideals (1915)
Robert Browning and Vedanta (1916).
Sleep and Superconsciousness (originally Sleep and Samadhi) (1918)
Development of the Will (1918)
What is Maya? (1918)
Health and Healing
 (also likely given under the title Healing in History) (1918)
Companionship of Pain (1934)

Poetry
Open Portal (2015)
My Song Garden (poetry for children)
The Holy Hour

Articles published in the *Prabuddha Bharata*
"Forest Schools of Ancient India" (1918)
"Swami Brahmananda" (1927)
"Has Man Free Will?" (1931)
"Memories of India and Indians" (1932) (6 installments)

Articles published by *Vedanta Kesari*
"Swami Ramakrishnananda, Sannyasin and Teacher" (1932–1933) (10 installments)
"The Individual and the Infinite" (1936)
"Living Presence" (1936)
"Scientist and Seer" (1938)

Table of Contents

Author's Preface. 9
Glossary 13
One: Vivekananda and the New York Vedanta Society
        Laura's Spiritual Journey Begins 15
Two: Laura's Family Background
        Beginnings in Cincinnati 27
Three: Laura's Formal Education
        1876–1882 41
Four: Laura's Family and Travels Abroad
        Sojourns in Europe 57
Five: Spiritual Training Under Swami Abhedananda
        Growth of the Vedanta Society 69
Six: Sister Devamata 1908–1909
        Part I: Madras 87
Seven: Sister Devamata 1908–1909
        Part 2: Calcutta 99
Eight: The First Centres in Washington, D.C. and Boston
        1909–1921 113
Nine: Years of Rapid Growth
        The Twenties 135
Ten: Sister Devamata
        Author 159
Epilogue 176
Spiritual Legacy
        Section One: The Divine 179
        Section Two: Life: Birth, "Death" and Re-birth . . . 186
        Section Three: Building Character 224
        Section Four: Living An Inner Life 271
        Section Five: Spiritual Practice 340

Appendix A 455
Appendix B 459
Appendix C 469
Acknowledgments. 487
Index 489

Author's Preface

This biography was written over a period of ten years, but more earnestly so, in the last five years. Two reasons motivated its completion. A biography of Sister Devamata is long overdue, as asserted to by many in the Ramakrishna-Vivekananda Vedanta tradition. This omission now stands corrected.

Secondly in the early 1990s Reverend Mother Gayatri Devi, then minister of the Cohasset Vedanta Centre, granted my request to spend the three months of my summer vacation living and working at the ashrama. Over a period of two years, no other opportunity for spiritual growth of this type was available. With the publication of this book, my sense of indebtedness to her has been repaid.

The Vedanta movement in the West can trace its strong literary roots to its earliest years, due in large part to Sister Devamata. It was her articles that appeared in the early journals of the Ramakrishna Order, the *Brahmavadin* (1895-1914) and the *Prabuddha Bharata*, begun in 1896. She also submitted articles to the *Vedanta Kesari*; begun in 1914 and considered a continuation of the *Brahmavadin*. In her articles, descriptions of Swami Vivekananda's work in New York during the years 1895-1896 are the only source for much of what we know of those early days.

Some of Devamata's books are classics and still in publication today, such as, *Days in an Indian Monastery* (1927) and *Sri Ramakrishna and His Disciples* (1926). A number of books that carry her teacher's name, Swami Paramananda, are the result of her effort, including the popular *Book of Daily Thoughts and Prayers* (1926). Paramananda's letters and sayings were the source, and Devamata's organization and editing were the means for its publication.

Devamata's spiritual interest and experiences are the truest measure of her life. She would have it no other way. This dedication to the spiritual marks the importance of the second half of this book, in which Devamata's writings on spiritual topics have been organized. Her words are edifying and provide a wealth of spiritual guidance for seekers, whether newcomers or long-term aspirants, as well as students of human life. Every thoughtful mind will be inspired.

Synopsis of Biography

Laura's Role in the Early Years of the Ramakrishna Mission in the West

A highly educated and cultured young woman, Laura Franklin Glenn was born in the Midwest in the nineteenth century. Possessing many talents and practical good sense, she was well prepared for the work which absorbed her. She began serving the cause of Vedanta as an active member of the first Vedanta Society of New York under Swami Abhedananda, Vivekananda's brother monk, for the six years 1901 to 1907.

She became the first disciple of Swami Paramananda, the assistant minister of the Society. In 1907, he initiated Laura giving her the name Devamata, a Sanskrit word meaning, "Mother of the Gods."

As described in chapters six and seven, she traveled to India in December of 1907 and stayed until September 1909. In India she came in contact with great souls, the first monastics and householder disciples in the Ramakrishna lineage, who treated her with love and affection. Their blessings, a rare treasure, accelerated her spiritual life. She maintained an ongoing correspondence with them over her lifetime. This included the Holy Mother, the Divine consort of Sri Ramakrishna.

Swami Paramananda began his work in Boston with a series of lectures at Huntington–Chambers Hall near Copley Square. His first lecture was on Sunday, January 24, 1909; Devamata was then still in India. Upon returning to the U.S., she became devoted to assisting him in his work over the next thirty-four years at the centres he founded in Washington, DC, Boston, and later in California. In the early years, during Paramananda's absence due to extensive tours, Devamata was given charge of the centres in Boston and DC. She became the first American woman to speak from a Vedantic platform. By invitation she also lectured to clubs, associations, and churches of the time, such as the Boston Browning Society and the Unitarian Church in Boston. In the 1920s, Paramananda gave opportunities to other women, monastic and lay, as full partners in his work.

Sister Devamata's Service in the Later Years of Her Life

To her younger sisters in the community, Devamata was a novice mistress and rather strict disciplinarian. Her sense of humor, however, combined with her familiarity with Indian scriptures and mythology, made community gatherings, formal or informal, very entertaining. Devamata stepped down from her leadership role due to her physical problems, and became revered "Senior Sister." Her tremendous will power gave her the strength to surmount her numerous physical handicaps and continue to share in the life and routine of a community. In 1921, for example, she supervised the renovations of the home of the second Vedanta Centre in Boston and in 1928, she insisted on supervising the construction of the Temple of the Universal Spirit at Ananda Ashrama in La Crescenta, CA.

Appendices

Appendix A explains the research done on four topics in Devamata's life. These topics were researched in an attempt to ascertain their validity. The topics have been noted in many literary citations in which Devamata's name is mentioned.

The four topics are: the identity of the minister that Laura and her mother visited while attending a family funeral in the fall of 1893; her family's stated relationship to Benjamin Franklin through her mother Elizabeth Franklin Glenn; Laura's actual birthdate (September 16, 1862); and the possibility that she joined an Anglican/ Episcopal community of sisters, for a short period of time, in order to answer the call within to a religious life.

Appendix B contains five writings of Devamata that are rarely found in the literature of the day. They are: her foreword to the first edition of *Days in an Indian Monastery*; her preface to the first edition of *Inspired Talks*; her foreword to *The Spiritual Teachings of Swami Brahmananda* (1931); her speech on the inauguration of the Bangalore Math in India in 1909; and lastly, her foreword to the first edition of *Book of Daily Thoughts and Prayers*.

Appendix C contains the endnotes for each chapter. Acknowledgements are also given.

Glossary

The following glossary is intended to help the reader with Sanskrit terms and names. Topics are arranged by chapter.

Chapter One

Brahmacharya and Sannyas: The two steps normally taken in the process of becoming a monastic, both steps include vows. A female is referred to as a brahmacharini and then sannyasini, a male becomes a brahmachari and then a sannyasi.

Four yogas: Four methods or pathways used to advance one spiritually. *Karma* yoga is advancement by means of work. *Bhakti* yoga emphasizes devotion to the Godhead as a way of union with the Divine. *Jnana* yoga is the path emphasizing knowledge. *Raja* yoga employs meditation and control of the mind. The end and aim of all four are the same.

Ramakrishna Order: An order of monks who follow the teachings of Sri Ramakrishna. 'Swami' is simply a title which distinguishes them as monks.

Sri: A title of respect.

Swami Abhedananda: A monastic disciple of Sri Ramakrishna and Sanskrit scholar, who was requested by Vivekananda to take up the leadership of the Vedanta Society of New York in 1897.

Swami Vivekananda: (vee VAY ka NAN da) The foremost monastic disciple of Sri Ramakrishna. Vivekananda founded the Ramakrishna Math and Mission and introduced Vedanta to the West at the World's Parliament of Religions in Chicago in 1893.

Vedanta: An ancient Eastern religious philosophy (sometimes referenced as a religious tradition) relevant to all countries, all cultures, and all religions, and inherently liberal. Among its tenets are the following: the existence of a Godhead, the Divinity of man, the brotherhood of all mankind, and the harmony of religions.

Chapter Five

Swami Paramananda: He was initiated into Sannyas at a young age by Swami Vivekananda. He set foot in America at the age of twenty-two to assist Abhedananda at the New York center.

Swami Ramakrishnananda: A monastic disciple of Sri Ramakrishna, he was both the founder and minister of the Mylapore Center outside of Madras, the first center of the Order in India.

Chapter Six

Swami Brahmananda: Sri Ramakrishna recognized Brahmananda (as a boy, Rakhal), as his spiritual son. A disciple of Ramakrishna, he became the first President of the Ramakrishna Order and was reverentially referenced as Maharaj.

Chapter Seven

Darshan: Being in the presence of a deity or person of high spiritual regard.

Divine Mother: An aspect of the Godhead which is represented in female form.

Siddhagopi: Master Mahashaya (M) refers to Devamata as a siddhagopi after meeting her in India. A gopi is a maiden and a siddha is a class of perfected beings.

Sri Sarada Devi: (1853–1920) The spiritual consort of Sri Ramakrishna, she is also referred to as Holy Mother. She spent her days at Dakshineswar in service to Sri Ramakrishna and in her home village of Jayrambati, as head of an extended family.

Yogin-ma: An attendant of Sri Sarada Devi and woman disciple of Ramakrishna.

Chapter Nine

Swami Shivananda: A monastic disciple of Ramakrishna, who upon the passing of Brahmananda, became the second President of the Ramakrishna Order.

Chapter One

Vivekananda and the New York Vedanta Society
Laura's Spiritual Journey Begins

The World's Parliament of Religions, part of The Columbian Exposition (World's Fair) of 1893, drew religious leaders from around the world. Swami Vivekananda, a Hindu monk, journeyed to Chicago to take part in this global event, and successfully introduced the Vedanta philosophy to the West. Of all the speakers he was the most widely acclaimed for his oratorical ability, his learning, and his message of religious harmony.

After the Parliament, Vivekananda undertook a lecture tour across the country. New York City happened to be a stop on his East Coast tour. At the Waldorf Hotel in that city, he gave his first lecture on April 24, 1894, entitled "India and Hinduism."

The city was a metropolis of the Western world; people of all nationalities and races crowded its sidewalks. Cable cars and horse-drawn transit vehicles, both cabs and trams, plied its busy streets. Vivekananda would have taken a cable car on Broadway to attend the theater, and as he traveled around the city, he likely crossed the Brooklyn Bridge. Opened in 1883, the bridge was hailed as a technological feat of its time.

The twilight of the nineteenth century was the golden age of the independent inventor in the United States; a record number of patents were issued. New York State was the hub of this activity. Thomas Edison designed and installed the first large central power station in 1882. His electric lamps lit up New York City. In 1892 Alexander Graham Bell transmitted the first vocal message by electricity to Chicago and George Eastman founded the Eastman

Kodak Co. of New York. In his laboratory, Nikola Tesla worked on his alternating current system.

After a stay of several months in the city, Vivekananda's correspondence with his brother monks in India conveyed his initial reaction.

> New York is a grand and good place . . . the head, hand, and purse of the country. The New York people are very open. [They] have a tenacity of purpose unknown in any other city.[1]

After attending the Greenacre Religious Conference in Eliot, Maine in the summer of 1894, Vivekananda returned to New York City and began to build on the foundation that he had laid for his work in the West. In November he formed an organization, the Vedanta Society, though a bit reluctantly since organizing was not in his DNA. He realized however, it was necessary for his work to be carried on. He did not view the organization as the foundation stone of a new religious society, per se, for he believed that Vedanta was a teaching that could be adopted by the followers of any established religion. By and large, the fledgling organization consisted of officers only, with no real leadership. In December 1895, he set up an Executive Committee to "take up the secular and business side of the Society."[2]

Vivekananda's Lecture Tour Ends

In the beginning of 1895, Vivekananda's work assumed a new trajectory when he took up residence in New York City. He and Leon Landsberg—his right-hand man and disciple to whom he later gave monastic vows—rented two rooms at 54 West 33rd Street. The Vedanta Society now had its first home. Morning classes at the center began on January 28; the *Bhagavad Gita* and the four branches of Vedanta (referred to as the four yogas) were the subject matter for those daily classes. Evening classes were added later. By demand, question-and-answer sessions were introduced, giving attendees an opportunity for in-depth understanding. Early in his New York stay, a number of parlor talks were arranged by his high-society well-wishers. Private and invitational, they served to introduce him to the society of the day—scientists, poets, artists, and scholars.

The lodging at West 33rd Street was not in a good neighborhood and the accommodations were shabby, according to a number of accounts. Financial considerations and racial prejudice were likely influential in the choice of lodging. Though contented, Vivekananda was advised that ladies would never come. As word spread, however, men and women from all levels of society came to the classes. Once all the chairs were filled, they sat on the stairs and on the floor. He did not charge for his teachings. Therefore, when donations in the basket at the door did not cover the expenses, he hired a hall and gave a secular talk on India for the general public. For these talks, a charge was levied.

In a letter to his disciple Sara Chapman Bull, dated February 14, 1895, he expressed his satisfaction.

> I am very happy now. Between Mr. Landsberg and me, we cook some rice and lentils or barley and quietly eat it, and write something or read or receive visits from poor people who want to learn something, and thus I feel I am more a Sannyasin now than I ever was in America.[3]

Sarah Ellen Waldo attended Vivekananda's first lecture in his lodging on January 28. One of the earliest workers of the Society—indefatigable by any standard—she ably assisted him throughout his stay in the city. She wrote, "There was nothing I would not have done for him."[4] In the summer of 1895, she followed him three hundred miles north to Thousand Island Park in New York State, which is located on an island in the St. Lawrence River. During the seven-week retreat there, she took notes of his teachings in longhand; these notes were later compiled as *Inspired Talks*. At this time, she received initiation from him. Haridasa, the name Vivekananda gave his new disciple, suited her well; it means "servant of the Lord." She later became *Brahmacharini* Yatimata.

Early in March of 1895, Laura Franklin Glenn was walking up Madison Avenue in New York City when she spotted a notice in the window of the Hall of the Universal Brotherhood. The announcement read, "Next Sunday at 3 p.m. Swami Vivekananda will speak here on 'What is Vedanta?' and the following Sunday on 'What is Yoga?' "[5]

Having some familiarity with the spiritual teachings of India, she was intrigued. She had read and studied Mohini M. Chatterji's translation of *The Bhagavad Gita* (1887), "looking up all his references to parallel passages in the Bible;"[6] Sir Edwin Arnold's poetic masterpiece, *The Light of Asia* (1879), on the life of Lord Buddha; and Sanskrit scholar F. Max Muller's English translation of the twelve principal *Upanishads* (1884). It is not surprising that Laura had familiarity with the spiritual teachings of India through her readings; she was interested in spirituality and religious life from an early age.

In addition, she recognized the name of the speaker listed on the announcement. It just so happened that Laura, her mother, and her younger sister had attended Chicago's World Fair in June 1893 with every intention of returning in the fall for the Parliament of Religions. The passing of a family member changed their plans. During their travels for the memorial, they were the guests of a Swedenborgian minister, the Rev. Louis H. Tafel of Urbana, Ohio.* He had just returned from the Parliament of Religions. In an animated voice he praised one speaker in particular "who stood out above all others, because of his learning, his eloquence, and his impressive personality." In response to Laura's eager question, "Who was he?" the minister replied, "A Hindu—Swami Vivekananda." As she read the notice, one and a half years later, Laura recalled her conversation with Rev. Tafel and the name of the speaker. As she wrote, both "remained vivid" in her memory.[7]

Vivekananda's First Lecture Season

Laura arrived early at the Hall of the Universal Brotherhood on Sunday, March 14. Though she had a background knowledge of Eastern spirituality, this was her introduction to Vivekananda's teachings and the Ramakrishna movement. Her reminiscences summarized her observations and reaction to his lecture that day.

> By the time three o'clock had arrived, hall, stairs, window sills, and railings, all were crowded to their utmost capacity . . . Vivekananda passed in stately erectness up the aisle to the platform. He began to speak; and memory, time, place, people, all melted away. Nothing was left but a voice ringing through the void. It was as if a gate had swung open and I had passed out on a road leading to limitless attainment. The end of it was not visible; but the promise of what it would be shone through the thought and flashed through the personality of the one who gave it. He stood there—prophet of infinitude.[8]

This was a turning point for Laura. She, and on occasion her Irish setter, attended the rest of Vivekananda's classes and lectures in New York City over the span of two seasons—namely, January to early June 1895, and December

---

*See 'Notes and Research' in Appendix A for clarification.

1895 to March 1896. Throughout this time, she experienced a reticence that prevented her from approaching or speaking to him. It has been documented that his lectures often created reactions ranging from shyness to sheer exhaustion in those present. In the way of an explanation, she noted,

> There seemed to be an intangible barrier. Was it created by shyness or a sense of strangeness, or by my elder sister's prejudice? She had no sympathy with my Oriental studies and often said she wished I "could get salvation nearer to home."[9]

One evening at the close of a lecture, Vivekananda approached her, saying, "You come so faithfully, yet you never speak a word." Leaning over, he laid his hand on her dog's head and called him a true yogi. Laura noted that his touch sent "a quiver through" her dog's body.[10]

From June 18 to August 6, 1895, Vivekananda delivered a series of inspired talks to a small group of dedicated individuals at the cottage of Mary E. Dutcher, in Thousand Island Park, New York. Though Vivekananda had invited Laura to Thousand Island Park, she wasn't able to attend. She and her mother were planning to travel to Europe for the summer to be with her younger sister, Helen, who was studying art abroad. Those plans changed once it was known that her sister Cora and brother-in-law Edward H. Bell, who resided in England, would be in the United States for the summer. According to the *Cincinnati Commercial Gazette*, Laura spent the summer with them in North Carolina, where Edward was designing special decorations for Vanderbilt's Biltmore palace.[11] Laura's mother did sail to Europe in July. However, she returned a year later.

Swami Vivekananda in 1895, the year Laura met him.

Second Lecture Season

During Vivekananda's stay in Paris and London (August 24 to November 26, 1895), the Vedanta Society relocated to its second home, two rented rooms on the first floor of 228 West 39th Street. Vivekananda's morning classes resumed at this address on his return to New York in early December. Both beginning and advanced classes were offered on the same day. Every week topics rotated through the four yogas—*jnana* (knowledge), *karma* (work), *raja* (discipline of mind), and *bhakti* (love).

These four yogas were also the weekly class topics for his first season in the city. Marie Louise Burke, famed author of the six volumes of *Swami Vivekananda in the West, New Discoveries*, distinguishes between his approaches to teaching the yogas. In the first season, she notes that he lays the foundation by explaining each of the yogas in simple, modern language. With regards to the second season, she wrote,

> When one considers Swamiji's [Vivekananda's] teachings as a whole during this second season in New York, one finds him marking out a way for the active modern man and woman, such as had never been defined before. He gave them [the yogas] a new turn, [that] made them fully relevant to and redemptive of [this] age . . . which called for a new model of spiritual struggle.[12]

After closely examining his lectures on the four yogas given in the second season, Miss Burke further clarifies her statement as follows:

> [Swamiji's] combination of yogas harmonizing nonattached activity, renunciation, the inviolate freedom of the Self, the equal divinity of all beings, and the dedicated and reverent service of man as God Himself was as unique in the history of religion as the modern age is unique in the history of the world. It was fully in keeping with the time-spirit of the age—rational, compassionate, active, and meditative. It was, moreover, a path that would produce a type of human being such as the new age demands . . . Whatever their way of life, they would be men and women of high spiritual ideals, of selfless love for all, of strong will with the ability for effective and beneficial action, and the capacity to give their lives

freely in the service of their fellowmen. Such was the new man of Swamiji's vision.[13]

In these new quarters on West 39th Street, no private bath or kitchen was available to Vivekananda. Consequently, he inquired of Ellen Waldo, "The food here seems so unclean, would it be possible for you to cook for me?" She eagerly acquiesced. In describing her task, Laura wrote,

> She lived at the far end of Brooklyn. The only means of transportation was a jogging horse-car, and it required two hours to reach Swamiji's lodging at 39th Street... Undaunted every morning found her on her way at eight o'clock or earlier; and at nine or ten at night, she was on her way home again. When there came a free day, the journey was reversed. It was Swamiji who traveled the two hours [to her home] and cooked the meals.[14]

A faithful group attended his talks throughout the winter season of 1895–96. Laura describes the faithful followers "as relentless as they were earnest." She continued,

> If he suggested tentatively omitting a class because of a holiday or for some other reason, there was a loud protest always. This one had come to New York especially for the teaching and wishes to get all she could; another was leaving town soon and was unwilling to lose a single opportunity of hearing him. They gave him no respite.

Expressing a sentiment that they all held, Laura finally stated, "We were almost sorry that there were only four yogas. We would have liked to have six or eight, [so] that the number of classes might be multiplied."[15] Vivekananda's increased popularity also meant that New York newspapers paid close attention to him now. Articles reported on the influential citizens who attended his classes and the content of his lectures.

In December 1895, Josiah John Goodwin, a twenty-five-year-old British stenographer, was hired to take notes of Vivekananda's talks. He was able to keep pace with his rapid speech; his notes became the material for the Society's early publications. The first two pamphlets, *The Ideal of a Universal Religion* and *The Cosmos*, were published in January of 1896. After working one week, he refused any pay and subsequently became devoted to Vivekananda and his cause. In India he became a *brahmachari* and helped publish the *Brahmavadin*—the first journal of the Ramakrishna Order. Started under the advice of Vivekananda, it was launched in 1895 in India.

To handle all publishing details—editing, printing, and distribution of his books—Vivekananda formed the Publishing Committee of the Vedanta Society in February 1896. His disciple Sara Bull, who was visiting New York at that time, was designated as chairperson. Her managerial ability, business acumen, and generosity of heart made her a good choice. She was given the power of attorney to conduct the committee's business. However, Vivekananda himself gave the stamp of approval for all the early publications.

His closing lectures of the winter season of 1895–96 were delivered in a large arena, Madison Square Garden, which had a seating capacity of twelve hundred. On the second floor in the concert hall, he delivered lectures to capacity crowds on February 9, 16, and 23. The last lecture of the three was entitled "My Master: His Life and Teachings." Newspaper announcements of this lecture placed it "under the auspices of the VEDANTA SOCIETY,"[16] which indicated a growing public awareness of the Society's presence in the West. Laura draws us a picture of the scene that afternoon,

> He began his lecture with a long preamble; but once in his subject, it swept him. The force of it drove him from one end of the platform to the other. It overflowed in a swift-running stream of eloquence and feeling. The large audience listened in awed stillness and at the close many left the hall without speaking. As for myself, I was transfixed. The transcendent picture drawn overwhelmed me. The call had come, and I answered.[17]

Laura's 'answer' may be inferred from her summary of his work in the city. It certainly reflected her newly formed focus on spiritual life as well as a sense, on her part, of the magnitude of Vivekananda's mission. She remarked,

> The time of hearing was over, the time of pondering and practicing had come. As we dwelt in memory on the Swami's teachings and tried from day-to-day to put them in our life, we came to feel more and more that a mighty comet had swung into our hemisphere, shone for a season in our heavens, and swung out again, leaving a line of light behind it. Its radiance still lingers.[18]

Vivekananda left for India via Europe in mid-April 1896 with J.J. Goodwin by his side. Before he left, his lecture "The Real and the Apparent Man" was published in pamphlet form. In addition, the Vedanta Society published its first book, a collection of his lectures on karma yoga, indicating that it was now officially operating as a publication entity for the propagation of Vedanta literature.

At the insistence of her sister Helen, Laura joined her in Europe in the late summer of 1896 after Vivekananda's departure. She returned three years later in early August 1899.

Vivekananda's Second Voyage to the West

Vivekananda and his party arrived in the U.S. for his second visit to the West in late August 1899 and immediately traveled north to Ridgely Manor in Ulster County, New York, for ten weeks of rest. On November 7 he was back in New York City, meeting with his old friends. He was honored at an informal reception at the Vedanta Society, then located at 146 East 55th Street. The Society was progressing well under the stewardship of Swami Abhedananda, who was a direct disciple of Sri Ramakrishna. He had arrived in the city in August 1897 upon Vivekananda's request. Under his leadership, the Vedanta Society had been incorporated under New York State laws as a nonprofit in October 1898.

Later in the same month, Vivekananda journeyed to the West Coast, stopping at Chicago for a week. While in the West he wrote to Abhedananda, "I am trying my best to get one of you for a flying visit to this Coast—it is a great country for Vedanta."[19]

By the time he returned to New York City six months later, in early June 1900, the Vedanta Society had relocated to 102 East 58th Street. For the first time, the Society's income allowed it to rent an entire house for its headquarters, a modest house in a good neighborhood.

A factor stabilizing the Society's income was the Board of Trustees' decision in March 1900, while Vivekananda was on the West Coast, to open a membership roll. Dues were set at $12 a year or $250 for a lifetime membership. Nonmembers would be charged a nominal fee for classes. Many of the early supporters of the Society, largely Vivekananda's students, were highly displeased with this Board decision. Charging a fee for spiritual teachings was not a practice in keeping with the tradition. Though informed of the fee controversy, Vivekananda would not take sides. He believed that organizations and all they entail, like fees, are inevitable in the West.

Additionally, he believed in Abhedananda's freedom to follow his own inner guide.

Upon his return to New York City, Vivekananda expressed satisfaction that the Society finally had a house for its use. He resided there, giving lectures on Sundays and classes on the *Bhagavad Gita* on Saturdays, through the month of June.

At the breakfast table one July morning, Vivekananda designed what later became the emblem of the Ramakrishna Order. Laura wrote about this event in an article for *Prabuddha Bharata*, a journal of the Ramakrishna Order, begun in 1896. The story was narrated to Laura by the Vedanta Society housekeeper, Mrs. Crane. Laura wrote,

> Swami was sitting at the breakfast table... when the printer arrived. He said he was making a circular for the Society and wished to have an emblem to go on it, could the Swami suggest something? Swami took the envelope from a letter he had just received, tore it open and on the clean inner surface drew the waves, the swan, the lotus, and the sun circled by a serpent—the four Yogas wrapped about by eternity, it seemed. He threw the bit of paper with the design on it across the table and said, "Draw it to scale." Henry Van Haagen, the printer, was an able draughtsman as well as printer. He converted the rough sketch into a finished drawing.[20]

Original black and white emblem of the Ramakrishna Order created by Vivekananda and printed on each monthly circular of talks given by Swami Paramananda and Sister Devamata.

Vivekananda explained the idea behind the design in a letter dated July 24, 1900, to Josephine MacLeod, who was devoted to his work. In summary, the wavy waters in the emblem represent work, the rising sun signifies the dawn of knowledge, the lotus depicts love, and the serpent is indicative of yoga. Through these means—work, knowledge, love, and yoga—the vision of the Supreme Self (the Swan) is obtained. The four yogas in visual form!

Vivekananda finished up his time in New York by editing a pamphlet on his lecture "My Master," which was a composite of his 1896 lectures in New York and in England on this topic; preparing a second edition on karma yoga for publication; and setting up a trust fund to handle the publication and administration of the proceeds from his books. Vivekananda and Abhedananda also made a number of outings around the city, including to Coney Island, the Bronx Zoo, and Central Park. They always had an entourage. On July 26, 1900, Vivekananda left for India via Europe aboard the French steamer S.S. Champagne.

There is no written record of Laura having attended Vivekananda's welcoming reception in November 1899, or his city classes held on weekends in the summer of 1900 (June 9 to July 2). According to the 1900 U.S. Federal Census taken in June 1900, she was staying for a brief time with her sister Cora and husband, who lived in the village of Scarsdale in Westchester County, New York, located just north of the city.

Laura Becomes a Member of the Vedanta Society

Laura spent the winter of 1900 in Boston. By the fall of 1901, she had returned to New York City and officially became a member of the Vedanta Society. She authored an article for the *Brahmavadin* dated November 22, 1901. Commenting on the Society's growth in the West, she wrote as follows:

> Never since Swami Vivekananda began his teaching in New York has it been possible to send such encouraging news of the Vedanta work as at the present moment. There is indeed every indication that it has entered upon a new and broader field. The first seven years [1894–1900] were necessarily probationary and formative. Now the work of organization is accomplished, and the society is not only being accepted as an established fact in the community, but is receiving recognition from many unexpected quarters. The membership likewise has increased with unaccustomed rapidity.[21]

This stands in contrast to Laura's description of the Society after Vivekananda's first visit to the West; she then referred to it as a "so-called Society" and "a loosely-woven organization." She noted at the time, "little was accomplished towards giving the group a permanent form."[22] The growth can be attributed to Abhedananda's extensive efforts to expand the movement during the years between Vivekananda's two visits (April 1896 to August 1899).

Vivekananda left his body on July 4, 1902, in India. On October 26, a commemorative service was held at the Vedanta Society of New York. Abhedananda opened the service with an address during which portions of letters from India describing Vivekananda's passing were read. After this, personal friends and disciples of Vivekananda paid glowing tribute to his mission and to the sublimity of his teachings, as well as their importance to humanity.

A year later Abhedananda spoke in appreciation of Vivekananda at the Carnegie Lyceum Hall in New York City. An eight hundred seat theatrical and recital venue, it was located on the lower level of Carnegie Hall. As Abhedananda was prone to do, he held aloft the banner of Vivekananda, saying,

> As a man, his character was pure and spotless; as a philosopher, he was the greatest of all Eastern and Western philosophers. In him I found the ideal of Karma-Yoga, Bhakti-Yoga, Raja-Yoga and Jnana-Yoga; he was like the living example of Vedanta in all its different branches.[23]

Chapter Two

Laura's Family Background
Beginnings in Cincinnati

L aura Franklin Glenn was raised in the Midwest, specifically, Cincinnati, Ohio. The city boasts of seven hills with many gorgeous views of the Ohio River. Locals called it the "Queen City," since it was larger and more prosperous than any other city in the Midwest. The reference to Cincinnati as the "Queen of the West" was first made by the poet Longfellow in the mid-1850s. In his poem "Ode to Catawba Wine," he praised the quality of the wine from the vineyards along the Ohio River.

The origin of the city's name can be traced to a citizen of the early Roman Republic, Lucius Quinctius Cincinnatus. Being civic minded, he left his work to serve as a leader in the military and afterwards returned to civilian life. The Revolutionary War Veterans of the Continental Army saw themselves in Cincinnatus, hence the name of the city.

The Glenn Family in Cincinnati

The first Glenn family in Cincinnati was Laura's paternal grandparents—William Glenn (1800–87), of Scottish descent, and Alice Elsie Miller Glenn (1804–91), of English descent. They met and married in Dearborn County, Indiana in April 1825, and became the parents of eight children. In 1842 the family moved to Cincinnati, Hamilton County, Ohio. It was then a town of about 40,000 residents with cornfields and pastures surrounding it. William began a wholesale grocery business, becoming the city's most prominent and the largest-merchant trader in the Ohio Valley. The Wm Glenn and Sons, Wholesale Grocer's firm thrived for over forty-five years until William's son closed it down two years after his passing.

In the early years, consignments came in on boats to the city's wharf on the Ohio River, which runs southwest on its way to the Mississippi River. Later, merchandise was transported in and out of the city by rail. The *Indianapolis Journal* of July 18, 1887, reported that William had been "identified at some time with nearly every railroad entering the city, either as an early stockholder or a member of the Board of Directors."[1]

The Cincinnati Chamber of Commerce dated back to 1839, but operated as a loose-knit group of business associates that rented rooms for meetings. To consolidate business interests, William helped charter a Chamber of Commerce and Merchant Exchange in 1850, which formalized the organization. Finally in June 1887 the cornerstone of its building was laid; William's son James (Laura's father) was the driving force behind its construction. Its opening in 1890 was part of the celebration of Cincinnati's centennial year. The ground floor was leased to different commercial interests; the second floor was the exchange hall; and three stories of offices and clubrooms soared upward from the level of the exchange.

William was a stockholder in several major newspapers of his time, and his investments in real estate grew substantially over the years. Numerous real estate holdings were listed in his will and testament. Since the margins on grocery trade became less each year, the firm's name (Wm Glenn and Sons) was retained but its purpose changed to real estate interests.

Throughout his life, William was devoted to supporting the work of St. Paul's Methodist Episcopal Church. He was the president of the Board of Trustees. In the seventeen pages of his will that were probated July 27, 1887, in Hamilton County Probate Court, he left $7,000 to support the local missions of the church; $2,000 for the Preachers Relief Society; $1,000 for the Church Extension Society; and $1,000 for the Women's Home Missionary Society. An equivalent amount of money was willed to nine other civic societies that were working in Cincinnati.[2] In the memory of many, William was a man with a large and generous heart. This was a justifiable sentiment even if based only on the fact that $1,000 in 1887 is equivalent in purchasing power to $27,136.59 by the 2020s.

His bequest of $1,000 for the Women's Home Missionary Society was bolstered by his daughter Elizabeth Glenn Dymond's contribution to establishing the Glenn Industrial Home in his memory. It was inaugurated on April 1, 1891, with the purchase of a "stone-front residence of fifteen rooms with a large two-story brick building adjoining." Operating under an independent General Board of Managers, over time it supported "three separate kindergartens, a Young Men's Club, a reading room, evangelical and temperance meetings, Mother's meetings, a poor closet, sewing and cooking classes, and the Glenn Auxiliary to the Women's Home Missionary Society."[3]

William purchased a family lot in Cincinnati's Spring Grove cemetery, which was started in the 1850s. His large plot is marked by an impressively tall memorial statue. He and Alice, their eight children, Alice's mother, and many of their grand-children (e.g., Laura's sisters) as well as great-grandchildren were interred there.

William's wife Alice survived him by four years. She and William celebrated their 50th wedding anniversary at their home on 371 W. 7th Street—one of the most elegant houses in the city in 1875.

Alice was born in Lancashire County, England, in 1804. Her family and most of the extended Miller clan emigrated to the U.S. around 1818–19 and settled in Dearborn County, Indiana. The end of the Napoleonic Wars in 1815 had resulted in periods of famine and chronic unemployment in England. In 1819 the Peterloo Massacre occurred in Manchester, which is located in Lancashire County. Cavalry charged into a crowd of 60,000 or more who had gathered to demand reforms. This event is the most likely reason for the exodus of the Miller clan from England.

The memorial statue at the site of William Glenn's plot in Cincinnati's Spring Grove cemetery.

During William's lifetime, Cincinnati transformed from a commercial trading city to a sizable industrial city. His son James Miller Glenn, Laura's father, lived through a much more tumultuous period when the city experienced a rapid increase in population.

By the 1870s Cincinnati ranked third in manufacturing among U.S. cities. Throughout the 1880s, a general dissatisfaction simmered throughout the country due to the poor labor and living conditions of factory workers as well as systemic corruption in government and big business. The Cincinnati riots of 1884 were among the worst in U.S. history. A nation-wide progressive movement arose to address the problems caused by industrialization, immigration, and political corruption.

James Miller Glenn: William's Son and Laura's Father

Born on a farm in Indiana, James M. Glenn (1829–1911) was thirteen when his family moved to Cincinnati. He completed his graduate studies at Woodward College High School in Cincinnati. Opened in 1831 as a high school, it was granted collegiate powers five years later. After graduating, he worked as a freight clerk for steamboats on the Ohio River for three years.

James Glenn and Elizabeth Franklin were married March 29, 1859, in Pickaway County, Ohio. In the *1860 U.S. Federal Census*, he listed his occupation as a merchant, with $12,000 invested in real estate and $35,000 in personal property.[4] During the Civil War, he was a member of a militia called the Squirrel Hunters that defended Cincinnati from attacks by the Confederate Army. By 1866, he was well established in the grocery business with his father and brothers.

Marriage portrait of Laura's parents, James Glenn and Elizabeth Franklin, 1859.

James was elected director of the Southern Railroad Company in June 1868 by the stockholders of the Cincinnati, Lexington, and East Tennessee railroad companies. That same year he was one of five business associates who formed the Franklin Mining Co. of Cincinnati, which was incorporated for the purpose of mining in the Colorado territory. Later he owned gold and copper mines in Montana.

In addition, he consistently represented the Grocer's Association on behalf of commodities like sugar, molasses, and rice. With his father, he was a member of the Cincinnati Chamber of Commerce, and in 1894 he became its president.

The *1870 U.S. Federal Census* of June 3, lists his household as consisting of his wife Elizabeth, four children, four servants, and his mother-in-law Martha Franklin. At the time of the census, Cora was nine (b. June 1861); Laura was seven, (b. September 1862); Wilmer was one (b. November 1868) and Helen had just been born.[5] Laura turned eight in September 1870.

James was involved in every aspect of civic life in Cincinnati. For example, he was a councilman on the Board of City Dads; he was appointed Fire Commissioner; he was elected as director of the National Insurance Co.; he was stockholder of the Fifth National Bank and later became its vice-president; and he served as chairman of the Finance Committee of the Ohio Republican Party. Additionally, he volunteered to be on any committee that was formed to oversee the visit of a distinguished military general or a state official. James's ambition gave him very little rest.

James owned several buildings in the downtown area, including the Glenn Building, the Ebersole Building, the Wilmer Building, the Potter Building, the Dakota Building, and the Nevada Building. Most were elegant stone structures that housed commercial interests, but some were hotels or apartments. In January 1890 the immense Nevada Building was totally destroyed by fire. The headline in the *Xenia Daily Gazette* read: "A Great Fire Causes a Loss of Over $300,000."[6] The seven-floor building housed sixteen different businesses—a tailoring establishment, real estate office, barber shop, plumbing shop, saddler company, laundry establishment, jewelry shop, printing shop, paper-box factory, shoe manufacturer, and lithographing company.

The Nevada Building was rebuilt largely as an apartment building, but it did house several businesses. Eight years later, the building was set on fire by arsonists. This time the financial loss was insignificant, for a newly installed alarm brought firemen to the scene early.

Having studied architecture and construction in his student years, James aided in the construction of a massive stone and brick municipal building. Completed in 1893, City Hall was a four-and-a-half-story structure, with a nine-story clock tower. The May dedication included a parade, speeches, and fireworks. The Romanesque-Revival style of architecture employed in constructing the building was attributed to the influence of architect Henry Hobson Richardson (1838–86). His style became known as Richardson Romanesque.

In an interview for the *Commercial Gazette* published May 1892, James explained why his many buildings in the city soared skyward. The article also quotes him as having "faith in the city's future." To him, Cincinnati was "one of the most substantial cities on the continent." He explained,

> She is the most prolific of any other in all the material that manufacturers demand and backing up these as a mainstay is her surrounding agricultural districts. We get coal here almost as low for manufacturing papers as they can at Pittsburg. We have iron cheaper. It is the best and cheapest market in the U.S. for all kinds, nearly, of manufacturing woods, and the largest tannery in the world evidences her advantage in tanning barks. Businesses will always be isolated on the lower levels, and the residence city will cover the hills, not only on this side of the river, but on the other also. The residence city is designed to be entirely separate from the business city and as a residence city, both for that reason and her airy, picturesque features, she will be, and probably is to-day the finest residence city in the world.[7]

In May 1895 an article in the *Cincinnati Enquirer* named a dozen wealthy men of the city. James was listed among those who were, "away up in the hundreds of thousands and to whose door the gaunt figure of want is almost certain to never come." The article also noted that "many [of these] would come under the list of millionaires could an inventory of their properties be taken but, as a rule, very rich men . . . do not want the exact extent of their wealth known."[8]

A write-up appeared in the *Cincinnati Enquirer* the summer of 1896 that represented a rare departure from the praise that James usually received. At times humorous, but with a tinge of sarcasm, the article outlined a failed venture as follows:

> The *Tribune*, a cheap morning paper, after struggling since 1893 for attention and existence was merged last night with the *Commercial Gazette*. The new publication will be known as the *Commercial Tribune*. The moving spirit in the enterprise was Mr. James M. Glenn, who for many moons has labored under the delusion that it would be an easy task for him to win success in journalism. . . . [He felt] the field

was ready and the time ripe for a new morning paper. After a struggle of 18 months everybody except Mr. Glenn was convinced that his forte was not in running a newspaper. Fully $500,000 was sunk into the venture.

The article went on to describe his efforts to try again, only this time with a set of personal friends as investors.

> Mr. Glenn, however, had not lost confidence in his own capabilities, nor had the power deserted him of convincing others that he could fill their coffers with great treasures. . . . Articles of incorporation were taken out under the name, *The Tribune Co. of Cincinnati*. . . . Talent was imported, facilities extended and, in fact, everything was done that experience and money could do to make the paper a success. The result was merely to increase the losses.[9]

On November 27, 1911, the *Cincinnati Enquirer* reported, "James M. Glenn, 82 years of age, still one of the most active business men of the city, having but a few minutes before declared he never felt better in his life, was stricken with paralysis while in the office of Charles A. Hinsch, President of the Fifth-Third National Bank."[10] James passed away at Christ Hospital on December 4, 1911. At his funeral service at St. Paul's Methodist Episcopal Church, a large delegation from the Chamber of Commerce, the Commercial Club, and the Queen City Club were in attendance.

In his will, a several-generational trust, he was generous to his married daughters Cora Nelson Bell and Helen Glenn Marx. They each received three-tenths of his estate after all debts and financial expenses were paid. The remaining four-tenths were to be evenly divided between his daughter Laura and her brother Wilmer, and given in yearly quarterly installments. Eighty percent of what remained of his father's estate was willed to Cora and Helen, and their issue. His wife Elizabeth Franklin Glenn received a $5,000 allotment. Overall, his estate was valued at $500,000 at the time of his passing.[11] In terms of buying power, this amount is equivalent to approximately $14,557,315 by the 2020s.

Elizabeth Franklin Glenn: Wife of James Glenn and Laura's Mother

The daughter of Nelson D. Franklin and Martha Lush Triplett Franklin, Elizabeth was born June 22, 1840, in Circleville, Ohio. She was an alumna of Wesleyan Female College in Cincinnati which was founded in 1842 to educate young women. The *Cincinnati Enquirer* notes that it was the "first college to be chartered for women in the world . . . and this alone casts great honor on the state of Ohio, to say nothing of Cincinnati."[12] In 1869 its name was changed to Cincinnati Wesleyan College.

Elizabeth was a member of the college alumnae association, which was founded in 1852. The association was active in the community; for example, in 1882 it pledged to raise $5,000 for "the maintenance of one of Cincinnati's objects of interest."[13] To achieve their goal, a three-day event was held, and donations were accepted. As secretary of the organization, Elizabeth was a member of the executive committee in charge of the project.

A souvenir entitled *Alumnae* was published by members of the association to preserve in writing the complete history of the college. Beginning in May 1842 with a meeting of the founding Methodist ministers, the souvenir ended when the college closed its doors in October 1892.

As members of high society, the Glenn family's comings and goings were always newsworthy. They frequently entertained socially and the newspapers commented on Elizabeth for her "exquisite" taste and "grace." In December 1890, her youngest daughter Helen made her formal debut in a reception held in her honor, at their family mansion on West 7th Street. The *Cincinnati Enquirer* covered the "delightful and charming event" in great detail, calling it the "most elegant reception ever given in Cincinnati."

Laura in her youth as identified by Srimata Gayatri Devi, who knew her.

In part, the article read, "The lovely home was arranged with bright holly everywhere in rich profusion, with a joyous riotous commingling of brilliant-hued chrysanthemums, and tall palms waved a gracious welcome." Since it was a family event, everyone was mentioned in the article. "Mr. Glenn stood near the door extending perfect greetings." The names of guests were announced as they arrived. "Mrs. Glenn and her trio of beautiful daughters received in the front drawing room. . . . Mrs. Nelson Franklin and Mrs. William Glenn [Elizabeth's mother and mother-in-law] were both in black silk gowns with a fichus of white lace." Wilmer Glenn, Laura's brother, assisted in entertaining the "crowd of notable people." The article gave special attention to the debutante: "Miss Helen Glenn stood at the right of her mother, and was a lovely picture in a toilet of white crepe de chine, mixed with the most delicate shade of lavender and carried a superb bunch of La France roses."[14] A band enlivened the occasion.

The three Glenn sisters— Helen (b. 1870), Cora (b.1861), Laura (b. 1862), left to right.

Three generations of the Glenn family owned this Nantucket house for over eighty years.

James and Elizabeth first visited Nantucket, an island off of Cape Cod, Massachusetts, in 1867 with their first two children (Cora and Laura). It became the family's summer vacation retreat. Eventually, the Glenns bought a house at 43 Pearl Street, which later became India Street. The house was in the family for over eighty years; it was sold in 1961.

During the latter 1800s, women of social standing were relatively independent of their husbands. As the breadwinner, a man's circle of influence was the business world at large. Men worked long hours; wives therefore had the leisure to travel. In the 1880s and 1890s Elizabeth traveled extensively with her daughters, in particular to Nantucket for the summer months.

In the summer of 1883, Elizabeth and her eldest daughter Cora, the wife of Leicester Sargent, vacationed on the island. Cora and Leicester had been married a year earlier in New York City at St. Thomas Church; Laura was the bridesmaid. In August of that summer, Leicester, his brother, and two friends sailed by yacht from New Haven, Connecticut, to join Cora and her mother. An unexpected storm swamped the yacht. All four were lost at sea. The *New Haven Daily Morning Journal and Courier* reported, "The sunken yacht was discovered . . . near the entrance to Buzzard's Bay."[15] The whole family was devastated; Cora and her father identified the bodies.

Eight years later, in the summer of 1891, Elizabeth vacationed at the Glenn house in Nantucket with Laura. Over the years at Nantucket, Elizabeth and her husband James corresponded. A significant number of her missives were full of motherly concern for their son Wilmer. She wrote that he was "falling back into his old habits" and needed to gain "self-mastery." In one letter she concluded with

Letter written by Elizabeth F. Glenn to her husband James while summering in Nantucket, 1904.

hope, "I must bear the grief with greater courage... and lean upon... Providence [who] can right all wrongs, correct all evils." In another missive, she expresses confidence that "God will hear and answer them [her prayers]."[16]

Reading Elizabeth's replies to James, it is evident that periodically he requested her to accept a reduction in her monthly income. In the beginning she did agree, but in later letters she held the line, noting that her funds were spent on the children to "[make] their life struggles as light as possible." She added that neither she nor they "should have to be disadvantaged by losses in his foolish business ventures."[17]

It might have been to supplement her income that Elizabeth bought, under her name, two houses in Nantucket. They were remodeled and then sold. One of them, on Ash Street, was bought in 1882 and sold in 1893. The other was at 85 Main Street. According to the Nantucket Preservation Trust, that house was sold in 1919, six years after it was purchased.

Laura's sister, Helen Glenn and her son Robertson Ward in front of the family's Nantucket house.

Over the years, Elizabeth upheld the family's summer tradition with her grandchildren. During the summer of 1902 she vacationed on Nantucket with her grandson, J. Robertson Ward, (nicknamed Happy). In his unpublished autobiography, he wrote that Elizabeth fell and broke her hip that summer. Staying through the winter on the island to assure her full recovery proved to be a challenge because the house was not winterized. They returned to the mainland in the fall of 1903.

Elizabeth sailed to Europe in the summer of 1895 aboard the steamer *SS Normannia*, an ocean liner operating between New York and Hamburg, Germany from 1890 to 1906. Helen, her youngest daughter, had sailed to Germany in September 1894 to study art in Berlin. Helen's passport, applied for through the U.S. Embassy in Berlin, stated her intention of returning to the U.S. within two years. It was issued October 5, 1894.[18] In her role as mother and moral safeguard of home and family, Elizabeth would have been anxious to touch base with her twenty-four-year-old, unmarried, daughter alone in Europe. Elizabeth returned in June 1896 after a year abroad.

Like other women of social standing, Elizabeth was involved in church-sponsored charitable work as well as in women's clubs. The local Methodist church had several charitable missions in the city. In general, church activities had a denominational emphasis, which was meant to demonstrate faith in practice. As for women's clubs, they advanced beyond their initial purpose of self-culture and social opportunities. As the Progressive movement spread in the country (1890s to 1920s), the idea that women had a moral responsibility to improve public policy took hold, especially among Protestant Christian women. Progressive clubs were formed to take up the prevailing issues of the day. In 1895, four progressive women's clubs were reported to exist in the city of Cincinnati.

At a meeting of one of Cincinnati's progressive clubs in January 1895, Laura read a paper on Working Girls' Clubs. She presented the history of these clubs in the country and practical methods of organizing them based on her earlier experience with them while in New York City. Laura was an influence on her mother, for within a few months the *Cincinnati Enquirer* reported that a Working Girls' Club would be started at the Glenn home on March 26.[19]

At the beginning of the 1890s young women constituted about twenty percent of the workforce, particularly in Cincinnati's clothing, textile, and canned food establishments. By the end of the decade, they were the majority of workers in manufacturing jobs in the city. This was happening across the country. These young women were unskilled and cheap labor, earning at most half the wages of a man, and working in settings largely free of family supervision. This unprecedented social change fueled anxiety about their well-being and moral protection.

The involvement of society women in organizing Working Girls' Clubs was therefore welcomed. Society women had the ability and time to arrange for meeting rooms, bring in motivational speakers, and organize group activities. As for society at large, it accepted working outside the home as "excellent training for those virtues of thrift, industry, and self-control which turned a girl into a woman."[20] These same virtues were needed by a woman to be a better helpmate to her husband, a fact not lost on the upholders of societal norms.

The first National Convention of the Working Girls' Clubs was held in New York City in mid-April 1890; it was a three-day event in the Metropolitan Opera house. Two sessions were offered daily on subjects relating to clubs; for example, "What do Working Girls Owe One Another?" and "How to Make a Club Self-Supporting?"[21]

After Elizabeth's husband passed in 1911, she lived with her children for varying periods of time—Cora in New York; Laura in the Washington, DC, area and later at the Boston Vedanta Centre; and Wilmer in Connecticut. As specified in James's will, their family home had been gifted to the Methodist Episcopal Church as a home for girls—the homeless, disabled, or poverty stricken.

In Elizabeth's will, which was probated on May 21, 1921, Laura and Wilmer were the executors and sole beneficiaries of her estate. She was buried in Eastford Grove Cemetery, Windham County, Connecticut along with her mother Martha (d. 1899). Later her son Wilmer and his wife were interred there too.

Glenn plot in the Eastford Grove cemetery in Windham County, Connecticut. The two graves are those of Laura's grandmother, Martha Franklin and her mother Elizabeth, left to right. Later her brother, Wilmer D. Glenn, and his wife were interred there.

Nelson D. Franklin: Laura's Maternal Grandfather

A farmer and politician, Elizabeth's father Nelson D. Franklin (1804–87) was a well-known and respected citizen, and a large landowner in Circleville, Pickaway County, Ohio. He was born in Kentucky about 1804 to Mary (Polly) Nelson Franklin and Major Anthony Franklin. Nelson's maternal grandmother was Roberta Daniel Nelson. Based on a practice of naming children at that time, his first name (Nelson) was his mother's maiden name, and his middle name is likely Daniel, the maiden name of his maternal grandmother.

Nelson's wife, Martha Lush Triplett Franklin, was born in the Shenandoah Valley of Virginia about 1806. In the *1860 U.S. Federal Census*, their household consisted of Nelson, Martha, and four children, Jesse (b. 1828), Spencer (b. 1838), Amherst (b. 1842), and Laura (b. 1846).[22] Their eldest daughter Elizabeth (b. 1840) had married James Glenn in 1859, therefore, she was not listed in the census as a member of Nelson's household.

In 1834 Nelson was elected County Auditor, and later County Treasurer. He won election to the Ohio State Senate in 1842, representing Fairchild and Pickaway Counties for two years. As a senator, he served on the Public

Institutions standing committee. He later presided at the State Convention held at City Hall in Canal Dover, Ohio, on January 8, 1844. When endorsed by the *State Journal* for another term as state senator, he declined to run again.

Years later he was elected to the State Assembly under the Democratic Republican party. In an article in *The Cleveland Daily Leader*, it was clear that he was held in esteem. The author wrote, "In the Ohio Assembly, sessions of 1856–57, Pickaway County was well represented by one of her sensible, intelligent, honest, well-to-do, Republican farmers, NELSON FRANKLIN, of Circleville, familiarly known in a circle of congenial House chambers as 'Gov. Franklin' because Franklin and Pickaway Counties are in the same Congressional district."[23]

Early in June 1865, Nelson's eldest son Jesse was shot while on a journey to the Far West. Jesse died the next day at age thirty-seven, and the offender was arrested but later released. Jesse was buried in the sands of Moore's Ranche, a boarding house and trading post on the Santa Fe Trail. This incident likely contributed to a change in the dynamics of the family, for five years later, according to the *1870 U.S. Federal Census*, Martha was living with her daughter Elizabeth. The subsequent census reveals that Nelson was residing in Carthage, Jasper County, Missouri, and living alone.[24] His daughter Laura Franklin Thomas happened to reside in the same county.

Before Nelson moved to Missouri, he sold his livestock and farm equipment. The *Circleville Democrat* carried news of the sale. "Sixteen head of horses, fifty head of cattle, twenty to thirty stock hogs, corn in the shock, one ox wagon, and one wheat drill" were all listed for sale.[25] Nelson's property and rent income were put in trust for his children; his son-in-law James Glenn was the trustee.

Nelson died in 1887, in Missouri. According to the New York City Department of Records, Martha passed away in the Bronx in New York City at age 94. She had been residing in a home for the incurable.[26]

Through Nelson D. Franklin's maternal grandmother, Roberta Daniel Nelson (1758– 1813), the family can be traced back to the shores of England using Ancestry.com. Three generations of his forefathers are in the Daniel family. The generation previous to Daniel (Joseph Smith and Mary Ann Cocke) came from England in the 1600s.*

---

*See 'Notes and Research' in Appendix A for the paternal lineage of Nelson Franklin.

Chapter Three

Laura's Formal Education
1876-1882

Gender-specific institutions accepted women for collegiate study beginning in the latter half of the nineteenth century. These prestigious and highly selective East Coast liberal arts colleges included Vassar, Mount Holyoke, Smith, Wellesley, Bryn Mawr, Barnard, and Radcliffe. The Seven Sisters, as they are called, promoted an education as intellectually rigorous as any solely male Ivy League institution.

Compared to other girls of their time, Laura and her sister Cora, had a rather exclusive and definitely advanced education. Their formal schooling began at the Bartholomew English and Classical School in Cincinnati. It was established in 1875 to service "young ladies and misses." Three levels of instruction were offered—namely, the primary course for ages seven through nine, three years of preparatory courses for ages nine through twelve, and six years of collegiate courses for college-bound students. The *First Annual Catalogue* of Bartholomew listed eight students in the primary course, twenty-five students in the preparatory courses, and sixty-three in the collegiate courses for the school year 1875–76.[1]

Laura and her sister Cora were listed as students only in the *Second Annual Catalogue* of Bartholomew (1876–77). Both were enrolled in the collegiate-course track; Cora was in the fifth year and Laura in the fourth year of a six-year program. In the 1877–78 academic year—between their studies at Bartholomew and their first year in college—they had a wide choice of girls' finishing schools in Cincinnati.[2]

Vassar College

Laura and her sister Cora enrolled in Vassar in Poughkeepsie, New York, in 1878. Vassar was founded as a girls' Christian college in 1861 by Matthew Vassar. Though not sectarian, by and large, it was under Baptist control. Its curriculum was modeled after Elmira College in Elmira, New York, one of the first women's colleges.

Students' letters sent to family and friends in Vassar's early years indicated that student life was regimented; every hour was scheduled. In October 1866, Irene Anderson wrote to her brother with details of her daily schedule at Vassar. Her letter notes that students rose at 6:00 in the morning. This was followed by: breakfast at 7:00, beds in order by 7:30, silent time for prayer 7:40, chapel at 8:00 for an hour, first class at 9:10 and second class at 10:10. Classes at 11:10 and 12:10 completed half the day. In the afternoon, dinner was at 1:00. This was followed by a class at 2:15 and then 3:15 with recreation at 4:00. Tea was taken at 6:00 in the evening. Chapel at 7:00 for an hour, study hour at 8:00, silent time at 9:00, and time with friends at 9:20 completed the day. Students returned to their room at 9:45 and retired at 10:00.[3]

Laura at age 15 (1878) entering Vassar College; photo taken at Vail photo studio in Poughkeepsie, NY. She turned sixteen in September. Cohasset Archives.

According to the *Sixteenth Annual Catalogue of the Officers and Students of Vassar College* dated August 1, 1881, the hours of rising and retiring, the warming and ventilation of rooms, the choice and preparation of food, the sanitary regulations of the College, and the regimen of personal habits were all carefully directed "for the health of the students." Weekends were filled with chapel services, Bible-study classes, letter writing, academic study, and exercise. Outdoor exercises included walking miles of trails, and boating or skating on the lake, depending on the season. Indoor options were the use of a well-equipped gymnasium and a bowling alley.[4]

As the years progressed, rules slowly loosened. Students were given more options in their daily schedule and in class choices.

By the time Laura entered Vassar, there were a number of organizations that engaged students in extracurricular activities. Laura was a member of the Philalethean (literary) Society. It was a very active group during her time at Vassar. It organized weekly exercises consisting of readings, critiques, and music for its members. With elaborate costumes and scenery, one-act plays written by the students themselves were presented to the campus community on what was called Philalethean Night. The society's name eventually became just Phil.

Other organizations at that time included the Students' Association, Floral Society, Missionary Society, Shakespeare Society, Society for Religious Inquiry, and sport societies. *The Vassar Miscellany*, a student magazine, also had begun publication.

In its early years, due to the difficulty and expense of travel, Vassar was largely a residential college for students coming from all over the country and abroad. Most students stayed on campus for their winter vacation, which included Christmas and the New Year. At these times, elaborate events were organized (e.g., an on-campus masquerade party or an off-campus adventuresome sleigh ride). Excursions for students and faculty to the estates of local trustees or college associates were also organized for a day of leisure and good food.

Vassar College Main Building.
Main Building of Vassar in 1800s with Vassar lake and students rowing.
Identifier, Vassar: 08.05.04

Vassar Curriculum

The *First Annual Catalogue of Officers and Students at Vassar Female College* from 1865–66 listed the admission requirements—namely, a student must be over 15 years of age; provide testimonials of character; and pass exams in Arithmetic, English Grammar, Modern Geography, and American History. English, Latin, and one other language were required.[5]

The entrance exams for admission to the freshman class were a three-day affair. Starting at 9:00 in the morning, exams continued until 5:00 with a one-and-a-half-hour break for lunch. They were held at the college, in Boston, Chicago, and Cincinnati.[6]

Student room on campus: ca.1878
Gas lamps, couches, desk, pictures and books.
Identifier Vassar: 08.15.01

After the disappointing results of the first entrance exams, preparatory courses were introduced to bring students up to a collegiate level of study. There was no standardized school system at the time. Girls seeking admission came with a variety of educational experiences; some had been taught at home.

The *First Annual Catalogue of Vassar* listed nine departments each headed by one of the original professors. The departments were: Rhetoric and English Language; Ancient and Modern Language and Literature; Math/Natural History/Chemistry; Astronomy; Natural History; Physiology and Hygiene; History and Political Economy; Philosophy; and the Extra-Collegiate Department, which included vocal and instrumental music, art, and physical training.[7]

The specific courses required for each semester (over a four-year period) were specified in *The First Annual Catalogue*. They were as follows:

1st Term	2nd Term
First Year	
Latin: Cicero, prose composition	Latin: Livy, topography of Rome
French: English into French	French: conversation
Algebra	Algebra: complete and start Geometry
Elective: History of Greece and Rome	Elective: Ancient Criminal History
Elective: Review of English grammar	Elective: Analysis: English
Throughout the year there will be exercises in English composition and reading.	
Second Year	
Latin: Horatio, Roman Antiquities, composition	Cicero's philosophical works
Geometry: complete & start Trigonometry	Botany and Zoology
Rhetoric	Elective: Medieval History or Conic Sections
Expectations over the year: exercises in writing essays (biographies and historical) and rhetorical reading.	
Third Year	
History of English Language and Literature	Natural Philosophy
Geology and Mineralogy	Physiology and Hygiene
Physical Geography	Practical Ethics
Elective: Astronomy	Elective: languages
Elective: languages	Elective: Political Economy
Elective: Logic	Elective: Critical Reading English Poets
Fourth Year	
Mental Philosophy	Moral Philosophy: Evidence of Christianity
Chemistry	Elective: Aesthetics
Elective: English	Elective: General History of Literature
Elective: Philology [now Linguistics]	Elective: Philosophy of History
Elective: Natural Theology	Elective: Fed. and State Constitutions
Expectations over the year: essays and recitations.[8]	

When Laura attended Vassar, students had the freedom to choose their courses of study beginning in the fourth term. Decidedly more options were added to the originally prescribed courses found in *The First Annual Catalogue*. Students could elect three areas of study, each requiring five recitations a week.

Maria Mitchell

Maria Mitchell, 1865: Vassar College astronomy professor, 1865-1888. Identifier, Vassar: 08.13.02.

In both their junior and senior year, Cora and Laura studied Astronomy under Maria Mitchell. When Laura was a first-year astronomy student, Cora was a second-year student.

Maria (pronounced "ma rye a") Mitchell was the first professor hired by Vassar. Having already a world reputation in astronomy, she raised the prestige of the nascent college. In 1847 atop the roof of her father's place of employment, the Pacific National Bank in Nantucket, she discovered a telescopic comet—one too distant to be seen with the naked eye. Previously uncharted, it was subsequently named for her. In light of

Vassar College Astronomical Observatory Building. The first building to be constructed at Vassar. First-year students about 1871-74 working with portable equatorial telescopes outside. Identifier, Vassar: 08.06.03

her accomplishment, she was elected to the American Academy of Arts and Sciences in 1848 and to the American Association for the Advancement of Science in 1850. She was the first woman to be so honored and the first professional female astronomer in the U.S.

At the age of seventeen, she pored over books written by renowned mathematicians and astronomers of the time. There was no school for her to enroll in for the advanced study of either subject. Later she would write, "A book is a good institution! To read a book, think it over, and to write out notes is a useful exercise. . . . The greatest object in educating is to give a right habit of study."[9]

Professor Mitchell and her father (an amateur astronomer himself) moved into the Vassar observatory, which was

Interior of the Vassar College Astronomical Observatory Dome in 1889, with a large equatorial telescope and ladder. Professor Maria Mitchell is seated on the left. Vassar: 08.07.07

the first building to be completed on campus. The observatory had a 12-inch refracting telescope, the last one made by the celebrated New York telescope maker Henry Fitz. In the U.S., it was second only in size to the telescopes at both Harvard and the Dudley Observatory in Schenectady, New York. It is now at the Smithsonian.

Professor Mitchell's life's aim was to do original investigation of the heavens; however, it gave way to a keen interest in the higher education of women. Her observation of naturally occurring phenomena (e.g., an eclipse) was now simply done in the company of her astronomy students, which provided them with direct field experience. Some of their original research was even published.

The professor instructed her students in the use of all the instruments and then let them work on their own—lecturing was not her style. The beginning classes used a small portable-equatorial telescope that was located outside on the grounds during the day. In her senior class, each girl was taught separately. Their observations of the sky were often during the night in the dome on top of the observatory. The observatory contained a meridian circle

Vassar College astronomy classroom with telescope on tripod, chart, desks, table, chairs, blackboard, and globe. Vassar: 08.07.04

with a collimating telescope, a chronograph, and an equatorial telescope. She described their program of study.

> The girls work wholly on planets, and they are taught to find a planet at any hour of the day, to make drawings of what they see, and to determine positions of planets and satellites. They learn to know the satellites of Saturn (Titan, Rhea, etc.) by their different physiognomy, as they would a person.[10]

To "her girls," she would say, "I cannot expect to make astronomers, but I do expect that you will invigorate your minds by the effort at healthy modes of thinking. . . . When we are chafed and fretted by small cares, a look at the stars will show us the littleness of our own interests."[11]

She believed that the girls leaving Vassar College were the best educated women in the world. She was referring to the broader education they received—not an education of a textbook, classroom, or apparatus. She did her part, in this regard, by putting "her girls" in touch with the outside world. She used letters from astronomers in the U.S. or Europe, stories of her travels abroad, and accounts of scientific conventions to broaden her students' outlook. The observatory was also the setting for the discussion of politics and women's issues. Leading women of the day, such as Julia Ward Howe, the suffragette, were invited to speak.

In these ways, Professor Mitchell exerted a substantial influence on her students, who were her daily companions. Based largely on student feedback, her influence was described as being formative, character-molding, and unceasingly progressive. Both Cora and Laura were exposed to her open-mindedness during their two-year study of astronomy.

A week before commencement, beginning in 1870, Professor Mitchell's graduating pupils were invited to a dome party, which is still a popular tradition at Vassar. Small tables were spread under the dome around the telescope; the flowers on each table were from her garden. At the party, she read a poem that she had written. Each student was alluded to in a few verses, in a more or less personal tone. As one student wrote:

> At the time it was read, though it seemed mere merry nonsense, it really served a more serious purpose in the work of one who did nothing aimlessly. This apparent nonsense served as the vehicle to convey an expression of approbation, affection, criticism, or disapproval in such a merry mode that even the bitterest draught seemed sweet.[12]

Having serious health issues, Professor Mitchell retired from Vassar in 1888. She passed away the next year at her family home in Lynn, Massachusetts. In her honor, a World War II Liberty ship was named the SS Maria Mitchell; the Hudson Rail Line ending near Vassar was named the Maria Mitchell Comet; and the observatory in Nantucket became the Maria Mitchell Observatory.

In 1886 Vassar graduates established *The Alumnae Maria Mitchell Chair of Astronomy*. On this celebratory occasion, stories of "her oddities, her kindliness, her paradoxes, [and] her unconventional sincerities" were shared in "memory of a life of high seriousness of purpose, and of a direct and most human comradeship."[13]

Laura's Experience at Vassar

Both Laura and her sister Cora started at Vassar College in the fall of 1878. Cora's transcript listed her as seventeen years old that year; Laura was listed as sixteen years of age. That would place their birthdates at 1861 and 1862, respectively.* Having entered Vassar at the sophomore level, Cora graduated

---

*See 'Notes and Research' in Appendix A for details on Laura's birth date.

as a science major three years later. Laura graduated as a science major in 1882, completing four years.

According to Laura's transcript, she was enrolled in the following science courses: Botany, Chemistry (two semesters), Physics (two semesters), Astronomy (four semesters), and Mathematics (four semesters). She also took Logic, Rhetoric, Literature Criticism (two semesters), Philosophy (two semesters), Latin (three semesters), English composition (seven semesters), and Music (eight semesters).

The two sisters attended a few of the same classes together—namely, English Composition (both semesters), one semester of chemistry, and one semester of Latin. Except for one class, Cora and Laura took the same courses in their junior year. One year ahead of Laura, Cora led the way—a fact descriptive of their personal relationship too.

In addition to their regular courses, every Vassar student was required to take one of the arts, that is, vocal and instrumental music or drawing and painting. Cora enrolled in singing. Laura chose to play the piano; she had two lessons a week and daily practice for forty minutes.

Originally entitled the *Vassar Miscellany* and later the *Vassar Quarterly*, a student-oriented monthly publication was begun in 1872. Events happening on-and-off campus, political opinions, literary works, and book reviews were covered. All Vassar's publications including the *Vassar Miscellany* are available online in its archives.

The diary of Ann Wyman, Laura's classmate, is one such publication online. It described the Sophomore Social held February 10, 1880. The evening program was a "burlesque in three acts, followed by collation [light meal] and dancing."[14] It consisted of students and sophomore faculty exchanging roles—a student with another student or faculty, and faculty with another faculty member.

The setting for Act I was the sophomore literature class. The diary describes the role assumed by each student in the class.

> Viva Buckland representing Miss L. F. Glenn asked, "Prof. Backus, what was the color of the coat that Chaucer's great-grandfather wore to that party he went to?" To which Miss Foos (in the role of Prof. Backus) replied "Well, really, Miss Glenn, I believe, I don't know. I think it was either blue trimmed with pink or pink trimmed with blue. I have forgotten which. I will make a note of it and look it up."[15]

Act II was performed in the Latin class and the setting for Act III was a faculty meeting. The diary described the attire of the individuals in each act and their actions. The finale of the night was described as follows:

> Presently Miss L.F. Glenn came in, dragging a little wagon full of apples and corn-balls. She was dressed like a little Irish boy, with red wig, old hat, calico tie, red skirt, grey gym drawers. She looked too funny. She was followed by Miss Warden, dressed in an old calico and faded shawl, with brown hair in front and great bonnet. On her arm she carried a basket holding, a peck of peanuts, and a box of candy kisses. We feasted on these and bye and bye they brought in ham sandwiches, olives, coffee and whipped cream. We had a nice feast and more dancing and then gathered around the piano to sing. We sang "Here's to '82, We'll see what she can do."[16]

At another sophomore gathering—a Mother Goose party—Laura was Mother Goose. In her diary, Miss Wyman described Laura as wearing "a yellow shirt with black geese on it and a red figured overdress and a tall pointed cap."[17] Many other nursery-rhyme characters were also represented in costumes.

Laura belonged to one of the three chapters of the Philalethean Society. In the *Vassar Miscellany* of February 1881, a review was given on the performance of Edward Bulwer-Lytton's comedy *Money* by the society's members. Bulwer-Lytton was a British writer, politician, and critic, whose *Money* was first performed in the U.S. at the Old Park Theater in New York City in February 1841. In the college production, Laura played the role of the supporting character Clara Douglas. A review of her performance was given in the *Miscellany*.

> Miss Laura Glenn as Clara Douglas showed a minute and faithful study of her part, as an outgrowth of which was the grace and naturalness of her acting. At times, there was a lack of sustained expression of face and voice and a slight tendency toward "posing" but, as a whole, Clara Douglas was made what she should be; a graceful, lovable, unselfish girl.

Hearty congratulations were also offered to the entire cast. "[All the] characters were well presented . . . and it can be truthfully said that, it was a pleasant play, pleasantly acted and with the important accompaniment of a new and very charming stage setting."[18]

Laura's 1882 graduating class at Vassar. Laura is holding a tennis racket, bottom left. https://commons.wikimedia.org/wiki/File:Vassar_College_class_of_1882.jpg

In the April 1881 issue of the *Vassar Miscellany*, a review was given of Laura's piano presentation on campus in Society Hall.

> In the performance of the sonata for piano and violin cello by Saint-Saëns, Miss Laura Glenn added to her former accurate technique, a depth of tone, and more expressions than she has ever shown before; there was evidence of careful study in the beautiful pianissimo and crescendo passages.[19]

Every year in May, the junior class of Vassar took the senior class on a surprise excursion. When Laura's junior class treated Cora's senior class of 1881, *The Kingston Daily Freeman* (published in Kingston, New York) detailed the adventure: "by carriage, steamer, train, and finally for the last half-mile by stage, the group was conveyed up twenty-five hundred feet to the top of Summit Mountain," located in the Catskill Mountains of New York. One hundred twenty-five students and guests were treated to an elaborate meal at the Grand Hotel. During the ceremony at the hotel, Laura toasted the chairperson of the event in a poem which was described as "original and laughable." The chairperson responded in kind. "An enjoyable day was had by all."[20]

As part of her own commencement program in June 1882, Laura gave a piano performance entitled "Prophecy." The following July issue of the *Miscellany* credits her presentation as being "exceptional in its graceful delivery and real kindliness of spirit."[21] It is worth noting that Laura was listed on the honor roll of her graduating class.

During one of the commencements in the early 1880s, conceivably Laura's, Professor Mitchell sang a few verses of her dome poetry to the tune of "Auld Lang Syne." The verses didn't mention the name of any specific student—though her verses often did—but Laura was likely one of the five students alluded to in the poem. This conclusion was largely based on the title of Laura's senior thesis, "The Five Rings of Saturn."

Laura's graduation picture taken at Vail photo studio in 1882. Vassar: [Ph.F] 11.15

Professor Mitchell's verses were:

> While Saturn's ring is poised aright
> And Saturn's moons still glow
> The five who watched them many a night
> Will not from memory go.[22]

During her Vassar years, Laura attended the Episcopalian Christ Church in Poughkeepsie, New York, which was a mile from the campus. In its records, Laura was listed as having received confirmation in 1880, one of the earliest indications of Laura's religious temperament. According to the present archivist of the Episcopal church, Rev. Henry L. Ziegenfuss was the church rector then and taught Laura's confirmation classes. He also performed a variety of ministerial services for Vassar students, according to the *Vassar Miscellany*.

It has been stated in present-day literature that Laura tried her vocation in an Anglican religious order. Since St. Mary's Episcopal Convent in Peekskill was only forty miles from Vassar, it would have been a possible choice for Laura. It was founded by the Episcopal Church in 1872—the first convent of the Anglican Order in the U.S. Upon inquiry, however, no record of her joining was found.*

---

*See 'Notes and Research' in Appendix A for details on the religious order Laura likely joined.

Laura as Alumna

The summer after her graduation, Laura teamed up with Cora to participate in a program at the Vine Street Opera house in Cincinnati. Throughout the 1880s, opera houses and hill-top resorts were places of amusement for residents and visitors. There were ten opera houses listed in Cincinnati in this period. Hill-top resorts boasted gardens, dancing theaters, and esplanades overlooking the city.

Every week the *Cincinnati Enquirer* published the Vine Street Opera house program. "The accomplished Glenn Sisters" were listed on the program for a week in July along with jugglers, a wire act, fun-makers and a minstrel show.[23] Based on their Vassar College transcripts, it is most likely that Cora sang and Laura played the piano.

Laura in New York City at the time of her sister Cora's wedding in the early spring of 1882. Laura was the bridesmaid. Vassar: [of Ph.F] 11.15

Vassar kept track of its alumnae under "Class Notes" in the *Vassar Miscellany*. Questionnaires were regularly sent out to alumnae inquiring as to their activities or changes in address or name. Those on the college's mailing list received the *Alumnae Magazine* and letters that contained news of their class and the college.

Through a classmate, Laura requested to be taken off the Vassar mailing list early on. In her March 1938 reply to a communication from the college, Laura explained her position, writing, "I received the forms of questions to be filled out but I have a strong feeling against being tabulated and put on record, so I did not answer them. I am enclosing a list of my writings which is the only part of me that I care to have made known."[24]

In a *Biographical Address Register*, printed around 1938, only Laura's name and address are given. Over the years, only her publications were mentioned under "Class Notes" in the *Vassar Quarterly*.

Chapter Four

Laura's Family and Travels Abroad
Sojourns in Europe

In the latter half of the nineteenth century, the U.S. was advancing as an industrial power and witnessing the beginnings of mass transatlantic travel. An unprecedented number of affluent upper- and middle-class Americans journeyed to Europe for personal and professional reasons—pleasure, education, health, and business. Because money and time were both needed for international travel, these people were able to claim special social and cultural standing.

Writers offered advice on different aspects of traveling abroad—what luggage would be needed, what to wear in general or on specific occasions, and how to manage Europe's tipping system. Metropolitan newspapers wrote frequent editorials on the travel scene. Travel commentators proclaimed Americans as world wanderers. In 1870, travelers abroad were fewer than 35,000 a year, but by 1885 they surpassed 100,000 a year.[1]

Every year from 1885 to 1900, one or more of Laura's immediate family was sailing abroad, returning from abroad, or residing in Europe. Laura's sister Cora resided in England from 1889 to 1896, with her second husband, Edward Hamilton Bell. Laura's mother traveled with her daughters to Italy in 1887 and spent one year, 1895–96, in Europe. Her sister Helen lived abroad from 1887 to 1890, and also from 1894 to 1899. Laura herself traveled to Europe three times during these fifteen years and lived abroad for well over eight years. Laura and Helen each received a generous allowance from home while abroad—an advantage of being born in a wealthy family. In subsequent years, European trips by family members were less frequent and of shorter duration.

During these fifteen years (1885-1900), Laura's life was still closely tied with that of her sisters and mother. They summered together in Nantucket and traveled to Europe together—Laura and Cora (1886), Laura and Helen (summer 1896), and Laura and her mother (early 1896). While abroad, they traveled in socially prominent circles.

1885–90

The Glenn family memorabilia—in the possession of Laura's great-grandniece S.M. Newell— contains Cora's personal journal. According to the journal, Cora and Laura sailed to Europe in July of 1886 and visited Antwerp, Rotterdam, Amsterdam, and Hanover; they stayed in Leipzig in east-central Germany for a month in mid-summer, 1887. Elizabeth and Helen, Laura's mother and younger sister, arrived in Europe that same summer. In her journal, Cora wrote, "we all went to Munich, Italy, and then to Paris."[2]

From Laura's writings and the "Personals" in the *Vassar Miscellany*, which kept track of Vassar College graduates, more highlights of Laura's years abroad can be pieced together. Spain was one country on her itinerary. Laura wrote of beggars in the streets of Seville during Holy Week "crying out their needs or attracting attention by gong or bell." More than twenty years later, she recalled this particular scene during a temple festival in Bombay, India. The temple in Bombay "stood on a high hill and the steep road to it was lined on each side with the blind, the deformed, the hungry and the sick."[3] The scene was much like the one in Seville.

Of the many things that she gathered in her travels abroad was a rare Spanish hanging several centuries old. Laura wrote that it had hung in a Spanish church and "sanctity pervaded it." It had been woven and embroidered by monks of the Dominican Convento de San Esteban of Salamanca in Western Spain, opened in the mid-thirteenth century; "even the embroidery silk was the product of their own silkworms," she noted.[4] Every aspect of the hanging—its handcrafting, its sacred use, and its long association with the Dominican monks—was an assurance that it had priceless value in her eyes. In later years, it found a home in another holy space—her private chapel at Ananda Ashrama in California.

The *Vassar Miscellany* of October 1, 1887, announced that all three sisters—Cora, Laura, and Helen—were in Italy at the same time.[5] In the introduction to her book *Sri Ramakrishna and Saint Francis of Assisi* (1935), Laura described her arrival in Assisi and her pilgrimage around the city.

> I had fled from the noisy, crowded Holy Week observances at Rome and reached Assisi just in time for the Easter Vesper Services and Benediction. In the great piazza of the city, facing me across the square, stood a pillared church, once a Roman Temple to Minerva. Through its broad, open doors I could see the high altar blazing with hundreds of lighted candles, and in front of it [stood] priests in rich feast-day vestments intoning the sacred office. The square outside was crowded to its edges with simple villagers, who had come from the whole countryside round about to attend the service.

Laura continues the narrative by writing that "each morning of Easter Week," pilgrims "toiled up the sheer paths, singing as they climbed." She made "a pilgrimage with them to all the places sanctified by association with St. Francis." Full of "exalted inspiration," she writes, "we knelt and prayed where he had prayed, we stood where he had preached, we bowed our heads where he lay entombed."[6]

At the guest inn that adjoined the monastery and church of St. Francis, Laura met Paul Sabatier. This French clergyman and historian wrote the first modern biography of St. Francis of Assisi. Having read his book, Laura was pleased to meet him and hear about new information he had uncovered in his research on the Franciscan Order and Saint Clare of Assisi. She notes that he was "one of the few who had free access" to the Franciscan library.[7]

Elisabeth and Cora returned from abroad early in 1888, leaving seventeen-year-old Helen in Europe under Laura's care. According to the *Vassar Miscellany*, Laura and Helen studied music and art, respectively, in Munich the winter of 1888–89. Helen wrote to her mother that she spent "many happy evenings dancing with dashing young officers and handsome music masters."[8] The two sisters then summered in Berlin.

From September 10–19 and October 20–30 of 1889, Laura and Helen were registered at Hotel Baudy in Giverny, Normandy, France. According to the hotel register, Helen and Laura had adjacent rooms on both occasions. Helen's age was given as nineteen and Laura's as twenty-seven.[9] Giverny was a small hillside village along the Seine River some forty miles from Paris. The village was the site of an artist colony founded by the French Impressionist Claude Monet (1840–1926). Artists from all nationalities flocked to Giverny in the late nineteenth and early twentieth centuries to study Impressionism and take advantage of Monet's lovely gardens to paint nature scenes. On the grounds, Monet also created a pond of water lilies for his creative inspiration. Eventually he bought a tract of land adjacent to his and enlarged an existing little pond, reshaping its banks, and planting weeping willows, iris, and bamboo around it. Lastly, he built a Japanese footbridge across it. The bridge appeared in several of his paintings.

Helen painted for several weeks at Giverny. Her work included murals on the studio walls of John Leslie Breck, an American artist, who resided at the colony during this time period. He painted Laura's portrait during their second visit in October. Entitled *Portrait Sketch*, it is now in a private collection in the U.S. Adopting Monet's style of loose brush strokes, ordinary subject matter, and bright colors, Breck returned to the U.S. in 1890 and advanced Impressionism as an art form.

Laura and Helen spent the winter of 1889–90 in Paris. The *Vassar Miscellany* notes that early in 1890, Laura was attending lectures on history and literature at the Sorbonne and Helen joined the women's class at the Académie Julian, a private art school in Paris teaching painting and sculpture. At the time, women were not allowed to enroll for study at the prestigious school of fine arts in the city, the École des Beaux-Arts.

Helen met Frederick MacMonnies at one of the evening parties that she attended. A major figure in American art, particularly as a sculptor, he was married to Mary Fairchild MacMonnies, a reputed American painter and pupil of Auguste Carolus-Duran (1837–1917). They had three children. Without regard for his family, though, he pursued a relationship with Helen. Their affair began at the end of her stay abroad.

At age sixteen, Frederick studied sculpture for four years in the New York studio of Augustus Saint-Gaudens (1848–1907), a renowned sculptor of the Beaux-Arts generation. At the age of twenty-one, he studied at academies in Munich and Paris. France became his second home, and at the École des Beaux-Arts in Paris, he received training in the fundamental principles of his art. Setting up his own studio in Paris in 1888, he submitted his work to the Paris Salon, which was recognized as the foremost art tribune of the day. He won awards in 1889 and 1891 for his sculptures, the first American to be so honored.

In 1891, Frederick received a commission to work on a fountain for the 1893 Columbian Exposition (World's Fair) to be held in Chicago. His large sculpture, centered on a vessel named the Grand Barge of State, was the centerpiece of the World's Fair. In her biography *A Flight of Fame, The Life and Art of Frederick MacMonnies*, author Mary Smart gave a detailed description of his design of the Grand Barge, writing,

> The great barge sat high out of the water . . . with Victory trumpeting the arrival from the bow, and Father Time using his scythe as a rudder at the stern. Eight maidens . . . were at the sweeping oars: the four on the starboard side representing Music, Architecture, Sculpture, and Painting; the four to the port exemplifying Science, Industry, Agriculture, and Commerce. Escorting the barge were [dolphins] plunging as they were ridden by youth and mermaids whose infants triumphantly blew on conch shells to echo Victory's trumpet.[10]

The barge transported the seated figure of Columbia, representing an enthroned America. The weekly journal, *The Critic*, noted that the "beautiful figure expressed in a way the restless, self-assertive, triumphant energy of the Republic."[11] Mary Smart concluded that the allegorical fountain, which was widely recognized as a triumph of artistic work, "vaulted him into a heady life of a world-class sculptor."[12]

As previously noted in chapter one, Swami Vivekananda journeyed from India to attend the World's Parliament of Religions, which was one of more than twenty congresses hosted at the World's Fair. Arriving in Chicago in July 1893, six weeks prior to the opening of the Parliament of Religions, he had ample opportunity to view the extensive exhibitions at the fair, including the Grand Barge of State. For the twelve days that he stayed in Chicago before leaving for Boston, he visited the World's Fair daily. Reportedly,

> He was struck with amazement at the wonders he saw. Here all the latest products of the inventive and artistic mind of the entire world had been brought to a focus, as it were, for examination and admiration. He visited the various exposition palaces, marveling at the array of machinery, at the arts and products of many lands, and, above all, at the energy and practical acumen of the human mind as manifested by the exhibits.[13]

On September 27, 1890, Laura and Helen arrived in New York harbor from Liverpool, England, aboard the steamship *City of Chester*. Helen's debut party, described in chapter two, was the motivation behind their return.

In her journal, Cora stated that she married Edward Hamilton Bell on November 28, 1888. The next year, the couple traveled to England, staying with his family in London. U.S. newspapers reported that they married on June 9, 1889; a second ceremony may have been conducted in London, though Cora's journal made no mention of it. At the time of their marriage, Cora was twenty-eight and Edward was thirty-two.

1891-95

Laura resided in New York City off and on in the early 1890s. She invariably stayed with her sister and husband, Cora and Edward Bell. Though the couple lived in London, they maintained an apartment at 48 East 20th Street in New York City. The apartment accommodated their extended stays in the U.S, which were due to projects that Edward was commissioned to do.

In 1891 they purchased a residence in Scarsdale, just north of the city in Westchester County. Scarsdale was changing from a rural town to a residential suburb at the time. The arrival of the railroad in the mid-1800s made accessing New York City rather easy. Laura likely resided with them during the time she was attending Swami Vivekananda's lectures in the winter of 1895 and spring of 1896.

Helen Glenn moved from her family home in Cincinnati around the end of 1891 and stayed with the Bells. Scarsdale served as an idyllic setting for Helen's artistic talents to find expression in landscape painting. During her stay abroad in the late 1880s, she had visited the rugged countryside of Barbizon, a French village, which inspired a generation of artists in objective landscape painting.

One of the first projects that brought the Bells to the U.S. was Edward's commission to design a series of five stained-glass windows for the grand staircase of the newly built City Hall of Cincinnati. The April 15, 1893 issue of *The Critic* described the artistic project as consisting of one large window and two smaller windows on either side of it. "The large window contains a group representing Cincinnati as a crowned and enthroned female in red between Law as an old man in purple and Order as a young man in a lion's skin, while

Commerce as a girl in blue, reposes at her feet. The other windows contain figures representing Labor, Abundance, Agriculture, and Liberty who, torch in hand, accompanies Peace with her olive branch."

The author concluded the article with his assessment, "Mr. Bell shows himself to be an intelligent designer."[14]

The Bells were in the U.S. in the summer of 1895 for another major commission. Edward was chosen to design the architectural decorations for the Biltmore Mansion in the hills of Asheville, North Carolina. The construction of the 250-room residence of George Washington Vanderbilt II (1865–1914) had been a six-year project. Housing four acres of floor space with 35 bedrooms, 43 bathrooms, and 65 fireplaces, it was the largest undertaking in residential architecture in the country.

Learning of the Bells' plans for the summer of 1895, Laura decided to travel to North Carolina to be with Cora while Edward worked on the project. Initially she had planned to travel abroad with her mother that summer. Consequently, she met up with Elizabeth in England in April 1896, after Swami Vivekananda returned to India. It was a trip of short duration for Laura. The UK and Ireland Outward Passenger List of 1890–1960 has Miss L.F. Glenn leaving Southampton, England on May 9, 1896, bound for New York. Weeks later her mother returned to the U.S.

According to the *1900 U.S. Federal Census*, the Bells moved permanently to the U.S. in 1896. Cora's profession—translating from German and French into English—necessitated her travel between Europe and New York. In 1890 W. S. Gottsberger and Co. of New York published Cora's English translation of a collection of Georg Moritz Ebers's fictional work, *The Elixir and Other Tales*, which combines history and fantasy. Another translation from German that she worked on was Ernest Eck Stein's popular romance novel, *Hertha*, published in 1892 by the same New York publisher.

As for Cora's translations from French, *The Memoirs of Madame de Staal de Launay* (1853) was one of the most noted. These memoirs provide us with a view of the court and courtiers and an account of the manner in which the author spent her time while imprisoned in the Bastille. Cora's English translation was published in 1895 by Dodd-Mead and Co. in New York. In 1893 she began translating the four volumes of the *Life of Marie Antoinette* (1879), authored by Maxime de La Rocheterie.

In the *Saturday Evening Mail*, an article entitled "Women Translators and their Meager Rewards" named seven women as prominent in the translation field. Cora Hamilton Bell was one of them. The article stated the requisites of a good translator—namely, a "thorough knowledge of the foreign language, a copious English vocabulary, a good English literary style and the power to enter into the spirit of the foreign author."[15]

Wilmer Dilworth Glenn, Laura's brother, also traveled abroad during the timeline of this section, shortly after graduating from DePauw University in Greencastle, Indiana, in 1892. The college was founded in 1837 by the Methodist Church. Originally called Indiana Ashbury University, its name changed in the 1860s with a bequest of philanthropist Washington C. DePauw. The College Catalogue of Beta Theta Pi fraternity listed Wilmer as a member. Having graduated as a mining engineer, he took a two-year business trip abroad as a coal-merchant.

1896-99

Characteristically strong willed, Helen successfully persuaded Laura to accompany her to Paris in August 1896 as chaperone, despite the fact that Laura had returned from Europe just a couple months earlier. Had Helen lived alone in Paris, societal gossip would likely have ensued, resulting in her becoming an embarrassment to her parents. Journals frequently carried articles warning girls of the dangers in Europe—particularly in Paris. "Glamorous courtesans and Romeos" made major European cities "fraught with danger for unsuspecting American women."[16]

In August, Laura and Helen rented an apartment in Paris. When Helen informed Frederick of her arrival, he immediately began arranging for their rendezvous. They had begun a love affair in the final months of her earlier visit to France. Discretely addressed love letters over the intervening years had kept the embers of their affair alive. In the fall of 1896, Laura and Helen were registered at Hotel Baudy in Giverny from September 10 to September 19.

Helen returned to Giverny later in September, likely with Frederick. At the time, he signed a lease for an ancient priory on a three-acre walled estate in the village so that his wife and daughters could live there year around, away from Paris. Keeping his relationship with Helen a secret from his family was uppermost in his mind; Helen had also insisted on secrecy. Once he had relocated his family home to Giverny, Helen would be able to visit him in his Paris studio unhampered.

*Laura and Helen rented an apartment in Paris, 1896.
Both pictures of Laura were taken there.*

Helen found herself pregnant in early 1897. Frederick arranged for her stay in the Paris countryside with paid caretakers. He wrote to her and visited her there. Though Laura, Helen's chaperone, had her own residence, she did her best to support Helen without hovering over her.

During this time, it is likely that Laura visited cathedrals relatively close to Paris. In an article that she wrote later entitled "What is True Worship?" she delineated the different ideals and forms of religious worship that she had encountered. In the article, she compared the Gothic splendor of the Roman Catholic cathedrals at Rheims and at Chartres (both near Paris) to the grey barrenness of a Dutch Meeting Room.

There was a *Couvent de l'Assomption* in the village of Auteuil that Laura likely encountered while bicycling through the villages in and surrounding Paris proper. Founded in France in 1839 by Mother Marie-Eugénie Milleret, it was a half-cloistered convent under the patronage of Mary, the mother of Christ, in her mystery of the Assumption. The objective of the religious order was to educate the daughters of the rich. Auteuil was reported to be a village where the nouveau riche bourgeoisie liked to live.

The nun's manner of dress likely influenced Laura's future self-chosen habit. The nuns wore a full-length gown made of a coarse woven fabric, with a knotted cord hanging from the waist at one side. A white hood covered the head and shaded the face, forming a cape that covered the shoulders. A white veil was thrown over the head.

There is no written evidence that Laura resided at the convent but taking part in its routine of prayer and perpetual adoration in the chapel would have appealed to her. The Catholic convent was assumed to be the setting for the birth of Helen's son in October 1887, with Laura by her side. In her diary Helen wrote, "I can't imagine loving God more than my son."[17] She was most likely referring to Laura's deepened interest in spiritual life sparked by Swami Vivekananda's lectures, which Laura had attended for two seasons in New York City.

Shortly after Helen gave birth, Frederick sent Laura, Helen, and their son to Florence, Italy for a few months in order to "keep [his] two families from colliding,"[18] author Mary Smart writes. The city was known for a number of famous artist residents, including two eminent Victorian poets, Robert and Elizabeth Barrett Browning. The Brownings resided in Florence from 1847 until the death of Elizabeth in 1861. Their fifteenth-century residence, Casa Guidi, became a house museum after the passing of their son in 1912.

Laura's lifelong appreciation for the genius of Robert Browning may have originated from her stay in Florence at this time. Twenty-five years later, she addressed the Boston Browning Society. The title of her address was "Robert Browning and the Vedanta." An article of the same title was published in the monthly journal of the Boston Vedanta Society around the same time. In the article she analyzed nine of Browning's poems, addressing the correlation between his "deep insights" and the teachings of Vedanta on the topics of Maya, the three states of consciousness, and the power of a man of God. She wrote of his unshakable faith in a personal God and alluded to his belief in the presence of God in everything. She also explained why some of his lines of poetry may "fall with a shock on uncomprehending ears."[19]

In 1899 Helen decided to return to the U.S. after finally realizing that Frederick would not leave his family and marry her. Laura sailed to New York on July 30, 1899. Helen returned five months later with her son, J. Robertson Ward, with a convincing story of his adoption by her after her short marriage and death of a husband.

Laura stayed with Cora and Edward after her return from France. According to Cora's diary, Laura was in Boston for the winter of 1900, staying at the Berkeley Hotel, now Revolution Hotel. The Mother House of the Society of St. Margaret was located in Louisburg Square on Beacon Hill in

Boston. Laura likely contacted the Society and even tried her vocation there. In the spring of 1901, she returned to New York and became a member of the New York Vedanta Society. She took up her own apartment in the city at this time.

After 1900

Edward Bell's talents as an architect and landscaper were evident in the construction of his family's country home, named Longcroft, in the village of Mamaroneck, New York around 1900. Among the rocky hills of Westchester County near the Connecticut shore, it was founded on Quaker Ridge—a solid rock 200 feet above sea level. The November 1903 issue of *House and Garden* featured Longcroft as "the seat of Edward Hamilton Bell."[20] The article covered all the details of the construction, for example, the blasting of rock for the basement and the landscaping of a fourteen-acre estate. Helen and her son resided at Longcroft upon their return from France. *The American Art Annual of 1903-1904* listed Helen as an art supervisor and teacher in metal work, specifically jewelry, and gave her residence as Longcroft.

Laura's great-grandfather, Alexander Glenn, immigrated to the U.S. from northern Scotland before the American Revolutionary War. A large estate in the town of Linlithgow, Scotland, named Longcroft, had been in the Glenn family for 1,100 years—hence the name of Cora and Edward Bell's country home.

In the *Yearbook of the Art Societies of New York, 1898-1899*, Cora and Edward H. Bell are both mentioned as supporting a number of art societies. The 169-page yearbook provides a complete record of the proceedings and major undertakings of the nine most important art societies in New York in 1899. Edward was a member of the Board of Directors of the Municipal Art Society and was a resident member of the Architectural League. Cora was a member of the Municipal Art Society as well as the American Fine Arts Society.[21]

Edward's numerous artistic talents ensured him a wide circle of acquaintances that included famous artists and actors as well as well-known politicians. In an envelope labeled "Edward Hamilton Bell" in a box of the family memorabilia, letters therein indicated the correspondence that he enjoyed with Stanford White (American architect), Maxfield Parrish (American illustrator and painter), Alla Nazimova (Russian-American actress, screenwriter and producer), Stanley Baldwin (British Prime Minister), and Secretary of War William Howard Taft in the Theodore

Roosevelt administration. A wedding invitation was also among the letters—Edward and Cora were invited to the wedding of Alice Roosevelt, daughter of President Theodore Roosevelt in 1906. In her journal, Cora writes that her husband sat at the table with the Roosevelts, and she was seated at another table between William Howard Taft, and Woodrow Wilson, then President of Princeton.

By 1910, Cora and Edward were living in Manhattan. According to the *Real Estate Record and Builder's Guide* (Volume 73) found on Google books, their country home (Longcroft)was sold in 1904 for $35,000. Edward became the art director of the New Theater in Brooklyn. The *Brooklyn Daily Eagle* published an extensive write-up entitled, "The New Theater and What it Means to Dramatic Art." The article called the New Theater "the single biggest step . . . that has yet been undertaken . . . in this country to secure the theater's rightful recognition as an educational institution."[22] Its intention was to establish a resident company of actors and operate a repertory theater. Edward designed scenery and costumes for a number of actors and producers of the New Theater. With his colleagues, he also authored the poetic drama *The Piper* as well as the comedy *The School of Scandal*.

In 1914, Edward's research interest in Asian art took him to the East. Departing Yokohama, Japan, aboard the *Mongolia*, he arrived in San Francisco on December 29 of that year. He compiled a catalog of Asian works of art that were in private Japanese and European collections. His resulting contribution to the *Catalogue of National Treasures of Paintings and Sculptures in Japan* (1915) earned him recognition as a co-author with Ichisaburo Nakamura. In Edward's publication *The Blackstone Collection in the Field Museum of Natural History in Chicago* (1914), art objects of Chinese and Tibetan origin were featured. He authored *Notes on Landscapes in the Arts of the East and the West* (1919), *The Buddhist Architecture of Japan* (date unknown), and *Chinese "Grape and Seahorse" Mirrors* (1926). They were all highly illustrated books.

Chapter Five

Spiritual Training under Swami Abhedananda
Growth of the Vedanta Society

Swami Abhedananda became minister of the New York Vedanta Society in 1897 with definitive goals in mind; namely, "to arouse the interest of the good people of the city...to persuade them to help ... in making the Vedanta Society a powerful religious organization ... [and] to find ways and means for making a success of the Vedanta work in New York which was started by Swami Vivekananda." In no small measure, he accomplished these goals. Under his leadership, the Vedanta Society became a public institution with its message spread far and wide and Ramakrishna-Vedanta a respected religion in the U.S.[1]

Swami Abhedananda was minister of the New York Vedanta Society, 1897 to 1910.

October 1897 to November 1898 was the first season of Swami Abhedananda's lectures in New York City. Lucid, well-reasoned, profound, and powerful were adjectives used to describe his presentations. His approach to lecturing was scholastic and largely impersonal, by and large attracting intellectuals. He drew audiences of several hundred. By the summer of 1899, he was lecturing throughout the New England states in addition to New York City. In the December 1901 issue of the *Brahmavadin* (1895–1914), Laura wrote, "invitations to talk and lecture were everywhere pressed upon him."[2]

In one-on-one philosophical discussions with renowned scientists, statesmen, scholars, and broad-minded religious leaders, he impressed his listeners with the breadth and depth of his knowledge, and awakened in them an interest in the teachings of Vedanta. These teachings and his dynamic personality were cited in articles carried by respected New York newspapers.

Abhedananda's first book, *Reincarnation*, was published by the Vedanta Society in 1899. Consisting of three lectures on reincarnation, it proved to be very popular. His use of straightforward and simple language, free from technical and Sanskrit terms, helped greatly in this regard. Over the next five years, more books and pamphlets based on his lectures were published, thereby significantly enriching the Ramakrishna-Vedanta literature available to the public. Book orders poured in from states across the continent and countries around the world in the beginning of the new century.

During Abhedananda's earliest years in New York, Laura was living abroad. Soon after her return in 1899 and through the winter of 1900, she lived in Boston. She had left the "hurried life" of New York City, looking forward to a life, she wrote, "in seclusion and silence" in Boston.³ Considering her active life abroad from 1896 to 1899 chaperoning her sister Helen, Boston gave her distance from her family and their questions about Helen and her son. She also might have looked into the Society of St. Margaret, headquartered in Boston.

While Laura lived in Boston, she had her first mystical experience. Some thirty years later, she wrote about it. This lapse of time is, in itself, an indication of her reluctance to reveal her deeply personal experiences. Realizing that the "day" of her life was coming to a close, however, she gave way to the "oft-repeated urge from within and from without" to commit her spiritual experiences to written form. Her decision was supported by the realization that "even the witness of lesser devotees has value to strengthen the faith of men and lend them the courage to go forward."⁴

One afternoon as she sat in the living room of her Boston apartment, agitated by thoughts of her future, two figures suddenly stood before her. She recalled,

> The face of one shone with a super-earthly smile, which seemed to shed an effulgence over His whole being. In quiet tones, he spoke these words: "Do not grieve. You have work to do for me." Then both figures vanished, but the sense of their presence lingered for many days.⁵

She returned to New York City in the spring of 1901. This date coincides with her submission of articles to the early journals of the Ramakrishna Order as well as agreeing with the date of her thirtieth anniversary in Vedanta (May 1931). After becoming a member of the Vedanta Society, she helped in the publication department. When Sarah Ellen Waldo (Ellen) stepped down from her publishing responsibilities, due to acute problems with her eyes, responsibility for the publication department passed to Laura. Her first assignment was the completion of the work that Ellen had begun—editing the two volumes of Swamiji's *Jnana Yoga* (1902).

As head of the publishing department, Laura was extremely busy. A report published in the *Brahmavadin* in January 1903 summarized the magnitude of the work. Drawn from the minutes of the annual meeting, the report read as follows:

> Nowhere was the expansion of work more apparent than in the publication business of the Society. The statement of the twelve months ending with December 1902 showed that 5,250 pamphlets and over 2,500 volumes had gone into circulation, while the gross receipts had much more than doubled. For the first time, publication expenses were paid for by the profit from sales instead of private donations.[6]

On one occasion, while consulting with Abhedananda on an upcoming publication, Laura noticed a photograph hanging over the mantel in his room. The personage in the photograph was one of the two figures that had appeared to her in Boston. Approaching the fireplace, she abruptly inquired, "Of whom is this a picture?" Abhedananda replied, "It is my Master, Sri Ramakrishna." One can imagine the impact of this moment on Laura—identifying one of the figures in her earlier Boston vision. Her devotion to Ramakrishna at that point took wing. He became the "subject of my meditation," she wrote.[7]

To accommodate an overflowing audience in 1901, the Society rented the Carnegie Lyceum Hall for Sunday lectures. In Abhedananda's first lecture in January 1902, he ushered in the New Year by outlining the religious need of the time. He affirmed:

> The twentieth century needs a religion with no scheme for salvation, no need for heaven or hell, no fear of eternal punishment. The twentieth century needs a religion free from

sacerdotal institutions and free from all books, scriptures and personalities. The twentieth century needs a religion with a concept of God, not personal, not impersonal but beyond both, a God whose supreme aspect will harmonize with the ultimate Reality of the universe. The twentieth century religion must accept the ultimate conclusions of all the philosophies of the world.[8]

In the winter of 1901–02, Abhedananda traveled to the West Coast for three months on a lecture tour. Using the initials L.G., Laura wrote in the January 1902 issue of *Prabuddha Bharata* that "he was able for the first time to perceive how far his field of influence extends. At every turn, indeed, he met with well-wishers and friends—those who had heard him lecture, or who had read his pamphlets."[9] During the summer recesses of the years 1902 through 1904, he traveled to Europe and lectured in several countries: Italy, Switzerland, Belgium, England, Scotland, France, Holland, and Bavaria (which is now in Germany). The message of Vedanta was thus spread over a large geographic area.

Laura describes one of the celebrations of Sri Ramakrishna's birthday that was held at the Society. If her memory served her right, this particular celebration occurred a year after her return to New York from Boston. In this case, she would be describing the celebration held in 1902.

> Of the fifty or sixty members who attended the celebration, scarcely one tasted food or drank water from before sunset on the previous evening until after sunset on the evening of the birthday.... All day we sat on the floor of the classroom without a mat or cushion, meditating, praying, or listening to the reading of sacred books. There were brief recesses, but a hush of holy silence was upon every heart and there was little conversation—that little being in low undertones.[10]

As the last hour of the celebratory day approached, she described what happened as follows:

> The stillness of the room was breathless. Something impelled me to open my eyes and there, on the platform amid the masses of flowers which had been brought in as offering, stood the Living Presence. It was the same figure that had come to me in Boston. The smile on the face was the same

Spiritual Training under Swami Abhedananda 73

and there radiated from it the same power, the same gentle benediction. The figure stood there for a few seconds with hands outstretched in blessing, then was gone.[11]

It was most likely in the fall of 1902 that Laura "entered on a course of intensive spiritual training" under Abhedananda's guidance. The training included the practice of posture and breathing exercises, and a grounding in the art of concentration and meditation. Her regime entailed great regularity, careful diet, and above all firm resolution. She wrote, "I charted my day as a sea captain might chart his voyage. I rose early, ate lightly, had fixed hours for spiritual practices and stated hours for publication work, which involved much editing, typewriting, and proofreading. Some time was spent at the Society house attending to book orders."[12]

At this time Laura lived alone in a studio apartment on Madison Avenue. At the hour of evening meditation in her private shrine, she had a vision of Sri Ramakrishna on each of three successive nights. On the first night, the figure of Ramakrishna was "a colossal figure made of pure light, with glistening garments." She laid her forehead on his feet and lost outer consciousness. The second night, "he cast off his body and stood clothed in light. A subtle tenderness lingered like a fragrance about Him, taking away all sense of awe or fear." Lastly, on the third night, "his body seemed only a lantern, in which burned a dazzling flame sending out broad beams of light all about Him."[13]

Though no words were spoken, the silence of each night was "charged with meaning." Laura conveyed her sentiment in words: "I had learned that whether clothed in an earthly body or manifest in super-earthly glory, Sri Ramakrishna was a living Presence, moving among men and women, to aid and to bless, to guide and to shield, in the fullness of His love."[14]

Abhedananda asked Laura to compile the sayings of Sri Ramakrishna in February 1903, a date based on Laura's accounts as well as the publication date of the book. She promised to have the collection in print before the summer set in. Delighted with the nature of her task, Laura described the process involved.

> I went, column by column, through long files of old periodicals, searching for a word or a sentence that might have fallen from Sri Ramakrishna's lips. I read carefully various small collections, some of them out of print. I exhausted every possible source and finally brought together nearly seven hundred sayings. . . . I decided to classify them into

> chapters with marginal headings and as far as possible to arrange them to make consecutive readings. It was a long and arduous labor, yet one I was reluctant to leave even for an hour. I rose at dawn and worked far into the night. . . . Day after day the glowing words burned deeper and deeper into my consciousness. I walked in their rhythm, I ate with them sounding in my thought, I slept with them on my lips, I was consumed by them.[15]

When typing the final copy of the manuscript in her apartment one morning, she felt "a tapping on my shoulder." Being alone and focused on her task, she assumed it was condensed moisture falling from the skylight. A second tapping however made her turn quickly. She saw Sri Ramakrishna standing just behind her on the left side. Describing him as "impressively living," she writes, "No light shone from Him, only the radiance of His smile made him luminous. He was dominantly a living human Presence. He remained a brief moment, then disappeared."[16]

For clarity, Laura explained the nature of her visions as follows:

> These were not psychic visions, they were not dreams, they were not imaginations, nor was the Great One who came in them an apparition. He was a pulsing Presence, a living personality. The warmth and radiance of His Being were clearly perceptible; in my being also, when the Presence came, there was a peculiar unaccustomed glow, sometimes the glow preceded the Presence, as if to herald its approach, sometimes it came with it; but always its influence lingered after for hours and even days.[17]

Swami Vivekananda stated that visions and experiences are "an aspirant's milestones on the way to progress" towards the goal.[18] They have the ability to elevate the heart of a spiritual seeker with new strength and insight. Neither is, however, an indication of spiritual depth or necessary for spiritual unfoldment. In judging spiritual progress, Vedanta states that the true indicators are, in fact, the degree of steadfastness in one's spiritual practice, the lessening of all worldly desires, and one's strength of character.

The *Sayings of Sri Ramakrishna* was at the printers in late 1903. Laura's alertness to exhausting all sources was such that "even after the manuscript had gone to the printers, I kept running down another Saying to insert. . . . Mr. Drummond, the printer, used to beg me not to find any more."[19]

In the Preface, Abhedananda noted that an "attempt . . . has been made for the first time to classify and arrange in logical sequence the Sayings which were published in the *Brahmavadin* and the *Prabuddha Bharata* as well as in *Ramakrishna, His Life and Sayings*, by Professor Max Muller, all having been carefully compared with the original and revised."[20]

Laura was also given the responsibility of conducting meditation classes at the Society. Mr. W.H. Starick, a member of the Vedanta Society since 1901, recalled, "Miss Laura Glenn was our teacher at the afternoon meditation class in 1903. As I have always said, she was as a hen taking care of her brood. She also had the gift to impart spirituality. From the time we left New York and went to Atlanta, she kept the correspondence between us and the Society."[21]

In the February 1904 issue of *Prabuddha Bharata*, Laura delivered an overall review of the work of the Vedanta Society under her initials.

> Few beyond those who have watched the organization from the beginning can appreciate through what vicissitude it has passed and what an inexhaustible store of determination, courage and perseverance it has needed to bring it to its present condition. . . . A religion like Vedanta, attempts no compromise, but boldly preaches practical renunciation and non-attachment, must necessarily find a limited number of followers at the outset and these will inevitably be among the thinking class than among the rich. The Vedanta Society has therefore had to make its way slowly; but this very struggle has undoubtedly meant added vigor.[22]

In April 1905, the Society began to publish its own journal, the *Vedanta Monthly Bulletin*. Its purpose was to spread the spiritual truths of Vedanta and to coordinate the efforts of individuals and groups far and wide. The contents of the bulletin varied each month. The annual memorial services held at the center were described in detail, including the speeches given on these celebratory occasions. Reports from the Vedanta centers in India and the U.S. were published. New books for sale by the Society were announced; some press reviews were given. At other times, questions and answers were published or an address that Abhedananda delivered before a club or an association in New York City. In 1909, the journal's publication was suspended due to financial constraints.

The *Brahmavadin* (June 1905) reprinted an article from *Broadway Magazine* entitled "Vedanta and the Swami in Manhattan." Its theme was the Vedanta Society's progress. The magazine's reporter observed that the swami has "secured" a strong following and placed the Society on a "solid financial" standing; furthermore, the Sunday morning lectures "have an average attendance of about five-hundred, drawn from varied ranks of life—the banker, the broker, the man of letters, the artisan, the woman of fashion, and the wage earner."[23]

On Tuesday evenings from November 13 to December 19, 1905, Abhedananda gave a series of lectures under the auspices of the prestigious Brooklyn Institute of Arts and Sciences to "an audience of professionals, critics and serious students" who were thoughtful men and women. The lectures were published by the Society in book form under the title of *India and Her People*. An extraneous lecture, "Women's Place in Hindu Religion," was also included. This book was "one of the most authoritative and concisely complete histories of India in circulation in the West."[24] It corrected the false impressions circulating about India and its religious beliefs in the milieu of the time.

1906–07

After nine years as minister of the Vedanta Society of New York, Abhedananda sailed for India on May 16, 1906. This was his only return to India in his twenty-four years of teaching in the U.S. (from 1897 to 1921). On May 14, he was honored at a reception. On behalf of the Society's members, the secretary, Emily Cape, read a farewell address that expressed everyone's deep appreciation for his work. In part, it read,

> With infinite wisdom, patience, courage and tenacity which have characterized your efforts at every step, you began to build, stone by stone, the solid structure of the Vedanta Society as it stands today. . . . You have been to us an ever wise and ever loving master and teacher. . . . Everywhere you have brought hope, gladness, strength and spiritual light. Never can we pay the mighty debt we owe to you, except in striving, day by day, nay hour by hour, to embody in our lives the lofty truths you have taught us.[25]

In December 1906, Abhedananda returned with his new assistant, Swami Paramananda, just before Christmas. A charismatic-monastic disciple of Swami Vivekananda, Paramananda was only twenty-two when he set foot on American soil.

Laura was one of the three Society members who met the steamer that cast anchor in New York Harbor. She immediately recognized Paramananda as the second figure in her Boston vision. Describing his demeanor upon disembarking, she couldn't have known how very apt her words would remain over the years. "He was calm and perfectly at ease and he maintained that same quietness and simplicity when an hour later he faced a large portion of the congregation who lingered at the Society . . . in the hope of seeing the arriving travelers,"[26] she noted.

In the early days of Paramananda's arrival, she observed that he "filled the house with joyousness…as he moved through the halls there was always a murmur of song on his lips, and [an] unvarying brightness of mood and bearing."[27] Cheerfulness remained the high note of his character.

At Vivekananda's birthday celebration at the Vedanta Society early in 1907, Swamis Abhedananda, Bodhananda, and Paramananda spoke at different intervals throughout the day. Previously an assistant to Abhedananda, Bodhananda headed the Pittsburgh Center. Abhedananda opened the evening service by addressing the entire scope of Vivekananda's work—namely, the "inspiring influence of his writings, the institutions founded by him or in his name, and the spread of his message through dedicated, inspired workers."[28] Laura was also asked to speak. In her address, she reminded everyone of the true strength behind Vivekananda's message. She remarked,

> Every word he uttered he had first lived in silence, in meditation, and in action; and it was because [they were] thus weighted with experience that his word had so much effect. We must learn to be disciples, to understand the truths we hear, to live them, and then we will never have to speak them. It is after all Swami Vivekananda's life which speaks strongest for him.[29]

Abhedananda was a man of indomitable energy, and he kept to a very busy schedule throughout 1907. One of his projects was to publish in English the original manuscript of *Ramakrishna Kathamrita*. Authored by Mahendranath Gupta (known as M), the two Bengali volumes provided detailed accounts of the daily life and verbatim conversations of Sri Ramakrishna. They had been published in Calcutta in 1902 (first vol.) and 1903 (second vol.).

When M sent his manuscript to Abhedananda, he authorized the swami to edit and translate it into English. On Monday, October 7, Abhedananda took the manuscript, entitled *The Gospel of Sri Ramakrishna*, to the printers. His was the first edition of the *Gospel* in the English language. In the preface of the work, published in pocket format and dated December 15, 1907, Abhedananda wrote,

> At the request of M, I have edited and remodeled the larger portion of his English manuscript; while the remaining portions I have translated directly from the Bengali edition of his notes. The marginal headings, foot-notes and index, as well as the division of the 'Gospel' into fourteen chapters, were added by me. I have endeavored to make every word of this edition as literal, simple and colloquial as possible.[30]

In the March 1908 edition of the *Vedanta Monthly Bulletin*, the *New York Herald*'s review of *The Gospel of Sri Ramakrishna* was published in its entirety. The newspaper review was cited in the bulletin as an example of the considerable attention that the secular press paid to the publication of the *Gospel*. A picture of the Panchavati, where Ramakrishna attained communion with the Divine Mother, was also published in the *Herald*.

On Saturday, March 2, 1907, Abhedananda purchased a four-story house for the Vedanta Society at 135 West 80th Street. The Society took occupancy that year under a $15,000 mortgage. The March 1908 issue of the *Vedanta Monthly Bulletin* describes the house as having "rooms for classes and lectures, a library accessible to all who are sincerely interested in our work, a room for publications, and last but not least, a home for our wise ones from the East."[31]

Members of the Society occupied these quarters without first installing the deity and setting aside a room for worship. This was no small omission for the spiritual seekers traveling the path of devotion. Paramananda took it upon himself to establish a shrine room where he performed simple, daily ritualistic worship.

This incident highlighted the friction that existed between the two different groups of devotees at the Society. Abhedananda was an erudite scholar with broad academic interests. He leaned towards the spiritual path of knowledge. His students were by and large from intellectual circles. Through reasoning, they practiced discrimination between the real (the Self) and the unreal (the world) that tended to an all-embracing unity (or monism). In contrast, Paramananda had a warm personality and was predominately inclined to the path of devotion. This path encouraged the devotee to establish an intimate relationship with the Divine through prayer, song, and ritual. By intermingling aspirants of different, though equally valid paths, conflicts were bound to surface in the community. This is especially true for students in the early years of their spiritual training when counter influences are disruptive. Those who are well established in their spiritual path have a more balanced view of the yogas as blending in one's life, as opposed to being independent. As pointed out in Chapter One, Swami Vivekananda called forth a new vision of spiritual life where the four yogas combine to produce a type of human being that could meet the demands of this age.

It is also worth noting that the approach of each swami to the work was decidedly different. By nature, Abhedananda was more or less reserved. He operated on a large scale, which assured the Society of sound financial support, based on large membership numbers. The swami felt he had to reach out, to plow new fields, both far and wide. In contrast, Paramananda was personable and approachable. He took no interest in organizational concerns like membership numbers and fund-raising drives (e.g., concerts). He would rather tend the growing plants. In the establishment of any movement, both approaches have their value.

A write-up in the July 1905 issue of the *Vedanta Monthly Bulletin* pointed out the need for a summer home for the membership away from the city. A farmhouse property in the Berkshire Hills of Connecticut was purchased by Abhedananda to serve that purpose early in 1907. It was located on what is now Town Street in Cornwall, 107 miles from New York City. An old house with eleven rooms, several barns, (large and small), and sheds stood on the property that consisted of 370 acres of rolling hills and pastures. Sixty-five acres of tillable land afforded ample opportunity for farming, and water was available from a spring on the side of a hill. As building projects got underway or renovations on the house were needed, someone having the prerequisite training would make an appearance. In this way, the ashram or Peace Retreat was kept in repair without hired labor. A variety of fruit trees and a kitchen garden "kept the table well supplied for summer guests."[32] A horse was purchased, followed by cows, chickens, and pigs for marketing. Within a few years, the ashram was self-supporting.

The *Monthly Bulletin* of April 1907 described the rationale for this purchase as being a "retreat where earnest students can enjoy the beauties of nature and find peace and harmony."[33] Society members discovered in short order its real role—a school for the study of karma yoga. As a member put it, "we learned to worship by thinking through our problems at our work." Sister Shivani, an ardent disciple of Abhedananda and author of *Swami Abhedananda in America*, further explained, "those who were best fitted for the path of reason found their every challenge in work and labor. Those best organized for labor were impelled by hidden forces within themselves to pit their acumen upon the keenest adversary. And the Bhaktas [devotional types]—sometimes I think they had [it] best because they gave the best. To them obedience made all things simple."[34]

After Abhedananda left the New York Vedanta Society in 1910, he resided with his students for nine years in this old New England farmstead, with its oil lamps, wood fires, and outhouses. His diary records that he worked along with his students, whether it be planting the garden, working at the stables, washing the dogs, picking fruit, or laying the foundation for a chicken coop.[35] He thus taught practical Vedanta through his actions, a significant change for an erudite scholar. For his students, the path of knowledge gave way to karma yoga, thus making their work an application of practical Vedanta. The ashram was closed in 1919 when Abhedananda moved to California before returning to India in 1921.

Devamata

In line with Laura's natural inclination, Paramananda was devotionally inclined. His early influence on her can be seen in the write-up of the Publication Committee's annual report, published in the February 1907 issue of the monthly bulletin. Unlike the report given in January 1903, previously quoted as being statistically framed, this report confirmed the importance of the publication department in reaching beyond "the voice of the swami" and "beyond the limits of the public hall doors," while acknowledging that "the foothold which Vedanta has gained in this country is shown less by the number of direct followers, or the extent of its book sales, than by the way it has everywhere modified and transformed existing modes of thought; and this can never be set down in figures."[36]

March 19, 1907, represented a turning point for Laura, a milestone in her spiritual journey. On that day, she was initiated by Paramananda and given the name Devamata, a Sanskrit word that translates to "Mother of the Gods." Considering her first vision in Boston, Laura must have perceived this event as wrought by destiny, that is, providentially ordained.

During this time, Devamata experienced opposition to her spiritual interests on two fronts. Her father, a member of St. Paul's Methodist Episcopal Church, adamantly opposed her involvement in Vedanta. He claimed he would disinherit her if that involvement deepened. Her initiation was certainly a sign of an increased commitment. He later retracted his statement and included Devamata in his will, even though marginally so. Secondly, Abhedananda's staunch supporters railed against her. As leader of the Society's meditation classes and head of the publication department, Devamata had an integral role in the day-to-day operation of the Society. Her articles in the journals of the Order spoke of the growth of the Society into a "sturdy deep-rooted plant" through the "tireless care and devotion" of Abhedananda.[37] Consequently Devamata's initiation by Paramananda appeared to be a shift in allegiance, bordering on disloyalty to Abhedananda.

Swami Paramananda in 1913

It is not surprising then that she wrote, "it was a moment of grave crisis with me and Swami [Paramananda] sought to sustain me in every way possible. His frequent words, stirring and vital because they came from one who lived them, carried me over the difficult places and made the darkest hours bright."[38] For his part, Paramananda expressed regret to her that he was the "outward cause of most of the suffering [she] had to undergo." But he added, "then again I think that everything is done through Her [Divine Mother's] will."[39]

In another letter to Devamata, he expanded along the same lines.

> When we ... try to defend ourselves by fighting or disputing with our opponents we ... forget the protecting hands of our All Blissful Mother. Do not forget for a moment that we are all her children, good or bad, all her children. If She does not

protect, there is no other power that can save us and when She protects, there is no power that can do any harm to us."[40]

To remove Devamata from the strife that embroiled her at the Vedanta Society, Paramananda arranged for her to spend time in India. He wrote to Swami Ramakrishnananda, head of the Mylapore Center in Madras, whom he had studied under for four years and with whom he had an intimate association. The twenty-one letters written by Ramakrishnananda to Paramananda shortly after the latter left India (1907–10) expressed the elder monk's solicitous concern for the young swami's health and spiritual well-being.

Ellen Waldo corresponded with Ramakrishnananda quite frequently. In a letter dated December 17, 1907, she addressed Devamata's forthcoming trip to India, which was booked for the end of the month. She wrote,

> I feel sure that your association with her and your spiritual teachings will be a great good to her. . . . She is highly educated and unusually cultured, has had fine literary training, speaks several languages and is devoted heart and soul to Vedanta. She is in every way fitted to do good work in India and to be of great help to you in many ways. I am sorry to have her go so far away, but there seems to be no place for her here in New York.[41]

Ellen's letter holds out the possibility that Devamata would permanently stay in India to help with the work there, just like other Western women disciples of Swami Vivekananda. She added, "I hope the climate will suit her and that she may be able to do good, helpful work in India."[42]

While in India, Devamata likely informed Ramakrishnananda that she felt Abhedananda was displeased with her. Abhedananda's position at the time was stated in a letter that he wrote to Ramakrishnananda on July 20, 1908. "Why should I be displeased with her [Devamata]? As she has taken refuge in the Master she has to love and move according to the Master's will—this is my belief and conviction. It is no body's fault O'Mother. May the Master lead her along the path of righteousness and keep her in perfect peace. This is my prayer."[43]

Abhedananda left for a visit to London in June 1907, leaving Paramananda in charge of the center until his return in September. In 1908 and 1909, Abhedananda spent six months each year in Europe. He established a branch of the Vedanta Society in London. His absence from New York City, however, began to negatively affect the center's membership numbers and income.

During Abhedananda's absences, Paramananda spent summers in the Connecticut Berkshire Hills ashram enjoying nature and teaching informally. The first summer that the ashram was open, the monthly bulletin noted the changes that were made on the grounds. "Trees were felled and others planted, and the stream was enlarged to form a swimming pool." With the help of swamis Paramananda and Bodhananda, a small garden was planted to "yield enough vegetables to supply the table bountifully." The livestock at the time consisted of one horse, named Rudy. He was "employed in hauling cut wood, meeting the train, and other work."[44] Grass was cut for hay for his winter feed.

Discoveries were made. "A splendid rock was named after Ramakrishna and a special point of interest was a cave named Sarada." A brook named after Brahmananda ran through the property. It served as a primitive laundry. An "impressive sweeping view of the surrounding country" was revealed at the summit of Echo Mountain, within walking distance of the ashram.[45]

On occasion a matter at the center required Paramananda's attention, so he would return to the city for a short period. During one of his stays at the center, Devamata describes an incident that led to the inception of the Indian Fund. She notes that after a lecture Paramananda made an appeal to the audience for the "famine-stricken souls of India."[46] Eventually the collected funds, amounting to 200 rupees, were sent to President Maharaj in India for famine relief.

Encouraged by the outcome of this appeal, Devamata wrote that Paramananda began an ongoing Indian Fund with a nickel. She described the incident.

> We took a candy box, cut a slit in the top, printed on it, "For the hungry of India," and placed it at the door of a small private chapel ... Before long there was more than fifty dollars in the box; and it was touching to see the Swami's delight when a few weeks later he tied the dimes, quarters, halves, bills and one shining gold piece in a handkerchief and gave it to me to carry to India.[47]

Over the ensuing years, Paramananda continued to send funds to India. With Ramakrishnananda's help, some needs of Holy Mother and the direct disciples of Ramakrishna were met. The stream of aid flowed more rapidly as time progressed. The Boys' School in Madras, charitable dispensaries in Dacca and Allahabad, an orphanage in Murshidabad, the Home of Service in Benares, and a hospital in Hardwar, as well as famine and flood relief were a number of causes Paramananda supported financially.[48]

Devamata spent the summer of 1907 in the Catskill Mountains of New York, near Jewett, upon the invitation of a friend. Her days were usually spent in nature, "wandering over the hills or through the woods" in the area, "memorizing the Bhagavad Gita" as she walked. Her love of nature was second only to her love for Ramakrishna. It was during one of her rambles through the hills that she lost the small photograph of him that she carried in her Gita. Much to her disappointment, despite an exhaustive search she did not find the picture. She wrote, "From that day, the hills of Jewett were sacred to me—somewhere in their tangled grass lay hidden a holy face."[49]

Inspired Talks

Overall it was a restful time for Devamata. Solitary activities filled her days—walking, editing, and meditating. She also spent time with her friend Ellen, who was residing nearby. She had enjoyed the tranquil environment of the summer in upstate New York since the late 1880s, when she and her mother vacationed there.

For several leisurely summer afternoons near the end of Devamata's stay in the Catskills, the two women sat on the veranda of the farmhouse that Ellen was renting. Ellen read her notes of Vivekananda's classes at Thousand Island Park, some forty-three pages in number, while Devamata listened attentively. At the conclusion of the reading Devamata stated, in no uncertain terms, "It is a crime for you to keep these notes to yourself. They belong to the world." Leaning forward in Devamata's direction and holding out her book of notes, Ellen said, "If you are willing to take them and work on them and bring them out, I am glad to pass them over to you. If I tried to do anything with them, I should be thinking all the time how lacking they were."[50]

Devamata returned to New York City to pick up her typewriter and a supply of paper then traveled back to Jewett where she hired a "room in an isolated house on the edge of the village" that afforded her solitude, and set about editing Ellen's notes over a period of six weeks. She detailed the process.

> Every afternoon I took my Bhagavad Gita, Miss Waldo's notes, pencil and paper, and walked to the solitude of a distant hill. Here for several hours I worked on the notes, undisturbed save by the call of a bird or the tap of a falling leaf. It seemed as if Swamiji worked with me, so readily did the unfinished sentence finish itself and the broken paragraph round itself out.[51]

Each morning Devamata typed the notes that she had written the previous day on Ellen's veranda. She recalled, "Ellen read them and grew more and more delighted, more and more content that the notes were to be published."[52] Though Ellen was not interested in the publication details of the book, she did suggest a title: *Inspired Talks*.

A duplicate copy of the typed notes was sent to Paramananda at the Connecticut ashram to keep him apprised of her efforts. Devamata notes, "In a day or two would come a letter from him containing comments and with them personal thoughts and counsels . . . gentle words of deep devotion!"[53] For her own edification, she copied all the inspiring passages of his letters into a notebook. Eventually, it dawned on her to compile them into a book. The passages grouped themselves under five titles—namely, devotion, purity, steadfastness, fearlessness, and self-surrender. In the foreword of the resulting book she writes, "nothing of this was written to the Swami, but when I returned to New York in September the manuscript was laid in his hand. His joy was childlike and lovely."[54] During the next months, the contents of the manuscript were arranged in chapters. The opening prayer was taken from the Bhagavad Gita. The Sanskrit salutations and litany to the Divine Mother at the end were translated by Paramananda.

The *Path of Devotion* was published in November 1907 and met with immediate acclaim. Its subtle power lies in its simplicity; it speaks directly and convincingly to the heart. According to a review in the February 1908 issue of the monthly bulletin, the swami's words emphasized the "value of looking for help not from the world without but from deeper and deeper within yourself." It also pointed out that "the conception of God as the Mother of the Universe, a thought associated especially with the teaching of Sri Ramakrishna, is beautifully developed."[55]

It was the first book authored by Paramananda to be published. Devamata also transcribed his New York lectures for his second and third books: *The*

True Spirit of Religion Is Universal and *Vedanta in Practice*.[56] They both appeared in 1908. The material for his fourth book, *The Way of Peace and Blessedness*, consisted of his letters to Devamata while she was in India. Prepared for publication in 1911, it was "humbly and gratefully dedicated to the sacred and loving memory of Swami Ramakrishnananda," who had passed that year.[57] Several quotes introduce each of the six chapters of this 105-page hardcover.

Devamata sailed for India from New York Harbor on December 28, 1907, aboard the steamer *Siguria*. She carried with her the manuscript of Vivekananda's talks given at Thousand Island Park. Regarding his spoken words, she wrote,

> Those glowing words. . .spoken at Thousand Island Park on the banks of the St. Lawrence River, hidden for long years in Brooklyn, prepared for publication in the heart of the Catskill Mountains nine miles from any railway, now traveled through the Suez Canal, past the sandy bluffs of the Desert of Sahara, across the continent of India, to take form as a book under the burning sky of Madras![58]

Devamata also carried with her a large case of the newly published edition of *The Path of Devotion*. In a letter to Paramananda dated January 30, 1908, Ramakrishnananda praised the book, a copy of which had arrived at the Mylapore Center "on the birthday of Swamiji." Regarding the book, he wrote "Truth is its life, consciousness its substance and love its soul, a supremely pure heart is its birthplace and the Lord's lotus feet are its goal."[59]

Lastly, Devamata carried Paramananda's blessing, "You are going to the land of great teachers. If you meet one whose disciple you want to be, do not feel bound by your relationship with me."[60] Paramananda freed her to choose another as guru. After all, she would be with the Great Ones of the lineage.

Chapter Six

SISTER DEVAMATA
1908–1909

Part 1: Madras

The thirty-seven-day journey was climaxed by a night in which Devamata kept vigil, watching and waiting. Peering out the porthole of the ocean steamer, she caught her first sight of India in the dawning hours of a new day. It was the beginning of February 1908. Due to a low tide, docking in the Bombay harbor was on hold. To avoid further delay, however, she set out for shore in a small boat with a fellow passenger.

After traveling two days, she arrived at the Madras rail station in the early hours of the morning, and was deeply touched by the warm reception. Swami Ramakrishnananda, head of the center at Mylapore, and a delegation of Indian gentlemen greeted her. The many carriages then set out for the new monastery. Consecrated on November 17, 1907, the center was the first permanent building of the Ramakrishna Order in the Madras area. Devamata described the scene when she reached the monastery.

> Swami Ramakrishnananda first led me to the Shrine, then to a large table at the far end of the hall where breakfast for me only had been set out. He was as loving and watchful as a mother with a home-coming child. He kept laying fruit after fruit on my plate, refilling my tea-cup and urging me to eat with such persuasiveness that I was forced to overstep the usual limits of my morning meal.[1]

The Swami's solicitous motherly concern was evident throughout Devamata's stay. He cooked all her food out of fear that the monastery's brahmin cook might overseason it, thereby creating digestive problems for her. Visitors had to meet with his approval so that she wasn't overwhelmed with a large number of unannounced guests. Likewise, all invitations were handled by him, whether it be to speak at a public meeting or to visit a home. In the hot months, he would arrange a carriage ride for her along the seashore to escape the heat.

A few days after she arrived in Madras, Sri Sarada Devi (Holy Mother) sent Her loving greetings. She addressed Devamata as "my daughter." Ramakrishnananda translated the note, written in Bengali, and ending in Mother's blessing: "May you live long and along with all my other children may you remain ever merged in bliss eternal!"[2] Swami Brahmananda, first President of the Ramakrishna Order, also sent her a letter of welcome. He expressed hope that the Lord "grant you peace of mind and heavenly happiness."[3]

Ramakrishnananda wrote to Paramananda on February 20, shortly after Devamata had arrived. His letter was full of assurances.

> Miss Glenn is well here. We have chosen a nice house for her. She is very careful and intelligent. Do not be worried about her. . . . She attended the Monday and Thursday class at the Math and took notes of what was said.[4]

Devamata's firsthand accounts of her two-year stay in India poignantly captured the essence of the spiritual life of a nation and its people, from its temple festivals and religious observances to its social ceremonies. These accounts were finally compiled in a book *Days in an Indian Monastery*, published in 1927.* The Indian women and the Indian home were also described in great detail. Since the book had been undertaken with Ramakrishnananda's encouragement, she viewed its completion as a sacred obligation. The book interweaves her Indian experience with the Swami's inspired teachings.

In Swami Tapasyananda's book entitled *Swami Ramakrishnananda, The Apostle of Sri Ramakrishna to the South*, Devamata's contribution to preserving Ramakrishnananda's teachings is described by C. Ramaswami Iyengar, who was Ramakrishnananda's right-hand helper. He wrote, "She it is that recorded every word of what he spoke and took notes on his class lectures; and it is to her that we owe the preservation of his invaluable teachings which are so original and soul-stirring."[5]

---

*Devamata's original foreword of the book is in Appendix B.

Besides class lectures, Devamata recorded Ramakrishnananda's informal instructions, which were not limited to the evening hours after service. She was the benefactor of his spiritual wisdom while sitting on the upper verandah of her living quarters, or standing in the hall of the monastery. She pointed out that surrender was a topic which he consistently addressed. Since he lived what he preached, his words carried the power to influence the mind and heart of the devotee. As she stated, his words were etched "deep into the heart."[6]

There was also the teaching that required no words. At the time of worship in the monastery's shrine, the fervor of his spirit uplifted Devamata's thoughts "entirely above the world and material concerns."[7] Forgetting himself

Swami Ramakrishnananda, head of the Mylapore Ramakrishna Math, India

in the exuberance of devotion, he would joyously cry out, "Jai Gurudev, Sri Gurudev."[8] For him, Sri Ramakrishna was a living presence. Those in attendance would join in the repeated cry, which seemed to have no end. During a festival, she witnessed him dance with the devotees in the monastery hall. She described one such scene. He approached the altar "in slow stately turns . . . and not once did his eyes leave it or an arm cease to point towards it. The fixity of his concentration could not fail to stir the deeper emotions. He seemed the embodiment of rhythmic prayer, the spirit of worship incarnate."[9]

Eager to learn, Devamata was persistent in posing questions. How could your words be so real and living? How can we hope to understand? Ramakrishnananda would provide a simple, straightforward answer, sharing unstintingly the vast richness of his thoughts. He was best in an informal mode of teaching, a conversational style. When he was indrawn, his eyes no longer seeing, her questions went unanswered or the conversation would be brought to a close, sometimes abruptly, with four words: "Sister, go and rest."[10]

Her enthusiastic actions, made in good faith, were not always welcome. On one occasion during his absence from Madras, she tidied the bed in his room. Upon his return, he conveyed his displeasure with a scolding for her intrusion into a monk's quarters.

As recorded in *Days in an Indian Monastery*, Devamata was roused from a rest one afternoon by the call "Mother, Mother." She walked to the door. Finding no one, she proceeded to the veranda. A man in the banyan tree nearest the door was stripping an entire branch of its leaves. She drove the trespasser away by clapping her hands and calling out. Hearing of the incident, Swami responded, "You were sleeping, your subconscious mind was uppermost, so you were able to hear the appeal of the tree for protection . . . that man who has the inner eye opened sees that the whole universe is palpitating with life."[11]

Located across the way from the monastery, a spacious house had been rented for Devamata's use. Due to unforeseeable circumstances, however, she was initially housed in a nearby primary school building. A month after her arrival, the rented house was ready for occupancy. Sri Ramakrishna's birthday on March 3rd was chosen as the auspicious day for the move. A small procession made its way from the monastery to her new residence, with Ramakrishnananda carrying her holy pictures. The entrance and the verandah of her new dwelling were auspiciously decorated with branches, leaves, and fruit. After stooping to touch the threshold of the door, everyone then made their way up to the second story. A makeshift altar had been set up, and straw mats served as seats. On his own initiative, a conservative South Indian brahmin from the neighborhood chanted Sanskrit verses from the scriptures. This action, like no other, sanctioned her presence in a neighborhood where all houses were occupied by brahmins.

In the morning, Devamata would wake to Ramakrishnananda's voice repeating the sacred name on the monastery roof. In *Days in an Indian Monastery*, she described her daily routine in detail.

> I rose at four and kept the first hours of the day for myself. At half past six, I walked to a lovely garden a mile away . . . to gather my day's supply of flowers. I had my first meal about nine. The morning offering in the temple was brought to me between ten and noon. I did not eat until half past twelve or one, the food was never cold. The air kept it warm . . . At half past four or five I went over to the monastery to do my part towards keeping it ordered and clean. The evening service came at the sunset hour. The hour or two after arati was the time when the Swami Ramakrishnananda often gave

his teaching. At half past eight or nine, instruction ended. [Afterwards I] usually walked round the four streets of the Temple ... for about forty minutes.[12]

During her evening walks, hearing chanting coming from a temple or songs with drum and tamboura from a nearby house, Devamata said that she "dropped back into Epic India," imagining the appeal of Lord Krishna's flute or the call of Chaitanya to praise Lord Hari. At eleven o'clock each night, she could be found recording by candle light all that Ramakrishnananda had spoken that evening. It was later that he would comment, "Sister, how did you do it? As I read your notes, I felt that I was speaking."[13]

Maharaj Visits Mylapore Monastery

Ramakrishnananda was persistent in requesting President Swami Brahmananda, reverentially referred to as Maharaj, to visit South India to sanctify the Math. Though a bedroom in the monastery was renovated for Ramakrishnananda's use, he left it unused in anticipation of Maharaj's eventual stay. He slept in another room that was used partially for storage.

In October 1908, Maharaj began to journey south, staying in Madras for six months. Devamata and Rudra, a brahmachari, were put in charge of preparing for his coming. In words of profound respect, Ramakrishnananda reminded them: "when you see him [Maharaj], you have a glimpse of what Sri Ramakrishna was. The self in Swami Brahmananda is entirely annihilated. Whatever he says or does comes directly from the Divine Source."[14] When asked if Maharaj will give a talk, he recoiled at the very idea asking, "What is there in hollow talk? Here is the man ... who can give religion and lead man to God."[15]

Devamata and Rudra undertook their task with great zeal. Every nook and cranny of the monastery was cleaned. The monastery was a one-story building with a high foundation, reddish stucco siding, and a roof terrace. The layout of the main building was simple—four rooms and a large hall that opened into a courtyard in which was located a building housing the kitchen, dining room, and bathroom. The hall was the Swami's office, sitting room for guests, and the bedroom of the resident monastic disciples. Two of the rooms were shrines—one for Sri Ramakrishna and one for Swami Vivekananda.

As the day of Maharaj's arrival approached, garlands were draped over the doors, the terrace, and the gate. Rudra made a large WELCOME sign of green leaves stretched across the roof. A heavy downpour the morning of his arrival tore the garlands and left the green leaves a dripping mess. Ramakrishnananda had traveled north to meet up with Maharaj. Arriving together at the Madras train station, they were greeted on the platform by a large enthusiastic crowd.

A month after Maharaj's arrival, Ramakrishnananda wrote Paramananda and noted that Devamata was extremely glad about the visit of Maharaj. In the letter dated November 5, 1908, he detailed her reaction, "How lucky she feels herself to have seen our President's holy self. She is sparing no pain to make him comfortable and you will be glad to hear that she has been blessed by him."[16]

At Maharaj's invitation, Devamata continued to attend the evening service in the monastery. His evening greeting, "Come in, Sister; are you doing well?" came across as both welcoming and caring. Without fail, these words brought her "a vivid sense of well-being and blessing."[17] After the evening service a group conversation would take place. Maharaj would ask about the work in the U.S., expressing his loving concern for Swami Paramananda. These evening gatherings often included stories of individuals who performed difficult physical feats, stories much in tune with Maharaj's boyish interest.

Sending for her one morning, Maharaj requested that she write a preface for Swami Vivekananda's *Inspired Talks*. Devamata had edited the manuscript and prepared it for publication the previous summer while residing in the Catskills of New York, and had brought it with her to India. Completing the preface, she read it to Maharaj. Unresponsive, he left the room. Thinking he was dissatisfied with her write-up, she was considering how to rewrite it when one of his attendants, holding a bottle of perfume, approached her. A portion of its contents was sprinkled over her head—Maharaj's unspoken sanction.

Ramakrishnananda read every page of the manuscript and added some footnotes. Both he and Devamata corrected the proof. In 1908, *Inspired Talks* was published in India. Devamata remarked, "Maharaj had the determining word in all matters pertaining to the form the book was to take—size, binding, paper, type. He supervised every detail." Being trained in book publication from her days as head of the Publishing Department of the New York Vedanta Society, she was surprised to find that if a difference of opinion arose between them, "he [Maharaj] was right and I was wrong."[18] The preface of the 2nd edition was written by Ramakrishnananda; it went to press in 1911.*

One day, Maharaj laid his shawl in her hands and inquired, "Sister, can you mend this for me? Some insect has eaten little holes all through it. I prize it because it was given me by Ram Babu."[19] Ram Chandra Datta was a devout householder disciple of Sri Ramakrishna. Known for his erudition, he was the first to preach publicly about Sri Ramakrishna around Calcutta. Pleased to help out, Devamata "tinted some sewing silk the exact shade, and darned each little hole with meticulous care."[20] When the shawl was returned to him nicely mended, Maharaj expressed his delight with her workmanship by showing it to everyone. He didn't voice his appreciation directly to her. Reflecting on this fact, Devamata concluded that a mere 'thank you' would have cheapened the service lovingly rendered.

During the month of December, Maharaj requested her to arrange for a Christmas party, "as much like a Western Christmas party as you can make it."[21] Her house was the specified site. The traditional evergreen decorations were replaced by green branches secured to pillars of the second-floor hall with garlands of mango leaves stretched between them. Plum cake and glazed fruit, suited for the holiday, were purchased. The Christmas altar stood in an alcove behind an arch formed by garlands of jasmine, which were draped and pulled back. Honoring Ramakrishnananda's request, bread and wine were placed beside the altar symbolizing the Christian Eucharist.

In late afternoon, Devamata began the service with a reading from St. Luke's account of Christ's birth. For a length of time during the reading, Maharaj lost all outer consciousness. The remaining portion of the service consisted of the waving of lights, burning of camphor, and singing hymns. After the assembled party had left, Maharaj narrated the following: "I have had a great blessing here this afternoon. As you were reading the Bible, Christ suddenly stood before the altar dressed in a long blue cloak. He talked to me for some time. It was a very blessed moment."[22] After this auspicious event, Maharaj moved into Devamata's house during festivals at the monastery. He disliked the noise and crowds on those celebratory days, preferring comparatively quiet surroundings and solitude. Devamata cleared the second floor for his use. His furniture and belongings were also moved in.

---

*Devamata's preface for the 1st edition is in Appendix B.

A Close-up ... Maharaj

Maharaj had a love for music whether vocal or instrumental. For him, music was sound-Brahman. Accordingly, Ramakrishnananda arranged for a leading South Indian singer to entertain Maharaj during his stay. The singer played the vina, his brother the violin, and his father the cymbal, all with "indescribable art," Devamata wrote. Having spent years studying music and having heard many great musicians, she possessed a well-trained ear. In further praise, she noted, "I seemed to be listening to something more plastic and melodious than mere human sound. Never did music give me a keener pleasure than on that late afternoon in Mylapore monastery."23

Maharaj introduced Sanskrit chants and hymns at evening service during his stay at the monastery. Out of respect, Ramakrishnananda continued the practice after his departure, in spite of the complete lack of able singing voices at the Math!

Maharaj also possessed a love for gardening. At Belur monastery, a tour of the flower garden was part of his daily routine; he addressed all the flowers by their botanical names. When visiting other centers, he encouraged the monks to plant flowers and fruit trees, and instructed them in watering and fertilizing them. In flowers he saw the worship of God in his universal form. At Mylapore, he requested a variety of flower seeds be planted in large jars. He enjoyed watching them grow, and exhibited a mother's tender care for them. Knowing that Devamata enjoyed gardening too, Maharaj would inform her of a particularly beautiful blossom. Through an attendant, he would even send a rare flower for her personal shrine.

Like Sri Ramakrishna, his disciples possessed a sense of 'fun.' Devamata discovered that this was particularly true of Maharaj. Requesting her to type a business letter to Swami Premananda, the manager of the monastery at Belur, he handed her some child's stationery which he had found. As requested, Devamata typed rather stern managerial instructions on the small sheets of pink stationery, decorated with a little flower on the top. Only three words actually fit on a single line so the letter could not be long. The many sheets were all mailed in a small pink envelope, which was covered with honorifics of Premananda to such a degree that the stamp had to be placed on the backside. Premananda would have been amused. Maharaj's fun-loving nature was widely known in the Order. Devamata noted that teasing and mimicking were ways Maharaj used to keep his mind on this earthly plane.

In April 1909, Maharaj left Madras for Puri. In later years, he blessed Devamata with a boon for having "served me very well" during his days in Madras. He confided to his attendant at the time, "In her next birth she should be born in India and spend her life as a brahmacharini devoted to Sri Thakur." When questioned about the boon by the attendant, Maharaj added, "She is just in the beginning of her devotional life."[24]

In the late twenties, Devamata was asked to revise and edit a manuscript of Maharaj's teachings in advance of publication. In the foreword of the book *The Spiritual Teachings of Swami Brahmananda*,* she vividly recalled the six months that she had spent in his sacred presence. She wrote,

> There rose before my mind once again the picture of that majestic, yet child-like, figure moving in the twilight shadow up and down the dim monastery hall at Mylapore; once again his gentle voice sounded in my ears; once again the benediction of his loving presence fell in refreshing shower over my spirit.[25]

The book was printed by the Madras Publishing House in 1931; the second edition was released in 1933. Consisting of thirty-six short chapters, this book presents his teachings in a question-and-answer format. The teachings were largely the product of informal conversations that he had at Benares, Kankhal, and Belur with young men of the Order, who were seated on the floor in front of him.

What did Maharaj's teachings convey? His teachings encourage the spiritual seeker to create a burning dissatisfaction within for things of the world; to lose oneself in prayer, repetition of the Lord's name, and meditation, in order to cleanse the mind and heart of impurities; to be steadfast in one's effort; and to mold one's character through service and holy company. Grace flows through his words. They possess a power and authenticity arising from their uncompromising directness. While presenting basic spiritual tenets, he holds aloft before each spiritual seeker a vision of their Divine nature. Though Ramakrishna's teachings to his monastic disciples were not recorded for posterity, they are reflected—in large measure—in the teachings of Maharaj.

---

*Devamata's foreword of this book is in Appendix B.

Bangalore Monastery

To escape the summer heat of 1908, a spacious house was rented for Ramakrishnananda and Devamata in Bangalore; the city had a more temperate climate than Madras. Every day Ramakrishnananda collected jasmine blossoms from the gardens, and Devamata strung the flowers to form a garland for offering. She had been given the privilege of caring for the shrine. When the number of daily visitors dwindled during the monsoon season, she received personal instruction from him on the sacred Indian epics.

Later that summer they were the guests of the Dewan (Prime Minister) of Mysore, Sir V.P. Madhava Rao. During this stay, Devamata was diagnosed with typhoid. Her stay in the Bangalore hospital proved to be an exceptional learning opportunity, providing her with a deeper understanding of the Indian ways.

Earlier in 1904, Ramakrishnananda had established a permanent foundation for the work in Bangalore by charging Swami Atmananda to start classes. The Dewan of Mysore was influential in securing a few acres in Bangalore for the Order to establish a monastery. The summer of 1908, he took advantage of Ramakrishnananda's presence and quickly arranged a ceremonial opening of the new center on the site. Per his request, Devamata drove the first stake to mark the newly chosen foundation. Actually, the foundation stone for the center had been laid by Swami Abhedananda in 1906, during his visit to India. Its location on the site was deemed unsatisfactory by the Dewan, hence the change. Ramakrishnananda was determined to beg for the money needed to construct the new building. Inwardly Devamata cringed at the very idea of begging, but when the Swami remarked that begging was a test of egotism, her inner reluctance gave way. Each day traveling by foot together, they solicited funds; she was assigned to make the appeal. Eventually the required amount was raised.

While Maharaj was at Mylapore, Ramakrishnananda requested him to dedicate the new monastery in Bangalore. On January 20, 1909, the dedication ceremony took place. Maharaj was given a royal reception. Pennants tied to poles lined the driveway and a decorated open tent with a capacity of 1200 was erected in front of the new building. The Dewan of Mysore made the opening remarks, welcoming Maharaj on behalf of the public. Maharaj gave a brief reply, in which he stated his delight in finding "that Bangalore has

Group photo taken in 1909 at the inauguration of the Bangalore Math in India. Swami Brahmananda is seated in the middle. Standing, unidentified, Swami Atmananda, Sister Devamata. Seated left to right, Swami Ramakrishnananda, Swami Ambikananda, unidentified.

been one amongst the foremost places to appreciate his [Sri Ramakrishna's] advent."[26] Ramakrishnananda then spoke of the meaning behind the advent of Sri Ramakrishna. In explaining the universal basis of Vedanta, he remarked as follows:

> Vedanta is merely a study of human nature. By studying human nature, Vedanta has been able to arrive at the conclusion that everyone has been aspiring after the three ideals—eternal life, blissfulness, and all knowledge. Vedanta is based upon this eternal verity sat-chit-ananda, and upon this every religion has been based.[27]

Devamata was the last to rise and address the gathering. Praising India as a land of spirituality, in comparison to the West, and extolling Swami Vivekananda as a spiritual teacher whose ideals both the East and West must strive to realize, she envisioned the new center as being the home of Sri Ramakrishna's children worldwide. Its work would be of benefit to the "common family of humanity."[28] Her speech underscored the reaction of those who met her in India. They would say of her: She loved India and all things Indian.*

---

*Devamata's full speech is located in Appendix B.

Bangalore Math at the time of its Inauguration on January, 20, 1909.

After the dedication, Maharaj unlocked the doors of the monastery. A temporary chapel was consecrated, a homa fire was lit, and prayers were offered. A number of Brahmins chanted verses from the Vedas. Flowers and prasad were distributed at the end of the day's program.

The Dewan held the hope that Paramananda would return to India with U.S. workers and establish himself on a permanent basis in Bangalore. On several occasions, he urged Devamata to write to Paramananda, encouraging him to do so. There is no indication that she did.

Meanwhile Devamata received a note from Paramananda which he had written in December 1908: "This is a line to tell you I am going to Boston and I leave New York on Friday. Pray to the Mother that this new venture which I am undertaking may be Her own work. May I feel that alone."[29]

The tension simmering over the years at the Vedanta Society in New York boiled over late in 1908. Upon a standing invitation from Mrs. Bull, Paramananda left for Boston. Within the span of a year, Abhedananda left the Vedanta Society, moving permanently to the Society's country retreat in Connecticut. President Brahmananda wrote Paramananda empowering him to work independently in Boston, and discharged Swami Bodhananda to head the center in New York.

Chapter Seven

SISTER DEVAMATA
1908-1909

Part II: Calcutta

The summer of 1909, Devamata journeyed to Calcutta to be in the blessed presence of the Holy Mother. Considering this to be the most salient event of her trip to India, the forty-hour train ride from Madras seemed endless. On arrival, she was greeted by Sister Christine, who brought her to the 'House of the Sisters'—the residence of Sisters Nivedita and Christine. Located at 17 Bose Para Lane, Bagh Bazar, its door was open to all. The 'Hours of call' posted on the door were 7–9 a.m., though they were commonly overlooked. Indian visitors were many and frequent—scientists, journalists, artists, public officials, and religious leaders.

Devamata occupied the bedroom, Nivedita and Christine were in the chapel, and the puja room downstairs served as the dining room. The rest of the house was used for school rooms. Devamata noted that "seventy-five little girls and about twenty older ones (widowed) attended" the school.[1] Christine served as principal since literary work absorbed most of Nivedita's time. Her publications helped to financially support the school. When Christine traveled, Nivedita taught the classes. She would give the English classes to Devamata to teach, and instituted new classes based on her observations in the West.

After school closed for the summer, Nivedita began to assist botanist Dr. J.C. Bose in editing his book on plant life. Dr. Bose arrived at nine each morning, and he and Nivedita worked until lunch. When Devamata, Nivedita, and

Dr. Bose had lunch together, the conversation inevitably turned to the wonders of nature.

In a private conversation with Devamata one Sunday afternoon, Nivedita related the story of her secession from the Ramakrishna Mission—the painful struggle between the political urge to free India and her spiritual desire to serve the Mission. She had to choose so as not to compromise the Mission by political activities. She chose India's freedom.

In separate letters written in July 1909, Nivedita wrote to her two dear friends Sara Bull and Josephine MacLeod, giving her first impression of her house guest.

> Sister Devamata is here, very, very charming, wears a costume like mine, so small and frail looking and absorbed in religious practices. Devoted to the Holy Mother and every step of Sri Ramakrishna and doing puja and things—and we enjoy so much having a third [person] so different in the house.[2]

With the intention of having Devamata reside in her house, the Holy Mother had prepared a room on the roof terrace; it had a distant view of the Ganges to the west. An illness in the household, however, altered this plan. Arrangements were therefore being made for Devamata to have her first visit (darshan) of Holy Mother. Not one for waiting, Devamata set out by herself to find Holy Mother's house (Udbodhan). She managed to do so with the help of a passerby.

Entering the building, Devamata climbed the stairs to her room on the second floor. She was alone. Devamata laid herself and the offerings she had brought from Madras at her feet. The Holy Mother repeated her name twice, mildly surprised by her unexpected arrival. The placement of her hand on Devamata's head as a blessing brought forth "a spring of new life [that] seemed to bubble up from my innermost heart and flood my being."[3]

Holy Mother seated in her shrine at Udbodhan, 1909, the year Devamata first met Her.

In *Days in an Indian Monastery*, Devamata described that first visit.

> She led me to the altar in the Shrine and after I had made salutation there, I took my seat on the floor, while she lay down to rest nearby. A Sannyasini (woman mendicant) came in and began to rub her body. . . . As I watched her the question crossed my mind, would I ever be worthy to serve her thus. Scarcely had the thought been formed before she motioned to me to take the Sannyasini's place. It was a benediction to pass my hand over her delicate shapely body, but the marble paving grew very hard as I knelt beside her. Again she divined the unspoken thought and made me sit instead of kneel.[4]

At seven every morning, Devamata arrived at the Udbodhan. She was given the privilege of making the Holy Mother's bed and straightening her room. Noticing that there were smudges of putty on all five French windows, which opened onto the front verandah, Devamata thoroughly washed the panes of glass. When visitors arrived that day, Holy Mother insisted on closing a window. The cleaned glass could be properly appreciated only by viewing the outside scene through the window.

One day the Holy Mother offered Devamata two mangoes, the last of the season. Wanting her to enjoy them, Devamata replied, "It would give me greater pleasure to have you keep them." Holy Mother immediately inquired, "Do you think it will give you greater pleasure to have me keep them or give me greater pleasure to have you take them?" Devamata's reply sprang from deep within, "It must give you greater pleasure because you have a larger heart to feel it."[5]

The Holy Mother's childlike nature surfaced when Devamata gifted her eight-year-old niece, Radhu, a jack-in-the-box. Holy Mother herself was delighted with the toy. Whenever it popped up, she mimicked the sound. The irrepressible, artless laughter that followed was evidence of her thorough amusement. On another day when Devamata arrived, Holy Mother and Radhu were stringing glass beads in order to decorate Radhu's baby Krishna. It was important to Radhu that her Krishna be properly adorned like the images in the temple. The Holy Mother helped decorate the small figure with worshipful devotion, viewing it as a sacred symbol of the Divine. It wasn't child's play to her.

Before Radhu left for school in the mornings, the Holy Mother would sit with others in her room and feed Radhu. Jyotirmayi Basu, her disciple, narrated an incident which involved Devamata. She recalled:

> One day when Radhu's meal was finished, Mother began to clean that place and we were watching it. But out of exuberant devotion, Devamata rushed to her, saying, 'Matadevi, Matadevi,' as she picked up Radhu's cup and plate and cleaned the floor. Seeing that Devamata's cloth touched the defiled plate, Nalini laughed loudly. Immediately the Mother signaled her with her eyes to keep quiet. When Devamata went to the wash-room with those dirty dishes, Mother said to Nalini: 'That girl does not know our language and custom and you laughed out loud! She might think that she had done something wrong. Thinking of this, later she will get pain.'[6]

Those devotees who came and went daily at Udbodhan were regarded by Devamata as her primary companions during her stay in Calcutta. Chief among them were Golap-ma and Yogin-ma, Holy Mother's personal attendants, as well as Balaram Basu's wife. From day to day the rhythm of the household didn't change—worship and meditation, domestic duties, service to devotees and neighbors, and a bath in the Ganges. Devamata bathed at the ghat used by Holy Mother and gradually became adept at changing from a wet to a dry sari without uncovering her body.

As a member of Holy Mother's household during her days in Calcutta, Devamata observed:

> She [Holy Mother] lived as they did, performing the same homely tasks, making no effort to distinguish herself from others save by greater modesty, greater gentleness and humility.... Yet beneath the veil of simplicity which enveloped her was a lofty majesty of bearing which caught the heart and bowed it in prayerful homage at her feet. The human covering was too thin to hide the radiance of divine consciousness beneath. She never taught, seldom ever counseled. She merely lived.[7]

Devamata's close relationship with Yogin-ma was revealed in her writings. She commented, "[Yogin-ma] possessed an uplifted, heroic quality and something of a warrior lay hidden in her nature. It was apparent in her manner, in her speech, in her step, in her whole temperament." Furthermore, she pointed out, "The hour of prayer in that upper chamber where the Shrine was, counted among the most precious in the day for me. Yogin-ma and I were alone—she before the shrine, I beside an inner window opening on the court. . . . She was very strict in conforming with all the usages and traditions of worship. I learned many things by observing her."[8]

Right before Devamata arrived, Yogin-ma had taken over the daily worship in the Udbodhan shrine from Holy Mother, and brought her own holy pictures and images with her. Since both pictures of Sri Ramakrishna were being worshiped, the puja was longer than usual.

Devamata recorded an incident demonstrating Yogin-ma's affection for her.

> One day she laid in my hand a small bag for my Rudrasha beads. It was a crude piece of workmanship, made of heavy dark cloth, coarsely sewn. Yet . . . I have cherished it through the years as a precious treasure, not only because it came to me as a token of love from one for whom I had great reverence and admiration, but even more because it was made by a hand that had touched Sri Ramakrishna's feet.[9]

In October 1909, Saradananda wrote Sara Bull in regards to a desire first expressed by Swami Vivekananda—to establish a Math for women on the bank of the Ganges with the Holy Mother as its center. He wrote,

> [Holy Mother] would like to see a convent started in the fashion of the Math, Belur, for women. Miss Glenn, who was here to visit the Holy Mother, and who passed here in the name of Sister Devamata . . . had also a talk with the Holy Mother about it and is very sanguine about the work. She has promised to help raise funds as far as she can.[10]

It was a commonly held belief, maybe hope, that Devamata would give her life to service in India as had Sisters Nivedita and Christine before her. In a letter written prior to Devamata's departure for India, Ellen Waldo had written Ramakrishnananda that Devamata "would do good work in India and be of great help to him."[11] Devamata's optimistic response to Holy Mother's desire to start a convent furthered the hope that she would return to India after a visit to the West. With foresight, the Holy Mother warned her, "be careful, if you get even the hem of your garment caught in the American work, you will not come back." This is, however, exactly what happened.[12]

Over the years, Devamata wrote to Holy Mother about the activities at the centres in the West and about the welfare of all involved in the work. The Holy Mother also dictated a number of letters to her using the appellations "sweet daughter" or "beloved child," and ending the letters with love and blessings. In the last correspondence that Devamata's received from her, Holy Mother noted: "You are my daughter, you are also my mother because you have prayed for my welfare to the Lord."[13]

Years later Devamata expressed her devotional attitude to Holy Mother through her insightful thoughts on the sublimity of her spiritual nature:

> Those who had the rare blessing of living with Holy Mother learned that religion was a sweet, natural, joyous thing; that purity and holiness were tangible realities; that the odor of sanctity was literally a sweet perfume overlaying and destroying the foulness of material selfishness. Compassion, devotion, and God-union were her very nature; one scarcely knew that she possessed them. It was through the soothing benediction of a word or touch that one sensed their presence.
>
> Such lives are like the lake or river. The sun may draw up its waters, but they fill again to refresh the earth. So these saintly ones in body may be lifted from our sight, but their holy influence falls back upon us to revive our fainting hearts and give us new spiritual life, new strength of purpose.[14]

A book of Devamata's poems entitled *The Open Portal* was published in 1929. Love of God and nature were the two dominant themes in the eighty-five poems. She set eighteen of them to music. The book's dedication read: "In loving memory of Srimati Saradamani Devi [Holy Mother] whose life was a perpetual song of exalted gladness."[15]

Dakshineswar Temple Grounds

While in Calcutta, a special occasion was her pilgrimage to the premises of the Dakshineswar temple garden; these grounds were made sacred by the presence of Sri Ramakrishna for some thirty years. Sitting on the floor of a flat-bottomed boat plying its way across the Ganges, Devamata was oblivious to her surroundings. She was engrossed in the stories of Ramakrishna's life narrated by Swami Saradananda and Yogin-ma, who accompanied her.

Arriving at the landing-ghat, she was guided around the Dakshineswar temple courtyard by her companions. They directed her to the places associated with incidents in Ramakrishna's life and repeated the words that He spoke on those occasions. These eyewitness accounts were an inspiration to Devamata.

A mere twenty-three years had passed since Ramakrishna's mahasamadhi; the temple grounds remained largely the same as in His day. Devamata was fortunate to be able to write: "I sat under the banyan tree (in the Panchavati) where Sri Ramakrishna attained the visions of eternity. I pushed barefooted through the brambles to the bel tree to which he had fled for deeper seclusion."[16] The Panchavati grove consisted of five different trees planted in five directions. As recorded in *Sri Ramakrishna The Great Master* by Swami Saradananda, the fig tree (or pipal) was planted and nurtured by Ramakrishna himself. The other four saplings—namely, the vilva (or bel), the amolaki, the banyan, and the ashoka were planted by Hriday, his nephew. It was the site of Ramakrishna's spiritual sadhana where he beheld various visions of God.

Ramakrishna would sit in the Panchavati with those who came to see him and talk of God. Near the Panchavati, a visitor caught sight of Ramakrishna playing leapfrog with his future monastic disciples, then only boys in their late teens or early twenties. The "boys" would also swing from the creepers and climb on the trees, with Ramakrishna joining in their merrymaking.

Devamata's first visit concluded with darshan of the Divine Mother in the main temple. It was dedicated to Kali, as Bhavatarini, the Savior of the Universe. Kali had many devotees in India before the time of Ramakrishna. The most well-known was Ramprasad, the great Bengali poet of the eighteenth century. His devotional songs, expressing a close relationship with Mother Kali, had become an integral part of Bengali culture. Ramakrishna's worship of the black-basalt-stone image of Kali in the Dakshineswar temple "awakened" the Divine Mother. He attained to the sweetness of Divine Union with Her.

Devamata's second visit to these hallowed temple grounds was in the company of Master Mahasaya, a soul of noble bearing who authored *The Gospel of Sri Ramakrishna*. His storytelling abilities and skill at detailed narration, much evident in the Gospel, enabled Devamata to visualize the scenes he painted. Even seemingly trivial incidents were holy to him. With tenderness he would point out where the Holy Mother had sat; where Ramakrishna had walked; and where He had gone into Samadhi. Master Mahasaya's actions were reverential—bowing down to the Ganges; touching his head on the verandah of the Holy Mother's room; and embracing a tree because it had the rare privilege of witnessing the enactment of the Divine play. Seeing the Dakshineswar temple grounds through his eyes, Devamata came away feeling that the grand play had happened only yesterday, for the divine joy and spiritual fervor that permeated the atmosphere in Ramakrishna's time were evident in Master Mahasaya himself.

For her third visit, Sister Christine and Devamata arrived by carriage to the temple garden. Their trip included visiting the spacious garden house at Cossipore in the northern suburbs of Calcutta, where Ramakrishna spent the last months of his bodily life.

On her last visit to these sacred grounds, Devamata was alone. She remained in Ramakrishna's room for a long time. Nivedita described his room as it was at that time. "All was as he had used it, the lounge beside the bed, a huge water jar in one corner, a few religious pictures on the wall and nothing more."[17] Devamata found herself lingering "under the banyan tree and on the verandah of the Concert House, half expecting that pervading Presence to take form"[18] before her. Would her thoughts at that time have shifted to the many stories told about Ramakrishna? Might she have consciously imprinted on her mind the scenes before her, so that years later, by means of remembrance she could visit these grounds again?

Association with the Blessed

During the weeks of her stay in Calcutta, Devamata frequently visited Belur Monastery, crossing the Ganges from the Calcutta side. Sister Christine accompanied her on her first visit. Swamis Atmananda, Shivananda, and Premananda warmly welcomed them. Time was spent in the shrine and the library. High tea was the occasion for an extended conversation.

There were two buildings on the monastery grounds at the time. The one-story house once occupied by Sara Bull, Josephine MacLeod, and Sister Nivedita when they first arrived in India in early 1898 had been remodeled into a two-story building that served as the monks' quarters. This building was consecrated by the Holy Mother on November 12, 1898. A newly constructed two-story building on the river's edge housed the shrine and prayer hall in a separate wing on the second floor. The kitchen and eating hall were located on the first floor of the wing. The main building accommodated a library and sleeping rooms. White walls, cement floors, and extreme simplicity were the norm. A large banyan tree at the rear of the monastery building served as a site for an outdoor shrine on festival days. This building had been consecrated on December 9, 1898.

To hear their stories, Devamata sought out all those closely associated with Ramakrishna, imbibing every scrap of information. One of those she frequently visited was Latu Maharaj, a monastic disciple of Ramakrishna. At the time, Latu was staying at the house of Balaram Basu, a devout householder disciple of Sri Ramakrishna, in Calcutta. Latu possessed a childlike nature, simple and frank. A playful bond was formed between them—the giving and exchanging of small gifts such as coconuts, oranges, mangoes, or English bread and butter. About him, she wrote,

> [Latu Maharaj] was a living embodiment of the Spirit of service. He was always a servant. He began life as the servant of man, contact with Sri Ramakrishna made him the servant of God, and after the master's passing, he became the servant of the servants of the Lord. Even his plain, thickset body seemed built for carrying loads and lifting burdens.[19]

Another monastic disciple of Ramakrishna, Premananda Maharaj, was also staying at Balaram Basu's house. He usually resided at Belur as the manager of the monastery. Fortunately for Devamata, he was staying in Calcutta during her visit due to a health issue. With burning fervor, he would speak of Ramakrishna or of the joy of serving the Lord's children. Sitting near him, the recipient of his spiritual wisdom, Devamata considered herself blessed. In a letter to her, Premananda offered his advice.

> My only message to you all is: Be His, absolutely and forever. In body, mind, soul, be His. In that becoming, everything that religion means and is will be realized. By becoming His only do you reach the goal of all human duties and responsibilities.[20]

Soon after she arrived in Calcutta, Devamata received an invitation from Girish Chandra Ghosh, the notable Bengali playwright and actor. With Swami Saradananda, she called on him, and answered all his questions about the work in the West. He spoke of his own spiritual journey—his first meeting with Ramakrishna, his persistent doubts and questions, and instances of Ramakrishna's motherly love.

Shortly before Devamata was due to leave Calcutta for a return to Madras, Holy Mother arranged a special party for her at Kankurgachi, where a temple was being built in honor of Ramakrishna. Twenty-five ladies were invited. Carriages were provided for all of them. Despite a rainstorm, they arrived safely. The rain suddenly stopped and they all enjoyed a picnic on the grounds. The party ended with an evening service at Holy Mother's house.

Back to the Mylapore Monastery

Two days later, Devamata returned to Madras and wrote letters to Nivedita, Maharaj, and Holy Mother. In a letter dated September 8, 1909 from 17 Bosepara Lane, Nivedita responded,

> It was nice to hear from you . . . the little spiders were all hatched, about 200 of them, and remain scattered over the wall . . . I do hope Swami Ramakrishnananda is better. . . . The Holy Mother speaks of you often. The first night, she pointed to your empty place with great pathos![21]

The Holy Mother also dictated a letter to her "sweet daughter."

> Your loving letters are duly in hand. Excuse me please not to answer you in time. I always remember you. Whenever I see the place you used to sit and meditate, your loving form comes to my mind. All the inmates of this house always speak of you. I am glad to learn in your last letter that Swami Ramakrishnananda is feeling better.[22]

From Puri, Maharaj sent his blessings. "Glad to receive your note . . . to hear that you have enjoyed your stay in Calcutta to the best content of your heart. I expected so of you."[23]

Devamata's regular correspondence with Paramananda kept her informed of his start-up in Boston beginning the winter of 1908–09. He wrote frankly of the physical hardships which he endured due to the winter weather, the prejudices encountered, the lessons learned, and the simple solutions devised to alleviate worrisome problems. He eventually wrote: "How I wish you were here to help me, but I leave your coming or staying entirely with you. If you are happy there, stay by all means. . . . I will try my best to do the work and if help does not come from anywhere, I will try to be content, thinking it is Mother's will."²⁴ In the end, Devamata could not deny him the help that she knew he needed. She was ready to leave India.

When she first crossed the Atlantic to India, she had written to Paramananda, saying in effect, no matter how great the distance that separates us, our hearts will cling together. Evidently her devotion to him hadn't waivered.

She wrapped up August and the two weeks of September taking notes on Ramakrishnananda's classes given to the boys at the Students' Home, a branch of the work that he founded out of sympathy for destitute children. On the day prior to her departure, Devamata wished to visit the temple in Triplicane, three miles from Mylapore. The imposing South Indian temple was dedicated to Parthasarathi (Sri Krishna as Arjuna's charioteer). It was in Krishna's capacity as charioteer that he spoke the sacred words of the *Bhagavad Gita*. Devamata had devotedly worshiped at temple festivals throughout her stay in India—in Bombay, Mylapore and Triplicane. She also had visited the ancient cave temple in Bangalore. However, Parthasarathi had captured her heart. She had attended a number of festivals at this temple during her stay in Mylapore and always with "a vivid consciousness of great power emanating from it." Her last visit heightened that awareness.²⁵

Swami Ramakrishnananda accompanied her to the temple, which remained open well beyond its normal closing time. After welcoming them, the Brahmin priest led them to the threshold of the inner shrine. Devamata "stood in silent awe."²⁶ The priest waved lighted camphor before the ancient Image, thus enabling her to clearly view the Lord; she bowed in devotion as had countless devotees down the centuries. A garland removed from the Image was placed around her neck and the flowers that had been offered in worship that day were placed in her silken shawl by other brahmins at the temple. Stained with sandalwood paste and pollen, the shawl remained a sacred memento over the years that followed.

To Devamata, Ramakrishnananda was a beloved teacher who played a dominant role in her Indian life, living as she was in his blessed presence. She conveyed her heartfelt feelings concerning him to Nivedita, who subsequently wrote to Josephine MacLeod, "Devamata is crazy about Ramakrishnananda, who is really her Guru. She adores him."²⁷ Nivedita admonished Devamata, saying: "What I have done for Swamiji [Vivekananda] you must do for Swami Ramakrishnananda. All the disciples must be recorded."²⁸

Both of Devamata's books, *Days in An Indian Monastery* (1927) and *Sri Ramakrishna and His Disciples* (1928) contain her reminiscences of Ramakrishnananda. Besides his teachings, these books also recorded his day-to-day interactions with devotees and visitors. The incidents cited aptly captured the essence of that great soul, thereby breathing life into what would otherwise be just words. She wrote that he met, "disappointment, criticism, condemnation, antagonism, waxing and waning of his work . . . with a smile on his face."[29]

Her belated memoirs of Ramakrishnananda, which contained unpublished material, appeared in the *Vedanta Kesari* in nine installments from February 1932 through May 1933 under the title "Swami Ramakrishnananda—Sannyasin and Teacher." These nine articles were published in the book, *Swami Ramakrishnananda, The Apostle of Sri Ramakrishna to the South* by Swami Tapasyananda in 1972.

While in India, Devamata also transcribed Ramakrishnananda's lectures, which were published in two small books; namely, *The Universe and Man* and *The Soul of Man*. The former consisted of lectures given by him in 1907, when the first permanent building of the Ramakrishna Math in Mylapore was consecrated. With the printing of M's original translation of *The Gospel of Sri Ramakrishna* (1907), the first edition of *Inspired Talks* (1908), and the aforementioned two small books in 1908, the publishing work of the Madras center was inaugurated.

Before she left India, Swami Virajananda, a disciple of Vivekananda and future president of the Ramakrishna Order, wrote to her from Mayavati. Along with some transactional business, he interjected his appreciation.

> It pleases me so much to see how under your strenuous labor and organizing method of work, the publication dept. of the Math there is making such nice progress and gives the Math a greater usefulness to the public. Getting out Swami Ramakrishnananda's books, especially, is a very excellent idea, as you know he would never have cared to do so himself.[30]

She would be sailing from Bombay on September 17, 1909. The Swami saw her off at the railway station in Madras on September 10 for her cross-country journey to Bombay. Before she boarded, he requested her to "come back in a year and we will write a life of Sri Ramakrishna."[31] As she settled into her seat in the train, he leaned through the window to give her a final piece of advice. From the warmth of his welcome to his concern on her departure, he was a solicitous mother.

In a letter to Paramananda dated September 9, 1909, Ramakrishnananda wrote,

> Devamata is much benefitted by her stay for more than a year and a half. She is very lucky because Sri Holy Mother, Sri Baburam Maharaj, Sri Rakhal Maharaj and others have blessed her specially. . . . The name [Devamata] that you have given her has become quite well-known. Everyone here knows her as Devamata. She feels very happy at that. Baburam Maharaj, Sri Master Mahashay and many others feel that she is a siddhagopi. Really, there is no doubt that she possesses much devotion to Sri Gurudeva. For this reason, Sri Holy Mother has showered her special affection and care on her.[32]

In the same letter, Ramakrishnananda notes that Devamata has a "slight tendency to boss" and gives way to some "exaggeration." In another letter, regarding her nature, the Swami states that she has "innumerable virtues" and "her minor faults will soon be rooted out by Their grace."[33]

From Bombay, she arrived in Genoa, Italy, on October 12 and boarded the new steamship Duca Degli Abruzzi for New York. The passenger list for 1820-1957 states that the steamer docked in New York harbor on October 25, 1909. Her age was given as 47.

Looking Back

Years later Devamata conveyed in writing her feelings about her pilgrimage to India. In the introduction to her book, *Sri Ramakrishna and Saint Francis of Assisi*, published in 1935, she wrote as follows:

> The most vivid [memory] is my pilgrimage to Calcutta and to the Temple of Dakshineswar, the very ground of which has been hallowed by the footprints of Sri Ramakrishna. So permeated is the atmosphere with his presence, the leaves of the trees seem to whisper his name, the river seems to murmur it as it flows by. That presence saturated my consciousness as

I moved from holy place to holy place in the Temple garden. ... The pilgrimage stretched out over months, and with each passing hour of it came a deepening realization of the spiritual grandeur of the One whose pilgrim I was.[34]

Chapter Eight

The First Centres in Washington, DC and Boston
1909–1921

Throughout 1909, Swami Paramananda's headquarters in Boston was the home of Miss Katharine Sherwood, a matron of Boston society and his staunch supporter. Classes in Massachusetts were organized in Boston, Waltham, Newton, Milton, and Lynn. Paramananda's first public lecture in Boston was given at the Huntington-Chambers Hall near Copley Square on Sunday, January 24, 1909.

Devamata returned from India at the end of October. On her sea voyage back, she wrote to the Holy Mother several times. In a letter dated November 3, Holy Mother responded.

> I am in due receipt of your letters. I can not express in words how I liked them. The mode of your passing the days en route is really admirable.... I have received the sandal box which you have sent me.... I like it very much. Be sure, my daughter, that the Lord is with you always and is taking care of you. I, too, always remember you... Your most affectionate, Mother."[1]

Devamata shared with Holy Mother the manner in which she passed her days aboard the ship, because she was carrying very special cargo. Before departing India in September 1909, she was at Belur Math when Swami Premananda handed her a small silver box containing a lock of Sri Ramakrishna's hair. As it happened, Premananda's mother was at Dakshineswar when a barber was cutting his hair. Laughingly Ramakrishna picked up a curl and handed it to her. Eventually she gifted it to Belur. Upon Devamata's return to America, a special service was held to honor the relic. A locket containing it was worn by Paramananda for some time. Eventually the relic was divided into three portions and installed in the shrines at the two centres established by Paramananda (Boston, MA and La Crescenta, CA), and in Devamata's private chapel at Ananda Ashrama in California.

Premananda also gifted Devamata a fan that Ramakrishna had used and the picture and throne that had belonged to Gopal-ma, a revered devotee of Sri Ramakrishna. The Holy Mother requested Devamata to return these three items to quell the concerns that were being expressed. Since this was the first time Ramakrishna's relics had left Belur, some questioned the practice.

Shortly after her return, Paramananda and Devamata visited Ridgely Manor, an estate north of New York City in Stone Ridge. On three separate occasions, Vivekananda had visited Ridgely Manor, which was owned by Francis (Frank) and Betty Leggett. The family members were ardent supporters of Vivekananda and Josephine (Joe) MacLeod, Betty's sister, did much to spread the teachings of Vedanta worldwide. On the passing of Frank Leggett, Joe had extended Paramananda and Devamata an invitation to visit. Paramananda's resemblance to Vivekananda, in Joe's assessment, earned him her admiration. Devamata and Joe had become acquainted in the early days of the New York Vedanta Society and ended up sharing a strong friendship.

Devamata could also evoke a strong dislike in those who knew her, due to her strong opinions and the strength of her personality. Even in her early days at Vassar, her classmates alluded to the fact that her presence was always apparent. People were rarely indifferent to her.

On December 6, 1909, Paramananda, Devamata, and Mrs. Reukirt, a New York friend, arrived in Washington, DC to open a centre in the city. Another harsh Boston winter would have been detrimental to Paramananda's delicate health. The house they leased at 1808 Kalorama Road would accommodate a meeting place for the public, the swami's quarters, and rooms for the workers. The only full-time resident worker was Devamata. Katharine Sherwood and Eliza Kissam were frequent visitors from Boston and New York, respectively. Eliza was given the name Satya Prana, a Sanskrit word meaning "truehearted."

Running a household was a new venture for all of them; Devamata was roused into action. Her resourcefulness, combined with her dedication and zeal, were deployed in managing the house and operating the centre. She performed the same function for Paramananda that Ellen Waldo had done for Swami Vivekananda.

Sri Ramakrishna was installed in a little chapel on the third floor on Christmas Day. Public services began the first Sunday of January 1910. Paramananda was very careful to avoid all sensationalism and oriental trappings in the services and his public interactions. Sunday service at the center consisted of an opening Peace Chant followed by readings from various scriptures, Paramananda's talk, music, meditation, and a closing benediction. This stood in contrast to the Sunday service at the New York Vedanta Society, which consisted of only lectures.

A letter from Ramakrishnananda dated March 3, 1910, conveyed a message from Holy Mother to Paramananda and Devamata. Her words were:

> I am immensely glad to hear that my beloved child, Paramananda and my dear choto Khuki [Devamata] have kept a shrine apart in the house which they have taken up for their residence and that they daily perform their worship and meditation in that shrine. My love and blessings to Paramananda and Devamata.[2]

For a firsthand observation of the centre's services, a Washington reporter from the *Sunday Star* attended the Sunday program on January 16, 1910. All his preconceived notions about a cult were dispelled. He wrote, "Bare floors, no furnishings, no ornaments, no draperies, no ostentation, no paraphernalia, nothing to suggest the atmosphere of the orient." He was furthermore surprised to find "the austere interpretation which Swami Paramananda put upon the teachings of Christ." In regards to Paramananda himself, the reporter expressed appreciation of his "lack of gestures and repose of manner [that] made him a restful speaker," and added: "the constant kindling of [his] very expressive eyes kept the listener spellbound."[3]

With the public response to Vedanta being lukewarm—the public was more politically interested—closure of the centre was discussed from the very outset. In the spring of 1910, Paramananda returned to Boston in order to sublet an apartment that he had previously seen as the first home of a Vedanta Centre in that city. He left Devamata in charge of the Washington centre, which entailed teaching Vedanta on a regular basis. For six to eight weeks in the early spring and in the early fall of each year, Paramananda returned to DC. During this time, Devamata would carry on the work in Boston. Between the two of them, both centres were covered.

Though Paramananda had entered the city quietly, unnoticed by the press, he could not escape the racial intolerance still prevailing in Boston. In an article entitled "The Heathen Invasion," the first sentence read: "Eve is eating the apple again." It exemplified the animus directed against pagan religions and the unfavorable categorization of a certain class of women in this country, and broadly speaking, of women throughout India. The twelve-page article was replete with pictures and proclaimed yoga to be "a way that leads to domestic infelicity and insanity, a promise of eternal youth to attract women and a teaching which grants spiritual merit to those who bestow gifts on the guru."[4] The author of this explosive write-up, though ignorant of Hinduism and other Eastern sects, was widely quoted in numerous articles published at that time. This furor against Eastern religions gradually subsided.

During Paramananda's travels in the summer of 1910 in the States, Devamata took over the work in Boston for two months, temporarily closing the Washington centre. During this time period, *The Boston Transcript* sent a reporter to interview her. The article "Sister Devamata Is Here To Work" was published August 6, 1910. Addressed as a "foreign priestess," she was quoted as saying, "I am not here to make any converts to Hinduism, nor to promote a creed, but to enlarge the atmosphere of belief." Later in the article, she added to that purpose—to "encourage the people of Boston to appreciate their own religion more." During the interview, the reporter noted, "she closed her eyes, and, with her hands crossed over her breast," she solemnly chanted.[5] According to the write-up, a similar incident happened a second time, suggesting either a pretentiousness on Devamata's part or the author's need to emphasize the mysterious ways of the East.

When she returned to the Washington centre, she advocated for keeping it open and even expressed the hope of opening a third centre in a different city. Knowing Devamata's penchant for work,

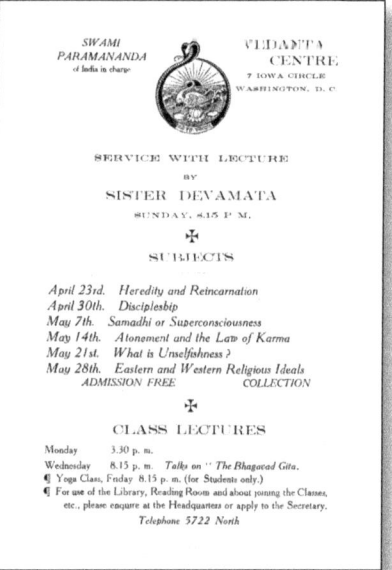

Circular announcing Devamata's lectures at the centre at 7 Iowa Circle in DC.

Ramakrishnananda spoke out against such a plan. In a letter to Paramananda in August 1910, he wrote, "Devamata understands the Lord's work to mean only opening centers and delivering lectures. . . . [She] may have devotion but it is veiled by clouds in the shape of her desire for lots of work."[6] In an earlier letter to Paramananda, he had addressed the topic of work at length. He pointed out that the body, being the Temple of the Lord, should not be neglected. Furthermore, he had admonished Paramananda to work only as his health permitted, and to avoid being deluded by the inspiration of the women.

Throughout 1910, Ramakrishnananda corresponded regularly with Paramananda. Each letter ended with a message to Devamata, addressing her as "My dear Sister." At times he requested her to write reviews of books published in Madras, so that, "we may publish them [reviews] in some of our Indian papers."[7] These missives were always full of loving advice and profuse thanks for her motherly care of Paramananda. In every letter, he also conveyed his love and greetings to Satya Prana and Miss Sherwood. He viewed them both as Paramananda's guardian mothers.

The books published in Madras were sent to Boston. Any income from the sale of these books in the U.S. was held in a separate account by Devamata. The circle was complete when these funds were sent back to Madras to support its publishing activities. Devamata was instrumental in starting the Madras press when in India and continued to actively support it from Boston.

In September 1910, the Washington, DC work was transferred to an apartment nearer to the center of the city. Paramananda realized that the large house on Kalorama Road required an excessive amount of care for its two or three residents. He moved into the apartment on October 18, and gave a Sunday service before leaving for Boston at the end of the month.

During his visit near Christmas, a large banquet was given for thirty-five members of the Washington centre to celebrate the holiday. Prepared and served by Paramananda himself, it became an annual custom in all the centres; it was known as the "Swami's Dinner." Each year it increased in size. By the 1920's, people traveled hundreds and some even thousands of miles just to attend. These banquets ended up dotting the calendar year.

When Paramananda toured Europe on his way to India in 1911, to have the holy company of Ramakrishnananda once again, the activities in Washington, DC were severely curtailed. Devamata was needed to run the Boston centre for the six months that he was abroad. Similarly, in the summers of 1912, 1913, and 1914, Paramananda lectured in Europe while Devamata kept the Boston centre running. The Washington centre eventually became a branch centre of Boston with a shorter season of lectures and classes. These classes were given by Devamata.

Each year both the *Evening Star* and the *Washington Herald* published her annual arrival in the city for her usual season of talks. Her lecture schedule and the respective venues were published. During the 1915 season, in addition to her classes, she gave a public address in the auditorium of the local library entitled "East and West—The Unity of Religions." It was an indication of the growth in interest on the part of the general public. She also wrote an article for the *Washington Times* providing an overall sketch of India—its early history, its religion, and its advancements in terms of scientific discoveries. She commented on the role of Western missionaries in the following way:

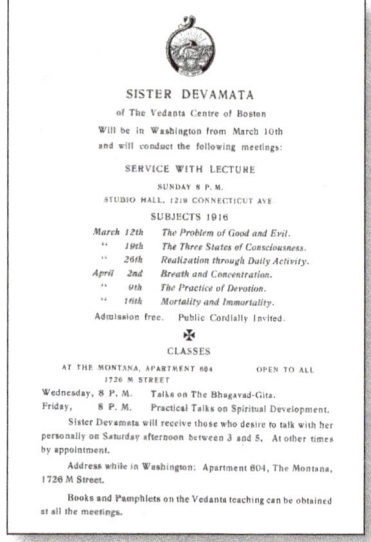

Circular announcing Devamata's lectures March 12 through April 16 of 1916 at the apartment that she rented for her stay in DC at 1726 M. St.

> Missionaries have done much good in remedying unsanitary conditions, yet they do not know how to approach the people. It is a very serious thing for a child to be told his parents are idolaters. . . . To shake a child's trust in his parents has a bad effect on any home. Religion is so closely connected with the family and its mode of living that the adoption of Christianity means that the convert becomes a social outcast and may never associate with his people . . . They [missionaries] can do their best work by living among the people and influencing by their example rather than by attempting to teach a new religion.[8]

Devamata gave two classes and three public lectures in Washington, DC during a week in April 1917, and private guidance for those who sought it. This visit marked the last program given in the city. When she left, she traveled to Los Angeles to take charge of the centre established there by Paramananda a year earlier.

The Boston Vedanta Centre Established

On Friday April 22, 1910, Paramananda moved into the first Vedanta Centre in Boston at 16 Saint Botolph Street. The upper level of the apartment consisted of a large studio and two adjoining smaller rooms for Swami's use. The downstairs floor, below street level, met community needs— a large dining room, a kitchen, a bathroom, a laundry room, and a storage room. At this time, Satya Prana became a sister resident, a second monastic under Paramananda. Later a community house was opened one block from the centre as a residence for Devamata and the sisters.

Returning from India in December of 1911, Paramananda was inspired with many new ideas for the work in the West. The centre launched the publication of a new monthly magazine entitled *Message of the East* in January 1912. It was published continuously for more than fifty years.

Devamata in 1912.

Devamata was the editor of the journal in its early years. Initially, the magazine addressed the philosophical objections to the Vedanta philosophy in the West. Reincarnation, desireless living, and working with no selfish motive were concepts often misunderstood or assumed to be opposed to Christian ideals. Practically every issue gave reports of the Ramakrishna Mission's charitable work in India, thereby highlighting Vedanta's humanitarian contributions. The section entitled "The Universal Message" appeared regularly. It consisted of quotes from philosophers, saints, scientists, poets, and mystics over the timeline of humanity, thus conveying the essence of the greatest thoughts of the world, whether Indo-Aryan, Greek, Persian, or Chinese. "The Universal Message" section helped fend off the vigorous campaign against Eastern religions in the Boston area in 1912 and 1913.

The twelve yearly issues of the *Message of the East* were eventually combined to form one volume. The index of this combined volume listed the entire content of all twelve issues under the headings— Editorials; talks by Swamis Vivekananda, Ramakrishnananda, Saradananda and Paramananda; talks by Sister Devamata; The Universal Message; and Reports.

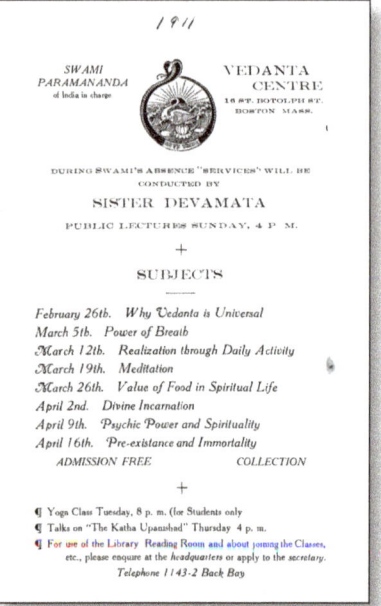

By 1914 a number of small books, bound in cloth, were published under Paramananda's name: *Concentration and Meditation, Faith as a Constructive Force, Self-Mastery,* and the *Creative Power of Silence* (later *Silence as Yoga*). They comprised the "practical series" along with *Spiritual Healing* and *The Secret of Right Activity*. The content of these publications was garnered by Devamata from Paramananda's lectures and letters written to her during his travels abroad. In his letters, he addressed her as "Mother dear," and signed as "Your son."

Circular announcing lectures by Devamata in Boston at 16 Saint Botolph St. centre, opened on April 22, 1910.

When it became evident that the Boston apartment was inadequate and a larger place was needed, quiet efforts were undertaken to purchase a new residence. The Boston *Christian Science Monitor* of January 1914 listed the real estate purchase.

> Final papers passed today by which Robert Treat Paine conveyed to Laura F Glenn property at 1 Queensberry Street, corner of Auburn Road, in the Back Bay Fens, consisting of 5,320 square feet of land assessed for 15,000 and a three-story brick building assessed for 17,400 . . . The purchaser Laura F. Glenn buys for immediate occupancy.[9]

The First Centres in Washington, DC and Boston 121

At the Queensberry centre, Sister Satya Prana, Sister Devamata, and Katharine Sherwood, left to right.

Swami Paramananda at the entrance of the Boston, Queensberry centre

Devamata in front of the Queensberry centre.

Dated a few days later, the same paper recorded a "transfer of property from Laura Glenn to Swami Paramananda in use of Laura F. Glenn et al. at Audubon Road and Queensberry Street for $1."[10] Laura used the funds left to her in her father's will very wisely in real estate purchases.

In the predawn hours of May 19, 1914, members of the Vedanta Centre arrived at one Queensberry Street. Alighting from their horse cab, they stood for a moment in silent prayer on the broad steps leading to the front door, carrying the holy things of the shrine. As they crossed the threshold of their new home, the first rays of the rising sun shed its light on the entrance as if signaling a new chapter for the centre. Paramananda spent the day in the shrine chanting and singing, while workers were moving about

Original Queensberry building when purchased in 1914.

the house with boxes. In the evening the members of the household, carrying burning incense and candles, proceeded through all twenty rooms, and every hall and stairway, invoking the blessings of the Divine. The Swami's living quarters were at one end of the house and a residency for the community and guests, with a separate entrance, on the other end.

Only three days later, a public ceremony took place and the home was dedicated to the all-loving Universal Spirit. Hundreds of invitations had been sent out. It was typical of Paramananda—getting things done in an incredibly short period of time, at the final moment.

Known as the Robert Treat Paine mansion, it was a respected landmark of the city. Robert Treat Paine Jr. (1866–1961), its original owner, was the grandson of a signer of the Declaration of Independence. Built for him and his wife in 1899, the red brick building—a Georgian Revival Mansion—was owned by the Boston Vedanta Centre from 1914 to 1925.

Taking up residence in such an imposing dwelling certainly aided in reversing public opinion of the centre. In the eyes of the community, it provided an air of stability and permanence to the work. People began coming to the centre as they would to any other church in Boston.

1915-1921

Devamata sketched a very picturesque snapshot of the setting of their Queensberry home.

> There were few buildings near it and open fields stretched wide about it—white under untrodden snow in January,

starred with daisies in June, orange with tansy in August, aglow with autumn leaves in October.... Song sparrows sang the first hymn at the Service on Sunday and all the week robins and black birds chirped and twittered in the vines which climbed the walls to the eaves. It was like a village church in the heart of an old-fashioned garden.[11]

There were two chapels in the house—one private and the other for public services. Both altars were designed by Ralph Deblois Flint (1885–1916), an artist of rare talents and a member of the community. For each chapel he employed a cabinet maker to do the initial woodwork but did all the carving and gilding by himself. The altar in the private chapel now resides in the Temple of the Universal Spirit in La Crescenta, California, and the altar in the public chapel found its home in the temple of the Cohasset Vedanta Centre in Massachusetts. Both centres were founded by Paramananda, the former in 1923 and the latter in 1929.

The altar at the Queensberry centre

In the twelve issues of *Message of the East* published in 1916, Devamata's activities for the year were listed as:

January issue: At the invitation of Reverend E. M. Cosgrove of the Second Unitarian Church of Somerville, she spoke on "Women and India."

February issue: She delivered a lecture before the Boston Browning Society entitled "Robert Browning and the Vedanta."

May issue: From March 9 to April 19, she was at the Washington, DC centre. In addition to the regular classes, she spoke twice at the National New Thought Center and lectured in Baltimore on the invitation of the Theosophical Lodge of the city.

August and September issues: For five months, June through October, she conducted services and classes at the Boston Vedanta Centre while

Paramananda was on the west coast, where he began a centre in Los Angeles. With the war raging in Europe, he had turned his attention westward.

November and December issues: Paramananda returned to Boston at the end of October for a month. On December 11, he was back in Los Angeles. He spent the midwinter months on the west coast, leaving Devamata in charge of the Boston centre.

During this year, she was also in charge of the busy publication department, in which packaging and shipping book orders to the west coast occupied hours of time. Transcribing and editing lectures for the *Message of the East* journal was another priority. In 1916, she authored: "Mortality and Immortality," "Psychic Power and Spiritual Vision," "Robert Browning and the Vedanta," "What is True Worship?" "God as Divine Mother," "The Nativity," and "The Value of Symbols."[12] These articles, published in the journal, often began as lectures. Collectively they reveal an insightful, highly intellectual and spiritually-grounded author. In the articles, she quoted Herbert Spencer, Thomas Carlyle, Goethe, Dante, Fröbel, and Emerson to succinctly clarify a point. Other times she referenced the lives of Krishna, Buddha, Jesus Christ, Ramakrishna, Zoroaster, Lao Tzu, and Confucius, to name a few.

Devamata at the Boston centre.

Devamata became a teacher in her own right, attracting followers differing from those drawn to Paramananda's more mystical approach. A staunch admirer stated: "When she lectured, students from local colleges sat on the edge of their seats, catching every word. She had much wisdom, had an answer for every question, and seemed to know everything."[13] Devamata was ever gracious and helpful to the public. The numerous letters of appreciation, which she received from congregants, were an indication of their gratitude.

During 1917 and 1918, Paramananda divided his time equally between Boston and Los Angeles, six months each. When he was on the west coast, Devamata led the community in Boston. When Paramananda was in Boston, workers were sent from Boston to carry on the work in California. In her book *Swami Paramananda and His Work*, Devamata comments on his continental commutes.

> On a moment's notice he starts on the long journey [cross-country] of nearly a week, stops at one or two points on the way . . . attends to what needs his special attention in Boston, conducts Services for two or three Sundays and is back to California within the month; or he reverses the direction and is back in Boston in the same interval.[14]

On his journeys to the Pacific Coast, he would stop for a few days in Louisville (Kentucky), Cincinnati (Ohio) or Gallup (New Mexico), cities on the transcontinental rail route. By and large, his talks were organized under the auspices of New Thought or some religious group, with an audience numbering several hundred. Study groups in these cities met regularly. While on the west coast, Seattle, Tacoma, San Francisco, and Portland were part of his itinerary. These stopovers attracted new community members.

Rhoda May Gladwell heard Paramananda speak in Los Angeles in 1916 and knew immediately that he was her teacher. He gave her the spiritual name of Seva. Edna Massman, born in Indiana, joined the Queensberry Street community in 1918 and became Achala. She was Paramananda's secretary, recording his talks in shorthand and transcribing them for publication. Georgina Frances Jones Walton was the fifth sister. She attended Paramananda's lectures in Los Angeles in 1918 and soon after joined the community as Daya. She became an ordained platform speaker on both coasts by 1920, and received monastic vows in 1921 along with Achala. Camilla Victoria Christians entered the community in 1919. She served as Devamata's secretary and personal aide. She was given the name Amala. That same year Mary Lacy Staib, later Shanta, became a member of the Louisville group and began visiting the Boston centre for months at a time. She entered the community in 1921, displaying an uncommon steadiness and balance. Alice Afsprung began attending Paramananda's lectures in Cincinnati in 1921. She joined the Ananda community in 1925 as librarian and became Vimala.

Seva, Achala, Daya, Amala, Shanta and Vimala are Sanskrit names that translate to service, unshakeable, compassion, purity, peace, and stainless, respectively. When making a commitment to spiritual life an individual may be given a name that exemplifies a quality they possess or one that they are working toward in their spiritual quest. When given monastic vows, each was addressed as 'Sister.'

The additional community members, a changing round of guests, and increased attendance at all classes including Sunday services, revealed the need for enlarging the chapel and the house at Queensberry. The six-month project was spearheaded by Devamata in 1921. She could be seen everywhere in the house, from the fourth floor to the cellar, directing the workmen. One day she consulted with a congregant, an electrician, for advice on lighting fixtures in the top room. The stairway to the room had not yet been constructed, but Devamata, undaunted, climbed out a third-floor window and scaled a ladder to the room. The man had to follow.

Brother Jack Miller, a young Jewish man from the Cincinnati group, helped her on the renovation project. Devamata gives an account of the resulting changes.

> The building was carried to the end of the lot at the rear, a vestibule was erected where the stoop had been, a wing was raised higher and a fourth story was constructed. Altogether were added six bedrooms, two bathrooms, a laundry room, a large and small storeroom, six storage closets, and a fourth-floor sun parlor. The dining room and cellars were enlarged and the seating capacity of the chapel increased. Also an entire new heating system of the most improved type was installed.[15]

The remodeling necessitated the repainting and repapering of the entire house. One of the changes was a new entrance porch lighted by Gothic windows. In the main window, the symbol of the Ramakrishna Order had been reproduced in stained glass with the Vedic text 'Truth is one, men call it by various names,' written below the windows.

The enlargement resulted in a spacious work room for the publication department. Printing facilities included a press, cutter, stitcher, and type rack. Invitations, circulars, and small pamphlets were now printed in-house. Copies of the monthly magazine and booklets were also bound. Devamata had spent a year in the bindery of a local press and likewise in a downtown print shop to gain practical experience.

By 1921 the monthly magazine had traveled to England, France, Germany, Switzerland, Africa, India, Ceylon, New Zealand, Australia, Canada, and throughout the U.S. The same year, the Los Angeles centre was closed due to erratic attendance, after which Paramananda turned his attention to the East and Midwest. In one twelve-day tour in November, he delivered twenty-two

*Renovated Queensberry centre.
Swami Paramananda can be seen in the top floor window.*

New entranceway to the Queensberry centre.

Devamata at Queensberry centre looking out a window in the entranceway.

lectures in seven cities in four different states.[16] During this tour, 1800 books and pamphlets were sold.

In Community

Paramananda viewed his mission as the "direct transmission of spirit to spirit," which changes and transforms a person's life. The verbal exposition of Vedanta, per se, was not his goal. The main thing, he noted, was "to sow the seed. Those who are ready will feel the living quality just from the presence without words."[17] He sought to give inspiration to all and to bind hearts together through the power of example and by appealing to the student's higher nature.

He furthermore held that the spiritual atmosphere of the centre should benefit anyone who entered. Instructing the community members similarly, he urged them to carry with them an atmosphere that impacted the lives of others who came in touch with them. When returning from India, Sister Christine visited the Boston centre. In a letter to Paramananda dated November 8, 1910, she wrote of the 'sense of sanctity' underlying every aspect of the centre.

> I shall always remember our visit to Boston with the sweetest feelings. I came there very much disturbed in mind but everything dropped from me as if by magic after the first day. . . . Everything—you, the house, the food and swatches of talk have a sanctity about it."[18]

All the sisters were avid diary-keepers. Their devotion to Paramananda prompted them to preserve his every word. Sister Achala's journal provides significant insight into Paramananda's teachings to the community members. She captured his informal and spontaneous comments whether in the community room, at the dining room table, or on the lawn under the stars. A sampling of his appeals taken from her journal, read as follows:

- Love is all. Its impelling power is greater than any power the human mind has ever conceived.
- Everything comes from the Divine Mother, even the smallest blessing. He never starts out to do anything, even a motor

trip for pleasure, without first asking the Divine Mother's protection.

- Living in a community is a great blessing. We learn to do for each other.
- We live in such a close circle we see each other's faults and failures more plainly, but be loving towards each other.
- The Divine Mother is all-tender. She does not remember our mistakes. She sees in our hearts the real spirit of our effort. She forgets our mistakes because she knows our heart.
- Renunciation means giving up the self and selfish ideas, low feelings and thoughts, pettiness and harshness.
- Pray for each other. Don't have unkind or hateful thoughts toward each other. Fellow feeling must go hand-in-hand with our meditation.
- Humility is the very foundation of spiritual life. Lose all sense of egotism.
- Be willing to stand tribulations. Be thankful for them. They are opportunities for you. Endure. Endure. Endure.[19]

Wanting the centre to be a spiritual home, not a rigid institution, Paramananda did not impose strict rules on managing the house. He viewed a consecrated life as leading one to correct conduct. "Make your own rules," he said, adding the all-important qualification, "then follow them."[20] He expected self-discipline.

The community's life followed a pattern. Each member began the day meditating at her private altar in her own room. Group worship conducted by Paramananda or Devamata followed. After breakfast, each set about doing their duties—gardening, cooking, cleaning the shrine, arranging floral

Devamata at the piano in Boston centre.

Two scores authored by Devamata for sale through Riker, Brown, and Wellington.

offerings, publishing *Message of the East*, or shopping for the community. Noon service was in common. After dinner there was time for personal chores. Vesper service was held after sundown.[21] After a light supper, they gathered together for community readings, singing, or listening to a play enacted by Paramananda, in which he even sang the songs of the play. Besides performances, he treated them to nonsensical stories and ludicrous attire. These were part and parcel of his spontaneous spirit, like that of a child, and often resulted in uproarious laughter among community members. In displaying such a lack of self-consciousness in these whimsical moments, he broke down that barrier in others.

Paramananda encouraged community members to be of help to their family. Devamata's mother lived with her in the early years of the Washington centre in 1911. Her mother was also a community member for a considerable number of months in 1919. During this time, she fell and was bedridden, which required around-the-clock care by community members until her bones mended. The Holy Mother wrote Devamata expressing approval of her mother's stay with her and appreciation of the care that was being given.

In her leadership role at the Boston centre, Devamata shared her Indian travel experiences with community members. She sensed a story's likely impact upon a certain aspect of spiritual life and employed it accordingly.

Devamata and her mother, Elizabeth, who was living in the Boston community.

Devamata in Nantucket

Girish Ghosh had narrated to her his initial doubts as well as the questions that he had posed to Sri Ramakrishna. This information was particularly helpful to new community members who themselves struggled with doubts. Since the direct disciples, whose holy company she had enjoyed, stressed the importance of service, their words on the topic spoke directly to the everyday lives of the community members, bolstering their spirits. Her numerous visits to the Dakshineswar temple grounds, and the words of Holy Mother were also profoundly inspirational to community members.

Devamata had a share of humorous anecdotes in her arsenal too, many involving Hindu tales. At meal times she would have the whole community laughing. She was equally amused. Even if retelling the same tale for the umpteenth time, she would find it amusing. This is much like Paramananda, who would always laugh at the punch line of a well-worn joke.

In her book *The Guru and the Disciple*, Sister Daya described Devamata's role as being that of a disciplinarian. Being set on establishing a perfect spiritual community, Devamata would become annoyed at any lapse of her sisters. Daya wrote,

> Her task was to establish the rule and discipline of the Centre's life. This she did with consecration and decision. . . . She taught the students that a heavy step or a high-pitched voice were evidence of rajas, or feverish restlessness, in other words, of ego! We were to learn to speak quietly, to move quietly, and

quietly shut the door. We were to demand nothing and perform even the lowliest task with joyousness. To be late for a public Service was for the Senior Sister a major offense. More than once, slightly delayed, I tried to creep unheard down the long flight of stairs which led to the chapel, but always a board would squeak, and I would arrive at the chapel door only to face a devastating glance of disapproval.[22]

Daya had commented, "[Senior] Sister was very active and seemed to be in every place in the house at once." An incident from Daya's early days in the community lends credence to her assessment. She wrote: "one day I had been assigned the task of dusting the library. As I dusted the books, the title of one caught my eye, and setting aside the dust cloth, I stood for a few moments engrossed in reading." It was the opportune moment for Devamata to walk in. Assessing the situation, she commented, "Are you serving the Lord or serving yourself?"[23]

Daya pinpointed the difference in the training methods of Paramananda and Devamata by using quotes from the New Testament to describe the approach of each. Devamata's quote was: "Whosoever will come after me, let him deny himself and take up his cross and follow me." Whereas she described the Swami's approach in the words, "Come unto me all ye who labor and are heavy burdened, and I will give you rest."[24] From Daya's vantage point, Paramananda was the indulgent parent and Devamata was the task master, who imposed on the new novices an austerity in keeping with her view of spiritual life—as a battle requiring endurance and uncompromising renunciation.

Devamata was no less sparing on herself. Using every free minute of time, Devamata darned socks between the two public services on Sunday. A guest reproached her for failing to rest on the day of the Lord. Responding, "Every day is the Lord's day,"[25] Devamata continued to stitch.

Paramananda would invariably remind her, "Some aspirants must express their devotion through austerity; they are unbending and critical of others in the spiritual life. There is another type which employs only mildness, gentleness, and humility in every task. Great souls belong to the second type."[26] Even his letters of the time from the west coast, though full of transactional details, would contain inspirational thoughts that served as reminders. He wrote, "May the Divine Mother keep you well in body and in mind and adorn you with humility and devotion."[27] But Devamata was given the same freedom as others in the community. In her case, it meant expressing her authoritarian nature.

In the long run, looking back, the sisters expressed their gratitude for Devamata's training. Daya understood this, at least in theory, in her beginning days in the community. In a letter to her mother explaining her decision to stay permanently at the centre, she wrote, "The special spiritual training and otherwise I am getting here is rare and I feel I must avail myself of it to the utmost. Being with Sister Devamata is a very special privilege for she can teach me so much that will be invaluable in my future work I may have to do."[28]

Life at the Boston centre, like in any community of beginning students, led to clashes of temperaments and ideas. Vastly different personalities living together became a source of friction. Clashes arose over practically nothing. The resulting frictional heat burnt away the mental impurities associated with the ego and sanded down the angularities of the character. It is said that only through struggle can a spiritual aspirant pass through struggle and grow spiritually. Community living certainly accelerates that learning process.

Regarding a spiritual centre, Sister Daya described it as "a hospital of the Lord where those fevered with the sickness of self are being healed by the tender touch of the great Physician."[29]

Sister Devamata, Boston, Revere Beach the summer of 1922.

The altars of the Boston Vedanta Centres, after the 1925 sale of Queensberry, are shown below. The Vedanta Centre moved permanently to Cohasset, MA in 1952; the last Boston centre was sold.

176 Marlboro St. 1925-27

875 Beacon St. 1927-29

32 Fenway, 1929-37

420 Beacon 1937-52

Chapter Nine

Years of Rapid Growth
The Twenties

Over the years, Devamata spent hours sequestered with Paramananda discussing publication issues and household concerns. In community matters, she was consulted in all decisions taken. By the twenties, the community membership had increased and others stepped up to assume responsibilities. She found it difficult, though, to relinquish her many roles. Sister Achala was a case in point. As Paramananda's personal secretary, she was able to take dictation, but Devamata continued to do so.

Devamata also challenged Paramananda's judgment, in particular, his travel arrangements or his request of another sister. This occurred often enough for the community to nickname her "But, Swami."[1] Though she was accustomed to having her way, these incidents were not always resolved in her favor, in which case, the mental adjustment was problematic for her. At such times, Paramananda felt her struggle and it grieved him.

From 1915 to 1926, a viral epidemic (encephalitis lethargica) occurred worldwide—in Europe, Canada, Central America, India, and the U.S. Commonly called sleeping sickness, it affected roughly five million people, a third of whom died. Those who survived had long-term health issues, which commonly had Parkinsonian-like signs. In the decades following the epidemic, estimates stated that a majority of Parkinson cases were post-encephalitic.

In March of 1922, Paramananda was summoned back to Boston from speaking engagements in his eight-city tour of the Midwest. Devamata had collapsed. She spent weeks in bed with no signs of recovering. Several months later she was diagnosed with encephalitis. When her illness took a turn for the worse, her physician declared her death imminent. In what appeared to be her last hour, she requested Paramananda's presence at her bedside.

In *A Bridge of Dreams*, Paramananda's biography, the bedside narrative is given as follows:

> She told him that she felt herself slipping out from the body, and implored him to save her. She pleaded that she knew she had brought this illness on herself by her ambition. Even though her yearning to live sprung not from any fear of death, but from her desire to remain with the Swami, she promised him that if she lived, she would never again trouble him by her attachment to him.[2]

"Paramananda was willing to let her go," the author comments, "but not in a state of darkness and resistance."[3] Vedanta holds that one's state of mind at the time of death is crucial to a good transition from the body.

Summoning the community to the dining room, Paramananda announced that they would hold a vigil for three days and nights in an attempt to save Devamata's life. Around the clock, members of the community took turns in the shrine room. He and Sister Seva began the vigil that evening, with him lying prostrate before the altar. During the night, an illness overtook him; it left his body, though, as quickly as it had entered.

Devamata knew nothing of the vigil. During the first night, however, she felt greatly relieved, as if a heavy burden had been removed. The next morning the attending nurse was shocked to find her sitting in a chair across the room, for on the previous day she had been too weak to move. Taking no credit for the reversal in her condition, her physician credited Paramananda and the residents of the centre.

After the three-day vigil, lights continued to burn in the shrine for nine additional days as members of the household entered and left at will. During this period, Devamata remembered a particularly bleak night of pain. As she recalled, "One night when I refused the ministration of the nurse . . . and all through the pain-weighted hours of darkness I kept my closed eyes fixed on that vigil flame before the altar, with the Swami's prayer-wrapt figure seated near to it. The power and blessing which came so lifted me that I seemed to float above the pain."[4]

In a letter to Paramananda dated August 23, 1922, Swami Saradananda, Secretary of the Ramakrishna Math and Mission, wrote, "May the Master who has been kind enough to bring her back to life and consciousness after your first night's vigil, complete her cure in His inscrutable ways and keep her with us for a long time yet in His great mercy and compassion."[5]

Throughout Devamata's months of convalescence, Paramananda was surprised to find that poems suddenly began to surge up from deep within, in a complete form. He would quickly jot down the words as they arose during the course of the day. Oftentimes numerous poems, as many as nine, came in one day. By August 1922, the number totaled eighty. In October they were published under the title *Soul's Secret Door*, which was lauded by even the most unlikely publications. It appears that his poetry reached corners that his books never could. Many readers were undoubtedly inspired to open for himself or herself the secret door of the soul.

Reflecting on the months of her recovery, Devamata wrote that Paramananda led her "gently back to life—through his prayers, through a brief daily reading of some sacred book, through holy words of encouragement and counsel, and above all, through his poems." His poetry made "so vivid an impression that often I could repeat [the poem] word for word after one hearing. The rhythmic lines of the poem drew my vital energies from the depths back to the surface of my being."[6]

His second volume of poetry, *The Vigil*, was published in 1924; a third volume, *The Rhythm of Life*, appeared the next year; lastly, *My Creed* was published in 1929. Devamata noted, "Spontaneous, fresh, imperative, it seemed to him not as his creation, but as a very special gift of the One Giver, and as such he always thought and spoke of it. In truth, he was swept by humility in the face of his own inspiration."[7]

In a letter addressed to 'Beloved Sister Devamata' and dated March 1924, Swami Shivananda, President of the Ramakrishna Math and Mission, wrote,

> I have gone through 'Souls Secret Door' by dear Paramananda. It is an excellent poem full of faith, love, devotion and purity. It helps many hungry souls and makes many more hungry. I see it is talked of highly in the U.S. Press. It is not less elevating than Tagore's poems, sometimes I think it is rather more.[8]

Devamata's recovery was less than perfect. She walked with difficulty, her speech was garbled, and her face was slightly contorted. She never again spoke on a public platform. Once a relentless disciplinarian of herself and others, she remained a semi-invalid for the last twenty years of her life. Her chief contribution became editing and writing. She continued to be consulted on community affairs and supervised a couple of major projects. As for her promise to Paramananda, she was unable to keep it and demonstrated even greater attachment to him.

Ananda Ashrama

Over the years, Paramananda dreamed of a spiritual retreat modeled after the forest ashramas of ancient India, which were traditionally the setting for students to learn from a teacher the highest spiritual truths. The quiet of nature was always sought—it drew man's thoughts Godward very easily. For this reason, the wide-open spaces, mountainous heights, and temperate climate of the west attracted Paramananda. He discovered the spot that he sought in the Sierra Madre range (Mother Mountains) in California. Located on a plateau five hundred feet above the valley of La Crescenta, north of Los Angeles; it commanded a view of the Pacific Ocean on a clear day. A half heir to her mother's legacy, Devamata provided the downpayment for the 135 plus acres, as surveyed from mountaintop to mountaintop in a straight line.

On April 2, 1923 a reception was held at the Boston centre announcing the recent purchase of land in La Crescenta, which would be used as a Peace Retreat. Paramananda named it, explaining,

> We shall create out there a place where a community of workers can live and express their talents along different lines—music, art, industry. It will not be limited to religion, although that will be the soul of it. . . . This is not a sudden change. For some time I have felt the need of a different line of action. Life is to be put on a simpler basis. It does not mean giving up anything, it means only expansion.[9]

Paramananda's vision focused on self-expression, selfless service, and spiritual practices. He dreamed of an ashrama where monastic women, men and women workers, families, and guests would all reside with minds and lives directed to the highest ideals. As for its mission, he stated, "My idea is not to bring here a Hindu creed or a Christian creed or a Buddhist creed, but to take the best out of all and embody the universal aspect of all. That is my dream.... People are of divergent types with differing ideals, yet they are all able to meet here and find something for their upliftment."[10] Clearly his mind was no longer on public work, such as lecturing.

Most of the property was mountainous land with canyons. There were nine canyons on the property. Approximately fifteen acres were tillable. The one house on the property was sturdily built of white stucco with a red-tile roof; other buildings on the property were cottages, barns, and garages. Several ornamental trees had been planted by the previous owner along the roadside, trails, and around the house. Orchards and vineyards had also been started by him without marring the natural setting. Devamata wrote, "The vegetation is almost as cosmopolitan and universal as the spirit of the teaching given under its shade."[11]

Water for the house was from a spring located at the top of the largest canyon. Stored in a concrete, roofed-in reservoir, a mile below its source, it was plentiful. To avoid waste, water conservation was the first job undertaken by Paramananda and his group of hardy pioneer women from Boston— Sister Daya, Sister Seva, and Mangala (Marguerite Mangala Morgan). The women were immediately engaged in cleaning away heavy brush and building stone walls.

Devamata was also one of the ashrama pioneers. The cold weather of Boston exacerbated her Parkinson symptoms, typically shooting nerve pain and muscle or joint pain. While other sisters moved between the centres, living on both coasts, she remained at Ananda Ashrama for the rest of her life, with occasional visits to the East Coast. Finding herself on the West Coast, only a year after her collapse, it is not surprising that during this time she "alternated between periods of independence and helpfulness and periods when she herself became one more care for the others to tend."[12]

Hiking the grounds in 1925.
At the top and coming down, Achala and kitty, Mangala, Amala, Hilda, Mary Lacy, Devamata, and Paramananda

Late in the afternoon on Sunday April 29, two weeks after taking possession of the property, the first public service was held on the grounds. Under the blue California sky, Paramananda spoke of that Great Unity which underlies all diversity and is the goal of all traditions. As he spoke, the nature scene surrounding him was picturesquely described by Daya.

> The platform upon which the Swami stood was grass. Locust trees in full blossom, masses of yellow broom, white syringa, wild sage, and the lupine made the air fragrant around him. Behind him, as in a Greek amphitheater, rose the hills, level after level, softly veiled and shadowed. . . . His Sanskrit prayers had a new majesty, heard out of doors with the undertone of nature, and his peace chant mingled with the peace of the hills and seemed to flow forth over the world below. All felt the spell of it and lingered till the long shadows told the lateness of the hour.[13]

New roads were built during the first summer, opening up previously inaccessible sections of the property; a row of cabins was constructed to accommodate a larger number of workers; and the first livestock were acquired—nine goats, two cows, hens, and a donkey. Corrals and pens were constructed for them. The animals supplied the ashrama with milk, cheese, butter, and eggs. The workers also tended the grape vines, irrigated the trees, planted a garden and harvested the abundant yield of the young fruit trees. The vicissitudes of nature also became apparent that first year—the destructiveness of the Santa Ana winds, the ravages of wild creatures like coyote and skunk, and the menace of brush fires on the surrounding hills.

In mid-September, Paramananda was back in Boston, returning to California in December with Sister Achala, Sister Shanta, and several others who could be spared in Boston. The book department and *Message of the East* journal were also moved west. With so few people left in Boston, the large Queensberry Street home was no longer necessary. In 1925, it was sold to the Boston Home of Truth. The centre moved to a smaller home at 176 Marlborough Street (for two years), then to 875 Beacon Street (1927–29), followed by 32 Fenway (1929–37) and finally established itself at 420 Beacon Street, overlooking the Charles River.

The first major construction was undertaken at the ashrama in May 1924. A twelve-room addition to the original stucco building served as the living quarters of the Sisters and women workers. It became known as the cloister, since it was designed under Devamata's guidance in the style of "a medieval Spanish cloister." The building consisted of "four wings, an enclosed courtyard, flagstone arcades with a pergola, arched patios, grilled windows, and beamed roofs, all constructed of unhewn stone gathered from the ashrama itself."[14] On a Sunday afternoon in early November, it was dedicated.

The nuns' cloister at Ananda Ashrama. Office, bedroom, and shrine of Devamata are in the building seen on the far right.

During the winter months that followed, weather permitting, an outdoor service was held in the new patio of the cloister. Sheltered from the wind, the patio provided a panoramic view of the mountains that formed a scenic backdrop for the Ashrama. At the beginning of each service Devamata rang the antique Benares bell—suspended from the beams of the porch—as a call to prayer.

Paramananda hoped to avoid hiring outside workers for future projects. Skilled workers began to show up as if in answer to his prayers. An electrical engineer, a skilled woodworker, a mechanic, a builder, and a handyman made their appearances just in time for the next major project—the construction of a two-story, fifteen-room guest house on a knoll below the cloister. However, working with Paramananda, a perfectionist with innumerable ideas, was a daunting task for the men. To be helpful, Devamata informed them of Paramananda's remarkable ability to accomplish a lot in a short time.

She recalled the record number of "books put through the press in two weeks, the number of the monthly magazines prepared and published in five days, successful entertainments organized in a few hours, or important enterprises set on foot overnight."[15] The workers were not impressed. Undertaken in the fall of 1924, the building was dedicated a year later, right after Christmas.

While the community house was still under construction, Paramananda launched the arts and crafts department. He led the way by instructing the sisters in molding incense sticks by using various Indian spices mixed with sweet herbs gathered from the ashrama grounds. Later leather bookmarks, artistic book covers, and calligraphy gave ashrama workers more opportunity for creative expression.

Ananda Ashrama celebrated its second anniversary on April 26, 1925, in an open-air temple that was constructed by numerous volunteers under Paramananda's supervision. A short distance from the cloister, a hidden sanctuary was the chosen site. Shut in on all sides by sage covered hills, great oak and sycamore trees, it was transformed in ten days. Brush and poison oak were cleared, tree limbs were pruned, and a new trail laid which led up the canyon. The canyon floor was filled and leveled at the site. At its entrance a rustic gate was constructed and steps were cut in the hard soil of the upward bank. A choir loft in a grove nearby added the finishing touch on the project. With a portable organ, the choir greeted the congregants, who took their seats on the redwood benches made for the occasion. The sycamores that had been cut down were used to form a partition behind the altar. Garlands of wild flowers were hung on it. The backdrop of the altar was a sheer cliff.

In September of that year Paramananda received a notice that a convention of the Ramakrishna Math and Mission would be held in the spring of 1926 at the head monastery of Belur. It was the first of its kind. Though Paramananda deemed it impossible to travel to India due to his Boston work, he was requested to reconsider and represent the North American work at the convention. When he agreed to attend, a formal reception was held in his honor at the Marlboro centre, the new home of the Vedanta Centre in Boston. He departed in early January.

While Paramananda was in India, Devamata received a letter from Swami Virajananda, a foremost disciple of Swami Vivekananda. He wrote,

> I cannot tell you how delighted I was to meet him [Paramananda] at the Math after nearly twenty-two years, and I found him as sweet and loving as before, as child-

like and unassuming as was always his nature when he was unknown to fame and honor. Just as years have lightly touched him, so have name, fame, and affluence.[16]

During Paramananda's trip abroad, Devamata compiled the *Book of Daily Thoughts and Prayers*. As far back as 1912 Paramananda had suggested the title of the book, whose contents would be dedicated to daily prayers and salient thoughts. If held throughout the day, these thoughts would aid the mind in the process of "continuous mindfulness." In the book's foreword, Devamata stated:

> I have garnered stray thoughts jotted down on scraps of paper lying on the Swami's desk or work table, or tucked in some book. I have noted vital sayings and set aside countless passages from letters. All the material used . . . was drawn from unpublished sources. The quotations from the Scriptures are from the Swami's translations. . . . They [words] have been classified and arranged in consecutive and cumulative sequence. The thought is carried forward from day to day, so that at the end of a month a new and defined impression will be made on the character.[17]*

Each page of the book contained the following: a holy thought, a verse taken from Paramananda's poems, a lesson, and an inspirational prayer. Every day of the year had its own page, and a different theme defined each month. The idea was to hold the mind steadfastly throughout the day on some holy thought to avoid the material overpowering the spiritual. The prayers were recorded by Devamata as they were uttered by Paramananda, unbeknown to him. Now in its sixth edition, the book has become a spiritual classic along with *The Path of Devotion*. It was first published in April 1926, just before Paramananda's return from India in June.

During his five-month absence, Devamata also wrote the first volume of *Swami Paramananda and His Work*, a biographical sketch from his early days in India up to the year 1926. His personality, habits, and methods of work were described in detail. Snatches of his letters to a number of workers were widely cited throughout the book. The worker most often referenced was Devamata herself, though not named. Of herself she writes, "To one who had grown harsh and critical and out of rhythm he wrote: 'All your earnest

---

*Devamata's foreword to the first edition of this book is in Appendix B.

service will surely enrich your life with true understanding. Remember that complete surrender makes us clear channels for the Divine.'"[18]

As this statement illustrates, faults or blunders which came to his notice were met with reminders. He reminded the worker of his or her contribution to the whole. In Devamata's case, her service was unparalleled and he commented on that fact. His statement also illustrates his habit of calling out the Divine in that soul to encourage forward motion on the spiritual path. His intent was not to correct, but to counteract such tendencies.

Upon his return to Ananda Ashrama, Paramananda found both books on his desk with handwritten notes slipped into each book, attesting to Devamata's devotion to her teacher.

In the *Book of Daily Thoughts and Prayers*, she wrote,

> This little book
> is laid at your Beloved Feet in humble
> worship and tenderest devotion.
> Preparing it brought to me new life.
> May it bring you joy and be pleasing to you.

and in the second book,

> The tribute of my life has gone into this Life.
> The devotion of my heart flows through every word.
> The fruits of my effort are now laid
> at your Holy Feet
> in devout reverence and holy worship.[19]

In traveling to India, one of Paramananda's goals was to find qualified assistants. Belur Math had long urged him to accept help due to his strenuous undertakings. He sought an assistant possessing idealism and simplicity with an ability to blend into community living. He saw in his niece Gayatri Devi, a young widow of nineteen, a person who met these requirements. Belur Math assigned Swami Akhilananda (1894–1962) to be his assistant.

Akhilananda and Gayatri Devi sailed with Paramananda to the U.S. on May 2, 1926. Assigned to the Boston centre, Akhilananda's traditionalism became a community problem. He mandated adherence to the guidelines enjoined by the tradition, whether it be in the shrine rituals or in the guidelines set down for initiation into sannyasa. When an SOS was sent by the community in Boston to Paramananda, who was not one to be bound by rules and technicalities, he interceded. By the end of 1928, Akhilananda moved on, eventually starting a centre in Providence, Rhode Island.

In February 1927, Paramananda was invited to take part in the opening of a radio station owned by a friend and neighbor in La Crescenta. Over the years, he had refused others who encouraged him to use the radio to spread Vedanta. This time he acquiesced to support his neighbor. His address became a weekly Wednesday night program. Its popularity resulted in a larger broadcasting station in Hollywood inviting him to give a series of Tuesday night talks. In June of the same year, he wrote Shivananda that he was seriously considering using an "aeroplane" for his transcontinental lecture tours. He did make his first flight some years later from Burbank to Boston, with a plane change in Kansas City.

The Temple of the Universal Spirit

In 1927, Paramananda's life-long dream materialized. The ground for the construction of the Temple of the Universal Spirit, or Viswamandir, was chosen at Ananda Ashrama. On Easter Sunday, the leveled ground was formally consecrated. In his address on that day, Paramananda stated his aspiration; he hoped that "the followers of all faiths and all paths might find a spiritual home within its walls."[20]

When the foundation was ready to be excavated, every member of the community, one after another, took a shovel in hand and dug up a scoopful of earth. For the success of the project, a vigil in the shrine began that day, with members taking turns sitting in prayer and meditation, as requested by Paramananda. Much of the construction work was done by the ashrama's brotherhood under the direction of a professional builder, and was supervised by Devamata, who had insisted on the responsibility. The stress of the project, however, made her tense and that had an ill effect on her daily state of mind—she was always irritable.

Devamata described the Temple building as follows:

Over the high doors of the Temple is the inscription in illuminated letters, 'Truth is One.' The same note of universality is sounded in every detail of the interior. In each leaded window is a stained glass inset depicting an historical place of worship representative of some one of the great religions of the world. . . . This was conceived by the Swami as an expression of his fundamental conviction that as the same light passes through all these windows—symbols of different creeds–so the One Truth shines in and through all religions.

Beneath the windows and alternating with them are arched niches further symbolizing the ideal of universality. Each niche contains passages from some one of the great Scriptures of the world, written in illuminated letters. Over each quotation is a symbol of the faith represented.

At the east end of the Temple was the sanctuary. The altar was dedicated to the Absolute and surrounded by the prophets of universality, Sri Ramakrishna, Sri Sarada Devi and Swami Vivekananda. It was entirely upon their teachings that the whole edifice stood.[21]

The Temple of the Universal Spirit at Ananda Ashrama with Swami Paramananda's quarters and library.

Altar in the Temple of the Universal Spirit at Ananda Ashrama.

The temple, Paramananda's two-story living quarters, and a library building—with a room for arts and crafts and another for the publication department—were constructed on three of the four corners of the foundation. Paramananda's living quarters was joined to the Temple walls by an arched arcade running to the right, as you face the Temple. From this building, a straight arched arcade ran to the library at the northwest corner of the Temple plot.

Even as the construction proceeded, Paramananda sailed to India via the Pacific in December 1927. Katharine Sherwood, who had been with him since the beginning of his work in Boston, accompanied him. The trip was a year-and-a-half after his return from India in June 1926. The distinguished Polish musician (Leopold Stokowski) and his wife, however, had urged Paramananda to accompany them to India for a few months to get a comprehensive understanding of Indian music. At the same time, he received a letter from President Shivananda requesting him to come to India. Shivananda's health was poor.

Sister Daya was assigned to take over the services in Boston and Gayatri Devi conducted the public services at Ananda Ashrama, the daily class for the household, and the classes in Los Angeles. Devamata conducted the morning worship in the cloister shrine. Paramananda also left her with his ideas and plans for the Temple's construction.

When he returned four months later in April of 1928, the Temple was still under construction and dissidence plagued the ashrama. His approach was once again to call out the Divine within each community member by noting their ability to change the whole atmosphere of the ashrama. "If we speak with the voice of love, or if the voice of love can speak through us, I am certain that nobody can go away from here with [an] injured spirit.... Love will conquer."[22] He did not focus on the misconduct itself. As mentioned earlier, fault-finding, scolding, or correcting were not his ways. His role was to inspire—to uplift minds.

The Temple of the Universal Spirit was dedicated on Sunday October 21, 1928, during the very popular festival of the Divine Mother that is celebrated especially in Northern India. Six hundred people attended the two services held during that day. Devamata composed the words and music of the anthem sung at both services. Three days later when the library building was dedicated, she wrote another anthem. On this occasion, she herself played the accompaniment.

President Shivananda sent his well-wishes on the occasion. In his letter of November 1928, he wrote, "I have been greatly delighted to learn that through Thakur's grace the dedication of Vishwa Mandir had nicely been celebrated. I pray that Thakur's high ideal of universal unity in the midst of diversities may be spread to all directions holding this temple as its prop."[23]

Paramananda at Ananda Ashrama. His dog was named Diana.

Paramananda and Devamata seated on the left in a group picture of a picnic on the grounds, 1929.

*The Sisters at Ananda Ashrama.
Left to right, Daya, Devamata, Seva, Satya Prana
and Achala. Devamata has her pincenez hanging around her neck.*

Sister Devamata on the grounds of Ananda Ashrama.

Sister Devamata and Swami Paramananda at Ananda Ashrama.

These various views of Sister Devamata were taken over her twenty plus years at Ananda Ashrama, whether it be selling items at the the Christmas Bazaar, roaming the hills, mending clothing, caring for the flowers, inspecting the grape arbor, or just posing for a picture on the grounds.

Years of Rapid Growth ✤ 151

Cohasset Ashrama

The decade ended with the purchase of twenty acres of wooded land on the south shore at Cohasset, Massachusetts, in June 1929. The property was remarkably natural, unspoiled, and isolated, even though the surrounding area was built-up. Some twenty miles from Boston and a mile-and-a-half from the ocean, Paramananda envisioned the location as a nature retreat for the Boston community.

A *Boston Globe* article gives us a glimpse of the original property. The entranceway is a narrow trail "which winds and twists through a tunnel of green foliage, like driving down into Alice's rabbit hole." One ends up in a "daisy field" in which the cars are parked. "Seventy-five feet up in the air on a huge glacial boulder is a portable house to which one climbs by winding steps cut out of the solid rock."[24]

In her first visit to the property, Sister Gayatri Devi described it simply as a "jungle" with poison ivy, cat brier, and other vines with prickly stems "climbing the trees and strangling them."[25]

From her perspective, Devamata narrated the rationale behind the purchase.

> As the Swami wandered over the hills of the Ashrama in California and breathed its clear air, he realized more and more the beneficent influence of the open spaces of the country, with the companionship of trees and growing things; the nude sky overhead, beneath the feet the soft earth; and he determined that the centre in Boston should have its Ashrama too.[26]

No doubt this was a factor in Paramananda's decision, but there were other more immediate considerations. Since his return from India in 1928, the dissension at the Ananda Ashrama was ongoing. Skirmishes due to annoyances and selfish demands were unsettling for one who made no secret of his peace-loving nature.

In addition, the increased attendance at the two Sunday services of the Boston centre and the Tuesday evening class, demonstrated a new momentum for the work that required his attention. He made train journeys across the continent ten times in 1929, spending more and more time in Boston.

Along the way he taught in Cincinnati, Louisville, Kansas City, Chicago, and other cities in the Midwest.

In an outdoor sanctuary, located in a shaded grove of pines on the Cohasset grounds, the centre was dedicated as Ananda Ashrama, informally called the Little Ashrama. Decorated with June wildflowers, a low rock served as the altar for the simple, ritual-free service, after which Paramananda cooked dinner for the fifty members who had assembled.

Service held on the grounds, Swami Paramananda and attendees.

Original house on the rock and parking lot

Saturdays became the community's day at Cohasset. Weather permitting, mornings were spent working on the property. Carloads of people arrived for the afternoon service under the pine trees. Lunch was served on the porch of the house on the rock. After that, many lingered on for the sunset meditation and supper. A new community house suitable for winter activities was the first building to be constructed.

Community members working on the construction of the new community house, the first building constructed on Cohasset grounds.

First altar on the mantel of the brick fireplace in the community house.

A Bluster of Storms

The U.S. stock market crash on Black Tuesday, March 29, 1929, started a worldwide economic downturn which was experienced in all industrialized nations across the thirties. During the resulting Great Depression, Paramananda faced a strained financial situation. For the first time, he found himself soliciting public support to make mortgage payments on both the Boston and California properties. People who valued the existence of the centres were asked to come forward with material help.

Like all households, the centres faced a new level of frugality in their daily lives. Food and water were the most crucial resources. The cows, goats, and hens at Ananda Ashrama provided enough milk, cheese, eggs, and butter to feed the community, and the canyon springs supplied the water. They also had two sources of income. The community's beehives were yielding a significant amount of honey; some was sold and some was used for barter. The arts and crafts of the residents also generated income. In both centres, the Christmas Bazaar was the major fundraiser of the year. It featured ashrama handicrafts, honey, baked goods, and donated items.

Devamata viewed herself as in the trenches, so to speak, with Paramananda. Since he was dealing with financial constraints, so was she. She spoke incessantly about the failure of the West Adam Street tenants in Los Angeles to pay their rent. Founded as the ashrama's city centre in January 1930, it was later rented out. Community members grew impatient with Devamata's constant concern regarding finances. Worry and anxiety were dual manifestations of Parkinson's disease, which was claiming more and more of her body.

Within Ananda Ashrama itself, another grave disruption surfaced at the same time. Beginning in the late twenties and climaxing while Paramananda was in India in 1933, an insidious slander campaign was waged against him. Fueled by the ire of a former resident who had voluntarily departed the ashrama, it rendered a severe blow to the work. Paramananda never responded to the charges leveled against him. He prayed that the offender's mind be calmed so that she would not inflict further injury on herself or others. To the community, he vowed to use the crisis to draw closer to the Divine.

As soon as one storm abated, another surfaced. One evening in November 1933, a fire engulfed the surrounding hills of Ananda Ashrama and with the aid of the Santa Ana wind, flared-up deeper into the canyons. In Boston, Paramananda was notified. A wired telegram from him informed the community not to take any chances with their lives. When the fire reached the fire break with the adjoining property, the community members prepared to evacuate. This precautionary measure was taken in case they were instructed to leave the grounds by the firemen. Devamata was the first to be seated in the car. Holy things and personal belongings were loaded in the trunk. The shrine was not dismantled. One or more of the sisters sat in prayer in the Temple throughout the night. Devamata, who remained in the car, was repeatedly urged to leave the grounds and take shelter in some place of safety, just in case. She refused: "If it sinks, I go down with it." She was "captain of the ship" and nothing could induce her to leave.²⁷ Firemen streamed in throughout the night. At one point, sixty-five men battled the blaze in a canyon behind the temple, with the ashrama brothers working side by side with them. At dawn, the blaze was quelled.

At sunset that very day, a gust of wind fanned the glowing embers on the hillside and set the fire blazing once again. This time, the shrine relics were gathered up, since the firemen didn't believe they could save the Temple. The sisters were directed to take refuge in the cloister and close all doors and windows. Throughout the night, they knelt in prayer as red-hot embers poured down on the house. To prevent its destruction, the firemen set their hoses on the building. By early morning, the worst was over. The Temple, cloister, guest house, barns, and cabins were spared. The fire had gone over them. Devamata wrote: "You cannot imagine the unity of love and life that was in our hearts. I never was so proud of people in my life as I was of the family on those two nights."²⁸ Surveying the grounds the next day, she summarized the scene: "Ananda Ashrama stands like an oasis in a desolate expanse, the only verdant spot for miles on the charred and blackened hills."²⁹

Six thousand acres had been destroyed and when a soaking rain set in a month later, so did the flood waters. Water seeped into the ashrama buildings and the familiar terrain which surrounded the ashrama was marred beyond recognition by gullies due to mudflows. The real devastation though was experienced in the La Crescenta valley below. The mud, boulders, and debris carried by the water as it roared down the hillside covered cars, downed trees, and crushed houses. In an impromptu service, Paramananda prayed for the people of the valley.

> O, Great Mother Heart, may always Thy will be fulfilled in everything, and may we never, never will anything but Thy will. May we learn to see The Divine hand through the beautiful and through the terrible. Under all circumstances may we never forget that Thou dost make us strong…to meet every situation…. Put us through anything, but grant us unshakeable faith, gladness of spirit and surrender unto Thee under all circumstances.³⁰

In her first book of poetry *The Open Portal* (1929), Devamata reflects a similar attitude in the poem "Hymn of Adoration." The eighty-seven poems in this book are divided into four sections: "Devotion and Aspiration," "Hill and Garden," "The Desert," and "Life." The "Hymn of Adoration" reads,

If life hurt or if it delight
   Lord, I adore Thee—
   Both come from Thy Hand;
   Thy pain shields a joy.

If world wound or if it caress
   Still I adore Thee—
   Both come by Thy Will;
   Thrust masks an embrace.

If man strike or if he protects
   Lord, I adore Thee—
   Both come in Thy plan;
   Blow too is a gift.

If life waving change into death
   Still I adore Thee—
   Both come at Thy call;
   Death heralds new life.[31]

Chapter Ten

Sister Devamata
Author

Throughout her years in Vedanta, Devamata exhibited an impressive aptitude for writing. Her literary works were all products of marked quality. During the period 1912 to 1920, she wrote articles for the centre's journal *Message of the East*. A number of these articles started out as lectures (e.g., "Robert Browning and Vedanta"). The Cohasset archive houses a list of over 140 lectures given by Devamata.

Over time, some of her articles became thirteen-page booklets that sold for twenty or thirty cents. Her earliest booklets were the following—*The Indian Mind and Indian Culture* (1912); *Practice of Devotion* (1913); *Eastern and Western Religious Ideals* (1915); and *Robert Browning and Vedanta* (1916). In 1918 several booklets were listed under her name—*Sleep and Superconsciousness* (originally *Sleep and Samadhi*); *Development of the Will*; *What is Maya?*; and *Health and Healing* (also likely given under the title *Healing in History*). In 1934 her last booklet, *Companionship of Pain*, went to press.

Her Books

After being stricken with encephalitis in 1922, she turned almost exclusively to writing. The viral disease had affected her body, but not her mental ability. Her major literary achievements were books dating to the late twenties and early thirties. In chronological order, they are—*Swami Paramananda and His*

Work, Vol. 1 (1926); *Days in an Indian Monastery* (1927); *Sri Ramakrishna and his Disciples* (1928); *The Habit of Happiness* (1930); and *Sri Ramakrishna and Saint Francis of Assisi* (1935). She also compiled and edited *The Book of Daily Thoughts and Prayers* (1926) that contained the informal teachings of Paramananda.

Her last book *Swami Paramananda and His Work* (Volume 2) appeared in 1941, a year after Paramananda's passing. It covered the multitude of activities that comprised the last fourteen years of his life, which included four trips to India. The story was told basically in his own words through his letters from abroad. She credited Sister Amala for her crucial role in publishing this volume—making working copies of Paramananda's letters, copying the entire manuscript, and taking Devamata's dictation. Devamata was not able to write with her own hands at the time.

A Great Teacher of India, Building Character, and *Shadows and Reality* were three other books that were authored by her, though little is known of them. The *Vedanta Kesari* did publish chapter six of her book *Building Character* in its August 1931 issue; it was entitled "Conscience and Character." In the introductory paragraph to the article, the editor noted, "The fluency of her style and sublimity of thought make her writings as interesting as they are elevating."[1] This same journal also published an abridged chapter of *Days in an Indian Monastery* in 1928 under the title "The Indian Woman and the Indian Home."

Chapters of *Days in an Indian Monastery* were also published in the *Prabuddha Bharata*—"Swami Brahmananda" (1927), and "Forest Schools of Ancient India" (1918). The journal carried some chapters of her book *Sri Ramakrishna and Saint Francis of Assisi* in its January, March, May, and June issues of 1933, at which time the book itself had not yet been published.

Her Poetry

Devamata published three books of poetry—*The Open Portal* (1929), *My Song Garden* (1930), and *The Holy Hour* (1931). The *Los Angeles Saturday Night* published a press notice on the release of *The Open Portal*. Its editor Samuel T. Clover (1859–1939) wrote:

> *The Open Portal* reveals that her poetic gifts are on fully as high a plane as her prose work. . . . [She] strikes many true lyrical notes and at times soars to holy places in the high hills. She travels the open spaces and the quiet solitudes of the soul and reveals them to humanity.[2]

Of the eighty-seven poems in this book, eighteen were set to music by Devamata herself. The scores of two of these; namely, "The Narrow Street" and "The Lotus" were published in Boston by Riken, Brown, and Wellington, Inc.

In her book *The Habit of Happiness*, Devamata describes a great musician who leaves nothing to chance in writing a score. She notes, "Tonality and time-beat, bar and double bar, crescendo and diminuendo, note-sequence and rests"[3] are all precisely indicated. Though not intentionally written to be self-reflective, any musician would agree that Devamata was describing her own work, for her scores were meticulously rendered.

Devamata also wrote songs for special ashrama celebrations. For the opening of the Temple at Ananda Ashrama; for example, she wrote "The Play of God." The Sisters sang it at the dedication. Music played a more dominant role in all programs in both centres over time.

Her second book of poetry *My Song Garden* differs markedly from *The Open Portal*, in that, it consists of poems for children—the little ones of the world. The book's presentation conveys, quite admirably, Devamata's artistic abilities and refined taste. Both covers of this seventy-one-page book are divided vertically, half green faux leather and half floral boards. Included are a number of simply amusing, reddish-brown illustrations by the author—birds, fish, trees, ships, chickens, the face of the moon, two angels, a vase of flowers, an old flour mill, a bridge in France, and the abbey of Mont-Saint-Michel in the Brittany region of France.

The poetry itself demonstrates that there was a playful child hidden in her personality. She put nine of the poems to music—"Daffodils," "Garden Manners," "Johnny-Jump-Ups," "Kisses," "Our Zoo," "Pansies," "The Pole," "Busy Thoughts," and "Where Baby Lives." The music bars were included in the book. She also choreographed a dance to go along with a few of her poems.

In the foreword of *My Song Garden*, Devamata wrote,

> I never had any children of my own, but I have borrowed many and made them mine by right of love. The name I bear means "Mother" and accords me the privilege of adopting

all the children of the world—big and little, grown-up and new-born. To the little ones I now dedicate this book, giving to each one a hug and a kiss, with the prayer that all those who read or hear these poems and hum these tunes may be brighter and sweeter, gentler and more loving to birds, trees, flowers and mothers.[4]

Her experience in 1915 might have been the impetus for this book of children's poems. Paramananda took Helen Lortais, a little girl of four, into the centre as a resident. She had no one to care for her when her father, the house janitor, was admitted to the hospital.

Devamata tells of Paramananda's childlike nature and his "joyous romps"[5] with Helen at bedtime. She would kneel and say her prayers, salute him as captain, and jump into bed. Devamata became Helen's surrogate mother for two years. When a distant relative took over her care, no longer allowing her to visit, it had a deeply-felt impact on Devamata, who had grown attached to mothering the child.

Her Later Articles

Most of her writings in the late thirties were articles for the *Message of the East* just as in the beginning years of her work at the centre. Of these, "The Power of a Holy Life" (1934), "Unselfishness and Selflessness" (1939), and "The Path to Realization" (1939) give a rare glimpse into the level of her spiritual attainment. Unlike her earlier articles, her references to and quotes of educators, leaders, philosophers, and saints were rather minimal. Her writing, though always appreciated for its inspirational quality, became markedly strengthened in these later articles by her experiences, garnered over a lifetime. Eminently practical and stronger in presentation, the articles remained very uplifting to a yearning soul.

In the article entitled "The Power of a Holy Life," she speaks of "the fulfillment of our effort ripened into being," a fulfillment entirely a matter of the inner life. She references the habit of inward gazing, the noble effort carried out through prayer ("prays when he eats, prays when he drinks, prays when he works, prays when he sleeps or wakes")[6] that leads to transcending our human nature. Written five years later, the "Path to Realization" continues the climb from this plane of human consciousness. "Consciousness expands,

expands and expands until the little personal-self drops away. . . . The body has been left behind, so there is neither sight nor other sense to perceive with . . . . The world is still relatively real, but it has no existence in itself; it is the shadow of the Almighty."[7]

In the early thirties, some of Devamata's articles were published in the journals of the Order. In 1931, the *Prabuddha Bharata* published her article "Has Man Free Will?" Six installments of "Memories of India and Indians" were also published in this journal in the spring and fall of 1932. This series of articles conveyed her intimate association in India with Latu Maharaj, Swami Saradananda, and Yogin-ma, as well as her involvement in the early years of the Vedanta movement in the West during Swami Vivekananda's visit.

Appearing as ten monthly installments, "Swami Ramakrishnananda, Sannyasin and Teacher" was published by the *Vedanta Kesari* from May 1932 to April 1933. The article contained details not previously recorded by her. In this same journal, three articles written by her appeared in the late thirties. The first was "The Individual and the Infinite" (1936), which addressed the need for an individual to consciously find completion in the infinite consciousness. The second was "Living Presence" (1936), which recorded her personal experiences over the years. Lastly, "Scientist and Seer" (1938) dealt with both objective and subjective research.

Early Thirties

In May 1931, Devamata celebrated the 30th anniversary of her work in Vedanta. The President of the Ramakrishna Math and Mission, Swami Shivananda, expressed his appreciation for her devotion to the cause of Vedanta in the West in a letter dated May 30, 1931. Addressed to "My dear Sister Devamata," he wrote,

> Your letter speaks so much of the work and I am joyous to feel how unselfishly you love it. I know what great a part you have played in it and still are doing with a frail body, but with a spirit which is getting stronger and stronger in conviction. Your connection with the work is not of thirty years existence, but I think your whole existence is related with it. Pioneers do not take birth but they come along with the birth of a

movement. The stage gets arranged—behind—the curtain of birth, as it rolls up, the characters come one by one to play their part in different climes and countries. You are one of such characters. Their distinctive features are [that] their heart impels them to join in the movement. Their joining requires no reasoning and [they do an] immense amount of good . . . to the movement, and they share the vicissitudes and fortunes of it with full faith in the cause. So to my mind your association with the work and with Paramananda have taken place at the will of Sri Ramakrishna. You are a blessed one—you will live so long as His Name will be honored here.[8]

Devamata viewed Swami Shivananda's letter as encouragement to preserve a written record of the most intimate and sacred experiences of her life. Breaking the silence of years, she shared her personal visions "in the hope that through it others may gain a deeper realization of the spiritual grandeur and boundless mercy of one of the greatest among the Great Ones who have come to earth as Saviors of men."[9]

She described one of her visions that occurred in the early thirties after the Temple at Ananda Ashrama was dedicated. Devamata formed a habit of praying for an hour in the sanctuary of the Temple after the household had retired for the night. She described the dimly lit inner sanctuary as a very "protecting space." One night as she knelt in prayer, the walls behind the altar "rolled back quite naturally, revealing the hills behind the building." She continues,

> As my gaze lifted from hill to hill, it was drawn to a blazing light on the highest peak. In the center of the light stood the living Presence [of Sri Ramakrishna]. The figure . . . began to descend towards the Temple. It did not follow the slope of the hill, but moved on a direct path of light. As it drew nearer, I could discern that the light which created the path came from the feet of the one who walked upon it. . . . The Presence radiated such tenderness of love that all sense of fear or marvel melted.
>
> It approached slowly . . . entered the Sanctuary through the open walls, which rolled together and took its place on the right side of the altar with the hand resting on it. . . . He

looked as when he walked visibly among men. He stood in smiling silence for a moment, then began to speak. What he uttered was spoken to the heart rather than to the ear and was meant only for the one who heard.[10]

Over the next four days when Devamata entered the Temple, the figure was still standing beside the altar. The Temple was charged with His Presence.

Years later she was persuaded by her sisters in the community to abandon her nightly visits to the Temple, largely due to the inclement winter weather. A private chapel next to her study in the cloister was set up with a lovely, centuries-old Spanish hanging on the wall behind the altar. This room had actually served as the original sanctuary of the household, prior to the construction of the Temple. When the chapel was finished many came to see it. They even brought friends to the door for a moment of silent prayer. Wondering whether her decision to share the chapel with others was a wise one, Devamata sought guidance in the Temple. She recounts,

> No answer came, but later when I opened the door of the little Chapel, I was amazed to find it apparently empty of furnishings. Only the hanging remained. Before it stood Sri Ramakrishna, his face alight with that radiant smile which seemed a very part of him. He held out his hands as if in tender greeting and said to me: 'This is the welcome I give to all who come here.'[11]

Devamata then understood why many eagerly sought to visit the chapel.

Companionship of Pain

On an early morning in February 1934, Devamata was offering flowers before a picture of Sri Ramakrishna to the left of the Temple platform, when pain became her teacher and companion for well over a year. Stepping backwards, she stumbled on the corner of an oriental rug and fell to the ground. Resisting the natural impulse to cry out, she was found by another sister sent to fetch her for breakfast.

At the hospital, she was literally sealed in a plastic cast. It extended from her waist to her right foot on one side and to her left knee on the other side. For three months she lay flat in her bed, unable to move. She was waited on throughout the day.

Though in a cast, she was determined to make the most of the situation. She dictated a booklet *Companionship of Pain* (1934), for which, the opening sentence read: "Out of pain comes power." An explanation followed: "He bestows his richest gifts there where suffering had made way for their coming." The whole booklet, though small, reveals her thoughts and actions during her months of recovery. The following portions stand out as quite revealing.

> Physical ailments are not a misfortune. They are often remedies—remedies for deeper sickness of mind or heart or character. They cure by chastening. They make us brave, strong, and enduring.
>
> Suffering, borne with courage and surrender, builds a larger man. It widens the vision, deepens the sympathies, and clarifies the understanding.
>
> Even the long hours of loneliness, which accompany illness, invalidism, and sorrow, may be made a product of benefit and blessing. Solitude is a great opportunity. In aloneness we make acquaintance with ourselves and learn to know our deeper nature.
>
> When the body is found to be inactive, we can still think, pray, meditate and commune with the Great One.[12]

Though not mentioned in the booklet, music undoubtedly aided in her recovery. For in her essay entitled "The Power of Music," Devamata noted, "acute pain can be transcended in hearing a symphony or some other exalting composition." She explained,

> Matter is in constant vibration. When the vibration is disturbed, the rhythm of the body becomes jangled and illness ensues. The regular beat of music restores the troubled vibration and the pain or malady is relieved.[13]

In the foreword of *Companionship of Pain*, author Maud Keck, a community member, addressed Devamata's physical trials when writing,

> Ten years of pain lie behind all that Sister Devamata wrote, years heroically spent. Everyone of them seems to have dug deeper; to have wrung something wiser and sweeter from

her. As if the Divine Artificer could not be satisfied with anything less than a spirit very finely wrought.[14]

When her cast was removed in May of that year, she was so stiff and sore that she couldn't walk. While sitting under a mulberry tree in the cloister patio, she penned a letter to Sister Daya dated July 26, 1934. She wrote, "I hope in ten days more I will begin to learn the art of walking. It is going to be tiresome, I know, but I shall be glad to be on my feet once more. The doctor says it will be a long time before I shall be able to walk alone."[15] In the autumn Devamata did take her first steps under the watchful eye of her companion—six steps from the bed to the wheelchair. The wheelchair gave her some mobility during her recovery.

One day, while seated in a corner of the cloister in her wheelchair, Devamata's facial expression attracted the attention of Paramananda as he passed by. He stopped and stooped down beside her wheelchair, and took her hand between his two fingers. It was a gesture recognized by the community as meaning, "Everything will be all right."[16] The next spring, she took her first steps alone.

The Living Presence

February 24, 1936 was the date that marked the opening of the one hundredth anniversary celebration of Sri Ramakrishna's birth. Between February 24 and March 15, Paramananda spoke at public meetings, banquets, receptions, colloquia, and special services in the east (Boston, New York, Providence, Washington, DC, and Chicago). On March 16, he left for the West Coast via Cincinnati and Louisville, and instituted the centenary celebrations at Ananda Ashrama.

During the centenary year, Paramananda purchased a new home for the Boston Centre at 420 Beacon Street. He viewed the purchase as an expression of homage to Sri Ramakrishna. Transformed into the Temple of the Universal Spirit, the house was first occupied in January of 1937. A front room on the second floor was used by Devamata as sleeping quarters and as a study for her writing, a fact indicating that she likely visited the East Coast when her health permitted.

In the *Vedanta Kesari's* centenary issue of February/March 1936, her article "The Living Presence" was published. It served as her tribute to the centennial celebration. The eight-page article described in detail all her visions over the years, from the early 1900's in Boston, to the early years of the New York Vedanta Society and finally at Ananda Ashrama in California. In the article's introductory paragraph, the editors of the *Vedanta Kesari* expressed their hope that its publication "will go to strengthen the faith of the numerous devotees of Sri Ramakrishna and reassure them that the Great Master is still a living presence in our midst, capable of being contacted by an earnest and prayerful soul."[17]

In these eight pages, Devamata never tried to analyze or explain the experiences she recorded. She took a broader view of visions in general.

> The Divine is present in every human heart. It is the eternal part of man. The forces of nature must be at its command, since to the Divine all things are possible. Why then could it not take form as a living Presence and become the daily companion of the devotee who through intensity of devotion calls it forth. It may appear in different forms, it may bear different names, it may come in different ways. That is determined by the devotee's conception of Divinity, but that it comes, there can be no doubt.[18]

Her formerly published chapters of *Sri Ramakrishna and St. Francis of Assisi* were released in book form, to honor the centennial anniversary of Ramakrishna's birth.

Correspondences—Cohasset Archive

While at Ramakrishna Math, Belur, during his first trip back to India in 1912, Paramananda received a letter from Devamata that solicited a warm response from him. Dated August 22, the missive was found handwritten in Sister Daya's notebook. He wrote,

Dear Devamata,

> Your letter of the 26th of June last was not only a joy to myself, but also was a source of new strength to many a Lord's devotees to whom it was read. The testimony of Thakur's loving

Devamata is on the east side of the cloister in one of the last photographs of her around 1938.

care, coming from such a distant land is really an inspiration. Those who are devoted to our Lord, wherever they happen to live, constitute our real kith and kin and here [on earth] the bond of relation that subsists between us all, will last through eternity.[19]

In reading the numerous letters sent to her during her years of service under Paramananda (1910–1940), it became evident that Devamata enjoyed a worldwide correspondence. She kept in touch with devotees and friends through letters of sympathy, words of congratulation, or updates on the centre's activities. She always included a few words of inspiration in her letters, which were doubtlessly appreciated. In response, one devotee wrote her, "your letter has done me a world of good."

She received missives from her associates in New York City such as Ellen Waldo and from the Vedanta Societies in San Francisco and Hollywood. When Paramananda traveled abroad, letters arrived from devotees in Switzerland, Italy, France, England, Germany, and New Zealand. Those letters told of his safe arrival, details of his visit, or requested copies of his books. In cities he frequented, a number of devotees wrote expressing the hope that a centre would be opened in their city.

In a box entitled "Letters from India to Devamata" in the Cohasset archives, correspondence from the Holy Mother as well as Swamis Ramakrishnananda, Premananda, Virajananda, and Shivananda are filed. Some of these missives are scattered throughout the pages of this book. In terms of frequency, the letters sent by Ramu (C. Ramaswamy Iyengar), a devotee of the Madras Centre, who was known to Devamata from her days in India, far outnumbered the others. Ramu always gave updates on the Student's Home in Madras which he had founded and was in its developmental stage during Devamata's stay there. Ramu also reported on Ramakrishnananda's health, and in a note written in 1911, he gave details of the Swami's passing. In a letter dated May 9, 1929, Ramu requested Devamata to revise the talks of Maharaj, writing,

> In the *Vedanta Kesari*, you must have noticed the spiritual talks of Swami Brahmanandaji published serially. General readers are asking us to publish these talks in book form.... You have had intimate and personal knowledge of his spirit and manner of instruction... I sincerely hope your love and devotion of Maharajji will make it possible for you to undertake this work.... I am sending in a separate cover all the articles serially arranged, about 130 pages.[21]

Shortly thereafter, Devamata received another letter from him requesting her to "kindly make it ready for the press including a foreword from you."[22] The resulting book, *Spiritual Teachings of Swami Brahmananda*, was published by the Mylapore Ramakrishna Math in 1931. A second edition was printed in 1933.

Devamata reached out through her written correspondence, and through personal, one-on-one contacts, especially during the latter years of her life. In the late afternoon on Sundays, an open house was held at Ananda Ashrama. Devamata could be found, unfailingly, in the living room conversing with visitors, who came to share stories and conversation. Tea was served.

Final Tributes to Swami Paramananda

The end came unexpectedly on Friday, June 21, 1940, as plans were being completed to celebrate the eleventh anniversary of the Cohasset ashrama. Paramananda was walking the grounds, when he fell to the earth. Those nearest came to assist him; he drew several labored breaths and became unresponsive. The doctor who was immediately notified could do nothing. The spirit had left his body.

The setting for his release could not have been more fitting. It was in keeping with Paramananda's nature and the words of Vivekananda in "The Song of the Sannyasin"—"The sky thy roof, the grass thy bed." The initial reaction of shock that swept through the community, touched them to the very core of their being. In the end, preparation for his memorial service, with its numerous details to manage, roused community members from their stupor.

Devamata would later address his passing by writing,

> He could not linger in his going—the momentum of his life had grown too strong. His spirit was tireless, but his body had grown too tired. It could do no more. Did he know that the end was approaching? I believe that he did. It was that which drove him on to give himself more and more freely, more and more completely—nothing must be left.[23]

Two memorial services were held in Boston. On Saturday afternoon, Swamis Yatiswarananda (Philadelphia) and Nikhilananda (New York) flew from New York to pay their last respects. Another service was conducted by Sister Gayatri Devi on Sunday morning. That same afternoon Paramananda set out on his last journey from east to west aboard the Santa Fe railroad 'Chief,' which he had used for his many transcontinental trips. Seventy friends gathered on the station platform to bid him Godspeed.

On June 26, Devamata received the oak casket at the door of Ananda Ashrama, thus maintaining the tradition of being the first one to greet him on his arrival from the east. He was laid in his room, head toward the altar. A vigil was kept throughout the night; and at five the next morning, the casket was carried by the ashrama brothers to the Temple for a final gathering of his spiritual household. After the two-hour service, the casket was borne to the Temple patio where the final service was held. Swamis Ashokananda (San Francisco) and Prabhavananda (Hollywood) conducted the fire sacrifice at the outdoor fireplace in view of the surrounding mountains and the beauty of nature. Fruit and flowers were laid on the fire, symbolizing the closing of a life.

After both Swamis spoke a tribute to one of their own Order, Sister Gayatri Devi spoke, after which Sister Daya read Sister Devamata's tribute to her teacher. Devamata was unable to do so.

> One of the great teachers of India, Swami Ramakrishnananda, a disciple of Sri Ramakrishna, said to me when I was in India, 'Paramananda lived with me for five years, in daily, hourly contact, and I was never able to find a single fault in him.'
>
> I, who worked with him in closest association for 34 years, can pay the same tribute, as also can another elder sister who

has known him as long—Sister Satya Prana. All the other sisters, brothers and workers, whether with him for a long or short time, bear witness to the inspiration and glowing example he held before them. His teaching was more than a teaching; his life was more than living; both bore a fragrance, a beauty, a convincing power that drew hundreds upon hundreds to his feet, to hear him and to love him.

We, the sisters, brothers and workers of the ashrama, stand anointed to carry forward the work in his spirit and in the spirit of his great Master, Sri Ramakrishna. With courage and deepest-consecration we pray that we may be clear channels through which he may still bless the world.[24]

Sister Lillian, a householder resident and ashrama nurse, wrote details of that day in her journal. Before the casket was taken to Forest Lawn Crematory, Lillian wrote, "Devamata [finally] spoke her first words—the measured reading of the poem 'A Lost Chord.'"[25] A poem published by Adelaide Anne Proctor in 1858, the last two of the seven verses are as follows:

> I have sought, but I seek it vainly,
> That one lost chord divine,
> That came from the soul of the organ,
> And entered into mine.
>
> It may be that Death's bright angel
> Will speak in that chord again,
> It may be that only in Heaven
> I shall hear that grand Amen.[26]

Two boxes filled with Paramananda's ashes were draped with a shawl and carried by Sister Gayatri Devi and Sister Seva around the Temple, stopping under each tree. Of the ashes, half was installed in a niche to the right of the altar in the Temple at Ananda Ashrama. The other half was placed in the Boston shrine, now at Cohasset. Eventually, a portion was immersed in the Ganges River in India.

The *Handbook of Daily Worship* at the Cohasset ashrama contains "The Guru Song" composed by Devamata, in devotion to her teacher. Chanted at the ashrama by celebrants during the morning service, the first verse (of four) reads:

Beneath the Guru's holy feet
I humbly take my place.
A rock of strength, a cooling shade
Within a desert space.
A home within the wilderness,
A rest upon the way,
From the burning of the noon-tide heat,
And the burden of the day.[27]

During the last months of her life, Devamata was by and large bedridden. She and Sister Amala finished the second volume on the life and work of Swami Paramananda; it covered the last fourteen years of his life. Published in 1941, the text is largely told by him through his various letters from abroad. Devamata dictated her written portions to Sister Amala from bed. During the last years of her life, Devamata burned the majority of letters that she had received from family members and disciples of Sri Ramakrishna, monastic and householder. Considering them to be too personal, she stated that her books and writings were all that she cared to be remembered for.

A Life of One-pointed Devotion Ends

Following a brief illness, Devamata passed from this earthly plane at Ananda Ashrama on December 15, 1942 after years of struggle against various physical handicaps. Her health was tracked through December by Amala in her personal diary. Community members referenced Devamata as "Sister"—her preeminent position in the community never in question. The diary's entries read as follows:

Tuesday, December 1: From her bed, Sister wrote some on a new article with Amala's assistance.

Thursday, December 3: Sister got a sore throat and cold.

Monday, December 6: In the evening, Amala found Sister in the living room looking "wretchedly, so thin, pale, and face drawn." Strong-willed Sister kept to her practice of attending evening gatherings of the community.

Thursday, December 10: Sister Daya began sleeping in Sister's study, keeping watch on Sister during the night.

Friday, December 11: Daya and Amala worked together to help Sister undress, use the bathroom, and get into bed in the evening.

Saturday, December 12: Sister enjoyed her supper, which Amala fed her with a spoon. Amala wrote, "She is so kind to me."

Sunday, December 13: Sister insisted on getting up and dressed. Dr. Sanford was called and arrived that evening; pneumonia was the diagnosis. Oxygen was ordered. A nurse spent the night.

Monday, December 14: Evelyn McMinn, close friend of the ashrama, served Sister throughout the day. Sister responded to the oxygen treatment well; "her color returned." Evelyn stated that Sister joked with her. The nurse came again in the evening.

Tuesday, December 15: In the morning, Evelyn cared for Sister, who talked of her ideas for a new article. Visiting Sister late afternoon, Amala writes, "Her face, eyes, and nose all had the mark of passing. . . . There was a feeling of expectancy in the community that Sister would soon pass."

At nine that night, Amala was called to Sister's room. Sister Daya had been chanting since late afternoon and others of the household came in, from time to time, and sang with her. Amala writes, "Sister breathed her last at exactly 9:12 p.m.—peacefully—to the chanting of Om Ramakrishna. A strong spirit full of fortitude and strength has gone from our midst."

Thursday, December 17: Abiding by Sister's wish, a private service was conducted by Sister Daya in the cloister patio. Daya sat immediately outside Sister's study. The screen of the study door was open and one could look into the study where Sister lay in her casket, "looking lovely under white habit and veil." There were two tall candles on either side of her head. She held a narcissus in her hand and a verbena flower was placed on her heart. Sister Daya "spoke from her heart on the release of death and its meaning in the light of expanded consciousness as well as of the significance of the life that had gone."

Friday, December 18: A note was received from Swami Nikhilananda, minister of the New York Vedanta Centre. He wrote, "Shocked at the bad news. My sincere condolences. May her life inspire all in faith, devotion, and loyalty. She has gone to the realm of the immortals."

Sunday, December 20: Sister Daya held the public Memorial Service in the Temple of the Universal Spirit with sixty in attendance. Flowers lined the outer steps of the Temple and filled the platform inside. Sister Daya spoke extemporaneously of Sister Devamata as one dedicated to the realization of Truth. Singing Sister's own compositions, the voice of the Sisters—"who loved her"—brought the service to a completion.[28]

In an article for the *Message of the East* entitled "In Memory of Sister Devamata," Glory Raye (Paramananda's student) expressed her feelings, writing,

> She was so much a part of the Temple—like the candles on the altar—like the tiny blossoms in the shrine . . . [and] an integral part of the service. Her slow halting steps being led down the aisle, the fleeting little smile she would give me as she passed, the small orange pillow she sat upon and the white veil that [was] so reverently placed behind her chair. Then [there was] her devotional attitude all through the service. She seldom took her eyes from the altar . . . There was the sweet smile of greeting she had for each one on leaving. I can still see the last turn of her head like a little bird, as her frail steps were led away.[29]

The immediate cause of death, as listed on her death certificate, was bronchopneumonia. Parkinson's disease was given as another medical condition.

Epilogue

Marie Louise Burke, renowned author of the six volumes of *Swami Vivekananda in the West*, noted (in chapter one) that Vivekananda redefined the yogas "fully in keeping with the time-spirit of the age—rational, compassionate, active, and meditative." She articulates the characteristics of this "new man of Swamiji's vision," as follows:

> Whatever their way of life, they would be men and women of high spiritual ideals, of selfless love for all, of strong will with the ability for effective and beneficial action, and the capacity to give their lives freely in the service of their fellow man."[30]

Devamata stands as an exemplar of Swamiji's new vision for men and women of modern times. Over the span of her life, she has demonstrated in action the characteristics mentioned above—one-pointed and intense devotion to a spiritual life, a kindness of spirit, a strong will with the ability for beneficial action, and the capacity to serve her fellow man.

The fruits of her life will live on through her writing and inspiration.

Spiritual Legacy

Introduction

Sister Devamata had a life of tremendous grace. She attended all of Swami Vivekananda's lectures in New York; received spiritual training from Swami Abhedananda; spent two years in India living across the road from the Madras Monastery and had daily conversations with Swami Ramakrishnananda; had a close relationship with Swami Brahmananda; gave personal service to Holy Mother in Kolkata; had close association with "M," Master Mahasay, who wrote the *Gospel of Ramakrishna* and helped him with its publication in India; helped Swami Ramakrishnananda establish the publishing department at the Madras Monastery; and maintained close relations with Swami Premananda and Swami Adbutananda, all direct disciples, as well as with Girish Ghosh. Thankfully, Sister Devamata had a brilliant mind and was a large vessel to receive these treasures and was an eloquent and clear writer so that what she shared in her books, *Days in an Indian Monastery, Sri Ramakrishna and His Disciples,* and *Swami Paramananda: Poet, Mystic and Teacher* are as timeless, inspiring and rich today as they were when they were experienced and written.

Sister Devamata never revealed much about her life and considerable accomplishments. She wished for her work to stand for itself, as she herself stated. The writing of her biography, therefore, required extensive research and makes its publication an invaluable contribution to the history of Vedanta.

Sister Devamata had a deep inner life whose fruits in the form of wisdom are revealed in her writings and in the lectures she gave in the Temple on both coasts. More than a hundred of her Sunday lectures were transcribed and published in the *Message of the East* over five decades. I have compiled, lightly edited them and organized them to form a wonderfully rich and useful guide for spiritual aspirants who desire to live "the larger life" in their chosen path.

Reverend Mother Sudha Puri
Vedanta Centre, Cohasset, Massachusetts

Section One: The Divine 179

Section Two: Life: Birth, "Death" and Re-birth. . . 186

Section Three: Building Character. 224

Section Four: Living An Inner Life. 271

Section Five: Spiritual Practice 340

Section One

The Divine

Who or What is God?. 180
God can assume any form or relationship . .182
How do we connect with the Divine? 184

The first question that the young Naren, who later became Swami Vivekananda, asked Sri Ramakrishna, was "Sir, have you seen God?" We all seek the confirmation that God does, indeed, actually exist, so it is so valuable for us to hear the answer to that question from those who have no doubt and who can help us along the pathway to our own experience and realization.

As water cannot rise higher than its source, so we cannot transcend the highest level of our understanding. What we are able to perceive in the world outside is measured by what we have perceived within. We can grasp only so much of the external universe as we have analyzed and understood within ourselves. The world we live in is our own world and as we find it good or evil, we draw the outlines of our own nature. So it is with our conception of God.

Who or What is God?

God is the whole. We see as much of Him as we choose to make room for in our consciousness. The God of each one of us is always the reflection of our own mental and spiritual development. If we remain on the plane of personality, bound by our lower self, we cannot hope to have any idea of the Absolute. So long as we cling to our human nature, our God must be a human God. Everywhere in the early stages of evolution, we find this tendency to merely inflate human attributes and powers and apply them to the Supreme. He is the Lord of Hosts, the Judge of Judges, the Ruler and Governor, the strongest of the strong — in other words, the largest thing we can think of, but always an expansion and extension of our own human personality. In fact, so long as we name God, so long as we speak of Him at all, we are speaking of a personal God; for out of our personal need language itself has grown. The story is told in the Chandogya Upanishad of a father who, wishing to test the knowledge of his sons on their return from the house of their Guru, asked each one: "What can you tell me of Brahman (the Absolute)?" The older boy replied by long quotations from the scriptures. "It is clear that you know nothing of Brahman." The younger boy, when questioned, hung his head and was silent. Whereupon the father, content, exclaimed: "I see, my son, that you have begun to have some idea of what God is."

It seems an irresistible tendency of the human mind to centralize the Supreme Power; to conceive It as a mighty Being seated at the heart of the universe and governing it by a mysterious wireless system, which no science is able to fathom or explain. We speak of "going to God" as if it were a far journey, beset with perils and discomforts; but in reality it is not possible to go from or toward God. He is an immediate Presence. Where we are, He is. We cannot escape Him. We cannot circumvent Him. He is both within and without us and on all sides of us — the essential and supreme fact of our existence.

The Infinite cannot be localized. It is not here rather than there, not in this more than in that. It is equally present everywhere. The Bhagavad Gita declares that "*Brahman* (The Absolute) is without imperfection and equal" and that those who perceive this equality, live in conscious union with the Absolute. Every created thing is an embodiment of Infinitude. It takes form in the Infinite and remains there, an inherent part of It. At no time does it emerge from It and become independent of It. If it did, it would be non-existent, for infinity and existence are identical. To go out of one is to go out of the other. And where would we go? There is no outside or beyond.

The Infinite admits of no definition. The Absolute can never be grasped by the relative mind. We must transcend ourselves to know God. It is in the rapt silence of the superconscious that the last veil falls and we behold Him face to face. Until then, mere abstraction is not a substitute for Infinity. Intellectual dissection, divesting God of form and definite qualities, does not bring knowledge of the Absolute. When we have stabilized our idea to the ultimate point of vagueness, made our deity a formless philosophic entity, if we analyze, we shall find that God is still a glorified image of ourselves, the furthest point of vision possible to us, that which we are striving to manifest in our individual life.

We can take only as much of the Divine as our limited mind can grasp. It is true wisdom to give to each one the idea of God which each one can comprehend. However primitive it may be, if served faithfully, it will lead to the Infinite. It doesn't matter where we fix our mind, even on the crudest clay image, the Divine is there.

We talk as if the universe were one thing and God another, as if to look for Him in creation were idolatry. But what sustains the universe? Where did the clay come from to create the image? What makes it possible for those particles to stay together as an image? What conceived even the simple idea which stands behind the image if it is not the Supreme? He is literally there, not because we place Him there, but because He exists there as the basis of every atom in the earth; and the truly devout worshipper can call Him out of that image as surely as out of subtler forms or realms. How foolish then to break the image and take away some humble soul's object of concentration. If she bows down with earnest, whole-hearted devotion, she has more chance of seeing the Divine even as the Absolute than the one who would break her image. Because it is not a question of getting a truer image, or of finding purer material out of which to make the image; it is a question of realizing an object in her own consciousness. And whatever starts us on the way, whatever helps us to make our mind one-pointed, that is of value and should not be destroyed. We should never try to impose our concept of the Divine on another or borrow theirs. Only that can be true for us which has sprung out of the depths of our own inner experience, the fruit of our own earnest searching.

As a matter of fact, there is no difference in essence between one aspect of the Divine and another, between the physical manifestation of God and the formless God, the personal and the impersonal. What is the personal God? Just as much of the Absolute as each one of us can comprehend with our own understanding; in other words, our own vision of the Supreme. Let our understanding widen and more of the Absolute will be comprehended and the personal God for us will grow proportionately vaster, mightier, more majestic. All spiritual growth is summed up in this, the uncovering day by day of more of the Absolute, moving towards the whole, passing from the particular into the universal.

To know the Supreme means to become one with It because only God can know God. "Does this mean I must lose my individuality?" the timid soul asks. Necessarily something must go. You have been a limited entity. When you go out into the unlimited, how can you expect to keep your limited nature unaltered? What is the thing that shuts God off from you? What is it that you have been trying day by day to conquer? What is it which you are striving to break down? Your own little personality. The barrier of your ego. It alone stands between you and God; and only as you transcend it can your consciousness expand. That which you are now, that which marks you as a person, how can you expect to take the Infinite into that? No, you must go out into It. This is inevitable, and some are frightened at the thought. They prefer to have only a little bit of God and all of themselves. Yet it is against this partial, limited condition of the little self that they are blindly struggling against; and it is the unrecognized longing for more and more of that undefined Absolute Good which causes all their unrest. But when they are told that they can get the whole of It, they draw back.

God can assume any form or relationship

God and the world are not rivals. They are not enemies. It is our contracted conception of both the one and the other that creates an apparent opposition. If, for us, the Divine is wholly personal, then He must dwell in a heaven and the world will be empty of Him, for a personality cannot be pervasive, it demands a specific abiding-place. If, on the contrary, the Divine is to us an all-pervading Presence, He is in the world as well as in the heavens and can be found wherever we seek Him.

As a pervading Presence He may manifest in any form and assume any relation. Whenever we take away any aspect of God, father or mother, friend, child or beloved, we impoverish religion and lessen for humankind the universality of the Divine. Each aspect meets the need of some soul striving to gain a closer relation with the Divine and to eliminate any one is to deprive the soul of its most natural approach to the Supreme.

There can never be a uniform conception of God. Try as we may to establish it by religious canon, we will restate the accepted definition for ourselves and out of it form our own God. We must never confound the reality of God with our idea of God. Your God and my God are not God. God is Unchangeable, our concept of the Divine is constantly changing; God is Infinite, our God, pictured by our finite consciousness, is, of necessity, finite; God never increases or diminishes in glory, but our God grows in majesty and power as we grow. God is the reflection of our own highest point of vision, as much of the Infinite as we grasp at any moment by our partial but evolving perception. As, however, we enter into a deeper union with the God of our conceiving, we make it possible for the Supreme Lord to reveal Himself or Herself to us. It becomes, therefore, a vital necessity of the spiritual life to establish the closest possible communion with the God we perceive, and this is most quickly and easily done by creating a definite relation with Him — that relation which meets the strongest need of our nature.

Even in the earliest Hindu scripture, the Rig Veda, the Supreme is spoken of as Mother as well as Father; in the Bhagavad Gita the Lord declares: "I am the Father of the Universe, the Mother;" while an ancient Sanskrit prayer runs: "You are our Mother, You are our Father, You are our Friend and Companion."

The Divine Mother of the Hindus, for example, is a cosmic Mother. She does not always come with sweets in her hands. She is the great Creative Force of the universe, — now preserving, now destroying; now caressing, now punishing; manifesting through every phenomenon of creation, terrible or benign. No phase of Indian teaching has been so grossly misunderstood by the West as this universal character of the Divine Mother, represented most often by the figure of Kali — a graphic metaphysical symbol of the Mother.

Kali is depicted a dark blue because blue seems everywhere the color of vastness in nature…the sky, the ocean. She stands on the body of her husband, Shiva, to indicate that all manifestation must rest on the Absolute, as waves on the ocean; and because the Absolute is unchanging, immovable, unaffected by creation, He lies apparently lifeless and unconscious of Her presence. Not only does She stand there, but She dances. Why? The Vedas tell us that "Out of bliss the universe has come." Creation is a joy to the Mother, as the painting of a masterpiece is a joy to the artist. The leap of the flame, the rush of the storm, the swirl of leaves in the autumn wind, the bursting of buds on the hillsides, these are the play of the Mother. She must have four arms, too, because fewer would not suffice to do all that She would do for Her children. Yet She is not always a tender Mother, for while, with one hand She protects, with the other She slays. She is a Mother who makes strong by discipline, who purges by pain, who takes away so that She may give more abundantly. And through it all She laughs and laughs loudly because She knows that Her glistening floating veil of creation only thinly masks the Eternal Fact of Being; that as out of the rotting tree trunk springs a new and richer vegetation, so out of a thousand deaths rises life untouched, out of countless sorrows emerges the Soul triumphant. If in the darkness of a crushing grief or failure this image of the Mother could take form before us and we could see the hand that blesses beside the hand that strikes, at once we would grow quiet and wait in patient confidence for the Supreme Maternal Love and Wisdom to accomplish in us the work of purifying and perfecting.

There is also a profound natural reason for laying stress on the Motherhood of God, — the mother relation is the one sure and clearly defined relation in nature. We may not know the father of any being born into the world, but the mother is always known. It is she who carries close to her heart the new life through the months of its pre-natal unfolding and an unseen cord binds the child to her through all the years of its earthly existence. To her is primarily entrusted the care of this treasure of manifested being and to her in particular measure is given the wisdom to preserve it. Buried deep down in the subconscious mind of every being is the recognition of this fundamental fact of human experience; if it can be drawn out and turned to account in the religious life, it will become a powerful factor in helping us gain a more real sense of our relation to God.

How do we connect with the Divine?

How can we connect with the Divine? Not by a sudden jump. In nature evolution moves in gradual consecutive steps; and the laws of nature are the same on all planes. Physical evolution has been a slow building up atom on atom; never a sudden expansion which would mean explosion, but a gradual spreading out of consciousness. And so must it be in the evolution of our higher understanding. We must begin where we are. At the present moment we are far from the Absolute in our consciousness. We are bound to this relative plane, to these perishable bodies and all that is related to them. We must be willing to let ourselves outgrow these ideas in which we are now so rooted. We must no longer live as if we were just a physical body. How can we get the least conception of that which is beyond body, if we live day by day bound up in this physical organism? We must transcend the body and whenever it tries to fasten itself upon us, refuse to be claimed by it. But mere denial will not do. We can accomplish nothing by a negative process, — first trying to destroy the body idea and then filling our mind with another idea. No, we must go within and find something higher that is not body. Seek the Divine and the rest will follow of itself. Let Truth drive out falsehood. Do not try to destroy the false and then go in search of the True.

Section Two

Life: Birth, "Death" and Re-birth

Wholeness of Life 187
The Three Worlds 188
Evil and Its Remedy 193
Life's Purpose 195
The Task of Living. 198
Have We Free Will? 199
What is Maya? 204
Universal Harmony 208
The Chain of Birth and Death. . . . 208
What is Death? 213
Mortality and Immortality 216
Heaven and Final Attainment. . . . 219
Stages of Life 221

These are the next big questions for most: Is there really life after death and what about reincarnation? Then, there are other perennial questions: What about evil? And free will? The purpose of life?

Wholeness of Life

Life is universal, it is not individual. It cannot be portioned out or possessed. Life is not in us, we are in it. We live in life, it does not live in us. Our existence is part of unbounded Existence. We are immersed in a shoreless ocean of Absolute Being, the manifestation of which is what we call life. It has its origin and its fulfillment in the Infinite. The law it obeys is made by a higher power. It passes through many changes of form, of circumstance of environment, yet it remains ever unchanging. It does not grow stronger or weaker, it does not ebb or flow; it is always without condition. It may seem to be caught in matter, but in reality it is free and unfettered, one with the essence of Being.

Even our body which seems so intrinsically to belong to us, is not ours. It is the work of universal forces and all the materials used in its building are borrowed from the universe. The universe also repairs and maintains it. It appears to be solid, but in reality science has found that even its bony framework is fluid. There is a constant ebb and flow; a constant casting off and replacing; a ceaseless mingling with the universal ocean of Life about it.

These processes are carried on without awareness on our part. We are little conscious of the interior functioning of our organism. We do not know when or how our food is broken up into its component elements and distributed according to the need of each organ. We cannot surprise the body at its task of growing or of renewing worn-out tissue.

The work is done by our own subconscious mind, it may be said. That is true, but the subconscious mind is the instrument of the universal Intelligence. It is the instinct-mind which operates through all nature. It fashions the pearl through the oyster; it gathers honey and organizes the hive through the bee; it directs the opening of the flower, the swelling of the fruit, the running of the sap. Wherever there are exactitude, skills, proportion and rhythm, we may know that the instinct-mind is at work.

We become a rebel only when our self-consciousness unfolds. Then we withdraw from the universe, create a little world of our own, and seek to govern it in our own way. Thus begins a long struggle between the universal Will and the individual will, between the part and the Whole, between the finite and the Infinite.

So long as we remain at war with the universe, we are cut off from our source of supply — from the source of our sustenance, our power and our strength. We are like a plant severed from its root. The reserve we have stored up may carry us for a time; but sooner or later disaster will overtake us. The widening of our consciousness should make us co-workers with the Whole, not rebels. The instinct-mind is inherently submissive, the conscious mind should be cooperative.

If our relation with the Whole is kept true and unblemished we shall not fail in any lesser relation. Christ taught us to seek first the kingdom of Truth and all else would follow. To live in conscious union with the Great Life is to partake of its pure and exalted qualities and to receive its support and protection. Epictetus says of this: "If all things that grow, nay, our own bodies, are thus bound up with the Whole; is not this still truer of our souls? And if our souls are bound up and in contact with God, as being very parts and fragments plucked from Himself, shall He not feel every movement of theirs as though it were His own, and belonging to His own nature?"

To attain conscious union with the Supreme Source our effort must be uncompromising and genuine; it cannot be intermittent or faltering. Confucius declares that superior people "are truthful even when they do not speak;" equally consistent must we be if we would manifest greater largeness in our daily living. Our every thought, our every word, our every impulse, must be measured up to the Whole not to any part. We need not destroy our small self-created world, but we must merge it in a vaster world; and as the raindrop mingles with the sea, so will our lesser life mingle with the Supreme Existence. When this takes place, all pettiness and littleness dissolve and our nature becomes purified and expanded.

Even the conception of Deity will alter. God will seem less personal and more a mighty Presence, enveloping and infilling all creation with Its power, Its wisdom and Its love. Those only who yield themselves up utterly to that all-pervading Presence, losing their littleness in Its vastness, will enter into wholeness of life and live truly. Thomas à Kempis writes: "Those to whom all things are one, who draws all things to one, and sees all things in one, they alone can be steadfast in heart and remain united with God."

The Three Worlds

Although in the West we talk more frequently of two worlds, the here and the hereafter, we are compelled to recognize scientifically that there must be three worlds. The future presupposes a past, and as a matter of fact, the present is only the point where past and future meet. We know that if there is a heaven there must be some state known as hell; and that point where they meet is our earthly realm. We read in the Eastern scriptures of those who conquered the three worlds; and in the Bhagavad Gita Sri Krishna says, "There is nothing for Me to accomplish. Naught is there in the three worlds unattained or to be attained by Me."

As a matter of fact, however, we live in three worlds every moment. The human soul stands, as it were, in its present embodiment, like a longitudinal section of the entire universe. In us at this moment lies the whole history of all the worlds. Just as we pass through the complete history of evolution in the prenatal state, so all during this life we are rising and falling between these worlds, repeating over and over again each age of ascent and descent, up and down that sliding scale. The wise concentrate their whole consciousness, their whole understanding, their whole realization in the now, in the present moment. They do not wait for some tomorrow to make a change of condition which will reveal to them a new world.

We set out to study and reflect today; to live and choose our worlds here and now; to determine in what realm we will exist, on what plane we will think and act, what we will manifest, for at every moment there is, in every germ, in every atom, the possibility of manifesting in one or all of the states or worlds. These three worlds correspond to what is known in Hindu philosophy as the qualities of nature, the three *gunas*; *tamas*, the dark and dull; *rajas*, the excessively active, and *sattwa*, the pure and serene.

When we first awaken from the lower state which we call *tamas*, we find ourselves heavy, dull, like one who is just waking from a sleep. Imagine someone who has plunged down into the depths of some sticky, thick substance like molasses and has been trying to rise and escape. As she comes to the surface how clogged up she must feel by that which has held her back! So are we when we awaken from this sleep of matter. Up until this point we live in the lowest realm, covered over by the material of the universe. We think that we are awake because we are aware of our striving to acquire more and more of material things. But so long as we seek in that lowest realm we are still asleep, still in the lower stage. As long as material things seem to be realities we are in the state of *tamas*; heavy and dull and cannot rise.

What can be done about it? When we wish to rouse ourselves after a night's sleep we move around and do all we can to cause the body to become active. Even so we must work with ourselves when we awaken from the sleep of matter and begin to discover the other worlds. It seems that very few people are living even in the middle stage world today, for this second world is the moral world and the human moral sense, for many, has not yet been awakened. Many large fortunes, for example, have not been gained by pure honesty; the very fact that the gain has been based on pushing others aside or on the survival of the fittest shows that it is not a moral act. Therefore, those who are living this sort of life are still on the lower plane. Whenever we are led to do something to gain for ourselves at the cost of someone else we remain on the lower plane.

Those who have placed too much value on material things must recognize, sooner or later, that they are living in the lowest realm, that realm which we call hell and which is a state of ignorance and egotism. The only thing in the world that can make us suffer is ourselves. It is the ego that creates all the hell that we can suffer. By a selfish act we may seem to gain today, but we have set ourselves at odds with every other self in the universe, and that whole army of selves is going to battle against us.

Go out into the cut-throat world of competition and ask who really enjoys it. They may think that it is a pleasure for a time, just for the exhilaration of the game, but how quickly they grow weary! Always looking over their shoulder to gain an advantage. Perhaps a sudden turn of fortune elates them for a moment; then comes another turn and they go bent with burdens. Why? Because they are living in the lowest realm. Nobody can be happy there. As long as we have any material ambition, as long as we set up any golden calf to worship, whether it is wealth, health, name, fame or power – anything that represents a return here and now in this material world — we are living in the lowest realm. We need never expect to be happy there, because we are in a state of constant anxiety lest someone should rob us. This is what hell is and to a great extent we are living in it now.

How can we get out of it? By just being human beings, and not following our lower instincts. It is the natural instinct of the wild animal to snatch food from another animal; it is the instinct of the wild animal to attack the one who hurts it. It is the instinct of the animal to fight, to kill. Are we going to permit such inclinations to be ours? If these instincts arise in us, even in subtle form, we still have our feet down in the lowest realm.

The human state is preeminently the moral state. If we wish to live in the middle realm, called by the Hindus, *rajas*, our standard of action must always be the moral standard. It cannot be, "Will I lose so many dollars?" but rather, "Will I lose my moral conviction? Will I lose my integrity? Will my sense of fairness be dulled?" When we come to the point where money, time, strength, and good opinion count as nothing beside the sense of moral uprightness, then we may know we have truly evolved into human beings and that is what is expected of us.

The middle plane is the plane of character. It is for the development of our higher moral consciousness, for the education of the moral being. If we have lifted ourselves to this plane we must continue to put the moral law into practice, for every day that we choose the lower rather than the higher, the false rather than the true, we keep ourselves just so much longer in a state of ignorance, *tamas*. Do not imagine that wealth, health or popularity can ever bring us the least glory in the sight of God. What does the greatest emperor in the world count beside a Buddha or a Christ? Even in our own community, what does learning count beside a person of character? We must realize this, for it is of genuine value to us: The power of distinguishing between right and wrong, real and unreal is the only knowledge that will stand as true when we become awakened. If our standards are false it is because we are still in the lower realm; if we pay court to others of money rather than to those of character it is because we have not risen yet to the middle realm.

Living in the middle realm, even at the topmost point, is not all of our duty. But do not imagine that we can even begin to be spiritual until we have learned to be absolutely upright in all our dealings; until we have learned to observe the strictest purity within and without; until we have become absolutely truthful in every word and thought and have learned to shrink from injuring the least of God's creatures. Only when we refuse to advance ourselves at the cost of the smallest or humblest of His children can we hope for spiritual vision. Practicing non-killing, non-injuring, bodily and mental discipline, we must keep ourselves unspotted by the world. This does not, however, imply staying away from the world. It simply means to remain aloof from selfishness and greed and all the things that tie us to the material realm — this *rajasic* plane is one of constant struggle with ourselves, our motivations, intentions and reactions.

Little by little, as our recognition of the spiritual increases, we discover a deep longing to attain to the higher plane and lesser things commence to drop away. The struggle then is no longer against the lower nature; no longer is the victory attained by battle as it is in the middle and lower realms. The whole conquest in this third world — the state of *sattva* — is made by keeping our eyes fixed on the Ideal. The conditions of outer life, the daily struggle, count for nothing when we are serving the spiritual Ideal; our whole life is focused on that one point. Then day by day our failures and successes make but passing impressions on us; even our own little human nature becomes of secondary interest. There is always that supreme Light and all values are measured against it. In the middle realm, whenever we pray or meditate we are concentrating on our own problems; we are trying to overcome some temptation or solve some difficulty. The whole thought is of ourselves, of trying to better ourselves. "Give me something — give me light; give me strength." But when we have passed out of the middle realm our whole thought simply flows out in adoration to the Supreme.

We can help ourselves reach that state by constantly trying to think of something higher and thus gradually lift ourselves into it. It is a condition of balance where we are not continually moving up and down the scale — sometimes happy, sometimes miserable; sometimes doubting, sometimes full of trust. Once we have attained the higher realm, the Self is always there watching and we no longer identify ourselves with the lesser. We see it but it does not touch us. We remain as a witness.

When we are in the lowest realm we are scarcely active; we are dull, and content to go the round of this fleshly, selfish life. In the middle realm we are always in battle, we cannot look on; our consciousness is caught in the struggle. But in the third realm we are the witness, calm, serene, mighty. Even that is, however, not the end. We may have performed our life's duties; we may wish to live with the utmost simplicity in quiet surroundings, but our consciousness is still in the material. For even our highest thought is an individual point of matter. By the practice of purity in the state of *sattva*, serene, detached, selfless, we can reach the very limits of this world. But it is only when all our desires have gone or have been gathered up in that one intense desire for God when the hunger for the highest overtakes all other hungers, when the love for the ideal transcends all other loves and we know that there is no duty on earth so great as the search for the Supreme, then and then only do we transcend the three worlds of creation and see God face to face.

We are meant to be eternal; we are meant to be infinite; we are meant to be ever-blissful. Until we are that we shall be given no rest, because the Soul within us is calling and it goes on calling until we are one with the Infinite — as Christ said, "One with the Father in Heaven," in conscious union with the

Divine, knowing ourselves to be part of That which is the source of all worlds and which eternally transcends them.

Evil and Its Remedy

Where does evil come from? If there is a Supreme Deity who is All-powerful, All-knowing, why so much sorrow and misery in the world? If an All-loving God rules in the heavens, why does He let His children suffer? Who has not asked these questions at some time and found no answer! Who of us has not beaten against this thing we call evil and felt ourselves baffled by it! Why? Because always we seek to escape it, never to understand it. In our tireless struggle against it, we forget to ask: What is it? Has it a real existence? Do we ourselves create it or does it come from God? Yet if we would but stop and analyze it, we would find, as the great sages tell us, that evil is only ignorance. It is seeing all things in the universe as separate parts, unrelated to the Whole. If a child, in playing with a crystal ball, should carelessly drop and cut her hand on the broken edge, she could as well cry out "Why does glass cut?" "Why do cuts sting?" Had she handled the glass skillfully and kept it whole, it would not have hurt her. So with us. We break the universe into many pieces and the jagged edges wound us. We look upon each fragment as an independent object and fail to see its true beauty and meaning. It is to this partial view of things that we may trace all our discontent and love of change; for we reach out instinctively for the perfect, the complete; and only when we have found a whole in which no part is missing will that unrest cease which is at the root of all our wrong-doing.

The problem with evil's cure, therefore, becomes the problem of piecing together a broken universe, finding the Whole in which all those parts belong. To do this we must discover the original plan; otherwise all our efforts will be fruitless — as fruitless as has always been the endeavor of those who through the ages have sought to rebuild the world without knowing the Architect's design. And where can the plan be found? In the mind and heart. Out of the realm of thought and feeling has come every individual conception which has later taken form, and from the same source has sprung the Universal plan. If, therefore we would know it, we must turn within.

But if it could be done that way, why did not Christ or Buddha once for all make such laws and create such conditions as to set the world right forever?

They had the power and wisdom and love, why did they change so little the general face of society? Because they knew that the only efficacious course was to draw us inward and to show each of us how to readjust our own world. Even dealing with such material questions as food, drink and clothing, Jesus tells His followers to "seek first the kingdom of God" — that kingdom within — and "all these things will be added." He would surely not have offered counsel that was not practical; but He had proved by His own experience that only as we live in contact with the inner Source will we have the light and strength necessary to master the difficulties of our outer life.

Every sincere effort to benefit humankind, however directed, must inevitably produce some good; but the result might be much richer were it not neutralized by lack of insight; for too often the very people who are most anxious to remedy social evils are themselves unwittingly the cause of them through their mode of life, their artificial standards and their unconscious ignorance. Can one blind person lead another to safety? Can one who does not know how to swim save another from drowning? If we are ignorant of the fundamental forces at play in our own nature, if we have not been able to establish our own lives on a sound basis of understanding, of wisdom, how can we expect to do it for others?

Through higher understanding alone can we meet the problem of evil. We may make law after law, but if we have not some evidence that we will gain more by observing than by infringing that law, we will break or evade it. Nor will prisons or even death teach us to obey. We will only learn to be law-abiding by seeing that those who make and keep the law are in every way happier, finer, nobler, better off than us. The true reformer or philanthropist must be not merely "God-fearing," but "God-knowing;" we must be "above the law" because we have conquered those desires and passions which bring us under it; we must be able to see and awaken the immortal soul even in the most degraded criminal, because we have already found it in ourselves. Until we have attained knowledge and self-mastery, we can never solve our neighbor's problem; we can only try to solve our own. But by doing this intelligently and bravely, we may show them how to attack theirs. This does not mean, however, that we are to live insulated lives, feeling no current of love, no desire to help. On the contrary, if we are sincerely striving for the highest light, we cannot help serving others at every step. All true growth indeed lies along the path of loving service. But we must constantly remember that we cannot carry another further than we have gone ourselves. We cannot teach what we have not learned.

Can we be sure in our present state of limited knowledge that the thing we call evil is evil, and that which we call good is good? Have we not seen in our own life that what seemed good at one moment, in the light of new experience appeared as evil? We regard poverty as a great misfortune, yet have we not been happy and miserable with the same income? Then money cannot be the cause of happiness. We cry out against the social order which denies a soft bed to every member of society. Yet every night thousands overwhelmed by grief or pain are tossing on the softest beds, longing for the morning. The remedy for our misery then must be beyond these material conditions; for change them as often as we may, the old social disorders reassert themselves in new guise. We all know that unless the cause can be eradicated, we may remove the effect a hundred times and a hundred times it will rise again. The root must be severed, the root of every outer wrong lies in the hidden depths of human nature. It cannot be reached except through our own inner being; and not until we have penetrated there, can we be sure that we have touched the real cause of the surface evil against which we are battling today. Therefore it is said in the Svetasvatara Upanishad: "Only when human beings shall roll up the sky like a hide, will there be an end of misery, unless God has been discovered in the heart."

Life's Purpose

We imagine that it is enough in life to have a worthy purpose. There is no doubt that any kind of worthy purpose gives stability to life. No one can be happy who is drifting, who has no aim from day to day, because life must have a definite course to bring any joy at all. But it is not enough to have a drifting purpose, and any purpose that is tied to this world must be a shifting one, because nothing in this world is stable. We may imagine, for instance, that if we gain a certain fortune we will be happy, so we turn all our energy toward gaining that fortune. We see money mounting up in the bank, and we have a sense of security and importance that we did not have before. Then something goes wrong with our health or with our family, and we find that money cannot buy us happiness after all. Then we imagine that if we turn to the spending of our money, that is to having some aim, some interest, as in art, for instance, so that we can have a purpose in spending money just as we had in gaining it, we will be happy. So we collect and collect, and still our heart is empty. Then perhaps we think if we begin to give away the things we have collected — a little philanthropy — perhaps that will make us happy. But there is always a rift.

It is not enough to have a goal, an earthly goal; we must have a supreme goal. As is so convincingly stated in the teaching of Vedanta, until we have chosen that supreme goal, life will always be a disappointment. Not only will our life be a disappointment, but we will be a disappointment to ourselves and to others.

No human life is worth living that is lived on a merely human level. We must have something that pulls us up constantly. We must have something that gives us a larger standard of measurement, and until we have that we shall never be able to bear even the stings and the pains of this life. People have an idea that they can cultivate fortitude, that they can cultivate concentration, that they can cultivate all these qualities merely by practicing, but actually nothing is cultivated except by a change of values. We may think that we can control our anger, for instance, that the next time a certain thing happens to us, we will remember to control ourselves and not grow angry; but if that thing is just as important to us the second time as it was the first, we will grow angry just the same. We cannot help it because our sense of values will betray us. If we do not wish to lose our temper the second time over the same thing, we must work and work until we have persuaded ourselves that the irritating cause is not worth a loss of temper. In other words, we must minimize it by getting a larger standard of measure. We must persuade ourselves that we are too big a person to lose our temper over such a little thing; we must change our point of view. To do so we must have some lofty aim toward which we are moving which will help us diminish our human reactions. When we come to look upon ourselves as children of the Most High, as spiritual heroes, we shall be ashamed to yield to the little things of this life and to the petty reactions of our own nature. There is no other way to acquire the necessary fortitude, control and surrender. It is by always keeping our eyes on the heights, by remembering that there is where we belong, that we may realize our divine heritage; for our aim is the realization of our Divine nature. This means that we are living here not to be merely happy, efficient human beings; rather, we are living here to outgrow humanity and to express Divinity. Of this we must remind ourselves every day and every hour of the day. We must make as the goal of all our effort, the highlight, as it were, of the picture of our life, this idea that we are God's, that we belong to the Infinite and to the Eternal, and that our real nature is pure and perfect. We must ever remember that we are evolving not to any small end of heaven or happiness, but to the eternal end of perfection, of knowledge of that highest bliss which can have no break nor change. When day after day we remind ourselves of that, shall we whine and fret over the little pricks of this passing life? No. They will seem too small to us. As we grow big they will lose their power.

Thus it is that the Lord Sri Krishna states, "He who worships Me, who is My devotee, who bows down to Me (that is, who keeps mindful of Me), he enters into My Being." That does not mean that such a devotee goes into a heaven and sings hymns and plays a harp and continues in a happy human existence. We enter into union with the Divine Being: we partake of all the qualities — the quality of unlimited knowledge, the quality of eternal life, the quality of unbroken happiness. Isn't that goal much more worthwhile striving for? Have we found such satisfaction in our mere human endeavor? Have the goals that we have set for ourselves, the human goals, given us such fullness of joy that we wish to continue to work for them? Have we found that when they were realized by us that they lasted? Our searching today is proof that those things which we have attained were not satisfying. The very rising of every new desire shows that the satisfaction of desire cannot ever be a lasting joy to us.

We are just like little children. Christmas comes and brings us a new set of toys, and we are delighted and happy and want to play with them all day long; in a week or two they are broken and spoiled; we are tired and we want more toys. So with life. We go on spending our effort, getting more playthings, playing with them, tiring of them and then striving again for more. How can we grow when we always live on this level? It is not possible. We must be ever striving, lifting ourselves by our thought, that is, if we would grow. Never shall we be content until we do grow because there is in us the immortal soul that is seeking expression; a Divine nature which will not be hemmed in eternally by the human, and that prods us on.

It is not the things outside which disappoint us and keep us from being happy. It is that eternal reminder within that this thing is too small for our happiness; even though we may seem to find something that is lofty, yet something within us says there is a loftier beyond. Even though we may find something that is going to last for ages, something within says there is something more lasting and eternal. So this soul within us keeps reminding us and reminding us on the long, long journey through which we have come, on the long journeys through we must go until we attain the perfection of our expression as divine children, as parts of the Infinite and Eternal. Let us be thankful that we are prodded; let us be thankful that the things here do not satisfy. Let us thank God every day and every night that He will not let us rest content short of Himself and what He alone can give us.

The Task of Living

All human beings have one supreme task, — the task of living — generously with others, patiently with themselves. Epictetus was asked on one occasion how a person could best disconcert his enemy; "By living the noblest life possible," was his reply. To live nobly means to follow a lofty ideal or principle in every relation and circumstance. Most often what others do to us, that we do to them. We react more than we act. If someone speaks harshly to us, we respond in harshness, if another shows antagonism, we grow antagonistic; we meet quarrel with quarrel.

The behavior of others should never regulate our behavior. We should never react. Each act of ours should be an independent expression of our own higher conviction. Confucius says: "To see the right and not to do it is cowardice." We are cowards when we imitate another's unworthy behavior, instead of obeying the loftier impulses of our own heart. We are cowards, running away from our human responsibilities, when we listen to the lesser rather than to the larger self.

If we would live nobly, we must be governed wholly by our higher nature. It alone is in close contact with the Supreme Existence and knows what It requires of us. It alone can overcome our smallness and weakness and make us stronger than ourselves.

We ourselves strike the keynote of our life. We set the scale of values by which it is measured. If we are rigid and resisting we magnify its difficulties and minimize its joys. If we are pliable and non-resistant, we minimize its hardships and magnify its pleasures. A Roman Stoic was once told that someone had spoken ill of him on the public square, reciting his shortcomings to the bystanders. His answer was "The man could not have known my other faults or he would not have mentioned only these." Such an unresisting spirit is invincible.

This human life is not an end in itself. It is not an isolated unit being dropped suddenly into space and time, and as suddenly dropped out again. It is a link in a chain of Eternal Existence. Its purpose reaches beyond the mere satisfaction of worldly desires or the increase of material possessions. Its purpose is to provide opportunity for growth and expansion — not for self-aggrandizement, however. As we expand, we include more and more of humankind, more and more of creation, until the entire universe seems too small an area on which to center our interest and our love. Our vision, thus grown vaster and vaster, unites us at last with the Whole and our life-task is accomplished.

Have We Free Will?

As we look at the world around us, we are impressed with the clock-like precision with which all things move — a precision so dependable that scientists find it possible to calculate to a nano-second the rising and setting of the sun, the revolution of the heavenly bodies, even the changes of the weather. Also when we look within ourselves, we see this smaller world of the body moving according to perfectly ordered law. If we try to lift it out of that law and make a law of our own for it, it slips from our grasp. Yet despite this relentless dominion of law, all of us do not seem to be bound equally by it. This variation in human affairs has led theology in every age and every country to ask the question: Have we free will? That we have a will, whether free or bound, is evident; for life itself is dependent on the play of will. If we do not will to move, we lose the power of motion. If we do not will to eat or breathe, we weaken and die. It is will which drives us to action; and without action, the Bhagavad Gita declares, the life of the body cannot be sustained.

When the volitional impulse comes in cosmic form, we call it law; when it comes in individual form, we call it will. This individual will is not free in itself. It is free to choose whether it will go with the law or against it; but it has no voice in determining the results of that choice. Thus we may build a fire on our hearth or on the floor of our room; but we cannot keep it from burning down our house if we kindle it in the wrong place. We are free to use our body as the instrument of our soul, or to misuse it for the gratification of our senses; but if we choose the path of pleasure, we cannot escape the suffering which is sure to follow. We are free to override our fellow beings, so far as our weakness will permit; but we cannot silence the hatred or avert the retribution which sooner or later must overtake us. In a word, we are free to determine our own action; but we are powerless to control the reaction resulting from it; because that is governed, not by the individual, but by the cosmic will. Those who defy the larger law and stubbornly insist on being a law unto themselves fall into greater and greater bondage.

The will to be free is an innate and fundamental instinct. Everywhere people are struggling for freedom, even to the point of killing to preserve it. So universal an impulse, common to all living beings must be based on an inherent right to be free. When we study the course of evolution, we see that each new longing has been the forecast and promise of an upward step in development. Thus the desire to see brought eyes, the craving to hear brought ears, the yearning for swifter motion brought wings. And since the ultimate aim of these and every new gain in evolution has been increased freedom, this primary desire underlying all other desires must contain within it also the promise of fulfillment. Not only is it inherent in nature, but it sounds from the lips of every world savior and prophet — the promise of freedom, freedom through knowledge of the law.

If, however, we are to realize freedom at any time, we must possess it within us now. We must be inherently free at this moment. Are we not conscious of it? Then there must be something in ourselves which is blocking the way to its full expression. God and nature are working tirelessly to free us. Every loss, every blow which falls and severs some attachment to material things is a cosmic effort to liberate us. The soul within us, too, is striving to break loose from the prison-house which we have built around it. How can we release it from its captivity?

At present there are certain laws of life which in no way hamper us, because observance of them has become instinctive. But there are other laws which still trouble us because we do not obey them naturally and spontaneously. We must make obedience to these laws equally automatic by steadfast practice of self-discipline; that is, by setting for ourselves special daily exercises which will teach us to obey them. Automatic action comes only through regular repetition. In creating the new habit there must be no indulgence in the old habit or yielding to the passing mood. Each time we lapse, we reinforce the old habit and lengthen our task. Even in so small a matter as rising early we know if we oversleep one morning, how difficult it is for the next several mornings to drag ourselves out of bed at the proper hour. We have lost the momentum of our cumulative effort and must regain it at the cost of much unnecessary labor. Any spontaneous act of will is the outcome of uninterrupted practice.

Honesty, truthfulness, justice are nothing but expressions of automatic volition; and until virtue has become automatic, we cannot be called moral.

When we begin our practice of obedience, through self-discipline, we must not try to cover too large an area all at once. It is better to start with what, in orthodox theology, is called our "besetting sin;" that is, with the weakest spot in our character, where most often we break through and fail. Sin is nothing more than rebellion against some cosmic law of which we have become vaguely or clearly conscious; and the amount of our knowledge of this law measures the degree of our sin, as also of our discomfort in transgressing it. Whenever we refuse to obey a law, we throw ourselves out of line with the universe and are battered and buffeted inevitably by the great cosmic forces moving in contrary direction. It is these multifarious, self-created blows, bred of our foolish push against the cosmic trend, which constitute our karma. We want something which according to the Divine plan belongs to another. The elasticity provided everywhere in the cosmic scheme for the play of relative free will, makes it possible for us to move a certain distance unimpeded; then the limit of cosmic indulgence is reached, the law asserts itself and we are thwarted. We have wasted energy in pursuing a futile course of action, we waste still more in useless rebellion and nothing is accomplished. The same amount of energy spent in searching out the law and learning to obey it would have brought a rich return.

Law is not a barrier raised to stop our liberty. It is a protecting wall to guard us from the dangers of our own ignorance. When that ignorance is great, the space between those boundary walls is narrow; but as we grow in knowledge, it widens and widens, until the walls completely disappear and we find ourselves in the unbounded open of infinity, with nothing to restrict our freedom. It is evident then that the will gains freedom as we grow in knowledge. It costs us no effort to obey the law when we know its true purpose and value. That is why the psalmist cried: "Give me understanding and I shall keep Thy law."

If we try to swim upstream the current is not to blame for our slow progress. Wherever we find our self-will pressing continuously against an unyielding obstacle, instead of battling with hot impatience to strike it down, let us begin to study it. Nearly always we shall find that we are opposing some cosmic law. Then, instead of challenging it, if we will ally ourselves with it, we shall experience new strength and freedom.

It would be a long and wearisome process, however, to acquaint ourselves and learn to act in harmony with every law on every plane of being. To shorten the work, the Great Ones have taught us a simple way which even the most unlettered can follow — the way of "Not my will, but Thine be done;" "Not I, not I; but Thou, but Thou." These few words contain the whole secret of free will. Those who can make them the law of their daily living will know no bondage or repression. The cosmic will and the individual will are both manifestations of the one Universal Supreme Energy. As long as the part wars against the whole, it must be baffled and defeated. When it goes with the whole, it partakes in fullest measure of the power and freedom of the whole. If God or the Infinite is with us who can be against us? But God can be with us only when His law is truly our delight and we live solely to do His will.

Will is not the driving power in any action. Behind every act of volition stands a desire. It is desire which determines the force and direction of the will. If the desire is strong, it gives a swift, sweeping volitional impulse; if weak, the impulse is abortive and ineffective. Again, if the desire is sordid and selfish, an act of self-will results; if the desire is lofty and in rhythm with the universe, we have an expression of cosmic will.

Midway between desire and will we find another factor — motive or intention. It is this element which lends moral color to the will. An action is ethical or unethical according to its motive. It is also this which leaves its stamp on the character. If the motive is a noble one, the character will be uplifted, however disastrous the outward action may appear to be. If the motive is ignoble, the character will be degraded, even though the outward success be dazzling. The human measure of failure and success is signally different from the cosmic measure.

Thus we see that will must be always a subject-faculty, driven by desire, modified by motive. Our daily experience proves it. We set our will in one direction and at the moment of action it veers and carries us in the opposite direction: — "The good we would, we do not; the evil we would not, that we do," to quote from St. Paul. The reason for this is that we work on the will instead of on our desire. If we would remain secure and firm in our purpose, we must deal with the primary cause of action, not with the secondary cause. We must not set our will; we must transform our desires. We must alter our mental attitude, our outlook on the world and on life. We must acquire "a new heart and a new mind."

Desire can never be destroyed or eliminated. It is a primal element of our nature, it is our prod to perfection, the impelling principle in all our evolution. Those who do not desire to learn make poor students; and they climb slowly who have no longing to reach the heights. Without desires there is no growth or progress. When great teachers like Gautama Buddha and Lao-tze tell us to root out desire, they refer to selfish desire, that which seeks outlet in acts of self-will. Utter desirelessness is impossible on the human plane, because on this plane there is always lack somewhere and lack induces desire. The state of total desirelessness can only be the outcome of union with the Ultimate. We attain it spontaneously when, through this union, we realize fullness or completion of being. The desirelessness preached by the Great Ones is a preparation for this higher state. It means loosening the ship from its moorings that it may sail out on vaster seas.

If we would have a well-ordered will, we must give place in our mind to constructive desire only. Like all created things desire is dual in nature. Harmful desires are as effective in dragging downward as noble desires are in uplifting. The will follows in either direction with equally ready obedience. Only when there is conflict of desires — a war between good and evil desires — does the will grow confused in its action. We must cultivate the habit of right desire, as we cultivate a taste for fine art or for the classics in literature and music. We do it in the same way, — by contact with that which awakens and nurtures such desire. We must read books which will stimulate our higher impulses; we must hear teaching which will help us to readjust our values and give us a right sense of proportion; and we must seek companionship with those who exemplify some exalted ideal in their daily living. Above all we must overcome the discontent and irritability we feel now when a desire is frustrated, and must learn to move in the serener atmosphere of lofty aspiration. This will not be difficult if we will but remember that we belong to the universe, it does not belong to us; and it is not for us to try to force it into a mold of our making.

Although will is subject to desire, it can be freed. Will is freed by gathering up the multitude of our desires and merging them in one supreme desire, — to live and act in harmony with the great Will of the universe. Then the last fetter of desire falls and the bondage of our little will breaks.

What is Maya?

Probably no part of Vedic teaching is so difficult for us to grasp as the conception of *Maya*. Interpreted usually as delusion, illusion, unreality, it would seem to reduce creation to an illusive dream. The idea at once calls out a protest from the practical person, accustomed to believe implicitly in the testimony of the five senses. What is there evasive or dreamlike in these solid objects which daily we see and taste and touch, one asks defiantly. The fault lies, not with the fact, but with its definition. *Maya* does not mean illusion; it means relativity. Everything in the manifested universe exists in relation to something else. It has no independent existence or independent characteristics. The outline which marks off one form does not belong to it any more than to the contiguous forms which it also defines. It is only a dividing line. If the object on one side changes shape, the form on the other side must be equally modified; that in turn alters the neighboring form; so the change is transmitted on and on throughout creation. And since there is always change somewhere, it follows that there must always be change everywhere; that is, absolute immobility nowhere. Take it in our own physical organism. Is the condition of our body ever static even for a second? If it were, in that second it would be dead; for on the material plane life and motion are synonymous; and motion means constant variation in temperature, size, weight and outline. The variations may be too minute to register, but they are none the less actual. This ceaseless alteration in the world of form is one of the fundamental qualities of *maya*.

What is true of body is more intensely true of mind. So fluid and susceptible is our thought that we can rarely determine what is ours and what our neighbor's. We think out some special style of dress and find the design in every fashion magazine; we evolve a new plan and meet a dozen people with the same idea. Thoughts move back and forth across our mind unbidden and unexplained. Even in the silence of some far mountain cave the world-thought beats upon us, transforming the stillness into a noisy thoroughfare. At last we learn that thoughts cannot be classified as "mine" and "others," but as human and Divine. Then we abandon the fruitless struggle to better our mixed human thought; and emptying the mind of self-thought, we pray that it may be wholly filled with God-thought.

In the realm of secular knowledge the bar of relativity defeats our most resolute efforts at precision and conclusive demonstration. Psychology teaches that knowledge is acquired through association of ideas. A new experience comes to us. The mind takes it up and compares it with previous experiences. If it finds others of like nature stored in the memory, it classes the new one in the same group, gives it a name and claims to know it. But what does it know about it? Only its relation to other things; nothing of it in itself.

In reality, through association of ideas we can never gain ultimate knowledge, because each new contact gives rise to a new modification. Therefore the unfamiliar object which we are studying and the objects with which we are comparing it are none of them at any time in their real, unmodified state. They are all constantly changing in relation to each new association. Take for example a color. We place it beside a pronounced blue and it looks purple; we put it beside purple and it looks blue; by the side of another shade it will take on a reddish tone; by still another it will appear black. What color shall we call it? And what is the color of that with which we compare it? How is it possible to have any fixed scale of colors by which to go? In the same way, who can determine what is beauty or what is ugliness? A shade which is exquisite in one combination of colors appears garish in another; a costume which is charming on one person loses all its grace of line on someone else; a building which is a triumph of architectural beauty in one setting becomes an offense to the eye in other surroundings. Some music jars on our ears; to others the same music is exciting and inspiring. Try as we may to coordinate and generalize, we cannot find a unit on which to base a world-ideal of beauty.

In the phenomenal world there can be no true generalization anywhere; for among all the objects or concepts which we gather into one group under a generic name, not any one is exactly like any other. Perfect repetition is not to be found in nature. Have we ever seen any two temperaments or faces or objects exactly alike? Untrained observers may imagine that they perceive identity, but the expert will always detect some infinitesimal variation. We know from our own futile attempts to make two sides of anything absolutely even, how impossible it is to produce undeviating sameness. This endless divergence or diversity which characterizes the external universe constitutes another fundamental quality of *maya*.

The subtler the substance, the greater also is the opportunity for variation. In gross forms an approximate identity may be achieved; but when we pass to the more mobile sphere of thought, it becomes impossible. In the realm of ideas the variations are limitless. No two persons can form precisely the same concept. The same word cannot mean the same thing to any two minds. There is, therefore, no chance of arriving at a permanent settlement through discussion. A temporary agreement may be reached, but it is at best an armistice. Every word spoken creates a new variation, which means a new difference to settle. Exact definition of terms will not allay the difficulty, for each will interpret the definition according to one's specific experience. Thus the term "hot" will convey a widely different picture to an inhabitant of India and a dweller in the polar regions. There is but one place where perfect understanding can be attained and that is in the silence of the higher consciousness, where thought-forms lose their peculiar personal bent and become pure abstract ideas.

How is it possible moreover to have any uniformity in the moral code, when the idea of good and evil on which it rests is wholly relative? Can we say that anything is absolutely good or absolutely evil? A soldier who sheaths his sword and turns the other cheek is a deserter. The one in private life who does it is a saint. Under one condition killing is heroism, under another it is crime. To a flooded district a heavy rain is a fresh calamity, to a drought-stricken land it represents rescue from starvation. Things are good or evil in relation to other things, not in their own nature.

Even in our daily experience how quickly a change of mood or circumstance will transform good into evil or evil into good. At one instant we are cold and wrap ourselves in warm clothes; at the next we are warm and they become an oppressive burden. Today we are tired and crave solitude; tomorrow that same solitude seems loneliness. What made us happy a year ago, at present wearies us; while what seemed then unbearable misfortune, we now regard as a blessing. This kaleidoscopic interblending of light and shadow, good and evil, happiness and misery, is another essential characteristic of *maya*.

Through all this never-ceasing change and endless diversity, however, perfect order and consistency are apparent. This is definite proof that the world about us is not wholly dream or phantasm. Where all things move with unfailing regularity, there must be some fixity and reality. *Maya* then is not illusion. It is the play of the Infinite in finite fragments, the pure white light broken into the multicolored rays of the spectrum. There could be no rays without the white light, hence their separate existence is illusory; but in relation to the basic light it is vital and inevitable. The very existence of the white light presupposes the existence of the colors of the spectrum, as the various colors presuppose the existence of the white light. That is the background on which alone they can manifest. So God or Ultimate Reality is the background of all created things. And since God is Infinite, there must be infinite variation in the modes of expression. No true artist ever repeats the same scheme of color or composition. No true musician ever carries the same melody from one piece to another.

Diversity, however, apart from unity is mere confusion; bound to it, it becomes the source of constant joy and loveliness. In relation to the whole, every created thing has its special place and value. Discord and harmony, pain and pleasure, darkness and light, all contribute their share towards the universal beauty. The jar and clash come in relating things to one another, or to ourselves; for in no way does maya so easily entrap us as by leading us to judge life and experience by personal rather than by universal standards. Through this mistaken habit all human beings continually weave a maya of their own, from which again they must free themselves. But why do we need to tear the net? Because it is the cause of all our misery. We do not cling to it, but to what we believe it to be. No one loves uncertainty. Don't we often hear: "Better the worst than this suspense?" No one loves instability. Doesn't the thought "It may not last" pour drops of bitterness into the sweetest cup of happiness? No one loves evasion; yet whenever we would lay our hands on Truth, does it not slip from our grasp? No one loves defeat; but however high we climb, are there not always heights beyond? On the plane of matter never can there be a satisfied ambition, for what is done never satisfies. It merely reveals fresh possibilities of achievement.

Our soul demands an absolute and will not rest until it has broken the entangling web of relativity which now holds it prisoner. This web is woven of a three-fold thread—the relation of things to one another, their relation to the individual consciousness, and their relation to the Cosmic Being. The first two must be illusory and unreal; because what has no independent existence cannot enter into independent relationships. Could two waves be related apart from the ocean? Taken from it, they would cease to exist. What would remain to relate? There can be but one real relationship and that is with God. When we try with all our heart to establish that, we move towards Reality and enter into true relation with all things. This is why we are taught to seek His Kingdom first. Seeking earnestly, we shall come to perceive ourselves and the whole created universe living and moving in Him alone; then the last thread of maya's web will snap; all sense of instability will drop away; and we shall see this world of incessant change and relativity transfigured by the all-pervading presence of the Unchangeable, the Eternal and the Real.

Universal Harmony

On the plane of created things eternal harmony cannot find full expression. Creation demands duality, the play of opposing forces, as an electric current requires a positive and a negative pole; and this means the presence of inharmony as well as harmony. In nature we find colors that do not blend, sounds that do not harmonize, and substances that will not mix. In the social organism are crucial differences, irreconcilable differences in human temperament and in national custom. Scientific invention may have seemed to efface them in part; but what we have gained is not harmony, but an outer uniformity, which has proved to be a mere cover for a greater inharmony. Peace and harmony cannot be attained so long as those who seek to establish them are at war within themselves.

The cause of this interior warfare lies in our unawareness of the origin and purpose of our existence. We look upon our life as our own. We regard our bodies, our powers and faculties as our personal property, whereas in reality they belong to the universe; we have merely the use of them. We did not come into being for ourselves; we came as parts of a great Whole, and we owe our loyalty to that Whole. Our one vital relation is with It; all other relations grow out of that and depend upon It. As parts of that Whole we are shaped and fashioned to take a special place and fulfill a special mission. To strive for another place and prefer some other task is to mar the order of the universe and throw ourselves out of rhythm with it. We are not forced to search out the task or place; we have only to surrender and they will come to us naturally and spontaneously. Then we shall be able to say with Marcus Aurelius: "I am in harmony with all that is part of your harmony, great Universe. For me nothing is early and nothing late, that is in season for you. From you, in you, and unto you are all things."

The Chain of Birth and Death

Something cannot come out of nothing. Such is the definite statement made in the Vedic scriptures; such is also the conclusive word of modern science. Nor is this a law for the gross material world only; it applies equally to the realm of consciousness.

What form the Soul takes up is determined by its state of development and by the use it has made of its previous forms. The principle is the same as that applied by any school or business in dealing with promotion. In these periodical changes of form and environment, however, there is no question of birth or death for the Soul. Travelers who spend a few days, months or even years at each station along a train route, have no sense of a break in their existence when they move from station to station; in the same way the Soul feels no interruption in the even flow of its life-consciousness in passing from one body to another. It means no more, so the Bhagavad Gita declares, than the transition in this body from childhood to youth and to old age. The mistake we make is in breaking up this deep-flowing, steady stream of living into fragments which we call "lives," whereas life in its real aspect is one unbroken, eternal, infinite existence.

The logical necessity for pre-existence becomes evident when we study our present earth-life; for even a little observation will show us that what we are today is the product of a pre-existence of yesterday; and if we trace our life back from one such small pre-existence to another, we shall reach a horizon line where the yesterday drops into another sphere of manifestation, out of which this one has risen, as a new flame leaps from the glowing embers when a fresh log is laid on the fire. It is not that we are, then as these self-conscious entities we cease to be, and again as other entities we come into new being. Never have we ceased to be and never shall we cease to be. The element of identity is constant and unchanging. Sometimes, however, our being is in visible gross forms; while at other times it is in subtle and invisible forms. But always we are. One of the meditations given in Yoga to strengthen this sense of identity is to carry ourselves in thought back to our babyhood and then to trace our life through condition after condition up to the present time, realizing how many different bodies we have worn even during this short span of years. Not one atom of that original body remains, scarcely one thought or desire of that infant mind. Our entire intellectual and moral outlook has altered; yet the consciousness of self-identity has never wavered. And so it will continue, firm and unshaken.

Future existence is as much a correlative of existence as is pre-existence. Eternity must stretch equally in both directions; for as something cannot come out of nothing, by the same law it cannot go into nothing. No entity can ever become a non-entity. If today we are vividly conscious of a sense of I-ness, it cannot be annihilated. The process by which we evolve from self-consciousness to God-consciousness is not one of destruction or substitution, but of expansion. Our self-identity expands and expands until it becomes commensurate with the whole. First we awaken to a unity of interest with a group of people we call our family, as we so far identify ourselves with their welfare that we literally love them as ourselves. Then this feeling widens to the community, the country, humanity, to every living creature, to the whole universe, and finally to the Infinite. We know ourselves at last as one with God, hence with no life or advantage apart from the whole. Only when we reach this point do we realize our true individuality or indivisibility.

Life as we perceive it at present is actually an endless chain of births and deaths. At every moment we are dying in some part of our being, and at the same moment in some other part we are being reborn. Not for the flash of a second is any human life static. It rushes and swirls like a mountain torrent; millions of molecules entering in, as many millions pouring out; every atom bringing its minute load of vital energy, emptying it somewhere in the organism and hurrying on. Thoughts, too, hastening in and out; so also emotions and sensations. Perpetual movement everywhere; never-ending change, or continual birth and death, for each change implies the death of what is and the birth of something else. Every death indeed necessitates a birth; because existence being indestructible and the change being in the form, not in the essence or substance, what leaves this place or body must reappear in some other form and place.

So long as our attachments, obligations and desires bind us to the physical universe, we cannot prevent this relentless alternation of births and deaths; for change is the very law and condition of material manifestation. The briefest interval of complete rest would mean stagnation and eventual dissolution. On this plane we have no choice as to whether we shall live or die. We can only determine to what we shall die and to what we shall be reborn. Every instant of time represents a death or a new birth. There is not one thought, not one word, not one movement of hand or foot, not one act of moral choice, not one breath even that does not sign a death sentence or a promise of life eternal. Are we dying to that which dies and being reborn to that which is deathless? Then we may be sure that every day death is losing its power over us, and there will come a time when we shall be able to walk over the waters or through a fiery furnace unmoved. Acts of heroism will cost us nothing then; for it is the little self in us which always plays the coward. The Great Self, fully conscious of its imperishable nature, is fearless. By this unfailing attribute of fearlessness, indeed, we may recognize the knowers of the Divine, so the Upanishads tell us.

Now we tremble when any danger threatens the body because deep down in our hearts we identify our life with it. What exists besides seems to us too cloud-like and intangible to rest our faith upon.

At whatever point we touch Truth, there we touch immortal life; because Truth and existence are one. The path of liberation, therefore, is the path of knowledge – knowledge of the Higher Self first and through that, knowledge of God. "Those who have no faith in this science of Self-knowledge, without attaining Me, return to the path of death and rebirth" it is said in the Gita. We must find something within us which defies time, space and causation; a something which not merely contains life, but which is life. It is plain that the body does not meet these requirements; nor yet the mind or character; for all are subject to the conditioning effects of time and space, and are bound by the law of causation. That something must lie deeper in the abysses of our being; and mere intellectual reasoning cannot penetrate to it, because it lies beyond. That which is life can be gained only by living. It is not enough to recognize that we are not the body, we must live as if we were not; that is, we must not make it the central motive in all our activity. We must not feel that our happiness depends on its comfort and pleasure; that our daily routine must be shaped according to its momentary state. We must look at it objectively, while we remain the subject; in other words, we must cultivate the attitude of a witness towards it, taking care of it as good workers do their instruments, but never yielding to its caprices or identifying ourselves with it.

Then once more we must push back the point of self-identity of objectifying our subtle body, that closer covering of mind, intellect and ego which still wraps the Soul when the gross body falls off. To confound our real being with this is as grave an error as to think ourselves one with our hands and feet or our senses. We must look upon it only as a finer tool to work with; a tool, however, of such intrinsic value that we cannot afford to neglect it or use it unwisely. The surest way to make it effective and also to detach ourselves from it, is to practice evenness of mind and mood. We must not let our consciousness sway and swing with each passing pain or pleasure, each chance word of praise or blame. The rhythmic play of opposites — heat and cold, light and darkness, the pleasant and the unpleasant — is inevitable on this plane. It is foolish to suppose that we can stop it; but what we can stop is our reaction against it. The Bhagavad Gita teaches that one who remains serene and unafflicted by these outer changes is the only one fitted to attain immortality. The reason is apparent, because to rise above them is to rise above our mortal nature. Only in the Soul can we "make for ourselves an island which no flood can overwhelm."

Growth in dispassion and serenity leads naturally to growth in Self-knowledge; for as the surface of the mind becomes calm, the reflection of the Soul within is no longer broken and distorted, and we behold the perfect image of our true nature shining in glory. Then by its transcendent light, as by a lamp, "we will see the real nature of the Supreme," we are told in the Svetasvatara Upanishad; "and having known the unborn, eternal God, we are freed from all fetters. For when God is known, all fetters fall off, sufferings are destroyed, and birth and death cease."

The fact of reincarnation comes to remind us that we are traveling a mighty journey, with perfection, unending bliss, infinite knowledge, eternal life as the destination. If we think of that, if we keep that in our mind, these stations along the way, the passing events of these little lives, will scarcely count for us. They only mark the progress of the journey, and we are content to stop and equally content to go on; what happens in between does not matter. Christ said: "Those who lose their lives for My sake shall find it," that is, we who lose the consciousness of this small fleeting, temporal life, gain the consciousness of that one unbroken sweep of eternal life — not an eternal life in some future state, but an eternal life that we have now; for that which is eternal, infinite and indestructible must be existent at this moment.

Reincarnation is not counted merely from birth to birth. Every day we are re-embodied. Every night we die and the way we live today determines our embodiment of tomorrow. If we have conquered self for one instant today, tomorrow we are a bigger person. If we have given way to the little self, given way to its demands upon us, felt a greater concern for this body of flesh than for that greater body of character, we have arrested our development. Stop and think of it. Every moment is a death and a rebirth. Are we determining these reincarnations in an ever mightier chain? Is each link bigger and stronger than the last one? Is each day's body and mind and soul-life a conscious widening and expanding of the one of the day before?

What is Death?

Death is the counterpart of life. Every moment that we live, we are dying. Life and death are merely two sides of a something which is change, and we know that without change life on this plane cannot continue. Whenever in the created universe motion or change ceases, disintegration begins. We play and work incessantly to prevent stagnation and induce change in our system; why then should we shrink from that culminating change called death and believe it to be an enemy? In reality, unless there were something constantly dying in us, we should cease to live. Life only comes from life. Each breath means that myriads of little creatures are offering themselves up for our life's sake. Our physical organism is a perpetual altar of sacrifice, on which the fire of old life burns that, like a leaping flame, new life may rise. When we enter into relation with the deeper facts of nature, we learn to look upon death as we look upon life; and we do not recoil from the consummation of the process without which we would not live at all.

Birth here must always mean death somewhere else; because it is no more possible for existence to spring from non-existence than for a positive quantity to come from the multiplying of zeros. The first little cry of the newborn baby does not announce a new life for the soul; it merely marks its entrance into a new environment and experience. The basic units of creation are eternal. Something cannot come out of nothing or go into nothing. It follows then that whatever is always must have been and always will be. And this applies to the individual consciousness as truly as to the material elements of the body. Forms change. Chemical elements compose, decompose and recompose elsewhere. Physical forces gather and scatter, making and breaking these created things to which we cling. But as we watch this ceaseless change, there is in us a self-identity which persists.

This sense of I-ness, like all other fundamental forms of being, cannot have come from nothing, nor can it melt into nothingness. It is as indestructible as the ultimate units of force and matter. It may expand until it breaks the bonds of selfishness and becomes as vast as the universe; or it may contract to the narrow limits of this body; but always it is there. It cannot be annihilated, because it is the vital part of us — the very witness of our existence...our consciousness.

Why then do we hold to life with such feverish anxiety? Because we have not yet convinced ourselves that it cannot be taken from us; and being our greatest treasure, instinctively we tighten our grasp upon it. Nor is this wrong. Nature meant us to cling to it, but not in the narrow personal sense in which we now conceive it. We think of it as something in us, which we possess. We must reverse our conception. Life is not in us. We are in it. We bathe in it. We are immersed in it. It covers us and flows over us in inexhaustible stream. It enfolds us eternally. It is the one thing from which we cannot escape, the one thing we cannot lose. Of what then shall we be afraid? Our fear of death springs from a false idea of what life is and where it is seated. We have identified it too closely with mere bodily existence. The body is only the outer garment of life. We put it on for convenience's sake, as we clothe ourselves when we go outside. It is of the greatest use to us and we should give it the best of care; but also we should wear it lightly, ready to throw it aside like a worn-out garment when its use is over.

Some people justify their attachment to this body and environment by saying that change of form involves loss of time. But children could as well claim that it would be an economy of time and effort for them to remain year after year in the same grade at school. These various life-fragments are like different school grades. In each we have specific lessons to learn; and when they are learned, whether in a few years or many, it is essential for our development that we pass on to other grades. The body we have at any moment is the product of an experience already out-grown. Our vision always stretches far beyond it; and every practice of austerity, every exercise in technique of any kind, is merely an attempt to make it respond to a larger and larger demand. When the limit of its power of response is reached, we should be glad to exchange it for a new one better adapted to our purpose.

If we are eternally existent, then why this age-long journey from form to form? The Soul has not plunged into the finite. It is as infinite today as before it began this apparent round of material manifestation. Its life is just as unbroken and continuous. These successive finite lives are like waves breaking on its surface. They cannot alter its nature. Still it is infinite and eternal. That is why our inner being gives such unwilling assent to the idea of death, and why we are so restless in this cage of the finite. All these countless lives through which we pass are solely to teach us that we are deathless, immortal, unchanging. Merely repeating it day after day and year after year, however, would not convince us. We must prove it to ourselves by living and dying many times.

To transcend death we must find, while still in this body, that inner principle of life which death cannot reach. It is useless, we know, to look for it in our body, since science tells us that all its particles are renewed in the short space of a year. That is, once in every twelve months physically we die and are reborn. We are not aware of it because it occurs gradually and in the same environment. But what reason have we to believe that that seemingly more radical renewal which we call death may not seem as natural and may not produce as little sense of altered condition?

The mind also cannot be taken as the seat of permanent being, for it is kaleidoscopic in its endless changes. A chance meeting, the reading of a book, a single occurrence may transform it completely. The same changefulness is apparent in our moral nature, for don't we see it growing as we grow? That which possesses the quality of persistent continuity must lie beyond — in that vital center of our being where we touch God or Pure Existence. This being so, shall we hope to cheat death by prolonging the life of this body? Or shall we escape from its haunting presence by giving ourselves to this ever-dying outer world? No; if we do not wish to be death's frequent companion, only one course is open to us — we must ally ourselves with the undying. It is not logical to suppose that nature would have led the individual life-unit on through eons of unfoldment to stop short with mere body consciousness or even mind consciousness. Of what use to perfect a machine and then grant neither sufficient time nor occasion to discover its true use and possibilities? The aim of life is not a perfect physical development. It is not the accumulation of learning, nor yet the development of a lofty standard of virtue. The ultimate end of life is to reveal to us the vital fact of our deathlessness. The instant that we realize this, rivalry, selfishness, all human weakness and struggle, will vanish; because they rest upon the erroneous belief that life and its opportunities are limited.

We need more than one body, however, to learn this lesson. We must outlive many bodies before we are convinced beyond all doubt that we partake of an imperishable, universal existence. So long as we consider ourselves isolated entities, each with rival interests and a little life of our own, death will press hard upon us, casting its shadow over our brightest joy. But when we realize the solidarity of life and interest throughout the universe, death will lose its power and sting. It is the little self which lives and dies. If we can forget that and lift our thought to a larger sphere, even while here in this body we shall live in the infinite and eternal.

Instead of recoiling from death, let us recognize its utility. Let us be glad that all these material things, which impede our free march onward, are destined to wear out and fall away. We should be too weighted with matter, were this not so. Change and decay create spaces for expansion of life. They make possible a richer fruition. The dead leaves of the autumn blanket and fertilize the ground for a new growth of the spring. So, as one bodily life falls, it passes on to the next one a store of garnered experience and understanding.

For the wise person death means a resurrection, not a burial. We see in it the promise of a more efficient bodily instrument to work with, of added attainment, of a wider contact with Reality. Like eager explorers, we set out joyfully on each new lap in the journey which is leading us steadily out of the realm of death into the full consciousness of life everlasting.

When death occurs, it does not reach beyond the physical; mind and spirit remain untouched. We are in the same state as we are here, when we become so deeply engrossed in our thought that we lose all consciousness of the body. If we would let our mind dwell less on our bodily conditions and sensations and more in the higher realms of our being, we too would feel the touch of death but lightly.

When this broader, more inclusive outlook comes, every expression of life is sacred to us. We do not break or pluck or tear growing things as if they existed for our pleasure; we do not walk heedlessly, not caring what we crush; we do not eat more than our body needs, unwilling to take even the most primitive forms of life unnecessarily. Scientists are recognizing more and more that there is no dead matter in the universe; that everything is living. A profound spiritual teacher of India declared often that trees, flowers and bushes were conscious beings without the power of movement from one place to another. The thought that all creation is alive and conscious should not oppress us; it should rather deepen our sense of the brotherhood of being.

Mortality and Immortality

How can we reach that inmost center and touch the Divine Power hidden there? We do not have to seek it. We are already united with It. From It comes our strength. From It comes our wisdom. From It comes our life. Without It we would not be existent, as a tree could not exist if there had not been a bud; as a machine could not take form if there were no engineer to conceive it. We do not need to search for that hidden Source of our being, we need only to become conscious of its presence. We do this by inward living, by setting a lofty standard for our thoughts and action and following it with undeviating consecration.

Actually the whole universe in the final analysis is deathless. All that we see is not death but change — the breaking up of a form, the falling apart of a compound. The science of physics long ago discovered that the sum-total of matter and force in the universe remains eternally the same. Should one atom die or drop out of existence, the equilibrium would be destroyed and the entire universe would crumble. Life and death in creation mean the melting of one form into another, the gross into the subtle, the subtle into a grosser or more visible form; but "the existent can never become non-existent" as the Gita declares, for where would it go since all that is must be existent? So it is with the human being. The Soul of the human being cannot die because it is an integral part of the Ultimate. At some point we must touch pure being, otherwise we would not exist at all; and that point of union constitutes our soul or real Self, while this rush and whirl of matter about us is what we call life and death. We are like an eddy in a river; the water flows on and on, but the force which creates the eddy remains fixed and unchanged. So long as we walk wrapped in a visible form we say that we are living, when we cast off the gross body we say that we are dead. In reality, however, the subtler the material form we wear, the more living we become, until we free ourselves from the last thin covering of matter and enter into Life itself.

Individual evolution falls apparently into two distinct states: the first is an evolution out of unconscious immortality into self-conscious mortality, the second is out of conscious mortality into conscious immortality. The soul or life-form through the first period seems wholly absorbed in developing a perfect instrument for mortal expression; having achieved that, it turns round and bends all its energies towards extricating itself from its own creation. But why should we thus entangle ourselves? It is a matter of unfoldment. The answer which Vedanta gives us is: We never have entangled ourselves, we merely think we have. In reality we are immortal at this moment, but we imagine ourselves as mortal because we are identifying ourselves with that which is not a real part of us. We believe ourselves to be our perishable bodies, whereas we are actually the imperishable dweller within.

Picture a bubble on a wave in the ocean. If it holds obstinately to the thought "I am a bubble, I am a bubble," then inevitably it will measure its life by the duration of the bubble. Let it, on the contrary, expand to the point of thinking itself one with the wave on which it rides and its life will stretch to the length of the wave's life. But let it suddenly realize "I am one with the ocean," and a thousand times it may rise and fall but never does it become less living; there is no ebb and flow in its consciousness of existence. The same is true of us. So long as we cling to the belief "I am the body," like the bubble, our life must seem fleeting. When we grow to identify ourselves with our soul life, the measure of our existence must lengthen; but when we awaken to the supreme fact that we are one with the Infinite Ocean of Being, then we know that our life is eternal. Yet always were we one with the Eternal; the change has been in our consciousness, not in the condition of our existence.

It is this delusive character of our present state of consciousness that has led the Vedic sages to liken human existence to a dream. Humans beings on this plane, they say, are neither wholly awake nor sound asleep. We wander in a twilight world between, a dream world in which reality and unreality mingle. We seem perpetually at the meeting point between the pairs of opposites — pleasure and pain, knowledge and ignorance, life and death, mortality and immortality; and the swift-flowing current of human activity buffets us back and forth between the two, unfolding within us by the very prod of circumstance, the higher faculties of discrimination and choice, and an ever-growing hunger for the Real. Those indeed whose vision has broken over the boundary lines between visible and invisible and who see far behind and far ahead in the Soul's Godward course, declare that our human state is the best for Divine realization. In our less evolved states, our consciousness is too deeply buried in matter; in the heaven state it is too engrossed in enjoyment; only in this intermediate human state has the living being the most favorable conditions for spiritual attainment, — enough of joy to give us courage to go on, enough of sorrow to remind us that the heaven we seek is not here; enough of light to allow us to push forward on our journey, enough of darkness to grant us periods of rest.

If we utilize to the utmost our present opportunity, this one incarnation would suffice to gain liberation. But we are not eager enough. We are not yet weary enough of our mortality. We are tired of the pain, but not of the pleasure; we shrink from the dishonor, but we covet the honor; we flee from death, but we cling to the transitory life with which it alternates; so we go on through birth after birth learning slowly and arduously the lesson of immortality. As long as there lingers in our hearts the least desire for gratification in the world of matter, we are allowed to return to satisfy it. This is all that reincarnation means, — the freedom to be a mortal through as many lives as we choose and an equal freedom to attain immortality here and now. Nor does this apply merely to this plane. The law extends on through all those planes we call heavens, which are only subtler forms of physical life; for the Lord tells us in the Bhagavad Gita: "All states of existence from the world of the creator (the highest heaven) to this world are subject to return, but those who attain to Me, the Supreme, they have no need to be reborn." They have discovered their indestructible nature and the true Source of their happiness, hence their journey is ended.

We cannot hope, however, to transform our consciousness in a day. We must acquire the habits of immortality. We must readjust our scale of values, change our standard of measurement in life. We must extend our vision by keeping our gaze fixed on the bigger things; by reminding ourselves that to our Soul a thousand years are as a day and that beyond that thousand lie other countless thousands on and on in an endless eternity of life. How quickly will the passing joys and sorrows of this small earth-existence dwindle and fade away!

Heaven and Final Attainment

The universal recognition that happiness is the goal of all individual effort has led every religion to posit a heaven; and because there cannot be a higher without a lower, so with a heaven has come a hell. These stand as outposts marking the boundary lines of the religious consciousness in its primary stages. As that consciousness expands, however, they diminish in importance; for belief in them can flourish only where there is a lack of the spirit of solidarity. Which one of us, of even normally decent feeling, would go off happily to an eternal heaven, knowing that some among our fellow-beings were doomed to an eternal hell? The very attitude of mind which would make it possible for us to accept such a reward, would prove us unfit to receive it.

Heaven as ordinarily conceived is a vacation place, a sort of celestial summer resort, where perpetual pleasure can be had without pain; where there is success without failure, praise without blame; above all, where families are reunited and live on eternally together without the bickerings and frictions which punctuate their earthly household life. Even after the old orthodox picture of hymns and harps and wings is outgrown, heaven still remains for us a place where we shall have all the advantages of humanity with none of its disadvantages. The Divine is left quite out of the question except as a central figure.

Next as the concept evolves, the geographical factor may be discarded; heaven may cease to be a place and become a "state of mind," but the "good time" idea persists.

Hinduism did not denounce this point of view. On the contrary, it swung so readily with it that it multiplied the heavens. One was not enough! No one region or form of pleasure could suit all types of people. There must be an endless variety of enjoyments and conditions; and it grouped and graded these through a succession of seven heavens. May we not find here the origin of our expression "seventh heaven?"

These celestial regions contained all degrees of satisfaction. There was the realm of the ancestors, where family and social relations continued; the realm of the righteous; the heaven of the gods; the region of celestial spirits; the sphere of the saints; the heaven of the highest sages, and the realm of the Creator, the region of limitless wisdom and illumination.

The Vedic sages, however, did not stop there. They knew that a state, whether localized or not, was, of necessity, perishable. It might extend through incalculable stretches of time, but at the moment of involution, when the manifested merged into the unmanifested and all creation reverted to a finer state, the heavens must crumble with earth and suns and planets. Only the Creator would remain — not because He dwelt supreme in the highest heaven, but because He was superior to all heavens.

Vedanta teaches that permanent happiness is a deeply interior state, independent of all things external. It cannot exist outside our consciousness, nor can it exist within it until we transcend clinging to form and whatever form implies. True happiness is born of one condition only — self-earned, conscious contact with the Supreme. How can we gain that contact? By lifting ourselves to that height of understanding where eternity and infinity will seem as normal to us as time and space are now; in other words, by learning to identify ourselves with the highest formless principle of our being and not with this fleeting form and name by which others know us.

When Lord Buddha saw the world as it was and realized that beyond the walls of his pleasure garden people were suffering and aging and dying, its sweet odors oppressed him, its loves and joys saddened him, even its kingly duties mocked him. His earthly paradise became a place of torment and he fled from it into the travailing world outside. The veil had been rent. He had seen into the depths and he knew that salvation for humankind did not mean escape from a hell and admission to a heaven. Knowledge alone would bring it. "Ye shall know the Truth and the Truth shall make you free."

Stages of Life

Life falls naturally into four stages. Growth, study and outward achievement fill the first three; the fourth remains undefined and optional. It would seem that in our closing years we are left free to choose between world and spirit; between continued outer achievement and the pursuit of inner culture.

The first stage, childhood, is the stage of instinct. The child follows its natural impulses. It has no decisions to make, no problems to solve. It lives in ignorance of the greater portion of its being. With the coming of the second stage, an entirely new area of consciousness is uncovered. The noted German psychologist, Carl Jung, calls it the "also I." This rouses in the awakening youth frequent inner conflicts. We seem to be two persons, one at war with the other. Added to these ceaseless struggles are many decisions and problems to meet, many adjustments to make. Adulthood brings a quieter note. Life settles into fixed grooves of family, profession, business or domestic duties, of social obligations and public service. These ripen the character and prepare it for higher effort.

The age at which these transitions take place is flexible. It depends upon the nature and the development. There are occasional souls who seem to pass over these transitions rather than through them and come out untouched by them. From the time the "also I" rises in their consciousness they lead their "real life." "Our real life is not the life we live," Maeterlinck says in his *Treasure of the Humble*, "and we feel that our deepest, nay, our most intimate thoughts are quite apart from ourselves, for we are other than our thoughts and our dreams."

There must be no overlapping in these transitions. We must not cling to the past or linger in the present, and neither past nor present should be allowed to prove an obstacle to the future. Each stage has its value, its purpose and its opportunities. To try to carry forward one stage into the succeeding one prevents our growth and throws us out of rhythm with our circumstances, and environment. It is as harmful to struggle to be a youth throughout life as it is to be a child. Both are signs of arrested development. Jung says in his book:

In the United States it is almost an ideal for the father to be the brother of his sons, and for the mother if possible to be the younger sister of her daughter:"…but "whoever carries over into the afternoon the law of the morning must pay for so doing with damage to the psyche, just as surely as a growing youth who tries to salvage childish egoism must pay for this mistake with failure in social development."

Life as it advances should be cumulative, not reiterative. Each stage should add to the accomplishment of the previous stage, not borrow from it. This is vitally true for those who are passing from middle life to riper years. At that time some fall easily into a dull routine, repeating themselves over and over; or they allow their lives to become a mere annex to a younger life, — that of a son or a daughter, or a grandchild. I would not undervalue the sacredness of human relationships or the privilege of service; but there are various ways of serving — a trivial way and a superior way. And the highest service we can render is to offer to the world a life rich in culture, in lofty aspiration, and in noble effort.

Older years should be marked by wisdom, dignity, and a gentle grace, not by an artificial youth which distorts and disfigures. Primitive tribes make the elders of the tribe the guardians of the law and the mysteries. To them is allotted the task of preserving the cultural heritage of the tribe. In ancient Aryan tradition also it was expected that when the children were grown and married, husband and wife should withdraw from worldly occupations, retire to the forest and devote themselves to spiritual culture.

How much deeper and nobler would be our social consciousness, if our elders would cast aside trivial concerns and strive to be keepers of the spiritual aspirations and standards of society. What a wonderful contribution they would make to their fellow-beings. Jung declares: "We moderns are faced with the necessity of rediscovering the life of the spirit; we must experience it anew for ourselves."

Those who have lived to riper years should be more creative than others, because they have a deeper experience and a wider vision to bring to their task. They are able to speak with authority. If our instrument of mind and intelligence has become dull, it is not the fault of age; it is because we have not kept it in condition during earlier years. Our higher faculties and forces have need of exercise. If we allow them to remain unused for a long period, we cannot expect them to be flexible and efficient. As youth with its study, its training and discipline, is a preparation for middle life, so should middle life be a preparation for age.

The body may weaken, but that only releases more of spirit. It leads us to transfer our activity to higher centers of interest.

Section Three

Building Character

Balance in Life	229
Cheerfulness.	229
Conscience	230
Courage and Endurance	232
Development of the Will	234
Forgetting	237
Forgiveness.	239
Friendship with Life	239
Generosity	242
Humility and Gentleness	243
Judge Not	244
Non-Resistance	246
Pain	250
Personality	253
Poise	255
Self-discipline.	260
Stillness	266
Truth Will Prevail	266
Unselfishness and Selflessness.	267

*S*ister Devamata emphasized the truth that good character is the essential foundation for the spiritual life. What does it mean to have good character? What qualities are essential and how do we build them in?

The soul wears two garments, the outer one of the gross body, and the inner one of character. The inner body contains the mind, the intellect, the moral nature and the sense of "I,"— the whole of our personal identity, in short, as well as the record of our previous lives. The question is often asked: if we have lived again and again, why have we no record of it? What better record could we have than the character we wear today? We write our thoughts and deeds deep into our being, and every time we move or speak we betray how we have lived down the ages. No recording angel is needed.

The substratum of the character-body is memory. The lightest impression made upon the mind is graven in the memory. The chance word we hear, the headline we glimpse, the fleeting wave of impatience or resentment, even these are duly set down. Not a scratch over the surface of our thought is ever effaced absolutely, although some are so lightly traced that they can be regarded as negligible. It is the frequent repetition of an idea or a desire which imbeds it in our character and makes it a dominating principle in our action. We wonder why our good resolutions break down so easily. It is because they are undermined by our actual life. Our resolutions are theories, while the disintegrating impulses are daily habits.

Yet these habits, however firmly rooted, can be wiped out by the persistent repetition of a counteracting thought. It is attention which lends strength to our mental impressions. The entire world might be in a ferment and we would know nothing of it if our attention were turned wholly elsewhere. Our first concern in shaping our character, therefore, should be to withdraw our attention from all destructive, weakening impressions. It is a very beneficial exercise whenever the consciousness of our limitation threatens to overwhelm us, to read or think of some holy life which illustrates the virtues we need to acquire. There is no quicker way of cultivating them; for what we think on, that we become.

If we wish to build a strong character we must never indulge in trivial, flimsy thought. We cannot be cowards six days in a week and expect to be heroes on the seventh. We shall be what our cumulative thought has made us. If we have not borne the little stings and pains of today bravely, we may be sure that we shall go down under bigger wounds in the future. It is the little things which test us; and one who would build enduringly must pay heed above all to the little things. If we are faithful in the small things of life, the Bible tells us, automatically we shall become master over greater things.

The cardinal qualities of compassion, fortitude, loyalty to the Ideal, spiritual courage, are all bred of patient practice in the commonplace tasks of each day. So often people complain that they have no time for spiritual pursuits; but it is the will which is lacking, not the time. All life is an open opportunity. It requires no more effort to think of God and His greatness than of our neighbor and his smallness. It is altogether a question of habit. You may say: "How can I think on two levels at the same moment?" The human mind always carries on two collateral lines of thought, —the line of the immediate experience and the line of self-consciousness, with a connecting zig-zag line of comparison between. Now everything which occurs reminds us of ourselves. Whatever we feel or perceive or think on, we refer spontaneously to the little self…its likes and dislikes, its advantage or disadvantage, its knowledge or ignorance. When we begin the training of our attention, our thought processes still remain dual, but consciousness of God takes the place of consciousness of self. All things are referred to the Ideal instead of the ego. Only when we cultivate this new habit are we able to provide a solid foundation for our character.

Ordinarily we associate character with morality, with struggle in the name of virtue. But a character which does not extend its reach beyond the ethical almost invariably is angular, harsh and unyielding. It is lacking in all the subtler grace and loveliness which should adorn the superior life. Probably nothing has done more to discredit virtue than the stern, uncompromising, puritanical practice of it by those who make ethical achievement the final goal.

I would not minimize the essential value of morality in human evolution. It is as indispensable to spiritual development as technique is to music. The exercise of choice and volition which it sets for us, do much to increase the pliability and vigor of the inner body and prepare it for the soul's use. But ethics alone cannot offer a firm basis for character because it deals wholly with the external, and all external things are shifting. The fundamental spiritual truths are the same the world over, but ethical laws vary from nation to nation and culture to culture. We are constantly readjusting our moral standards as our outlook on life broadens.

True character building is an interior process. Nothing we are at the present moment is the result of any superimposition from the outside. External conditions and surroundings have furnished merely the proper occasions for this unfolding of our essential being. We have grown as the branch does, from within our own root and stem. In every living creature perfection exists, out of sight perhaps, yet there none the less; and because perfection is stronger than imperfection, because the Infinite is stronger than the finite, that mightier principle of life prods us on and on, but we hold back. To this holding back are due all our aches and pains and miseries.

The growth of character is organic. Our part in the work is to hold our thought resolutely on higher levels. "I shall lift mine eyes unto the hills from whence cometh my help." Character draws its sustenance from the heights always. When we consecrate ourselves whole-heartedly to a noble ideal through contact with it, the deeper forces of our nature are set in motion and within us rises from day to day a new temple for the living God. We may not know it, but others see it and the world is richer for it.

We cannot escape perfection. It presses upon us with greater insistence and force than the atmosphere on our body. It is the law of our being which must attain fulfillment. Everything that happens to us, happens to this end; everything is made to serve it, even our rebellions and the barriers we set up. Nature converts all experience into chisel strokes to shape and fashion us. No opportunity is lost, no effort is wasted or overlooked. There is, therefore, little cause for anxiety as to our ultimate state, or for grief over our present one. This is the true significance of that reassuring promise given at the close of the Bhagavad Gita: "I will free thee from all imperfection. Grieve not."

It must not be imagined from this that perfection is superimposed from without, like a pasted picture. It is the fruit of the cooperation of the God within and the God without — two manifestations of one Supreme Power. The ground on which these two expressions of Divinity meet to accomplish their work is the character. The innermost essence of our being does not evolve. It is ever unchanged and unchanging. It exists in eternity, finds expression in time, yet never reverts from its eternal estate. It is like the geometric point at the center of a circle, which does not turn or shift, however many the circumferences (wide and narrow) drawn around it. This inalterable center of being is the Soul.

What is the relation of character to the Soul? Character is the interpreter of the Soul, the medium through which it contacts the outer world. Its nature is a composite one, made up of the perceptive faculties, the mind, the intellect, the moral sense, and the ego or sense of "I-ness." That which holds these component parts together as one united whole is memory. We are a continuous personality only because we remember. Memory and its correlate, habit, are the stone and timber of the structure of character. They have built into it all that is there. We need no recording angel in a geographic heaven to keep account of our thoughts and deeds. They are written large in our character. It holds a complete record of our life-habit of thinking and doing.

This record is more subjective than objective. The action of the world upon us leaves but faint trace; it is our reaction against the world's action which cuts the deep grooves in our memory. The more violent the reaction, the deeper the groove. That is why it is so difficult to forget an attack of anger or a feeling of hatred. If we would have noble characters, we must fill our memory with deeply graven records of generous, heroic impulses. We must write it full of exalted reactions which proclaim us superior to dishonor and insult, superior to failure and defeat, superior to loss and pain. We must be bigger than ourselves and transcend even our character.

We should not be discouraged if this habit of larger vision does not come to us at once. We must even bear in mind that as human beings we are unfinished products — rough-hewn statues awaiting the refining chisel of the Master Sculptor. Objects in the making do not always please. The half-cut diamond tells little of the polished gem. Like all else in creation, we are in process of becoming. We must watch our unfoldment with compassionate interest, therefore, and not apply to ourselves the measure of the complete product until the work is done. In art we judge only after the last touch has rounded out the marble, or the last brush-stroke has added color to the canvas. Why should we adopt a different method in judging living beings? When we take this attitude of mind, we learn to be more lenient and patient toward ourselves and towards others.

It becomes evident, then, that development of character without unfoldment of Soul-consciousness is like building without a foundation — we shall have a house on soft sand that will go down in the first driving storm. Character-building must be linked at every step with spiritual training if we are to have an enduring structure. We must be steadfast, heroic, strong; but strong and steadfast "in the Lord and in the knowledge of His might." We must not rest our strength on our changeable human nature. We must stand firm on principle or Truth, and both of these dwell in the Soul realm.

Any education that does not include spiritual development defeats its own end. Meditation, study of holy books, the practice of inwardness, should form as vital a part of education as learning to read and write and count. Soul-training must begin in the primary school and continue without interruption through all grades to the end of life. It is the one department of schooling in which no recesses or vacations may be granted. This may seem to put a heavy weight of responsibility upon us, but the weight lifts when we remember that it is the Soul that accomplishes the task, not we. It will reveal itself more and more vividly and flood the whole character with radiance, if we let it work unhindered.

Balance in Life

Balance is a fundamental requirement of nature. Root must be commensurate with branch, hollow must equal wave, heat and cold, light and darkness, pleasure and pain, must measure alike. If one side of the scale dips, something must happen to bring the needle back to the center. The universe will not allow its equilibrium to be destroyed. It demands balance of us. Our individual life forms an inseparable part of the Whole and must be lived for the welfare of the Whole. If our balance is disturbed, it will affect the Whole.

Our part in safeguarding the cosmic equilibrium should not be a purely passive one. That we cease to disturb it is not enough, we should actively protect it. The nobility of our life should offset that which is ignoble in the world. We should strive by our daily living to counter balance the evils of society, — greed, ambition, selfish competition, injustice, persecution and crime. We can do this only by the practice of self-denial, generosity, love and justice. We must cultivate a willingness to share and make room for others. Principle must count with us more than self-interest; and the good of the Whole, before our personal advantage.

Cheerfulness

The strong person is habitually cheerful. Despondency is like a dry rot which eats away the supporting beams of our character. All the fears and failures which induce dejection, taken together, could not do us so much harm as dejection itself. Swami Vivekananda declared despondency to be the most insidious enemy of the spiritual life. We would not willingly breathe poisonous vapors into our lungs, why should we any more lightly give room in our mind to the poison of despondent thought? Melancholy works slowly and heavily, hence it is not so difficult to combat as the hotter passions. When we feel it beginning to press down on us, we should meet it promptly. So far as possible we should keep actively occupied, preferably in manual labor, to stimulate our physical and moral circulation. Then, remembering that attention is the level by which we regulate the mind, we should fix our attention on some triumphant example of bigness and buoyant heroism and hold it there, until the constructive influence of the example catches us on its current and sweeps us out of stagnant waters into the free-flowing midstream again.

Conscience

There is something in our consciousness that acts like a high place in the road — it gives us a jolt every time we pass over it. It prods us to action and again it holds us back. It troubles our peace and disturbs our sleep, yet it brings great peace and induces sound sleep. The world calls it conscience; but that is only lending it a name; it does not tell us what it is. What is it? It cannot be the body because it disciplines the body; it is not the mind because it regulates the mind; nor can it be the moral sense since it governs all ethical action. It cannot be the ego for it is at perpetual war with ego; and it is not the character because it stabilizes character and provides for it a firm base. What is it then?

Conscience is as much of our higher or Soul-nature as we have made acquaintance with. Every human being possesses a higher nature, every human being has a conscience. Conscience cannot be killed or silenced. We cannot ignore or destroy the foundation of our being, our Soul. It is indestructible and will not be suppressed. Its voice may sound faint and far, but ever it calls.

All human beings are dual…we manifest in two spheres of activity, known commonly as lower and higher nature. Sometimes we seek expression in one, sometimes in the other; and this accounts for the inconsistencies and contradictions evident in our actions. It is not that we deny our previous standpoint. It is merely that we have moved to the other plane and our character is not sufficiently coordinated to join the two into a consistent harmony. This does not apply to the petty inconsistencies due wholly to whim and capricious self-will, but to those larger inconsistencies.

In speaking of higher and lower nature, we must guard against attaching a locational or an ethical significance to the terms. Lower does not necessarily mean immoral. There are those who lead the noblest, the most admirable lives, yet their consciousness has not awakened on the spiritual plane. They are wholly unaware of the great realm of Spirit, and its language sounds to them visionary and impractical. Their higher nature is unexplored, except as they touch it through the conscience. Virtue, not vision, is their aim. People of this type can be rigid and unbending. They listen obediently to conscience, but they interpret its dictates according to preconceived ideas of a self-made ethical code. Conscience governs their coming and going, but it makes them more puritan than saint. This is the natural outcome of a purely ethical standard. One feels in it a lack of the softening touch of Spirit.

The lower nature does not carry all the way. It is the lesser part of a human being. It includes the physical body, the senses, the mind, the intellect, the moral sense, and the sense of me and mine or the ego. It is the portion of us that grows, evolves, changes, is born and dies; whereas the higher or Soul-nature is birthless, deathless, unchanging. The lower nature is heterogeneous, multiple, frequently at war with itself. The higher nature is homogeneous and one only, hence ever peaceful.

Architecturally, we can picture the lower nature as the base and the higher nature as the crown; in reality, however, the higher nature is both base and crown. It is that on which our being rests, its foundation and support. It is also the highest point toward which all our effort tends. The lower nature is the channel of expression through which the higher nature reaches the outer world. That which connects them is the conscience.

Our spiritual unfoldment takes place spontaneously as conscience expands and discloses more and more of our higher nature. When the higher or Soul-nature is fully manifest, the purpose of all evolution has been attained and conscience, having accomplished its mission, becomes merged in its source. Along the way to this ultimate goal we pass through two stages. In the first stage, conscience is on one side and we are on the other. Everything that happens seems to create an issue between the two. Conscience interferes with our play and interrupts our work; it is an unceasing annoyance and we do our best to eliminate it; but it keeps steadily on with unperturbed persistence, reminding us of the higher laws of our being. Gradually, it breaks down our opposition and wins us. Then we pass to the second stage of our spiritual evolution, in which we are on the side of conscience and our higher nature and are struggling to subdue our lower nature. We long to express that which is lofty and noble in us, but constantly we are trapped and overcome by old habits and tendencies. This period of our unfoldment requires greater patience with ourselves. We are eager to press forward and escape from the trammels of the little self, but it still entangles us and pulls us back.

We must not be disheartened. We are fighting a winning battle. We are on the side that cannot fail to gain the victory. Nothing can withstand the power of Spirit. If we are brave and fervent and hold fast, all the odds are with us. Conscience and character allied with Spirit are sure to conquer.

Courage and Endurance

God does not shield us from the battle. He fights it with us. He wishes us to be heroic, not faint-hearted and weak; and we become heroic by battle, not by flight or shielding. If God carried us from the field always, we would soon learn to be cowards. Without struggle we cannot gain endurance and endurance is the measure of our strength. It is also the measure of our growth. In gymnastic exercises, those we do without fatigue merely keep us in condition at the point we have already attained. Increase of strength in muscle and sinew is measured by the stress-interval; that is, by the length of time we can continue after the exercise has become an effort.

The same law holds on the higher planes. What we do naturally and easily in our daily round merely maintains our present level of merit. We grow strong by enduring, and our endurance increases by anticipating our capacity, by striving to extend our endurance. Our will goes forward and draws our lagging character after it. There comes to everyone moments when life grays, day drops into night, and the treasure in our tightly-closed hand falls and shatters. These are the stress-intervals that measure our waxing strength and make for character. If we are patient and endure, the day will brighten and a more precious treasure will be laid in our empty hands.

Brave struggle never fails to strengthen. It gives us power to struggle harder, and with every battle won comes greater endurance. Our struggle, however, if it is to make us stronger, must be constructive. It must not spring from obstinacy or rebellion. Too often we cling stubbornly to the darkness and try to convert it into light; we refuse to come out from under the shadow. We fight against our life instead of with it; we battle with outer circumstance instead of with ourselves. We wish to bend conditions to our will, when we should adjust ourselves to them. We forget that the author of this drama of life is the Supreme Power, origin of all things. Our task is not to write the play, but to act our part in it as nobly and impressively as we can.

The only struggle that is productive of lasting strength is inward struggle. We cannot change the world, we cannot change others, we cannot change nature. The only thing we can change is ourselves. We may try to force the Universe to accept our plan, but it continues on its course unmoved, fulfilling the law of its being. We may imagine that we can modify the character of others, but in the end we find that each one of us must work out our own salvation. Trees, plants, and animals seem to respond more readily to our altering touch, but neglect them for a season and they revert. There is a deep inner law operating in every living and growing thing which influences and directs its development and determines its relation with the cosmos. No one can interfere permanently with it or alter its course. We can only cooperate with it. When we do this, we throw ourselves into harmony with humankind and with nature and there is no waste of strength through conflict or adjustment.

It is upon this hidden center of cosmic strength that our power of endurance rests. Our current store of energy supplies our habitual activities, but our endurance depends wholly upon the amount of our reserve. When we break under stress, it is not because we lack endurance, but because we have too small a reserve. It is because our daily life is so poorly organized that it leaves no overflow of energy, and our reserve is built up entirely by conservation of this overflow.

When we fail to harbor our forces, we are foreordained to defeat. At present we spill our energy in countless ways, by needless talking, by making unnecessary motions when we work, by giving way to emotional excitement, by overcrowding our day with engagements and duties. We should leave spaces in our life for living and not fill it with mere doing. We should exercise ourselves in silence, in serenity, in moderation. We should make our daily routine a preparation for the hour of test. We should strive to live in rhythm with our environment by meeting its conditions with unresisting cheerfulness.

There is no more effective way of conserving our energy and gathering a strong reserve than through the practice of non-resistance. In calm non-resistance lies our greatest strength. The person who resists and battles with life is broken as inevitably as the unbending tree is broken by the storm. Every act of resistance represents enormous wear and tear and loss of force. Instead of warring against our existence as it is, if we will ally ourselves with it, we shall transform our character and our environment and increase our endurance tenfold.

Development of the Will

The self-conscious or human plane is the plane of duality. We always see two—the self and the not-self. These two ever-present factors create a continuous division in our mental outlook. As human beings we are confronted at each moment by a relentless act of choice. An event occurs calling for a decision. At once two or more lines of action present themselves for our consideration. We compare and reason, weigh and measure, then weigh and measure again, exhausting all our energy in a perplexing, see-sawing calculation, until at last when we come to a decision, no force remains for the final act of volition and we fall short because our whole store of vital energy has gone into the preliminary process.

The root of this indecision and abortive action, however, lies less in the diversity confronting us on the outside, than in the play of duality within, born of a twofold standard of measurement. We cannot be wholly selfish, nor yet wholly unselfish. We consider the question at issue, first from the material angle of advantage, then from the moral angle of virtue. At one moment we give ear to the loud voice of public opinion; at the next we listen to the still small voice of conscience. An impulse rises and drives us in one direction; then suddenly a half-formed, spectral ideal stands in our way and warns us back. As we thus consider and vacillate, the possible benefits and disadvantages of either course of action multiply in our mind, until we find ourselves turning dizzily in a whirl of indecision regarding perhaps the smallest trifle, which should have been settled and dismissed from our thought an instant after its inception.

The first step towards correcting this weakness is to unify our standard and establish a single point of appeal. When we have done this, we shall soon find it easy to focus our energies and clearly defined acts of volition will result. Desire is the most potent factor in accomplishing this. Desire, indeed, lies at the very root of will. "As is a man's desire, so is his will," it is said in the Brihadaranyaka Upanishad. Whenever we have a dominating desire or purpose, that focuses the vital energy and generates a strong driving-power; but only as this becomes continuous, does the will develop.

Impulsive people are those who are swayed by changing desires and focus their energy in puffs. As a result they move fitfully, like a sailing-craft before a squally wind. But this kind of will accomplishes little, because it invariably sinks into periods of inertia. When, however, the desire is steadfast, it becomes an impelling force which commands nature and circumstance. We see it in the bodies of athletes, who train daily with their whole ambition fixed on gaining physical agility and strength; or in musicians, who practice tirelessly to develop their technique: both focus the life-force to such good purpose that sometimes the most discouraging physical disabilities are overcome. Whenever the energy is focused and carried forward to a fixed point, we have a manifestation of will.

Those who would increase their will power must set for themselves some specific exercises of this nature. They are as essential as the practice of technique in music. At no time perhaps in the ordinary routine is the will weaker than at the hour of getting up in the morning. Here then is the moment to begin our volitional practice. We should set a time for rising and hold to it resolutely, whatever may be the arguments of mind and body against it. Often we imagine that a sense of exhaustion indicates the need of more sleep. Coddling at such moments is the worst possible thing for us. The person who says to us: "You will feel much better if you get up," is the truer friend.

The daily religious practices, our meditation and sacred study, may also become valuable exercises of will if we perform them with unfailing regularity, without regard to our passing feeling. Laxness is a serious obstacle to spiritual growth. Only those who pull beyond the stress-point gain in strength. Those who let go and take hold according to their mood or circumstance advance little. A new habit can never be formed so long as we yield to the old tendency whenever it asserts itself aggressively. Resisting it now and then will not efface it; our effort must be consecutive and diligent.

In reality there is no act of life which cannot be converted into a volitional practice. Being prompt in meeting appointments; keeping strictly to our word even in the most trifling matters; completing what we begin; resolutely following out a course of action when once it has been decided upon; never procrastinating; cultivating economy of motion in working; precision and simplicity of expression in talking—all these may seem commonplace and even childish practices, but they serve as excellent five-finger exercises for the will; and if we make use of them, we shall see how rapidly we shall gain in resolution and vigor.

It is not enough, however, to learn to focus our life-force; we must also provide against its loss. Those who are striving to develop their will should be constantly watchful not to scatter or waste their energy; otherwise there will be none left to focus. We do this primarily by the gradual elimination of all non-essential elements from our life. At present the spaces between the inevitable occupations of our day are filled full of nonvital concerns and activities, which unnecessarily tax our vital force and will-power. As soon as we begin to remove these, we shall experience a fresh accession of strength and quietude.

In human life little gains and losses, pleasures and pains, victories and defeats, are the mere by-products of existence; yet to them is devoted practically all our energy, while the real product, understanding or knowledge, receives only our chance attention. Christ told us that we must know the Truth, because only the Truth would make us free. It is towards this above everything, then, that our volitional power should be directed; not for our own sake alone, but for the sake of the world.

When we learn to make this ultimate knowledge the ruling purpose of all our activity, our vital energy will become permanently centralized; and there will be no further need for the laborious efforts of choice and volition which now drag upon us and create so many wearisome struggles. The moment that our eye grows single, our being will be full of light; our mental processes will be instantaneous and will terminate automatically in unfaltering acts of will. This is why all the illumined souls who have come to earth to teach humankind have brought the same message,—"Not my will, but Thine." Apart from the Eternal Will, the individual will has no motive power. We may roll a wheel by little pushes of the hand, but it has neither force nor balance; attach it to a locomotive and its strength and steadiness become tremendous. Yet as a wheel its character and individual usefulness have not been destroyed.

Our will won't be annihilated through surrender; it will merely take its proper place in the scheme of things and share in the power of the Whole. Wherever we see the Divine Will in free action, we are awed by the unfailing wisdom and power and glory manifest through It. When we learn to cast aside our small personal measure of things and move in line with the great cosmic forces, obedient to the cosmic plan, we shall act with the force of the universe behind us, confident and unafraid because we shall know ourselves to be "strong in the Lord and in the knowledge of His might."

Forgetting

Memory strikes its roots down into the very depths of our being. Without memory we would have no continuity of life. Each sleep would be a death; each waking, a new birth. Our days would pass in blankness of unremembered hours. We would be always ending, always beginning. There would not be individuality, no personality associated with us. Each one of us would be a disjointed succession of separate, unrelated beings, with nothing to bind us into a single unit of consciousness. Being unable to remember who we were or who we are, we would have no self-identity.

Without memory we cannot know our fellow-beings, we cannot know the universe, we cannot know ourselves. All knowledge on the plane of created things is gained by comparison, by relating one object to another. One is longer or shorter, higher or lower, lighter or darker than the other; but if we cannot hold these measurements or qualities in our mind longer than for the flash of the instant during which they are observed, how can we compare the objects possessing them?

Having no power of retention, we are unable to accumulate experience and therefore we cannot acquire either knowledge or wisdom; for knowledge is assimilated experience and wisdom is digested knowledge. Neither can we grow. If we are unable to remember, it will not be possible for us to learn the lessons of our failures and victories, of our struggles and strivings, and upon these our growth depends. We shall have no moral standards, no faith, no endurance, no heroism, no loving kindness; for all these rest upon remembered experience.

Relations with our fellow-beings become impossible also when we have no memory. If we cannot recognize them from moment to moment as the same persons, how can we have any intelligent contact with them? They would be new acquaintances to us each time we met them. Neither could we have any continuous occupation — we would never know what we were doing. We could make no plans, no engagements and give no parties, for invitation, plan and appointment would be forgotten as soon as spoken.

Without the power to remember, our life would be completely isolated and lacking in usefulness. Should we not cherish our memory then as a sacred gift, to be held pure and inviolate — a sanctuary of lofty thought, where we go, before all else, to remember God and to forget ourselves?

Our usual habit is to remember first and to forget afterward. We write a record on the memory, then we try to erase it. The wise reverse the order. They make forgetting a preventive rather than a corrective measure. They challenge every impression that first gains access to the consciousness; and if it is trivial, non-essential, harmful or disturbing, they bar its entrance to the memory by substituting a new impression. They forget it by blotting it out. A text from scripture, the thought of a noble character, even the repetition of a potent word, will serve to do this. We must act quickly, however, to stop the invading impression before it registers. Once imprinted on the memory it is difficult to efface.

Remembering is the product of repeated thought. The more we dwell on an experience, the more firmly will it be lodged in the memory; and the more probable is it that it will repeat itself. Thinking constantly of failures and losses prepares the way for further losses and failures. Harboring resentment breeds fresh quarrel. Brooding darkens the mind and poisons the entire system. If we would lead wholesome, uplifted lives, we must forget our misfortunes and injuries, remember our benefits, and fill our memory with that only which is elevating and constructive.

It is not possible to do this unless at every moment we stand guard over our thoughts and above all over our emotions. A strong emotion must be controlled in the incipient stage. Once released, it can be neither curbed nor forgotten. Anger, hatred, antagonism, resentment, cut deep grooves in the memory, creating a picture which lingers long after the storm has passed. It may persist for years even and give rise to bitter hostility. We cannot afford to store such destructive impressions in our mind. No affront or injury will justify it.

Very few make wise use of the memory. It is more misused than used. We misuse it by filling it with trivialities, passing incidents, casual conversations, foolish gossip; facts and occurrences which should be forgotten before they are fixed in the thought by repetition. We misuse the memory again when we read or watch media indiscriminately. Sensational events act like a drug or an intoxicant and create haunting pictures in the memory which rise to distract us when we try to hold the mind on some serious subject.

Living in the past is another wrong use of memory. To dwell in ourselves as we were in childhood and youth fosters vanity, egotism, self-importance, and a tendency to exaggeration. The past gains glamor as it recedes; and in telling of it, we build fairy tales out of the most commonplace happenings. In the same way, we misuse our memory to nurse and prolong our griefs, believing it a disloyalty to forget them. Those who live in harmony with nature do not cling to their sorrows. When they are struck, they strive to heal the wound.

Character rests on memory like a superstructure on its foundation. A thought held persistently in memory grows into a tendency; this tendency, frequently repeated, becomes a habit; and out of our habits, mental, moral and physical, our character is built. If we would alter our character, we must go back to the initial thought and change that. We cannot have a superior character with an ill-stored memory, full of petty, inconsequential details. We must empty it of all sordid, belittling impressions and fill it with ennobling thoughts. Then only may we hope to be noble and uplifted in all our impulses and tendencies.

Forgiveness

Forgiveness is an unknown virtue to those of strong character, because they never find anything to forgive. Forgiveness implies a consciousness of injury, but if we were truly generous, we would excuse our neighbor's fault before it has wounded us. We would cover it over as a mother eagerly cloaks her child's wrong-doing. If we are offended, the fault lies in us; we have a sore place in our character which needs to be healed. When we are sound throughout, we take even the sharpest blow with equanimity. A sense of grievance is an unfailing symptom of weakness and egotism. It is we who need to be forgiven, not the one who has hurt us.

Friendship with Life

In all our dealings with the world there seem to be two distinct methods of procedure. One is to regard the obstacles and obstructions in our path as enemies and, when they are conditions caused by people, to fight them and if possible, to conquer them. The other is to regard them as friends and ally ourselves with them.

We often interpret non-resistance as passive endurance. But it is more than that. It is an active alliance through which we annex ourselves to the whole cosmic universe. Those moving toward God do not wish to eliminate any part of God. We wish to know God in every particular manifestation, in every experience.

If we read the lives of the great saints of India we shall find them calling the most hostile influences friends. Once Swami Vivekananda went to have a visit with the great saint Pavhari Baba, but before he was allowed to see him he was kept waiting all day. When he was finally admitted the saint apologized for the delay, but explained that he had been entertaining a friend of the Divine Mother, and had been listening to Her message. Later the Swami learned that the "friend" Pavhari Baba had been closeted with for so many hours was an attack of fever, and the message was the lesson he had been learning by it.

You may say it is a very dangerous doctrine which teaches one to regard fever as a friend. But is it not a friend? If you have a fever doesn't it mean that there is impurity within you which the fever is burning up, and that there is a lesson to learn which perhaps only the fever could teach you? Therefore, instead of tossing in discomfort, full of self-pity and rebellion, would it not be better to go within yourself and try to discover what that lesson is? Would not body and mind both benefit if you were to lie there patiently listening for the Voice of God in your soul to reveal the meaning to you?

The wise do not sit down and weep over every unfortunate experience that comes to them. They turn and face it and listen to it and ask what new gift of wisdom it is bringing them. They feel that it has come to them as a friend, to tide them over some point of weakness, to save them from some wrong or negative state, and so they sit down beside these experiences, as it were, as one would sit by the side of a wise friend and listen to her words of wisdom. When we approach life in this spirit, we are no longer afraid of what it may bring. We no longer fly from it or try to hide from it. Instead, we welcome it and take gratefully whatever it chooses to bestow.

For the most part, however, we resist nearly all the forces of nature. If it is too cold for us, we complain. If it is too hot for us, we complain. If there is too much rain, or if the road is rough, or whatever the discomfort may be, we avoid it and thereby we give it power over us. If, however, we go towards it, we shall find that there is no manifestation in nature that doesn't have its pleasure and beauty. If we relax we will feel the exhilaration of the cold. We will feel even the joy of heat in the very sense of suppleness it gives to the body. We will enjoy the storm if we unite with it as a friend. Every aspect of nature has something to share with us, and gives us something when we hold out our hands in welcome. When we fail to do so we are the losers. This is the way to draw near to God. We imagine that to draw near Him means drawing away from everything else, shutting ourselves off on every side. But those who have once realized union with God know that God will speak to them in the most unexpected places, through the most unusual channels. God is not in any one special locality, from which everything else is fenced off and excluded. He is everywhere, in everything. Not only is He in everything, but He is seeking to make Himself felt everywhere. He is ever longing to have us recognize Him. When we hear that voice in our heart and do not answer it, the worldly joys give us very little pleasure. But if we respond to the divine call, then even the smallest outward happiness fills us with joy because we find God in it.

To see an enemy in anything is to see something that cannot be united with God and ourselves. Let us therefore from this very day set out with one idea — to ally ourselves with the universe and to ally the universe with ourselves. The work of each one of us is first and foremost the integration of our own life and being with the life and being of the Whole.

It is a very good practice to cultivate in our hearts the spirit of friendliness, not to feel that if someone pushes us aside or takes our place, or stands in our way, that they are an enemy; but rather let us begin to feel that they are a friend. Also let us cultivate the same sense of friendliness towards every living being we see and begin to observe its noble traits and its points of contact with human life and feeling. Let us feel a relationship with the sun and the rain, and think of the pleasant things connected with them. The value of life with all its experiences cannot be over-estimated. No one who has this attitude of mind can ever be shut away from God's message. At every moment it is pouring into our hearts, filling them with new life, new light, new joy. If it is not pouring in upon us, it is because we lack the spirit of friendship towards God and His universe.

Let us try from this time on to cultivate it, to accept joyfully whatever comes as a loving messenger. Let us feel that God-unity with all living things, then we cannot fail to see the God-presence in our spiritual practice. We shall find that as we go about our spiritual tasks we shall be saying to ourselves all the time, "How beautiful life is! How great God is! How wonderful that I can be consciously one with Him and with His universe!"

Generosity

We measure life's benefits by what we receive, rather than by what we give. But giving alone enriches. Our giving, however, must not be from the residue of our resources and our interest. It must be fresh and fragrant and free from all grudging and calculation.

There is no store so scant that it cannot be drawn upon, no human beings so poor they may refuse to give. We may not have outward wealth, but we can share ourselves, our compassion, our good will, our appreciation, our forbearance, our cheerfulness.

It is not lack of resources that stops our more generous impulses; it is fear, fear that we shall not have enough left to meet our own needs and satisfy our own ambitions and desires. Out of this fear grows the most insidious foe of giving, — greed. Whenever we enter into competition with the cosmic will and seek to wrest from it more than belongs to us in the universal order, we are guilty of greed. Whenever we desire to have more than others — more honor, more praise, more importance, greater material advantages — if we are envious or jealous or discontented, we are guilty of greed. The seed of greed lies hidden in every desire and if we allow it to germinate, it will destroy our sense of proportion and stifle all our finer feelings.

The great cosmic Power is always seeking new avenues through which to pour Its benefits and blessings. The effort to keep blocks the channels and shrinks to a minimum the capacity to receive. Hoarding is always destructive. If we close up a room and leave no ventilation, the air will grow stale and poison us. If we put our food under lock and key and refuse to share it, it will decay and sicken us. If we hide away our material possessions, we impede the free circulation of cosmic resources and impoverish the whole human family, ourselves with it. The one who hoards is the most poverty-stricken among us. Circulation is the condition of life on all planes. The cosmos exacts free interchange and intermingling of its resources. We are not meant to be insulated units with a little store of our own, kept under lock and key and doled out at our convenience. We are chosen to be purveyors of God's bounty – open channels through which He pours His riches.

The abundance of the universe lies at our hand. Why should we close off a portion of it and limit our giving to that small supply? As much as we give, so much shall we receive.

Humility and Gentleness

In the Sermon on the Mount it is said: "Blessed are the meek for they shall inherit the earth." From the beginning of time we have striven to inherit the earth, but very few have tried the method of humility. Those who have stand as towering figures in the human world. Buddha, Jesus, St. Francis, Sri Ramakrishna, — in power and influence, what builder of empire or conqueror by arms can outrank these mighty ones and others like them! Their followers people the earth; their voices, though silent, still sound in every land.

The differences between the two modes of activity, force and gentleness, are fundamental. They operate on totally different planes. Those who resort to aggression to accomplish their ends call into play the grossest, most destructive form of cosmic energy — destructive for aggressor and adversary alike. Nature makes no distinctions. A disturbance in the cosmic universe endangers as much the one who attacks as the one who is on the defensive; and in the ultimate reckoning the victor is as great a loser as the vanquished. Victory and defeat do not count as weights on the cosmic scale. Whatever the outcome, those who live by the sword perish by the sword; and in moral and spiritual values their gains are losses. This is true not merely of warfare, but in all dissension and controversy.

Aggressive action may seem to triumph, but it is only for the moment. Worldly glory fades, worldly gains diminish. In created things there is a ceaseless evaporation which nothing can stop. Slowly but relentlessly they shrink and dissolve. There remains, however, a rich residuum of experience, which finds expression in a new-born gentleness and humility. Truly says Saint Augustine: "There is something in humility which raises the heart upward."

Our humility, however, must spring, not from self-depreciation, but from awe and reverence. It must rest on God's mightiness, not on our littleness. Our gaze must be upward, not downward. The humble ones see the best in others and forget themselves. There can be as much pride in self-condemnation as in self-praise. So long as we think of ourselves, whether to condemn or to commend, we cannot be truly humble. Egotism and humility cannot coexist in the same heart; one neutralizes the other.

The deeper our humility, the more exalted our spirit, and the more fearless. We are fearless because we live in close touch with the "All-Powerful" and thereby have command of a power that can pierce the strongest armor and blunt the sharpest weapon. It is not the power of material force, it is subtler, more baffling. It disarms and checks the blow by awakening a gentler spirit in the one who would deal it. This quick appeal to our higher nature is the safest and surest protection.

Humility and gentleness are twin qualities, they come and go together. Both are essential to spiritual living and to our daily contacts. According to the ancient Chinese classic, the *Tao Te Ching*, they are signs also of true wisdom. "The Sages," it acclaims, "shed a bright light all about them because they have no desire to shine; because they are free from self-assertion they attain superiority; because they do not boast their merit is acknowledged; because they are free from self-satisfaction their work endures; because they are non-contentious, no one in the world is able to contend with them." Proud, self-assertive people are noisy, quarrelsome and egocentric. They resent correction or suggestion and are perpetually at war to defend their rights and extend their possessions. The humble, on the contrary, are little concerned for their rights; their whole thought is to maintain a serene and noble spirit and to be at peace, inwardly with themselves, outwardly with all people.

In a medieval manual of prayer it is written, "My peace (says the Lord) is with the humble and gentle of heart." This peacefulness of the gentle heart is not a superficial fluctuating quality. It rises from the depths where humility also has its birth — humility and faith, not faith in a creed or sect or ritual, but trust in the All-Knowing and All-Powerful. If we do not believe in a power stronger than ourselves we dare not be gentle and we cannot be humble.

Trust lies at the base of all humility, all gentleness and all fearlessness. Our finer nature rests upon it: our noblest impulses spring from it. Without trust our life would have neither foundation nor stability. When our trust in the might and protection of the Divine deepens, our heart grows more humble, our spirit gentler and we no longer strive or wound, rather we seek to heal the wounds of the world and to lessen its strife.

Judge Not

When we judge others, we measure them by our standards, by our habits and ideals, which are wholly unrelated to them. They are the product of themselves and must be judged in relation to themselves alone.

It is true that outer influences play upon us constantly, but they affect us only when they are transmuted into our own being. As food must be assimilated and made a part of our body before it can nourish us, so the outside world must enter and be transformed into ourselves before it can alter our nature. All the changes that take place are interior changes; the outer merely reflects them. They are hidden, unperceived and often unsuspected. It may take months or even years for them to reach the surface and become manifest as new habits or a new outlook. A person of great reserve may never give full expression to them.

With the fundamental factors unknown, what value can our judgment have? We would not try to solve a mathematical problem without accurate data; yet we attack the problem of a character or an achievement with suppositions only as factors for our equations. Motive is the measure of both action and character, and motive is always veiled from us. We have nothing on which to base a judgment except our opinion and opinion is inherently unstable. It does not offer a safe foundation for either praise or blame.

The task of evolving is for every human being an unfinished one. It stretches far back into the past and far forward into the future: one lifetime does not suffice to complete it. How then can we pronounce upon its present accomplishment and call it success or failure? What is failure? What is success? They cannot be defined or classified. They are so interwoven, so interchanging, that it is difficult to differentiate them. What begins as failure, grows often into success; what promises to be a signal success, ends in defeat and sorrow.

Galileo knew the darkness of a dungeon and saw the record of his researches burned on the public square. Copernicus spent his closing years in a small peasant village in his native land of Poland, ostracized, silenced, and solitary. His one book containing all his observations, a book of three thousand pages which he edited and re-wrote completely five times with his own hand, came from the printer and was laid on his bed as he was dying. He would never know how the world received it. Yet viewed through the long perspective of centuries we cannot say that these heroic searches failed; nor can we say that they were successful; for success is too small a term to apply to the greatness which grows in magnitude as the years pass.

As our insight deepens and we become more thoughtful, we judge less and less. Why should we be so eager to express our opinion? "Judge not that ye be not judged. For with what judgment ye judge, ye shall be judged." Judgment breeds judgment. If we speak harshly of another, they will speak harshly of us, for their words are the direct rebound of our own. "Would you have others speak good of you?" Epictetus asks, "Then speak good of them. And when you have learned to speak good of them, try to do good to them; thus you will reap in return their speaking good of you."

The only safe ground on which to meet others is that of compassion, tolerance, and understanding. These silence all controversy and baffle all attack. They awaken loving kindness and friendliness where there might be antagonism. When we sit in judgment, we isolate ourselves, we feel apart from our neighbor and are sensitive to their judgment; but when we lose the habit of judging, no words of criticism or blame have power to wound us. We grow strong and enduring, quietness falls on our spirit and we are at peace.

Non-Resistance

Endurance is one of the chief measures of value in life. But how does nature accomplish it? By non-resistance. The tree bends and sways in the storm; the metal expands and contracts with each variation of temperature; the child lets itself go and survives countless falls.

This law of the natural world is also the law of the moral and spiritual planes. In calm non-resistance lies our greatest strength. For that reason Christ taught, "If someone strikes you on one cheek, turn the other." He would never have advocated a course that stood for weakness or defeat, but He knew that those who can turn their energies towards controlling their own passions instead of expending them in an answering blow will in the end prove master of the situation. As Buddha declares: "If one person conquers in battle a thousand times a thousand individuals and if another conquers himself, that one is the greatest of conquerors. Not even a god could change into defeat the victory of those who have vanquished themselves and always live under restraint."

The practice of non-resistance means conservation of energy, accumulation of power, clear vision, wise and carefully directed action, all the qualities, in fact, which make for strength. The person who habitually resists and battles is rent and broken as inevitably as is the metal which resists the rise and fall of atmospheric pressure.

The great majority, however, fear that if they begin to practice non-resistance they will be over-ridden in the struggle of life. True non-resistance does not mean cowardice or meek inaction, but controlled strength; the non-resistance we see in nature, which consists in a combination of elasticity and firmness — an ability to be pliable on the surface, but fixed at the root. It means a willingness to yield in the nonessentials, to hold fast in the essentials; to admit great latitude in variety of expression, while maintaining uncompromising loyalty to the Truth expressed; above all, a willingness to play fair, to care more for right than for our own rights, to be deliberate, thoughtful and generous.

The habit of non-resistance, however, cannot be acquired all at once. It must be developed gradually by regular practice, a practice based on definite method as truly as the practice of painting or music. We must reduce our task to its component parts and deal separately with each part. What is it that arouses our resistance and produces so much friction? The world, of course, in some form. Upon what does this created world rest? Upon time, space and causation. Manifestation necessitates a beginning in time, form means outline in space, and every effect pre-supposes a cause. Therefore our ceaseless struggles are in reality against these fundamental elements of creation, — time, space and causation.

At this moment every one of us is resisting time. That is why we are so hurried, so worn and anxious. There is scarcely anyone who does not work with one hand and with the other hold back the flying minutes, scarcely one who does not try to cheat the clock and double the length of each hour. We call upon the sun to stand still in the heavens while we pile up engagement on engagement, task on task, imagining that we are more useful and important if we do twenty things in a day breathlessly, even possibly imperfectly, than if we did only ten calmly and well. We must learn to stop this mad onrush. Let us ask of each hour no more than it can justly give us. Instead of trying to stretch its measure, let us rather reduce the number of our daily occupations. Having many interests is not a sign of greatness, multiplying duties is not a proof of spirituality. The spiritual life is the life of doing a few things thoughtfully and humbly in the sight of God. Should we lay a little less emphasis on our outer obligations and begin to fulfill a few of those long-neglected inner duties to our soul and God, we should see how quickly our daily routine would grow simple and free from feverish haste.

All these multifarious demands upon us are self-created. It is we ourselves who have woven this tangled web of obligations by our ever-changing desires and ambitions, or by our misunderstanding of what is of true benefit to humankind. We are so stressed and hurried, not because there is not time enough, but because we have forgotten that we are living in eternity. We should order our life more by routine, less by time; and we should make that routine as the engineer lays a track — with spaces between the rails to allow for expansion. How then shall we accomplish all that is to be done? We shall accomplish infinitely more, because our whole mind will belong to the one task in hand. Now we have broken ourselves into a hundred pieces and have only one small piece for the immediate duty. Our thought is busy with what has been crowded out of the hours that lie behind us and with all that must be crowded into the hours before us. We are trying to calculate and remember a multitude of things; preparing for another task while doing this one, because there is no hope of a quiet space between. If, on the contrary, we would learn to gather up the whole of ourselves into the present moment and, looking away from our clocks, say: "In all the world at this instant I have only this one thing to do, and my entire energy and interest shall go into it," we should have such power that our work would be accomplished, not only in half the time, but with an efficiency that would amaze us. When a period of extreme pressure arises, let us hold fast to the thought of eternity and remember that we live and move in That. Soon our breathlessness will leave us and we shall regain our quiet poise.

In our efforts to focus all our energy on each succeeding moment, however, we must guard against the error of magnifying its importance. Too often we lose our sense of proportion and let the passing experience of joy or sorrow loom so large that it blocks our higher vision. We see it as a finality, a something that stretches on in endless perspective. But to the Soul, in whose calendar "a thousand years are as a day," it is scarcely more than a flash. We measure it up so large because we are looking at the little things of life. Let us begin to fix our gaze on bigger things, — on this vast universe of revolving solar systems, in which this earth counts merely as a geometric point without length, breadth or magnitude; on the eons and cycles and centuries that have rolled on in the slow work of evolution; on the countless lives and forms through which the Soul has passed in its journey back to God; let us turn our eyes on these vaster things and the event of today will shrink to its proper proportion.

Next we must withdraw from this feverish battle to conquer space. To get there faster has become the ruling ambition of the modern mind. Everyday the race between miles and minutes is growing hotter, and in the contest, all the dignity, the grace and beauty of life are being sacrificed. Our homes have become mere bases of supply, places where we recharge our batteries and start on again. The family comes together as friends meet at an airport, each hurrying to catch their plane. The mania for skimming over the earth's surface has taught us to move over the surface of our minds, to do all things superficially. The habit of profound thought is gone. We seek escape from ourselves in change and motion. We run away from our problems. When grief or misfortune overtakes us, we fly to another continent to forget it; a second loss sends us adrift again. Would we but turn our steps to our own home, go into our place of sanctuary, close the door and try to be still, we would find a permanent solace for all our pain and unrest. Sometimes for this reason an illness proves a blessing to us, because it keeps us at home and allows us to become acquainted with ourselves. It enables us for a season to forget time and space to ponder on eternity and infinity.

Only those who have cultivated a taste for solitude and quiet contemplation, who have learned the joy of those far inner journeys to the secret places of the Most High, can stand unmoved amid the shifting fortunes of this outer world. The rest of us beat ourselves to weariness against the stern accomplishment of the law; for all our discontent, our suffering and disappointment mean nothing less than blind resistance to the consequences of causation. We demand of destiny results we have not earned; we refuse to accept the consequences of our own actions; we are envious and rebellious if we reap tares and our neighbor wheat, forgetting that the harvest is the natural fruit of the sowing. We base our happiness on that which dies, and cry out in anguish when death snatches it. We allow ourselves to be irritable and moody, critical and self-absorbed, then resent the indifference and selfishness of others. We are unwilling to admit that all these conditions are only the reactions of our own actions. If, on the contrary, instead of warring against this inevitable law, we should ally ourselves with it, we could in a short time transform our character and environment and gain just the results we covet. Are we eager for happier surroundings, for greater talent, for conditions more favorable to our aspirations? We have only to set to work and earn them.

Nothing can keep from us that which we have made our own by earnest effort, as nothing can give us what is not justly ours. Law and order govern the course of every atom in the universe. Creation is like a great machine in which each part has its special place and function, the whole impelled by one central force. When we try to move according to our individual will without regard to the universal law, we strain and wrench the mechanism and cause disaster to ourselves and others. Yet nature is so elastic that up to a certain point we are allowed our wayward course. If, however, we persist beyond that, then we are violently drawn back into our proper place and the readjustment manifests itself by some great upheaval in our outer life. Our own nature, that which we have made ourselves, determines just where we belong and only there can we live in harmony with the cosmic whole. Therefore "Better one's own duty, though devoid of merit," the Bhagavad Gita tells us, "than the duty of another, well performed. Better is death in following one's own duty; the duty of another is full of danger." If today, however, our place or duty is distasteful to us, tomorrow, by altering our nature, we can deserve another and more congenial one.

This practice of non-attachment, — of keeping our values true and giving way always to the larger point of view — will lead us gradually to that supreme form of non-resistance, surrender to God. The Divine is pressing on us from all sides. Through the ages It has sought to make Its presence felt by impelling us to ever higher grades of manifested life. But we are resisting that upward impulse, too jealous of our human estate, too fearful for our human duties and relations to yield ourselves up to the greater on-pushing Power. We may believe that we long for Truth or God, but what we are gives the measure of our desire; for at this moment we possess actually as much of God as we really want, just as we have in our lungs the amount of air we care to breathe. He is within us and all about us, waiting to give Himself in fullness to us. It is because we are resisting Him, warring against His will and love and wisdom, that we are not God-conscious today. Nor can we hope to gain the vision or attain to peace so long as we persist in our unreasoning battle. The lesser can never swallow up the greater, the finite can never overcome the infinite, the ego can never push out God. Therefore so long as we hold to our individual will, two principles will continue to struggle for dominion within us. Let us, however, cease our childish rebellion and, opening wide the door of our heart to the universal Lord, bid Him enter there as ruler; in an instant a flood of Divine consciousness will flow in and, sweeping away all our small human limitations, will make us at one with the infinite and eternal cause of all things.

Pain

Physical ailments are not a misfortune. They are often remedies—remedies for deeper sickness of mind or heart or character. They cure by chastening.

They make us brave, strong and enduring. Pain allied with spirit heals and exalts. It makes heroes of us.

The secret of happiness does not lie in absence of suffering, nor is it to be found in outer conditions. It is hidden in the depth of our own being. Happiness is the light we throw upon the world, not that which the world throws upon us. We see the universe by no other light than our own. It grows dark or bright to us according to the radiance of our Soul. The kingdom of joy is within, nowhere else. We make it or unmake it in our heart; the world merely registers it.

Those who bear the tests of life with unresisting spirit are the truly happy ones. Fretfulness, complaining, rebellion, darken the mind and double the suffering. Thomas à Kempis tells us: "If you bear your cross cheerfully it will bear you…if you bear it unwillingly, you make for yourself a load and burden yourself the more… Stand firmly and with perseverance. Be long-suffering and a person of courage." No one wishes to be a coward; rather let us be strong and brave-hearted. Let us not allow ourselves to be daunted, but let us do all things to the profit of our Soul.

Even the long hours of loneliness which accompany illness, invalidism and sorrow, may be made productive of benefit and blessing. Solitude is a great opportunity. In aloneness we make acquaintance with ourselves and learn to know our deeper nature. We uncover mysteries which otherwise would remain covered.

The thought world is our real world. It is there that our life centers. Our creative faculties, our imagination, our volitional forces, our moods, all have their origin in mind; and these determine the atmosphere and color of our day. Why then place such stress on the body and allow it to be the determining factor in our life? Why account it the whole of our being?

All avenues of activity are not closed when the body is forced to be inactive. Is it helpless? We can still think, pray, meditate and commune with the Great Ones. Is it inert? Our mind will carry us more swiftly than our feet wherever we desire to go. Is it restless and in discomfort? Surrender, and quietness will come.

Restlessness is the sign of rebellion, and unwillingness to accept life as it is. We gain nothing by it. We merely miss the benefit of an experience that otherwise would make for our strengthening. If we would surrender to things as they are, at once we would find ease of body and calmness of spirit.

Helen Keller gave proof of this in these words: "Observers in the full enjoyment of their bodily senses pity me, but it is because they do not see the golden chamber of my life where I dwell delighted; for, dark as my path may seem to them, I carry a magic light in my heart."

Suffering borne with courage and surrender makes us larger. It widens the vision, deepens the compassion, clarifies the understanding. It refines and consecrates. It transfuses the life with new power. Could Beethoven have reached the heights of tonal beauty that he did, had he not had those long torturing years of struggle with growing deafness? Would St. Francis of Assisi have had the same irresistible appeal as he tramped the highways of Italy, calling people to God, had he not gone with blinding eyes and faltering feet? Those who heard him knew nothing of the blindness, they felt only the power of his words. It was the touch of pain that ripened the genius of both saint and musician.

Bodily disabilities need not be an obstacle to creative effort. On the contrary there is a sacramental quality in the work of those who have striven with suffering as they worked. Nature seems to demand the tribute from the gifted ones. It is difficult to lay the hand on a single life of great accomplishment that has not passed through the fires of pain. Teresa of Avila, mighty reformer and inspired saint, struggled throughout her life with a heart condition. Charles Darwin for many years could work only one hour a day.

Endurance is a quality of heroes. There must be something of the Spartan in us, if we would live our life bravely. "We count them happy that endure," Saint Paul declares. We are part of a vast universe and must take our place in it nobly. A great purpose stands behind our life. To fulfill it we must pass through many kinds of experience, — hardship and ease, joy and sorrow, discipline and indulgence.

If we seek to escape the dark side, we cheat ourselves and become weaklings. When a flower has only sunshine, it bakes and withers. So do we wither in continued ease. If we would be brave warriors we must be steadfast and enduring, and not shrink from the fortunes of the day. The mystic poet, Kabir, says: "The brave never forsake the battle. The one who flies from it is no true fighter."

When we cease to beat against pain and accept her as our companion, we change an enemy into a friend and gain a staunch ally. Though at times she may press hard upon our wounds, she is full of tender yearning to make us perfect. Under her transforming touch the heart grows mellow, the thought deepens, the spirit rouses to new strength. Even death loses its terror and creeps upon us softly — so softly that we are hardly aware of its approach. Only the glory of a sunset tells us it is here.

There is a higher form of heroism with which we must make acquaintance. It does not endure; it transcends. Our mood is not the result of the play of the universe on us. It is shaped by our reaction against it. Pain may be inflicted despite us, but the suffering which arises from it is of our making. Pain is the world's action on us, suffering is our reaction to it. True heroism consists not in bearing the reaction, but in controlling it. We cannot hope to control the universe or curb its play upon us, but we can control our response to it. Everywhere in creation we shall find the same sequence of light and shadow, night and day, following each other in relentless alternation. But in that inner realm of our heart and mind, the realm of thought and feeling, there need be no shadow, no nightfall, for the light which blazes there is shadowless like the sun at noon and it has no setting.

Personality

We judge people by their bearing, their speech, their appearance and manner; or, in other words, by that subtle and undefinable something we call personality. But according to the Greek root, from which the word is derived, personality signifies a mask. To judge people by their personality, therefore, is to judge them by the mask they wear, not by what they are. It is true, that mingling with the personality are signs and proofs of the real person behind the mask; but only those can perceive these who have found reality within themselves.

We live on the surface of our being and know nothing of what lies hidden in its depths. Its origin, its purpose, its powers — of these we are wholly unaware. The larger part of our effort is expended on the outer. We are more concerned for our personality than we are for our character; for the impression we create rather than for what we ought to be. But impressions are impermanent; they fade and betray us. To make them lasting we must be what we would appear to be.

Personality is variable. It sways with mood and circumstance. If the mood be happy, the personality will shine and give a sense of lightness. If the mood darkens, the personality will cloud and grow heavy. This outer variation weakens the whole nature and impedes spiritual progress. The way to the Divine must be straight and undeviating. The Bhagavad Gita declares: "The steady-minded, undeluded knower of the Supreme, well established in the Supreme, neither rejoices on receiving the pleasant nor grieves on receiving the unpleasant. Those who are unattached to external contacts realize the happiness that is within the Higher Self."

Until we transcend the personal we shall be small-minded and a captive to our lower nature. All our struggles and limitations lie within the domain of the personal. To strive to overcome these one by one would mean too long and arduous an effort. The simpler and wiser course is to strike at the cause and eliminate that. We cannot wholly eliminate the personal. It is interwoven with our entire outer being. But we can reduce its importance by substituting an exalted Ideal for it, and referring all our thoughts and actions to that. This will break down the barriers of our little self-made world and allow us to live in the great world. Our outlook will grow vast and all our standards will lift.

To accomplish this we must create a close relation with the Ideal. This is done by meditation — not a rigid concentration of thought on a fixed point, but a gentle communing with something higher than ourselves. In the early morning and at the sunset hour we should go apart and learn to live with the Ideal. What we gain in these silent moments we should carry into all our activities and associations. Thus making the Ideal our constant companion, we grow less and less conscious of the personal.

We need not fear that in subordinating our personality we shall weaken or lose our individuality; on the contrary we shall gain it. Personality and individuality are not synonyms. They are opposites, as light and darkness, pain and pleasure are opposites. One obscures the other. Personality is made up of many elements, individuality of one. The definition of the word proves this. Individuality means undividedness or indivisibility. Only as we gather up our entire being into one do we come into the possession of our individuality. This is the advantage of holding a fixed Ideal. It fuses the many elements of our nature and creates a state of indivisibility or oneness.

On the human plane individuality cannot be attained. So long as we cling to human habits of thought, human ambitions, human prejudices and human weaknesses, we shall remain multiple and variable. It is not that we must cease to be human beings in order to become individuals; but in our consciousness we must rise to a higher plane of expression. Our life must be one of continuous aspiration and upward reaching. The effort must not be spasmodic or fitful. Day and night, in all moods and in all conditions, we must reach upward. And as the river quickens its flow on approaching the ocean, so must we quicken our aspiration as we draw near to the Most High.

In God-union alone is individuality realized in its fullness. Indivisibility is the property of the Infinite One. Only by rising to the highest plane of consciousness may we share in it. When we return from those heights, behold! The personality — forgotten, discarded — is still there, now self-forgotten, shining with the glory of the heights it has touched and radiating a light that will illumine the lives of many who walk in the dark places of the earth.

Poise

The cosmic universe has one supreme concern, — to maintain its equilibrium. This equilibrium is not an abstraction applicable only to stars and planets. It is a concrete responsibility resting upon each one of us. A great French scientist once said that no one could measure the mighty effect on the cosmos produced by the fall of an apple. Who can determine the effect of the rise and fall of our mood upon the worlds swinging through space?

Equilibrium is purely an inner condition. External circumstance and environment are never determinative factors in it. The proof is that in a disaster or any test of balance, one person will meet it unmoved, while another is completely undone. Circumstance and environment are the same for both; but one has, to use Gautama Buddha's words, "a conquest which cannot be conquered, a conquest which nothing in the world can overcome;" while others have not made the conquest of their own inner being and have become victims of themselves.

If we will observe ourselves from day to day, we shall find that our stability varies at different times under the same conditions. When we are in a sensitive mood, a trifle can overthrow us; let our mood change and we are calm in the face even of a heavy calamity. This shows that our self-possession is determined, not by the action of the outside condition on us, but by our inner reaction toward it. If we allow each passing circumstance or experience to stir our mind and create on its surface waves of pleasure and pain, approval or resentment, we can never hope to maintain our poise; but when our thought is properly stabilized, nothing can overwhelm us.

Stability of mind and mood is most easily gained by assuming the attitude of a witness. If we take our place on the heights of spirit and look upon life objectively, instead of subjectively, we shall have a totally different outlook. The small things which annoy us at present will dwindle to nothingness and the big things will appear small. This is the cosmic remedy for disturbed balance. Equilibrium is regained by a readjustment of values and values are adjusted by changing the perspective. A lofty point of view levels and reduces differences. If we look at the valley from a mountain top, trees, bushes, and waving grass all appear of the same size. When we look on life from the loftier standpoint of the whole, important and unimportant seem to us alike and we are able to face success and failure, honor and dishonor, with quietness of mind.

Poise, equanimity, balance cannot be acquired directly, nor can it be possessed as an isolated virtue. It is a bi-product, the spontaneous and inherent expression of certain fundamental qualities. If they are present, we are poised; if they are absent, we lack balance. It is difficult to say which of these qualities is most vital, but three stand out: they are flexibility, fearlessness, and trust.

Flexibility is essential. The rigid person goes down under the lightest blow. If we would maintain poise, whether of body or of mind, we must be pliable and adaptable. Nature does not shape the tree to resist the storm, she shapes it to bend without breaking. If we would hold our footing in life, we must adapt ourselves to every circumstance and condition. Non-resistance is one of the greatest safeguards of poise. To hold to principle and yield willingly in secondary questions is the secret of balance. Resistance creates turbulence invariably, but when under attack we can bend without breaking, we shall not fail to preserve our calm.

A person cannot be non-resistant and flexible, however, who is afraid; and no one can be truly fearless who has not a sense of the Divine. Trust in God and fearlessness lie at the very root of poise. Without a belief in higher protection we can never feel secure, and without the assurance of security we cannot attain evenness of mind. Divine protection, however, does not free our path from obstacles, it makes us strong to meet them. It does not change the course of our life and fill it with ease, it stirs in us a new courage to live it with all its hardships. There will always be severe tests put upon our poise, however great our trust; but if we will fasten our thought on God, the world may turn us as it will, nothing will be able to destroy our balance or the serenity of our spirit. Without steadiness, indeed, we can be of little use to ourselves or others. Under stress we may even prove a danger, because at the critical moment we may lose our balance and be the cause of a grave catastrophe. It is evident then that if we have any sense of responsibility towards the world or any desire for efficiency in our own life, we must labor diligently to cultivate this essential quality.

Nearly always when our equilibrium is disturbed, we blame it on people or circumstances. We believe that in other conditions it would have been perfectly easy to maintain our serenity. As a matter of fact, however, the outside has nothing to do with it. Why, in a disaster, are certain ones panic-stricken while others by their composure save the situation? The danger is equal for the terrified and for the quiet. It is because the external circumstance is never the determinative factor in our actions or states of mind. They merely test us and show us where we stand. Their power over us is much like that of a disease germ. If we are strong, we throw it out of our system and escape the epidemic; if we are weak, over-wrought and fearful, we take in the germ and succumb.

This makes it apparent that the degree of our self-possession is determined not by the action of the outside condition on us, but by our reaction against. If we permit each passing experience to stir our mind into waves of pleasure or pain, approval or resentment, we cannot hope to maintain that habitual balance which we call poise. All this unrest and discontent, this nameless distress and downheartedness, which so often sweep over us, are nothing but forms of mental seasickness caused by incessant rocking on the waves of our own mind; and if we can still its troubled waters, these painful sensations will quickly disappear, leaving us at peace.

It is wholly with our own thought that we have to deal in acquiring poise. When that is properly adjusted, the outer world can never overthrow us. And we adjust our thought by the practice of discrimination. The crucial point in this practice, however, is not how to discriminate, but when. We are all using our discriminative faculty, but not at the right moment. We begin to exercise it too late. We hastily call in our discriminative faculty to prevent the reaction. When a stone has been thrown into a lake, however, it is not easy to stop the circles widening to the shore; so when the surface of our mind is once broken and disturbed, it is very difficult to calm it. Even the discriminative faculty is crippled and functions haltingly. The time when its action is most effective is not at this tardy moment, to allay the disturbance; but at the very outset, to prevent it.

Discrimination should be the angel at the gate, with a flaming sword of wisdom, challenging every impression which seeks admission. None should be allowed to enter which has not come on an errand of primary importance. Nearly always it is the secondary things which destroy our balance. When large joys or sorrows overtake us, something heroic rises in us and we meet them in a big way. Perhaps it is because they cut deeper into our nature and rouse our Soul to action. It is under the repeated sting of petty irritations that our poise goes down — the little envies and jealousies and misunderstandings met in the daily round. But these should never be allowed to gain access to our mind. We should brush them aside as we would a gnat or a mosquito. We make ourselves vulnerable to them by our feverish concern for outer things. We take our desires too seriously, and we expend too much energy in weighing our rights and privileges against those of our neighbor. Our mind is kept in a state of constant agitation by these foolish calculations and it becomes easy for the least provocation to overturn it.

This is what is meant in the Bhagavad Gita when it says that thinking on external things, attachment for them arises; from attachment is born a desire to have them. If our desire is thwarted, we grow angry; anger so clouds the mind that we lose our true measure of values; this disintegrates our power of discrimination and when that is gone we are ruined. Such is the actual order of events whenever we lose our balance, but it usually takes place so swiftly that we are unconscious of the successive stages. A resolute and voluntary reversal of the process will give us the practice necessary to establish a habit of calm stability. We must exercise our discriminative faculty without ceasing. No trivial or destructive thought should be given lodging in our mind. Once within, it cannot fail to produce a reaction of like or dislike, desire or aversion, which not only will disturb our present balance, but through our memory will create a future menace to our serenity; for every time the impression rises, with it will rise the reaction of anger or distress and a fresh storm will pass over us.

But how to prevent the entrance of such disturbing thoughts? By meeting them with counteracting thoughts. Let the angel at the gate drive them away with his flaming sword. Does a complaining voice whisper: "Why must you always work while others play?" Let the discriminative faculty answer: "But do those who play seem really happier than those who work? Isn't there more discontent among the idle than among the busy ones?" Or does the voice say: "If you only had more money, think how free and peaceful you would feel?" Again let discrimination give answer: "Are the rich invariably at peace? Don't desire and unrest appear to increase with increasing riches?

And haven't there been many who have chosen a life of voluntary poverty and simplicity, believing it to be the way of peace and freedom?" If words of criticism or denunciation wound us, again let discrimination check the hot retort by the reminder: "You are what you are. Words cannot change you. If they are just, strive to profit by them; if unjust, they will surely die away, for Truth alone conquers, not untruth; and if you are faithful to the Truth, nothing can do you harm."

By such diligent practice of discrimination we shall gradually eliminate the false and illusory from our thought; and as we do so, our scale of values will adjust itself automatically. What once was all-important will dwindle into insignificance, while that which seemed of slight importance will grow real and vital to us. With this change in our standards, our selfish desires and attachments will diminish necessarily, and we shall find ourselves back at the starting point where the Gita warned us to guard our poise: — "Thinking of sense-objects, one becomes attached thereto." We return, however, fortified by a new measure of things and possessed of a new and invaluable habit of thought, — we have learned to look upon life from the vantage point of the witness.

According to the Vedic scriptures this is one of the profoundest lessons in attaining that serenity essential to all higher understanding. Only the witness can see clearly and judge calmly. The moment the sense of self-identity enters in, with it comes the twin sense of self-preservation and we are in the fight, swaying back and forth in grim struggle with some antagonist who threatens our rights or our possessions. This external world is a world of opposing dualities; and the continuous alternations of light and darkness, pleasure and pain, good and evil, desire and aversion, make of it a giant teeter-totter. So long as we cling to it, we must go up and down with it. Good resolutions to maintain a calm demeanor will avail us little; each rise or dip of the plank inevitably sends us up or down. We must let go our hold and watch it. Only then can we exercise freely our power of discrimination and learn the lessons the world has to teach us.

This attitude of witness, however, does not imply deadness or indifference. The Soul has been defined in Vedic scriptures as "the Witness or Looker-on, the Sanctioner, the Sustainer." As we cultivate this attitude, we move closer to our Soul and can draw more freely on its power and wisdom. There is nothing which will so quickly bring us into conscious union with the cosmic life and will. As the looker-on we perceive clearly the two sides of every question and being in no way involved ourselves, we instinctively stand for the universal right. When we gain this impartial point of view, poise becomes an easy matter.

So long as our way of solution looms larger than the cosmic way, we shall never be able to face a difficult problem without some degree of anxiety and uneasiness; for these will always be the fear that circumstances may go against us, and we shrink instinctively from sacrifice or defeat. Even our sincerest efforts at resignation will lack conviction. But when our moral sense expands beyond the narrow boundaries of personality and we are able to consider the abstract right of the question, we shall be able to meet it without confusion and anxiety. Whenever a trying situation arises, we should conserve our energies for the decisive moment, instead of wasting them on considering the various possible lines of action we may take to win our point. We should hold our mind firmly on the thought: "There is only one right way, right for me and for everyone involved, and that is the cosmic way. If I do not interfere, it will fulfill itself." Each time the mind reverts to its old habit of calculation and disquietude, we must draw it resolutely back to this one thought, the only safe one to hold whatever the problem before us. In this manner gradually we form a habit of moving according to the larger plan.

Self-Discipline

If we would cultivate self-control, we must develop character. We must devote our effort to the basic springs of action within, and pay little heed to the outer issue which stirs the surface of our being; that is, we must work on that inner something which makes the disturbance possible, instead of on the disturbance itself. Our practice must not be to hold back, but to go forward in nobility of spirit and convert our enemy into an ally by our fairness and friendliness. Generosity of heart and a willingness to yield do away with all need of control.

Whenever our balance is shaken or destroyed, it means that we have lost our sense of proportion. We are giving too large a place in the universe to some isolated incident or object and identifying ourselves too closely with it. This erroneous self-identity is the pivotal point of the whole difficulty. Theoretically we may believe that we are souls, but in practice we are bodies. The real accent in all our motives of action is laid on the physical. It is the needs of our body or of other bodies which consume our time and effort. The needs of our spiritual life are remembered only at rare intervals, if at all.

Our irritations are in greater part physical — someone has interfered with our comfort, we have not the ease or leisure we desire, our work is unsatisfying, people do not treat us as they should, we are lacking in health or grace or gifts. These are the grievances which keep our disposition raw and sensitive. Envy, hatred, malice, jealousy, anger, discontent, are all reactions of our physical being. They are the remnant of our subconscious habit when we snarled and snapped at some quadruped neighbor over a disputed bone. The bone seemed the largest thing in the universe to us then, so naturally we fought for it. Our present tempers and resentments may be less apparently brutal, but they rise from the same plane of our being; and until we have ceased to identify ourselves with that, we shall not escape from them.

So long as a thing seems vital to us we cannot help growing angry or despondent or anxious over it. Even the buzzing of a mosquito can make us lose our temper, if a night's sleep for the moment appears to be the most essential thing in life. And no amount of reasoning can alter the situation. We must proceed, not by the method of elimination, but by substitution. We cannot persuade ourselves by abstract reasoning that the present vital thing is of no importance. When we finish all our arguments, it is there just the same, pushing hard against the foundations of our self-control. We must bring in something else more vital, which by comparison will make the first thing dwindle into nothingness. In order to do this successfully we must form the habit of holding our thought on the truly vital things of life. This is the purpose of all higher study and meditation and holy association.

The physical organism will be much healthier and stronger when we pay less heed to it. Its vitality is decreased by keeping our attention fixed upon it. We should learn to treat the body like a useful vehicle or instrument — give it the necessary care, use it wisely and forget it. If it cannot be forgotten, then by steadfast practice we must dis-identify ourselves with its varying conditions and demands. The same method should be adopted in dealing with our subtle body — that inner body consisting of mind, intellect and ego.

Our likes and dislikes must no longer be the standard by which we determine our action. We must find a larger measure to live by. A great deal of our irritability, depression and impatience arises from indecision. But we shall never acquire decisiveness so long as we make our own comfort or discomfort, advantage or disadvantage, pleasure or pain, the basis of our calculation;

because these are shifting quantities. What is pleasant to us at one time is extremely unpleasant at another, the comfort of today is the discomfort of tomorrow. That which seems an advantage from our present outlook appears a great disadvantage when we view it from another angle. The habit of firm decision comes only when we refer the situation to some fixed point and the one truly fixed point in the universe is the Supreme Will. When all our acts of choice are referred to It, our life moves on in a strong unswerving current and we feel none of the rebellions against circumstance which now so often disturb our balance.

In reality there is no occasion for choice. So perfect and homogeneous is the cosmic plan that at every instant there is just one course to pursue. If we try to move along other avenues, we shall be thrown back again and again, until we are forced into the path which is the universal plan.

We can completely obliterate some weakness in our character by choosing as our object of meditation in our daily practice a strong counteracting picture; and it must be the same picture day after day until the source of the weakness is wholly effaced. In this way our meditation may be made to serve a double end. While on the one hand it is teaching us to gather up our scattered energies and direct them through higher channels, it may also wipe out past habits of thought and create for us a new scale of values…substituting the real for the unreal, the essential for the non-essential. No one can dwell persistently upon any word or act of a Christ, a Buddha, or any holy saint or prophet, without gaining unconsciously a new point of view.

Our thought is the material out of which we build our character. If it is flimsy and unsteady, we shall be like a house built upon the sands; the first rushing storm will throw us down. But if our mind is firm and one-pointed, the wind and rain of circumstance may beat upon us, but cannot shake us. It is not possible, however, for the mind to be fixed and one-pointed unless it has a definite point on which to fasten. And here we touch the innermost secret of all self-control. We can never be truly the master until we have a clearly defined Ideal. Our lack of control is due wholly to the scattered state of our energies. We are like an immobilized army. When the enemy strikes, it takes us unawares and routs us before we have had time to gather our defensive forces together. Also we invite attack when we are thus off our guard. But when our forces are fully mobilized and on guard, the very sense of calm impregnable strength thus created will silence the petty word or shame away the hostile action, and our occasions for irritation will be reduced immeasurably.

An Ideal is necessarily something higher and nobler and bigger than we are at the present moment. It represents our furthermost point of vision, and our heart cannot rest upon it from day to day without being transformed into its likeness. What we think upon, that we become; and as we think on God, in whatever form, we are recreated gradually in His image. Then we receive instinctively the relative value of the things of the world and the things of spirit, and the passing trials of the outer life leave us untouched. The whole universe cannot tempt us to sell our soul's peace and serenity.

If we haven't the will to rise, no one can uplift us. Should we be drawn up for a moment by a stronger influence, when that is removed, we shall drop down again like a stone slipping from the hand. There are within us two selves constantly contending for supremacy. If the lower self dominates, there will be chaos in our outer and our inner life and we shall be out of rhythm with our surroundings and our associates. If the higher Self is in the ascendant, our life will flow quietly and peacefully, even in the midst of turbulence and pain. Stressing this, the Bhagavad Gita declares: "Let a person raise himself by his Self, let him never lower himself; for he alone is the friend of himself and he alone is the enemy of himself. He who has conquered himself by the Self — he is the friend of himself; but he whose self is unconquered, his self acts as his own enemy like an external foe."

Without self-discipline we cannot raise ourselves. Often it is said: There is no need for us to discipline ourselves, life does it for us. But the discipline life gives is haphazard and lacks system. The lagging results we gain from our oft-repeated life-lessons prove how ineffective they are unless coupled with voluntary discipline of ourselves. Life gives us our lessons, self-discipline enables us to profit by them. We see this in these words of Marcus Aurelius: "Suppose any person shall despise me. Let him look to that himself. But I will look to this… that I be not discovered doing or saying anything deserving of contempt. Shall anyone hate me? Let him look to it. But I will be mild and benevolent towards every being, and ready to show even him his mistake, not reproachfully, nor yet as making a display of my endurance, but nobly and honestly."

Self-discipline is not a negative practice, it does not consist in reluctant self-denial; what it asks of us is complete and willing cooperation with our higher nature. Our better self must be in command at all times. Every thought, our every act, must carry us forward on a lofty level. We cannot be partial or intermittent in our effort. It will not suffice to strike now and then at some glaring fault, leaving other hidden ones untouched. Nobility must be written deep into every part of our being. We must cultivate a nobler bearing, we must think nobler thoughts, we must harbor nobler feelings, we must obey nobler impulses.

It will hasten our progress to fit our day into a framework of orderly routine. This will create a rhythm in our activity and give greater stability to our practice. The routine need not be a rigid one. It should consist of a wholesome mingling of recreation and work, of prayer and study, of service and rest. Body, mind, heart and spirit, all should have their place in it. No part of us must be left out, least of all our spiritual faculties. Without the softening and elevating influence of spirit, self-discipline is in danger of hardening and stiffening the character. We need the touch of God on our lives to lend them power and beauty and sweetness.

Our growth in self-mastery and knowledge of God is not unlike an experiment in chemistry. The chemist takes a test tube containing an unknown substance, pours into it an acid or an alkali, and a precipitate is formed; letting this settle, she drains off the clear liquid, applies another testing medium, and creates another precipitate. Thus she repeats the process until no reaction takes place, no precipitate forms, and she has the original substance free from all adulteration. So is it with us in our life-experiment. The unknown substance is the Divinity which pervades the universe and permeates our lives. The precipitate is the suffering we undergo when the hard blows of experience strike us and make our heart and mind troubled. It is as necessary to our growth as the precipitate to the chemical experiment. As the precipitate removes all adulterating substances, so the suffering we are called upon to endure carries off all that is alien to our higher nature. A wise medieval writer declared that if there had been any better way for growth than through suffering, the Great Ones would have surely told us of it; whereas by their lives and by their words they teach us there is no better way.

A time comes however when suffering ceases to be suffering, rather it becomes a welcome open path to liberation. So intense is our longing to know and be united with the Supreme, we accept joyfully any sacrifice that will make us more able to reach Him. We see that with every blow we grow nobler, with every surge of anguish scales fall from our eyes; and we have the promise that in the hour of triumphant vision even the memory of the troubled days and nights that have gone before will be blotted out. It was the realization of this that led St. John of the Cross to write these words: "You never kill but to give life; as You never wound but to heal. O Divine Hand, You have wounded me that You may heal me; You have slain in me that which made me dead and without the life in God, which I now live."

Occasions for discipline and suffering would be fewer if we ceased to relate the universe to ourselves and related ourselves to the universe. Now we try to measure its vastness by our small personal standard, comparing all that we see or hear with what we know, what we have, what we believe or what we feel. The element of self is ever present, vitiating our judgment and falsifying our values. Yet we have the power to eliminate it. When we look at a sunset, we don't think whether it is more beautiful or less beautiful than we are, we enjoy it in itself. So should we judge each person and each thing in the universe by its own standard free from the thought of the intruding self.

It is not possible to formulate general rules for the practice of self-discipline. The individual temperament and individual life-conditions shape them.

Self-control has little to do with restraint. It springs from a state of mind, not from an act of will. Self-control is not a problem concerning our relation to the outer world, as commonly supposed; it is wholly a problem dealing with our relation to ourselves. Unthinking people regard themselves as independent units entering into a purely external relation with the universe. If under stress they fall short of their standard in dealing with it, they believe that they must make an effort to improve their behavior; that is, whatever may be their inward state of mind, they must curb all apparent display of it and learn to meet every condition of life with outward composure and courtesy. If they feel anger surging up, they struggle to keep it down; if someone irritates them, they endeavor not to show it. Their whole practice in control is directed towards specific events or people and is carried on only at the moment when the test of endurance rises. When they fail in dealing with it, they try to improve their behavior, not their character.

Thoughtful people, on the contrary, do not wait for the hour of stress, nor do they devote their attention to their behavior. The control they exercise rests, not on isolated acts of will, but upon a continuous striving to build up a strong inner force which will sustain them under attack. A control that is based on suppression or concealment is not control. It merely delays the outburst of impatience or resentment. Calmness of manner can be counted on only when behind it stands calmness of mind, and behind calmness of mind must stand an enduring moral force. Behavior is admirable and dependable only when it rests on character, and character in turn must be upheld by a clear vision of fundamental values.

Stillness

Quietness is a salient quality of character. Lord Buddha says: "The gods even envy him whose senses have been subdued, who is free from pride and free from appetites; his thought is quiet, quiet are his word and deed, when he has obtained freedom by knowledge, when he has thus become a quiet man." The untrained mind is noisy, but those who live in unbroken awareness of the soul feel no impulse to boisterous argument or self-advertisement. They are confident that truth will prove itself, right will protect itself, that in due season the Divine will prevail over the human. They are generous by the very logic of their nature. They have touched the Source and they know that all the basic things of life are inexhaustible. There is more than enough for all; and however much is given, the Infinite still remains undepleted.

Truth Will Prevail

Constantly we are being told that Self-knowledge alone will make us free. The question naturally arises: How are we to gain this knowledge? Self is at the very root of our being; it is our being; therefore we cannot seek it as we seek things that are objective to us, but we can strive to identify the small personal self with the great Self within. The Upanishads tell us that we do this through Truth. Truthfulness is the first condition, and this does not mean merely telling the truth, it means having the sense of truth developed in us. At the present time we do not possess a fully developed sense of truth. If we did, untruth would be impossible to us. The reason we occasionally swerve from the way of truth is because at the moment something else seems more important. Telling the truth does not always mean expressing our opinion. There may be greater truthfulness in remaining silent. We must strive to cultivate a feeling for truth, not only through words but in all things.

There is nothing more harmful in the spiritual life than the habit of self-justification, because it so often means protecting the little self by untrue explanations, half-truths, or a juggling of trivial things in our outer existence.

False explanations make us slaves to custom and tradition. There are no excuses in the spiritual life. So long as we indulge in them we can never develop our instinct for truthfulness. The sense of truthfulness is the sense of sight by which we perceive truth. That is what is meant in the scriptures when they speak about seeing everything just as it is, with direct vision, or face to face. There is no reason for those who are striving to find union with the higher Self ever to follow anything but the right way.

To admit an error is the first discipline in spiritual living. One who is developing the sense of truthfulness stands right up and says: "I did it; yes, I said it; I acknowledge the mistake." There comes a time when we cannot say it fast enough. The quicker we admit that we are wrong, the more quickly we free ourselves from the effects of that wrong-doing.

Truth prevails, not untruth! No matter what the condition, we must never forget that truth is all-powerful. It is for us to remind ourselves and keep on reminding ourselves. For as long as we believe in the power of untruth, as long as we fear that darkness may overwhelm us, we are bound to grieve and to suffer. Once we say, however, that truth will conquer, and hold to that conviction, the result will be quickly apparent.

Unselfishness and Selflessness

Selfishness is not the outgrowth of evil tendencies in our nature, it springs from smallness of vision and a distorted sense of proportion. We view the universe as an assemblage of independent parts and strive to appropriate as many of the parts as we can. But the universe is an indivisible Whole. It cannot be divided. When we would break it up and seize some part, the part slips from our grasp and we find it still in the universe. Only as we leave it there and use it as belonging to the Whole can it be ours for a few brief moments. Such a thing as selfish possession may seem to exist, but compared with the timelessness of the universal, it is temporary and is bought at a high cost. We cling to wealth and health goes; we gain fame or glory and those who might enjoy it with us are taken from us. The universe reminds us in one way or another that we are holding to something that does not belong to us.

Only when we realize the integral nature of creation and surrender to it, are we able to rise from selfishness to unselfishness. Until then even our kindliest acts will bear the taint of calculation, and calculation lies at the very root of all selfishness. We shall expect gratitude, recognition, advantage of some kind. We cannot be unselfish until the Whole becomes our unit of measure. By a mere act of will this cannot be done. We must readjust our entire outlook, rebuild the structure of our thought, and change the habits of our life. Thomas à Kempis gives a simple and definite rule for the accomplishment of this. He calls it "The way of peace and perfect liberty." He says: "Be desirous to do the will of another rather than your own. Choose to have less rather than more. Seek always the lower place and to be humbler than all… Give all for all, ask for nothing, require back nothing. Abide purely and unhesitatingly in Me…. Let this be your endeavor, this your prayer, this your desire, to be stripped of all selfishness, that you may die to yourself and live eternally to Me."

Unselfishness is less an end in itself than a method of approach to a loftier expression of being; an exercise to prepare for the higher state of selflessness. This cannot be attained fully so long as we are on the human plane, since it is a purely spiritual quality; but the self can become so attenuated that it little influences the thought and action. We get flashes of it when a mother plunges into leaping flame to save her child, or when people sacrifice their own lives that others unknown to them may live. To rise above the self, however, we must transcend personality. The personal plane is the plane of difference, of contrasts and shifting moods; the selfless plane is the plane of evenness, unity and quietness. One may be personal in outlook yet be highly unselfish; but on the personal plane one cannot be selfless.

Those who have attained selflessness seek no return for their effort. Praise, gratitude, recognition, gift for gift, are to them like coins thrown to children. They serve, not for the reward they may gain, but for the joy of service. They love because it is their habit, as it is the habit of the sun to shine. So love pours from the selfless heart unceasingly, without thought of answering love. No special object calls it forth, it goes to all who come within the radius of its warmth. St. John of the Cross described this selfless attitude thus: "Those who act out of pure love, not only do not perform their actions to be seen of others, but do not do them even that God may know of them. If they thought it possible that their good works might escape the eye of God, they would still perform them with the same joy in the same pureness of love."

Selfish people can never be truly strong. They may have a short-lived strength bred of the focusing of their energy. Even by one-pointed direction of our ordinary, everyday power, we cannot fail to achieve prominence or success. That is why those who focus their energies for selfish ends appear to be strong, with the result that many say it does not pay to be unselfish — only selfish people get ahead. Selfish people go a very short distance, however, because the element of selfishness destroys the possibility of real accomplishment at the soul level. Swami Vivekananda said that our greatest work is done when we completely forget ourselves. There is a scientific basis for this statement, because the very moment we remember ourselves we have at once divided our forces by following two lines of thought at the same time, one going toward ourselves, the other going toward our task. We must never forget that so long as the ego is predominant, God is silent within us, and that the very moment the ego becomes silent, God makes Himself manifest. Voice of God and voice of ego cannot sound together. We cannot listen to both voices at the same time.

The question is: how are we to lose the self since the sense of I-ness is at the very base of our consciousness? The only way is to learn little by little to be aware of a Self that is greater than the self we now feel ourselves to be. We cannot blot out that lesser self, we cannot argue it out of existence, but we can expand it; and the way to expand it, especially at the beginning, is to transfer our consciousness to some other, some holier being. We can never see our own face, we can see only its reflection; so in the early stages of our higher development, we can never perceive the real, the true Self except by its reflection in those who have realized Truth in their own hearts. Each time that we read of a noble deed, each time our heart glows as we think of a Christ or a Buddha, each time there rises in us a desire to be like them, we are catching a reflection of our higher being. Therefore we must keep our thought fixed on some pure and holy one who reminds us of what we inherently are.

In our reading, in our daily contacts, in our thoughts we should always be seeking the Highest. So many of our thoughts now rest on the level, wandering idly over the little river bed of our ordinary life, in a meaningless flow. In those empty moments we should go and stand, in thought, before our mental image of some Great One, in order that we may remember our own true being. Everyone of us should have this inner Ideal, so that at all times we can go and gaze upon it.

It is by realizing our true nature, that is, by making it real to ourselves, that we gradually expand our self-consciousness and lose the little self in the great Self. Nothing of value will be lost; nothing real will drop off; we need not be afraid. Spiritual growth is not an exclusive growth; it does not cast anything out, but only glorifies and gives new meaning, new power to every part of our being. Now our senses betray us, but when our inner vision is clarified and quickened we shall hear more, see more, feel more. We shall go more deeply into the heart of things and shall perceive the Divine where now we see only the material. Every sense will be alert to catch a new beauty in God's universe, and to respond to it; nor will our intellect be blotted out. The one who is all-knowing from the spiritual level is not less intelligent than the one who is merely groping along purely intellectual lines; they are more intelligent, as a matter of fact, because they touch the Source, the basis of all intelligence and reason. We merely complete ourselves when we forget the little self. It divides us now, like a house divided against itself. That is what the spiritual life means — wholeness; the supplanting of our self-consciousness by Divine Consciousness.

So wisdom and power and love and joy are not lacking; it is we who lack the will, the power to take them in in their fullness; but we can develop that power as we develop any other power. If we want greater intellectual force, we think harder, we study, we go where we hear of things which develop our mental capacity; and when we want to develop our moral power we go out and do loving and kind deeds. Thus when we want to develop our God-power, we concentrate upon it; we study about it; we ask about it; we pray for it and we cry for it — and it comes. No one has ever sought it in vain. The *Bhagavad Gita* tells us that when one sets out on this higher path there can be no waste of effort, no loss of any kind. The very thought of God opens us to God, and God pours into us His great Divinity in all its fullness.

Section Four

Living An Inner Life

Hunger of the Heart	272
The Inward Life	275
The Veil of Ignorance	280
The Religious Life	282
Empty Vessels	284
The Power of a Holy Life	286
Ascent in Consciousness	289
Search for God	291
Spiritual Culture	292
The Hidden Source of Knowledge	295
Recognition and Realization	297
The Source of Power	302
Planless Living	303
The Spirit of Contentment	306
God-Union	308
Oneness	309
Whom the Self Chooses	311
Discipline and Discipleship	313
The Three States of Consciousness	316
The Path to Realization	322
Holy Living	324
Psychic Power and Spiritual Vision	325
Let Your Light Shine	330
The Life We Find	333
The Value of Symbols	335
God's World and the Human World	336

> Genuine spiritual life is all about "living the life." It is all about the spiritual principles that we have internalized, made our own, and demonstrate in all of our relationships and situations that arise in our lives. The degree to which we are able to manifest the Divine in our outer life, in our daily life, depends upon our inner life, our growing relationship with Truth, the Divine, the Supreme, the Higher Power.

Hunger of the Heart

In every heart there is a mute, nameless hunger. Each one of us imagines that it is peculiar to us. But no heart in the whole universe is without this hunger. If we could look beneath the smile we would know that no human being ever tasted complete satisfaction. We interpret that hunger in terms of our earthly desires. Some imagine that if they had more money and could have greater opportunities, greater advantages in the way of education or travel or of doing good to others, then the hunger would go. Others imagine that if they could gain more knowledge, go deeper and deeper into the secrets of nature, become learned, then the hunger would go. Some think in their loneliness if they had companionship, then they would no longer feel the emptiness, or if they had a position of importance, or even a sense of usefulness, the hunger would not be there.

It is really the voice of the Soul sounding in our hearts. Just when we think we are going to have some finite satisfaction, this voice whispers to us that we are infinite, nothing finite will ever satisfy us. Just when we think that these passing pleasures, these temporary relationships, these bodily loves will bring us satisfaction, then the voice whispers: "You are eternal, nothing temporary and passing can satisfy you."

We do not always hear the words of the voice, and if we do, we do not always believe what they say. But that is the hunger. It is the quality of our infinite, eternal nature calling to us to be infinite and eternal. Even if we could satisfy our hearts with all the satisfactions of the universe, if we could realize every dream today and every dream that a larger vision may bring us tomorrow, if the whole earth were at our feet, we would be just as hungry. That is why Christ said, "What shall it profit a man if he gains the whole world and loses his own soul?" That is why we have to satisfy this Soul hunger within us. We have to give ourselves to the life of the spirit.

That does not mean that we are to drop all our tasks and enter a cloister. No. The spiritual life is never an external life. It does not mean changing the least thing on the outside; it means changing our point of view, and making the new point of view habitual. It means that we always give God the first place, and that nothing must be allowed to make us forget our Soul life for our bodily life.

When we give God the first place we do not mean a small, limited conception of God. There must be no definition of the Divine, no preconceived idea of how we may give ourselves to It, no idea of how the Divine will act through us when we give ourselves. It means seeing that the Divine works differently through different beings, and that no matter how we may give ourselves, it is enough. It must be complete, uncalculating surrender of all our will, of all our forces, of all ambitions. We may go on with our earthly occupations, but they will no longer be our occupations. We shall continue always with the thought in our heart that, if it is not right for me, O Lord, I stand with outstretched hands to take the task You give me. I am ready to lay this one down, no matter how deeply my ambition may be set upon it: I am willing to go against the whole world's opinion and to bear ignominy, as the Christ bore death. That is the attitude of mind we must have.

We learn that God is our first and truest friend. We say from our hearts that sacred prayer, "God is our father, God is our mother, God is our friend, God is our companion." Nothing so quickly stops the hunger of loneliness, of unsatisfied ambitions, because that hunger grows from being separated from God. The Soul feeds on God, but it cannot if we are absorbed in things of the world.

We connect ourselves with the universe by our thought; if we think only of our body we feed our body and our Soul starves, but when we connect ourselves with God we feed our Soul and God takes care of our body and all our worldly concerns, and then there is peace in the heart. The sooner we realize this, the sooner will all unrest leave us — all this sense of incompleteness, of wondering what life is and whether it will bring us what we want. In place of the hunger there is a great peace, a great sense of fullness, of complete rest.

We shall be in the same circumstances, perhaps, doing exactly the same task and have no more success on the outside than we had before. But we shall not care, knowing that it is God's universe, that we are with God, and that He is with us while we are doing our tasks and doing them with Him. One task is just as sweet as another when we are with God. The most unpleasant spot, the most obscure position, is a glorified place if we are sitting at the Lord's feet, if only we could know it instead of rushing here and there trying to still the hunger.

We think first that the Divine is going to take us away from all that seems real and vital; that we are going to have to forsake our duty, our families and friends; but would God ever take us away from anything that is vital? It is true that He may break the narrow sense of duty and give us a broader one — one that includes not just one little group of people but all humanity. The little chain that binds us to earthly things may weaken and break, but we will find ourselves bound to the Eternal and Infinite, and because we are bound to God we have a new bond with each one of God's children.

A great teacher once said to me that we pray to God not really for what He is, but merely because we think we can get bigger earthly things by praying to Him than if we asked anyone else; but we do not really believe in His divinity and His divine wisdom. This feeling shows that we have no trust, we have no belief in the reality of God.

There is no danger in giving ourselves up to Him. He may not give us what our appetites crave for, but He will give us what will satisfy our hunger; we must take this attitude not only for ourselves but for every living creature. We must never judge what others should do. We must only see that they are God's children. May He work freely in every life.

We are all longing to ease the pain, to lift the burden, to do our bit in bringing greater peace and goodness to the world, but until we have brought it in our own hearts by daily and hourly communion with God, until we have let go of all things and fastened ourselves wholly to Him, we cannot possibly bring the least permanent help to any other life.

When our life is lived in God we may not know that we do anything but we are a blessing by the very fact of our existence. God is asking each one of us to loosen our hold on finite things, to quiet our restless minds, and to make our hearts still, and listen. Then He will give us our task, and with it peace for ourselves, satisfaction for ourselves, and peace and satisfaction for all others.

Let us hear the voice; let us make ourselves God's child, willing to be led by Him, to be used by Him, to ask nothing, but just to trust and to pray and to serve. Our whole duty is to love Him, knowing that He will teach us and direct us, and merge our life in His great life.

The Inward Life

We can never attain lasting happiness in the outer spheres of our being. The reason becomes apparent when we study our constitution. At the very base of the human organism there seems to be an insatiable desire for expansion. No matter what we have or what we are, our mind overlaps and craves for more. We move into a larger house and in a short time we have filled it and feel the need of more space. We inherit a fortune and imagine ourselves rich, but soon our wants have outstripped our income and we are coveting greater wealth. We spend years acquiring technical efficiency in some trade or profession and in the end we are as dissatisfied with our ability as we were when we began. In whatever direction we move, added knowledge merely intensifies the consciousness of a vague unknown beyond which lures us on.

The limit of expansion varies according to the density of the form of manifestation. In our physical organism it is reached quickly. Even though we may have innumerable opportunities for enjoyment, the body can take only so much and then it begins to deteriorate. Our senses grow numb and the further pursuit of enjoyment, instead of bringing joy, only serves as an irritating reminder that joy is denied. The pleasure-seeker is striving constantly for the sensation which is never fully experienced. Try as we may, we cannot force our bodily organism beyond its normal bounds. The scholar and the philanthropist also sooner or later come to the limit of satisfaction in their intellectual or altruistic life. The amount accomplished invariably seems painfully small in comparison with the energy expended. One part only of the human constitution appears to possess unlimited power of response and that is the spiritual nature. Here alone are we able to expand indefinitely and thus escape from the gnawing hunger for more. Every great teaching has proclaimed this truth and our own experience has confirmed it, yet still we go seeking our happiness on the outside.

Inwardness is the law of creation. Everywhere material manifestation shows a tendency to revert to a finer state. Ice melts into water, water evaporates into vapor; the solid rock crumbles into dust. When we move away from the grosser towards the subtler part of our being, we throw ourselves into line with the cosmic current and reduce the friction and distress of life at once. The effect is immediate. If conflict remains, it is in that part of our nature which is still tied to the external. God is all-power, all-peace, all-beauty. Just one touch exalts and sweetens us. And we touch Him the moment we turn toward Him. He is not far distant from us. We have only to enter that silent inner shrine of our heart and instantly there comes the soothing sense of benediction which His Presence alone can bring. Many recognize this and even experience it, yet they advance a thousand arguments in favor of outward living. The inner life, they say, is a selfish life. It takes us away from the strain and stress of human society. Those ones are most helpful who lead a useful active outer life. But is it selfish to learn before we begin to teach? We cannot give joy until we have found joy; and we cannot find true joy until we have found God.

God is the source not only of all that the unselfish are striving for, but also of all that the selfish covet. Therefore from the standpoint both of material and of spiritual advantage, the inward course is the wiser one. Our outer life will always be the projection of our inner. It will be just what we are. If we are peaceful and happy and illumined, it will be peaceful, happy and illumined. What is it now? Full of unrest, indecision, anxiety, uncertainty. But it is the reflection of ourselves. No change on the outside therefore can alter it. We must begin deep down within.

We need never be afraid that when we move toward reality, we shall sacrifice anything that is real; and the sooner we sacrifice the unreal, the better. There is no greater danger to society than ignorance; and so long as we remain ignorant of the spiritual realm, we constitute a part of that danger, because our sense of values will be shifting and our proportions false. The immediate and temporal will be our first concern, while the ultimate and eternal will be given a secondary place. Until we have known Truth, how can we know what is true or untrue? Until we have linked our life with the great Life, how can we be sure that the foundations of our daily living are safe? Until we have gained contact with Righteousness, how can we know what is really right or really wrong?

The spiritual life is the one life which must be wholly voluntary. Freedom is its goal and it must be lived freely. Unless our thoughts and actions are free offerings to God, they are not offerings at all. But people would turn eagerly to this deeper training, if they could be persuaded that it is to their advantage; and we can persuade them by our own daily lives. We ourselves, however, must have the conviction first. No one ever tested out the practical value of the inward life and found it wanting. Every mighty achievement has begun on the inside and worked outward.

Now the inward life serves us poorly because we live it falteringly. We are too ready to compromise between the inner and the outer. When the world serves us well, we trust in it; when it fails us, we turn to God. Sometimes we move inward, sometimes outward, thus we neutralize our own effort and are less successful than the frankly worldly, who are consistent and undeviating in their course. All success is the result of cumulative striving. Our conviction and resolution must be strong enough to carry us over the barren stretches. Athletes know that it is their "second wind" which takes them to the goal. No human heart is always brave and fervent; but the momentum of the strong hours will bear us through the weak ones, if we are steadfast and prayerful.

Let us begin to cultivate a yearning for the inner life. This means a yearning for contact with all that is holiest and loveliest and tenderest and highest. It would seem as if the longing for these things would be natural to us; but our life does not indicate it. The outward habit still dominates us. Yet a taste for God can be cultivated. As we cultivate a taste for art by studying the best pictures or hearing the best music. So we must go where we hear constantly about God. We must read and think about Him. We must seek Him wherever we are, whatever we are doing. There must be something in us calling ceaselessly to Him; and we may be sure that this continuous call will open a broad channel of communication with Him.

No one ever called to God with a sincere heart that God did not answer and pour out upon them His richest blessings. If we keep on calling, He will bestow that greatest of all gifts — Himself. But no one can receive the whole who does not give the whole. We cannot bargain with God in our inner life. We must give ourselves as fully in hardship as in ease, in failure as in success. When we can do this, we shall find that it is in the dread stillness of some great sorrow that we shall hear His voice; in the solitude of a lonely life that we shall taste His companionship. When the inward life becomes a reality to us, we shall not be afraid of affliction or hard work or pain; for we shall live close to that which never suffers or labors, but which feeds upon that "infinite bliss born of contact with the Supreme."

The gift of life involves a grave responsibility. We accept it casually and use it lightly, as a larger toy. When, however, we awaken to the value of the gift and there arises in our heart the desire to utilize it worthily, we are confronted with two paths to follow — a path leading inward and a path leading outward. In the Katha Upanishad we read:

> The good (or inner) is one thing and the pleasant (or outer) is another. These two, having different ends, bind a person. It is

well with them who choose the good. Those who choose the pleasant miss the true end.

The good and the pleasant approach a man; the wise man examines both and discriminates between them; the wise one prefers the good to the pleasant, but the foolish one chooses the pleasant through love of bodily pleasure.

The outer, or pleasant, is more obvious and immediate, therefore, it tempts us. The inner appears vague and intangible, yet in that inner is hidden all that is vital in human life. If we should receive a beautifully wrapped gift, we would not spend ourselves in delight over the wrapping and forget the gift. Yet that is what we are doing constantly. This universe of created things with all its beauty is but the wrapping; the priceless gift is within — the gift of life, the gift of wisdom, the gift of consciousness, and uncounted other gifts. The wrapping is perishable, the gift within is eternal.

The inner alone can bring permanent satisfaction. In India the story is told of a person who prayed for wealth and was given eight jars of gold. Seven were full, the eighth was only half full. He thought to fill this before he enjoyed the other seven. He tried with feverish persistence, but all in vain. He sold his house and lands, he disposed of all his possessions, but the jar was still half full. He died an embittered pauper with his jar unfilled. So it is with all those who move outward in their search for happiness.

Inwardness is a cosmic habit. All the treasures of nature are hidden and must be sought with labor. Her seeds are sheathed with a hard shell, her gold and precious stones are wrapped in baser ore and buried in the earth; all our gifts and qualities are also hidden in the depths of our being and must be drawn out by our own effort through struggle and strenuous striving. We expend our strength, however, seeking the outer. We mine the gold and jewel, we plant the seed, while the inner treasure is left latent and forgotten. Yet our whole value lies in the inner. The Katha Upanishad declares again: "I know that (earthly) treasure is transitory, for the eternal can never be attained by things which are non-eternal."

We belong to the universe, not to ourselves. From it comes the gift of life and the power to live it. As a farmer homesteads lands and must develop them, so we homestead our intellectual and spiritual gifts and must cultivate or lose them. We must go inward and upward not outward and downward.

We must learn to live inwardly. Our judgments and decisions must be based on inner, not on outer, values. We must judge actions by their motive, not by their result; we must judge others by their character, not by their manner or appearance; and human lives are to be judged not by their momentary attainment but by their aims and aspirations. If we cannot discern the inner within the outer, it is better not to judge at all; for all our evaluations will be distorted or wholly false and our opinion will fail to carry conviction. This is especially true in judging ourselves. We do not realize that the faults we attribute to others are more often our own faults, and the good qualities to which we lay claim are the qualities we lack. We must clarify our vision and stabilize our values, if we are to pass judgment on anyone or anything.

The unfoldment of the spiritual consciousness is vital. We are primarily spirit. The body dies and crumbles to dust. By our spirit we live, therefore we should acquaint ourselves first and foremost with that. Religious observances will not do it. We may be very devout and yet be wholly outward. It must be accomplished by regular spiritual practice. Now we are chiefly concerned with our outer duties. We give them first place. We have no leisure for inner spiritual study. But there is great waste in our outer thought-life. We begin to think of a task long before we take it up, we think of it while we are doing it, and we think of it after it is done. If we would concentrate our whole mind while we are performing the task, and neither anticipate it or dwell on it afterward, we would garner enough time for spiritual practice. A half hour devoted to holy thought in the early morning and again in the quiet of evening would lift the level of our whole day.

It is not enough to gain knowledge of our own inner spirit, we must go still deeper within and unite with the ultimate Source of all being. The Bhagavad Gita tells us that beyond this Unmanifested that turns the created universe in an endless round of evolution and involution, there is another Unmanifested which is eternally existent and is never destroyed even when all else is destroyed. That is the highest goal. When we reach that goal, outward and inward are gone and there remains only one vast infinitude. We do not cease to live, rather we live more fully, because we live in the infinite and partake of infinite life, infinite wisdom, infinite power and infinite bliss. We become one with the Imperishable and Eternal.

The Veil of Ignorance

The veil that hides the Truth from us is not over Truth; it is over our own eyes. This we must keep very clearly before us at all times. There is nothing hidden anywhere in nature. All the processes of nature are being carried on openly and may be seen by anyone who has the eyes to see. God has not hidden anything from us. The only thing that veils the highest Truth, the most hidden facts of life, is our own ignorance. God is eager and glad to have us discover all His secrets. He is calling upon us, begging us to understand everything concerning Him and His universe. If we do not respond it is our own fault.

Often the question is asked: "If it is true that everything is open to us and the veil is over our own eyes, why did God ever allow the veil to cover our vision in the first place?" The reason is that freedom is the greatest gift that God has given us. He does not force us even to be good. Merely for our protection, He has put a barrier or law on either side, so that we can move only within a certain limited space. But He gives us a long leash. He lets us discover everything for ourselves as far as is possible. In other words, we must cut our own way. We are given the same freedom, because we could not attain ultimate freedom if the privilege of freedom were wholly ours.

If we set out with determination to face towards God rather than towards the world, making the desire to know Him the supreme desire of our life, then this veil will wear out, just as a garment finally wears out. We shall not have to bother to tear it away because it will fall of itself. We are, however, constantly adding to it by clinging to the false things of existence, to the very things out of which the veil is woven, and thus we add to its thickness. We believe those things to be real which are not real. There is not a single relationship that we do not permit to take precedence over our relationship with God. If there is even one human call upon us, we listen to it rather than to the call of the Divine.

We have only to analyze our day to see how our spiritual duties are crowded into a few minutes while our secular duties consume hours. To make God our first concern does not mean, however, that we turn our life upside down. It means that we transform all other duties into God duties. Our life will adjust itself without any violence whatever, once we change our point of view.

Those who know the inner Principle, — the life of the life, the eye of the eye, the ear of the ear, the mind of the mind, they alone comprehend the

Supreme. They are conscious that God is within, that He is not to be discovered through mere mental theory, nor do they seek Him outside, knowing they shall not find Him there. Often we hear people say: "I am searching for God everywhere!" But they have not yet learned to go beyond the covering. What they see is the light of God playing on the external world, and they like this world with God's light upon it. The Reality, however, is to be perceived only within. This Eternal Being can be known in one way only, — by internal seeking. No amount of outer activity can bring vision of Him.

These two worlds — this outside world and the inner world where all is clear — must not be confounded. God stands on the boundary between the two. When we find Him by turning within, then both worlds are made known to us. We understand their relation and our relation to them. This awareness of God does not increase with our activities. Our activities may purify us, but it is only by that knowing that we shall tear the veil. The inner Self is all knowledge. The measure of our day should not be what we have done, but how much more we know of that infinite Mystery tonight than we did last night. Have we had the slightest glimpse farther down into ourselves? Have we for one moment caught a flash of that eye behind the eye, of that mind within the mind? It would be a wonderful practice, as we go about our daily tasks, if, occasionally, as we observe something we would stop and think: "Who saw it? These eyes did not see it. It was another, an inner eye. Of course, there was the mind that registered, that took account of the picture in the organ of seeing, but who actually did the seeing?" Likewise if every time we heard something we would ask ourselves: "Who heard?" and every time we thought something, we would stop and say: "Who thought that?" we would learn to become gradually mindful of our inner being.

We never ask a question in all sincerity that we do not grow a little. The trouble is that we move about our daily tasks so unconsciously that we never ask anything. We feel it is foolish to bother. The wise, however, feel just as good students feel in school. They are not interested merely in learning lessons; they want to understand. Pupils used to learn their lessons by heart; but now they are expected to give them in their own words and in their own way. They are expected to think about them. We should be able to interpret our life in a similar manner day after day. Of course to do this all day long would be too great a strain; but we can do it at intervals throughout the day, whenever we have a little leisure. When we are walking along the street, or sitting in the car, or waiting, we should begin to question: "Who is it that is walking or sitting or waiting?" and soon the answers will begin to come and our understanding to open. Thus we learn that it is not by rushing here and there that we are able to perceive the light. All our outer activities do not take the place of the search for knowledge.

The Religious Life

To pledge ourselves to the religious life, whether lived in the cloister or in the world, means to pledge ourselves to beauty, nobility and loftiness in every thought and act. Whispering a prayer, studying a scripture, entering a church or temple, these are not enough. Piety can never be a substitute for religion. Every impulse of mind and heart, every effort, must reach Godward. Religion must bind us back to our Source — that is the significance of the word.

Religion is not an end in itself. It is a means to an end — a method by which humanity attains its highest unfoldment. Forms, creeds, dogmas, rituals, are mere incidentals. They are in no way essential to it. As a fundamental method it has many different modifications — music, art, every craft and every science. To wage war over these modifications is as unreasoning as for two violinists to come to blows because of the variation in the manner in which they hold and draw their bows. Equally without reason is the so-called feud between religion and science. Religion is the supreme science; the science which interprets all other sciences and explains the ultimate mystery of nature which telescope and microscope cannot reveal.

The religious life is not a specialized calling, designed for the few; it is a universal vocation, the crown of human effort. It can be lived within cloister walls, in the home, or in an office. The place and circumstance are of secondary importance. It is the mode of living which characterizes it, — the sincerity, perseverance and fidelity with which we pursue it; how much holiness and energy we put into it from day to day.

A 15th c. anonymous writer declares: "This life is not chosen in order to serve any end, or to get anything by it, but for love of its nobleness, and because God loves and esteems it so greatly. And whoever says that he has had enough of it, and may now lay it aside, has never tasted nor known it; for those who have truly felt or tasted it, can never give it up again. And those who have put on the life of God with the intent to win or deserve aught thereby, have taken it up as a hireling and not for love, and is altogether without it. For those who do not take it up for love, hath none of it at all; they may dream indeed that they have put it on, but they are deceived. Christ did not lead such a life as His for the sake of reward, but out of love; and love makes such a life light and takes away all its hardships, so that it becomes sweet and is gladly endured. But to those who have not put it on from love, but have done so, as he dreams, for the sake of reward, it is utterly bitter and a weariness and they would fain be quit of it. It is a sure token of a worker that they wished their work were at an end. But they who truly love it, are not offended at its toil nor suffering, nor the length of time it lasts."

And the mystic William Law writes: "There is but one salvation for all humankind, and the way to it is one; and that is, the desire of the soul turned to God. This desire brings the soul to God, and God into the soul; it unites with God, it cooperates with God, and is one life with God." We debase our religion when we use it as mere sedative, a balm to ease our pains and soothe our distresses. It may do this incidentally, but that is not its purpose. Its aim is to make heroes of us, to fill us with strength and lift our endurance to the level of the hardest trial, "uncontaminated by pleasures, unharmed by pain, untouched by insult, feeling no wrong, fighters in the noblest fight." (Marcus Aurelius)

The practice of religion must involve the whole person. It must reach down into the depths of our being and up to its heights. The physical organism, the senses, the mind, intellect and moral sense, must be purified and sanctified by it. Above all it must awaken the dormant spiritual consciousness; for until that awakening takes place, our unfoldment is not complete. Every part of our nature must have its share in this awakening. Religion cannot be practiced partially or at intervals. We cannot go forward one moment and backward at the next moment, and advance.

As we pursue our daily practice, however, we must be watchful that it does not degenerate into a dull routine. Our aspiration must be kept living and fervent. There must be a constant up-reaching of the thought. We must wage continuous warfare against our lower nature — the weapon, self-discipline. Thomas à Kempis tells us: "When a person perfectly overcomes himself, it is easy to bring all things else under the yoke. The perfect victory is to triumph over ourselves. Those who keep themselves subject are truly conquerors and lords of the world."

God asks but one thing of us, — ourselves. He would have us yield ourselves up to Him without reserve or compromise. "Whatsoever you give besides yourself I regard not; I seek not your gift, but you." Of what avail is it if we offer God one thing when He asks of us another. A partial gift will not content Him. He would have us give all, that we may receive all.

Empty Vessels

To receive God's blessings in fullness we must empty ourselves of ourselves. This is the secret of spiritual attainment. Nature allows no vacuum in the universe. The moment a void occurs, it is filled. So it is in our little personal world. When we create a void, if we are facing Godward, God fills it; if we are facing toward the world, the world crowds in. God does not barter with us, does not force us to labor and earn His gifts. He asks only that we prepare a place for them and He will bestow them freely and in abundant measure. How may we prepare the place? A sixteenth century Spanish writer tells us, "Make no account of anything, however great and precious it may be, but only be well with God. . . . He who seeks for satisfaction in anything else is not keeping himself in a state of emptiness that God may fill him with His unspeakable joy. . . The immense benefits of God can only be received and contained in empty and solitary hearts. . . As the sun rising in the morning, enters the house if the windows are open, so God enters the emptied heart and fills it with His blessings."

Our task is to empty our mind and heart of self. We cannot cultivate the gifts of spirit. They do not grow within us from spark to flame as do moral traits. They are attributes of the Divine manifesting spontaneously when heart and mind are void of self. This self-emptiness however, must be complete. Divine gifts cannot mingle with human frailties. We cannot be half holy and half unholy, half pure and half impure, as we cannot have a glass of water with half the water in it bitter and the other half sweet. Nor can we overcome our faults by substituting spiritual qualities for them. They find expression on two widely different planes and have no common meeting-ground. We must conquer our defects and rise above them before spiritual gifts can enter within.

Emptiness of self cannot be attained by an act of will. It is acquired only by remolding the character; the character is remolded by redirecting the thought, and we turn our thought by altering our values. This is the order of practice we must follow if we would empty ourselves of ourselves. Our first effort must be to readjust our attitude towards the world. Material resources, material interests, material undertakings must no longer occupy first place in our concern. The spiritual must be more vital to us. Christ tells us that where our treasure is, there will our heart be also. There too will our thought rest, and what we think we become. Thought is formative and creates us in its image. Our character is the product of our thoughts. If we cling to the material, the fiber of our being will coarsen and we shall grow dense and body-bound. If, on the contrary, we allow the spiritual to dominate, our whole nature will become gentler, nobler, more elevated.

In abandoning self-willing and self-thinking we lose nothing; on the contrary, we gain greater richness of life. For the first time we enter into right relations with the universe and move in harmony with it. Our outlook broadens and deepens, our inner nature expands, and our whole being is filled with a calm that even the heaviest blow cannot break. When this stillness of spirit is attained our consciousness rises to a higher level, we become vividly aware of the presence of the Divine.

This stillness of spirit born of inner self-emptiness cannot exist without a corresponding outer-self-emptiness. We must make spaces in our daily routine — not for idle conversation or aimless activity, but for God. We must form the habit of turning the mind at intervals completely away from outer material concerns and fixing it on higher verities. Even from a practical standpoint, this emptying the thought and creating a void in our outer effort is of the highest utility. The Chinese philosopher, Lao-tze, illustrates this graphically in a passage from the *Tao Te Ching*. He writes:

> The thirty spokes of a chariot-wheel and the nave to which they are attached would be useless, but for the hollow space left for its contents.
>
> The door and window frames of a house would be useless, but for the empty spaces they enclose, which permit ingress and egress, and the admission of light and air.
>
> This teaches us that, however beneficial the material may be to us, without the immaterial it would be useless.

The material must rest upon the immaterial or spiritual, otherwise the whole universe will crumble; for spirit alone is stable and undeceiving. The material is deceptive and variable. We contact it through the senses and too often they bear false witness of what is heard and seen, touched and tasted.

We mistake a rope for a snake, a shadow for reality. If we would have a stable mind and a peaceful, steadfast heart, we must disentangle ourselves from the material and place our whole dependence on the spiritual. This does not mean that we must eliminate all material things from our lives. That is not possible so long as we live in a material universe and have physical bodies; but we must not make the material our treasure and set our heart on it. Nor must we accumulate and hoard. If we do, we shall fail of our aim. What we gather for our pleasure will rob us of our leisure hours and we shall labor more than we enjoy.

We need not cast away our material possessions — but we must detach our mind from them. We must lose the sense of ownership. The Bhagavad Gita defines persons of superior wisdom as those who are free from attachment and who neither rejoice on meeting the pleasant nor are vexed on meeting the unpleasant. In all circumstances they are serene-minded and unattached. We must lose our life to find it. To partake of the greater we must relax our hold on the lesser.

The early mystic, Jacob Boehme, writes in his book, *The Supersensual Life* "Your willing stops your hearing; (your willing) stops your efforts toward God through your own thinking upon earthly things and your attention to that which is outside you . . . Your life is in God, from where it came into the body, and as your own power wanes, the Power of God will then work in you and through you. When you are quiet and silent then you hear and see, in the same manner in which God Himself saw and heard in you before even your own willing or your own seeing began . . . "

Self-emptiness holds the promise of God-fullness. The blessings of the Supreme never fail us, they wait only for us to make ready to receive them. We empty ourselves of the lower self, and the Higher Self takes its place. We empty ourselves of the human and the Divine fills the void. We empty ourselves of the finite and the Infinite rolls over us in mighty waves. We empty ourselves of the fleeting, the perishable, and behold! The Eternal is there.

The Power of a Holy Life

We help the world by what we are, not by what we do. Our doing is merely preparatory. It is the five-finger exercise or the rough sketch. But true artists do not offer to the world the practice sheet; they give a finished production.

So should we give, not our crude effort, but the fulfillment of our effort ripened into being.

Nothing is more needed by the world today than holy living. The power it releases cannot be measured. We are told in the Bible that ten righteous ones would have saved Sodom and Gomorrah, and who can divine how much in these troubled times humankind owes to silent lives lived here and there in the quiet places of the earth? The philosopher and mathematician, Blaise Pascal, declares: "The serene, silent beauty of a holy life is the most powerful influence in the world next to the might of God."

It is not possible to calculate the far reach of holy living. Its radiation is cosmic and unbounded. Holiness, purity, exalted aspiration, loving-kindness — these create a radiant force in which we all share.

Holiness is the fruit of spirit. It cannot thrive where there is attachment to the physical. Bodily comfort and convenience are foreign to it. It grows by chastening, not by indulgence. It is a super-earthly quality and can live only in the pure atmosphere of the heavens. We rise to this higher atmosphere, not by transforming our human nature, but by transcending it. Our human nature and our spiritual nature belong to two different realms and are not interchangeable. Our spiritual nature calls for singleness or oneness of being. It is unchangeable. There can be no fluctuations of mood or temper in the realm of spirit.

Human nature, on the contrary, is changeable and dual. Like a pendulum marking the hours, it swings between pleasure and pain, joy and sorrow, weakness and strength. We cannot stop this swinging and swaying, neither can we alter its rhythm. Pleasure cannot be lengthened, pain cannot be shortened or discarded. They are but two aspects of the same fact of existence. If we would escape from one, we must detach ourselves from both. When we do this, we are lifted out of our human nature and the human in us gives place to the God in us. The God in us is always there, but He is veiled by our human nature. The moment we part the veil, He stands revealed.

When this revelation comes, the whole life is sanctified, and a new power is born; not a power to acquire or to achieve, but a greater power, — the power to endure, to sacrifice, to renounce, to love and to pray. Prayer is the refuge of a holy life. It seeks shelter in prayer as a ship seeks a safe harbor when the storm drives. Those who are striving for holiness pray when they eat, pray when they drink, pray when they work, pray when they sleep or wake. Their silences are supplications, even their speech sounds a soft overtone of prayer.

The prayer of holiness, however, cannot be a divided one. It must be directed to God alone and it must ask for God alone. Only thus does God give Himself in sanctifying fullness. So long as we have a worldly desire in the heart, so long as we grieve over loss, insult, failure or defeat, we are praying to the world and the world must answer our prayer; but our life will not be made holier by what we receive. Only when we cry out for God and nothing but God are we truly sanctified by our praying.

There comes a moment in our spiritual striving, however, when we are stripped of all asking. Our prayer grows mute; and we lie silent and passive before the altar, consumed with but one longing, — that as the candle flame fades away before the blazing sun of noonday, so may the flame of our being lose itself in the dazzling effulgence of the Supreme. This is the true prayer of holiness.

No less vital to holy living than prayer is self-surrender. But there must be no compromise in our submission. We cannot share the command of our being with God. God cannot rule on special occasions and give place to our rule at other times. Oscillations between self-effacement and self-assertion are not possible. If we would become perfect in holiness, the gift of ourselves must be complete and unconditioned. We read in Thomas à Kempis:

"If we give all our substance, it is nothing. If we practice great penances, yet it is little. If we attain all knowledge, still are we afar off. If we have great virtues and very fervent devotion, yet is there much wanting in us, especially one thing which is most chiefly necessary. What is that? That forsaking all, we forsake ourselves, that we go wholly forth from ourselves and retain nothing of self-love." "Forsake yourself and you shall find Me. Stand without choosing and without any self-seeking; and you shall always be a gainer. For ever greater grace shall be added to you the moment you resign yourself, provided you do not turn back to yourself again…"

Humility and holiness are synonymous. Self-importance has no place in a holy life. Vanity, pride and arrogance belong to worldliness; holiness rests in godliness. The way of holiness is open to all. Those who travel it move steadily godward. No miracle may mark their course, but their life itself is a miracle. Though they walk humbly and alone, without armor or weapon, they wield a power that is invincible. They conquer by the strength of sanctity.

Ascent in Consciousness

Human evolution is wholly interior. It is an ascent in consciousness. A boundless range of consciousness is at our command, but we do not possess it. We do not have a separate consciousness of our own. We partake of universal consciousness, as we partake of universal life. When, however, through steadfast striving we grow aware of this, our thought expands and mounts, wider and wider areas of consciousness come into play and we rise gradually to the highest plane of vision. With this expanding inner sight the entire life lifts; a new and loftier standard measures every thought and act; and all that is noblest and most exalted in our nature finds full expression.

In this upward climb the outer environment follows after, it does not go before. We ourselves shape it. The newborn child with its first cry begins to mold it. The place, it is true, is already determined; but place is merely the background against which the environment takes form. Environment is the consequence of the moods, the outlook, the habits and the taste of the one who lives in it; if a group — then it is a composite of the group-consciousness. Even a tree shapes its life conditions. The fallen leaves, decaying, supply the soil; the nature of the soil determines the kind of undergrowth that springs up around it; the nature of the undergrowth determines what animals will come to feed upon it, and they in turn fertilize the soil. Like humans, every living and growing thing sets the scene in which it plays its allotted part.

With this highly subjective element in the origin of our environment, our discontent and complaining become unreasoning and without foundation. We only have to alter our outlook and habits of thought and our surroundings will be transformed; — gloom will turn to brightness, rigidity to grace, unloveliness to loveliness. Consciousness and environment act and react upon one another. Every widening of the realm of awakened consciousness infuses the environment with new dignity and beauty; and the added culture of the environment lifts the consciousness to a higher level.

Consciousness is the binding force of the universe. It is the property of every living and growing thing, of all things moving and unmoving. Botanist, Dr. Jagadish Chandra Bose once defined plants as "conscious animals without the power of locomotion." Pioneer ecologist, Dr. Paul B. Sears in his book, *Deserts on the March*, declares: "The whole world of living things exists as a series of communities, whose order and permanence put to shame all but the most successful of human enterprises." We only have to observe the intelligent behavior of a tree, an ant or a bee, to recognize that every form of life is individually conscious. Science has proved that there is nothing inanimate in the universe; that all created things are living and responsive to stimuli. If this be true, then whatever exists must share in all-pervading consciousness and intelligence.

Through pure consciousness we touch the Eternal. Thought is in time; pure consciousness, in eternity. Time has no actual existence, it is merely a name we give to a succession of thoughts. When we become deeply absorbed in a task, we lose account of time and pass into the timeless. The German philosopher, Friedrich Wilhelm Joseph Schelling writes of this: "In all of us there dwells a secret marvelous power of freeing ourselves from the changes of Time, of withdrawing our secret selves away from external things, and of discovering to ourselves the Eternal in us, in the form of unchangeability. This presentation of ourselves to ourselves is the most truly personal experience upon which depends everything that we know of the super-sensual world. At that moment we annihilate Time and duration of Time: we are no longer in Time, but Time, or rather Eternity itself, the Timeless, is in us."

When we reach this lofty vision, our outlook is reversed. We no longer see God in the universe, we see the universe in God; we do not know causes by their effects, we know effects in their cause. The causal realm opens to us; we perceive all things in direct relation to their Origin, and we acquire a stable and irrefutable basis for all our knowing. It is on these higher levels of consciousness that deep meditation takes place, and the state of superconsciousness is reached. Thought is stilled, thinking ceases, mind is transcended, and the inner gaze becomes fixed. With unified force it penetrates to the uttermost depths of the object of meditation, a light flashes, and we perceive the hidden essence of that on which we are meditating.

This inward gazing or "staring" is described potently by the Flemish mystic, Jan van Ruysbroeck, thus: "In the idleness of our spirit, we receive the Incomprehensible Light, which enwraps us and penetrates us, as the air is penetrated by the light of the sun. And this Light is nothing else than a fathomless staring and seeing. What we are, that we behold; and what we behold, that we are; for our thought, our life, and our being are uplifted in simplicity, and made one with the Truth which is God, and therefore in this simple staring we are one life and one spirit with God." This deeper understanding cannot be reached by fitful effort, we must strive for it with the same ardor and fixity of purpose as we put into the accomplishment of worldly duties or into the pursuit of pleasure. "The more a person is at one with himself and becomes single in heart," Thomas à Kempis tells us, "the more and higher things we are able without labor to understand, for that we receive the light of understanding from above."

We are not alone in our upward striving, we are part of a chanting multitude moving Godward. Every noble thought sent out into space cooperates with us and sustains us, as we sustain and cooperate with the one who thinks it. The universal nature of consciousness makes the thought of the world one. This lays upon each of us a grave responsibility. An angry thought from us may push another far-away to crime, a despondent mood may break down another's hope and courage; while a thought of love and strength may revive a sinking heart and heal it of its loneliness. Our thoughts belong to the universe and register there. The reach of their influence cannot be measured. The greatest service we can render humanity and the world, therefore, is to guard our consciousness that it may be kept pure and unsullied; and our life, that it may be holy and dedicated to the Highest.

Search for God

In the Bhagavad Gita the Lord says, "Wherever there is a manifestation of glory, or power, wherever there is beauty to be seen, know I am that." Of course that is not the whole of God. It means that God is a little more visible there than elsewhere. At that particular point the veil of matter is a little thinner and God is more perceptible. He is everywhere.

Only those who yield themselves up utterly to that all-pervading Presence, losing their littleness in Its vastness, will enter into wholeness of life and live truly. Thomas à Kempis writes: "Those to whom all things are one, who draw all things to one, and see all things in one, they alone can be steadfast in heart and remain united with God."

In the best of each thing is the place to look for God. It is a great thing to know that wherever there is a best to us, there is God. If we form the habit of looking for the best in order to see God, by and by we will begin to see God everywhere and all things will seem to be best to us.

It becomes, therefore, a question of finding out where the veil is thinnest and where God can be most clearly seen. In the process it also becomes a question as to how we can wear the veil thin so that God can be seen at all times and everywhere, and all of the religious life comes to a process of purification. Christ has told us that the "pure in heart shall see God." He does not say that the pure in heart shall look to the place where God is, or see that place. The pure in heart shall see God everywhere. They do not have to go to heaven, they do not have to die, they do not have to change their mode of living. They will see God just there where they are. Hence the real journey, the real work of the devotee is just that — getting clean, being purified. The religious life is not an aggressive activity. It is a process of elimination.

Spiritual Culture

We can measure our spiritual growth and our spiritual sincerity by how far we seek higher things for their own sake. We find people approaching spiritual study from opposing angles. The majority take it up for what it will bring to them of health or happiness or powers; here and there is one who turns to it because truth and holiness and the ultimate refinements of life draw her with irresistible force.

Do we who claim to be seeking God feel this way? Are we sensitive to the lack of order and proportion in our daily living? Are we as careful as we might be about the neatness and fitness of our dress? Is our tread soft and gentle? Are we thoughtful about the way we move and speak? Are our words quiet, gracious and to the point? Are we scrupulously watchful in the accomplishment of each task? These are not negligible considerations in the spiritual life. Arjuna proves it when he asks Sri Krishna in the Bhagavad Gita: "What are the signs of a person of well-established wisdom? How does the one of steadfast wisdom speak? How does he sit? How does he walk?"

True spiritual culture penetrates to the minutest habit of life. There can be no veneer or contradiction anywhere. Our thoughts, our actions, our whole being must measure up to our Ideal. We are perpetually in the attitude of "taking the shoes off our feet" because wherever we stand is for us holy ground. In certain convents it is the custom to train the scholars, whenever they enter a room, to make obeisance in homage to the unseen Presence there. This may seem a foolish ritual, but any practice which keeps us mindful of the Divine has value. If some great personage were in the room, how careful we would be of our words and behavior. Won't the remembrance that a greater than all human great ones is present hold us on a higher level?

Our virtues are too much for others. Many of us keep our virtues on call to use when we come in contact with other people. They form a part of our social code; they are not imbedded in our character. That is why we have so much struggle in practicing them. Our springs of action go down too deep in our human relationships. We try to be honest in our dealings with others; we do not strive to become honesty itself. We are loving and kind in relation to others; love is not an essential element of our being. We concern ourselves too much with the practice of isolated virtues; we make too little effort to rise to the realm of virtue, as Emerson puts it. We do not cultivate the loftier attributes for their own sake. We are all things in relation to others; continual variation in our behavior. But this is not the lesson taught in the textbook of God's universe. Nature goes on her way without concern as to whether she is seen or heard. The sun shines because it is its nature to shine. Flowers bloom, trees bear fruit in the darkest tangles of the jungle; they do not wait for the passer-by. Everywhere creation is fulfilling itself in relation to a universal rhythm, a universal order and beauty.

We constitute a part of it and should follow the same law. We should train ourselves to be at all times that which we hope to express on special occasions. We should cultivate the habit of loving, the habit of living and working well. When we have done this, we shall be as unconscious of the world's baser, ruder side as the rose is unconscious of a foul odor. Even on the dung heap it perceives only fragrance. There can be no compromise, however. We must be big and noble and consecrated all the way through. The small human point of view must be discarded. We must not set our course by what other people say and think and do. We must look upon life, not in relation to living beings, but in relation to life itself — the all-embracing cosmic life. We must think of love, not in relation to what is lovable or unlovable, but in relation to love itself — the unchanging love of God. Work for work's sake, love for love's sake, truth for truth's sake, life for life's sake: this must be our standard.

How to attain it? It is recognized everywhere that the quickest way to acquiring culture is to associate with those who possess it. We may not find holy companions outside, but we may always have them in our thoughts. A Christ, a Buddha, a Saint Francis may go with us wherever we go and be the close comrade of our work and play. We must fill our memory with the words and acts of the Holy Ones. Our life must be mingled with the substance of their lives until it has taken on the same hue and radiance. To think deep and yearningly of anything is to make our whole system vibrant with that thing.

In time a permanent impression is graven on our consciousness and a new habit is formed. The love that can hang on a cross, or lay itself on a sacrificial altar in the place of animals destined for sacrifice, or eat and sleep with lepers, such a love is impelling and will transform us if we but open ourselves to its influence through daily remembrance of it.

We squander our mental forces on the tawdry things of life, — the scandals and accidents of the media, gossip, personal adornment, current entertainment. We imagine we can touch these things lightly and pass on; but each contact with them lowers our taste and deadens our higher sensibilities. Every able worker and thinker knows the value of contact with the leaders in their profession. One walk through the woods with a botanist will quicken a new sight in us; one visit to a gallery with a painter will open to us a new world of form and color. If we wish to cultivate the loftier qualities, we must seek out those places, those companions and books which make these qualities real and living to us.

Spirituality does not consist in sitting long hours in meditation, shutting ourselves off from our fellow-beings, choosing some peculiar diet and dress. It means clearing out the dross and refining every part of our being until no adulteration or mixture of attributes remains. That is what purity means, the purity which leads to God-vision. Our nature must be made up entirely of love, entirely of honor, entirely of patience, of endurance and compassion. And when we have reached that state of singleness, we can live in any environment, wear any kind of dress, follow any occupation. People spend too much time getting ready to be spiritual. They wait too long for some special condition or opportunity. Spiritual education is just as possible in the workshop, in the kitchen or in the field as in the cloister. There is no better school than experience. Every place and every condition offers untold advantages for the sincere seeker.

One rule, however, must be observed rigidly. We must never allow a thought to lodge in our mind, a word to linger on our lips, or an act to busy our hands and feet, to which we would not give a permanent place in our character. Each thought, each word, each act is the beginning of a habit which will lead either to our elevation or to our degradation. We cannot afford to be careless about anything. We must be as exact and uncompromising in our spiritual living as mathematicians in their computations. Accuracy and precision are fundamental elements in all research work; and where can we need greater exactitude than in the search after ultimate knowledge? The author, George Eliot, has defined genius as the power to take infinite pains, and this is preeminently true of spiritual genius. The spiritual life is a life of care in detail. It consists in lifting each small ordinary task to catch the glorifying light of Spirit. Christ indicates this when He admonishes His disciples to be faithful in the little things, if they would become rulers over greater things. One little self-indulgence, one unlovely thought, one moment's loss of temper, one word of ungenerous criticism, may undo the work of many days of spiritual practice. But also one whispered prayer, one quick call for Divine help, may avert a downfall and carry us out of danger.

The base of spiritual culture is cheerfulness, obedience, simplicity, forgiveness, tolerance, straightforwardness, courage, carefulness and unswerving commitment to the Ideal. When these qualities fill the whole heart, every part of our nature will manifest a refinement, a power of penetration and understanding which no amount of intellectual attainment can bestow. To grow in the knowledge of God means also to grow in Divine grace and beauty. The only way to knowledge, however, is through contact. Our thought must rest close within His thought, for it is to those whose hearts are fixed on Him, whose life is absorbed in Him, whose joy and content are in Him, that He holds out the promise: "To these ever steadfast and loving devotees I give that wisdom by which they come unto Me. Out of pure compassion for them, I, dwelling in their hearts, destroy the darkness born of ignorance, by the effulgent light of wisdom."

The Hidden Source of Knowledge

Knowledge is accumulated experience. It cannot be borrowed. As it is impossible to see through the eyes of another or to hear through another's ears, so it is impossible to know through another's mind. "If I look at a thing from another's point of view, I do not see it; only as I know it myself, do I know it," the sage, Chuang Tzu, declares. And Lao Tzu, his master, says: "The further people go out from themselves, the less they know."

Acquiring knowledge is an inward process, it takes place in our inner being. We may move outward to gather data: but the results of our observation, experiment and study, when gathered, must be carried inward, related to our individual experiences, coordinated and assimilated, before they become knowledge. Otherwise they remain merely information. Information is not knowledge. It is something superimposed, undigested, and unrelated to us. It gives a semblance of knowledge, but it is deceptive and leads us to believe we know when we do not. "To know and think we do not know is the highest attainment; not to know and yet to think we know is a disease," it is said in the Tao Te Ching.

If we would grow in knowledge, we must maintain a high level in our thought, our conversation and our study. Our reading and research must be fundamental. There can be no waste of power on trivialities or subjects of secondary value. To read merely to exchange our thought for the thoughts of someone else will avail us little. We should seek out such books as stimulate the mind and train it to think for itself.

So long as our effort to know is confined to the external universe, what we gain will always be shifting and inconclusive. Since experience is the test of knowledge, it cannot be otherwise. The universe is too vast to be covered by human experience. There will always be something beyond, which, when discovered, may overturn all our explanations and theories. How many able scientists have spent their whole lives building up an hypothesis, which their successors in the same field have completely demolished? A more practiced observation, a more powerful instrument, a fresh discovery may alter the whole outlook of science in a moment.

Yet despite all this instability and lack of conclusiveness, we have within us a power of intelligence which assures us exact and stable knowledge. This intelligence is not an individual faculty, it is universal. We share it with the tree, the flower, with the mother bird in the nest and the beast in the jungle. Wherever there is ordered action, instinct, intuition, vision, it is present. It is infinite as existence is infinite. Without it there would be no basis of communication in the universe; each human being would be insulated and mute. Even if we possessed an individual faculty of intelligence, constant use would exhaust it; and there would be no general source from which to replenish it. It is this universal transmitting medium which makes thought transference possible and inevitable; and which uncovers untruth and evil. Nothing can be hidden from that all-encompassing intelligence.

We bathe in this cosmic intelligence as in an ocean. The thought-waves beat against our mind, and pass. They come, we don't know from where; they go, to where we don't know. But beneath this restless surface lie still depths of unerring knowledge.

Those whose thoughts rise from those quiet depths grow silent. They do not argue or contend. They realize the deceptive power of words. It is told of an ancient sage of China that when he sat with his disciples, he did not speak; when he stood with them, he did not speak, yet they came to him empty and went away full. Higher knowledge needs but one language, — the unspoken language of living and being. The Ultimate, knowing which all else is known, finds expression only in profound silence.

Recognition and Realization

In all development there are three stages, — the stage of receptive instruction, the stage of reflection, and the stage of realization. First we hear of some fact in the universe; next we think about it, refer it to our past experience, reason as to its validity; and then, if we earnestly desire to know, we push on beyond mere belief in its validity to the actual knowledge of its reality. In material science, we consider it of little value merely to go through the second stage. The scientist who is content to sit in his study and theorize about the laws of chemistry or physics, without seeking practical proof in the laboratory, has little standing among his colleagues. It is indeed this which distinguishes scientific minds from ordinary minds: ordinary minds accept facts on hearsay; they are satisfied to read about them and idly comment on their interest; while scientific minds go out into the field, take the flower and study its structure and nature; or carry the unknown substance into the laboratory, and by analysis find out its component parts. Their constant effort is to pass from the stage of intellectual acceptance to that of conviction. For them it is not enough to recognize the plausibility of a theory; they demand the reality of a proven fact.

The great ones in every department of life are those who "prove all things and hold fast to that which is true." We admit this without question in the various branches of secular knowledge; but in matters of religion, curiously enough, it does not occur to us to insist on the same scientific standards. We consider it quite sufficient that our teachers shall at most attain the second stage — that of thoughtful recognition of the higher verities regarding God and the soul; while we remain placidly in the first stage of mere hearing about them. Yet exact knowledge is more necessary and imperative in this subtler realm of research than anywhere.

We should be more wary of the person who teaches religion without realization than we are of the physicist or chemist who would become an instructor without practical training; for there is more danger in spiritual ignorance than in any other. We recognize that the finer the forces of nature the more hazardous it is to handle them without knowledge. Always the subtle, hidden forces are most dangerous; and the most hidden, the most mighty of all, is the force of spirit. We are dealing with the very finest force of nature when we deal with people's spiritual being; and no one should undertake to direct or handle it who does not fully know its constitution.

Actually, we know nothing of our existence. We go on blindly, driven by desires and needs. From where we have come, where we are going — these are questions still unanswered. We hear of a heaven and a hell, a *Brahmaloka*, a state of nirvana, a condition of *mukti* or liberation; but for us they are mere idle speculations. We claim to believe in a God, yet our daily living proves us atheists; for if we actually believed that there was a God and that He was all that He is defined to be — the storehouse of power, of love, of wisdom, of everlasting happiness — how could we wait so long before seeking Him?

It is time that we woke up and strive with all earnestness to transform mere religious validity into religious reality. "What profiteth a man," Christ said, "if he gain the whole world and lose his own soul?" One thing alone in the final analysis is worth giving to the world, and that is Soul-consciousness. But how can we give it if we do not possess it? It is not possible. We must find our own life before we can give new life to any living thing. We must find our own Soul before we can tell anybody where the Soul is and how she may gain access to it. We have read enough; we have heard enough, we have speculated and talked enough…now we must realize the things about which we have been talking ever since Christ came into the world and other saviors before Him.

Religion is in realization, not in recognition. How do you know, for example, that Christ is a Savior if you have not tried to be saved by Him? How can you proclaim His redeeming grace to others if you have not proved its efficacy? Has He saved you from anger, from impatience, from ceaseless desires, from envy or discontent, from fear of death, from ignorance? Only when you have tested the power of His teaching in your own life can you know its true value. When you have felt the Christ spirit awakening in you; when you have begun to experience for yourself those things which He showed forth in His life; when, even facing death, you can say as He did in the garden:

"Not my will, but Thine," and then go forth unmoved by false accusation, so absolutely surrendered as not to speak a word even in self-defense; when you have been able to live one day as He lived, then you may say that Christ is a Savior, because He has done something towards saving you. You have proved His power. And then there will be no need for you to proclaim Him. Your life will do it.

The greatest things are always accomplished in the realm of feeling. That is why the Psalmist cried out: "I will feel after God, if happily I may find Him." We may think about Him forever and we shall not reach Him, for intellectual recognition alone is the fruit of thinking. The heart is the seat of the highest consciousness. The subconscious mind, so the great Vedic psychologists discovered, resides in all the nerve ganglia of the body; the conscious mind has the brain for its seat and instrument; while the superconscious faculties are resident in the heart. At the time of deepest meditation the whole activity is focused there; hence we read again the Psalms "Let the meditations of my heart be acceptable to Thee, O Lord." Also, it is said in the Maitrayana Brahmana Upanishad: "When one, having freed the mind from sloth, distraction and vacillation, becomes as it were delivered from the mind, that is the highest point. The mind must be restrained in the heart until its activities come to an end; that is knowledge, that is liberty." The preliminary processes, — concentration, discrimination, choice — take place in the head; but as the spiritual vision plunges deeper, ordinary intellection ceases, and a great fire kindles in the heart by the rising flame of which one apprehends clearly and directly all the ultimate verities of existence.

Every living being is equipped to attain this state of vision. In each life-germ is involved all the faculties necessary to perceive every truth regarding God and His universe; but by the faculties of one plane we cannot apprehend the truths of another. It is because even the most earnest seekers sometimes do not take account of this fact that, after vain efforts to know God through the intellect, they declare Him to be unknown and unknowable. It is easy for us to see that our bodily sense-organs, the fruit of our subconscious evolution, cannot reveal to us the higher truths of reason. To discern these, we must develop a new set of intellectual faculties. By the same law, mind or intellect cannot perceive the things of the Divine realm; for that again we must evolve spiritual faculties. Sri Krishna indicates this in the Bhagavad Gita when, referring to His own Divine Nature, He says to Arjuna: "But Thou canst not see Me with these eyes of Thine; behold I give thee Divine sight."

The process, however, by which each new set of faculties is unfolded remains the same through the whole gamut of consciousness. As it was the desire to perceive objects or forces impinging on the surface of the primitive body worn by the individual life-germ or Soul in the early stages of its manifestation, which impelled it to evolve eyes, ears, olfactory nerves and all the senses; as again in the human form it has been the desire to perceive and master the subtler laws and principles playing on his or her life and mind and character which has led that same individual to develop higher intellectual organs; so will it be an irresistible yearning to understand the subtlest forces of the universe which will bring about the evolution of the highest faculties, those of the spirit. But although the motive-cause throughout the journey remains the same, the direction taken is gradually reversed. In the first stage, all the disturbing stimuli being external, the life-germ moves outward and concentrates its whole activity in an effort to pierce various channels of communication with the external world. In the second stage the activity alternates; a disturbance outside sets up a corresponding disturbance in the inner, mental realm; and we move first outward, then inward, trying by alternating processes of observation and reflection, of experiment and deduction, to relate and coordinate the facts of both realms. In the final stage, however, the disturbing, impinging stimuli are all inner. A nameless, insatiable hunger of mind and heart, grief, disappointment, a thirst for Truth: these are the forces beating upon our deepening consciousness. In order to perceive and understand their causes, we must turn, and with the same energy we once spent in piercing the sense channels outward, we must now cut new channels inward to the core of our being, where at last we will stand face to face with the Ultimate Reality and know the ultimate cause of all things. Then our task of evolution will be finished. Whatever work we do thenceforth will be a free offering to the world. But until that point is reached, through all our activities, however philanthropic or humanitarian, we are only learning lessons which in the cosmic economy are also used to bring benefit to others.

The task is a mighty one and it cannot be undertaken in any haphazard or half-hearted way. We must set our whole will and desire towards it. We must be as eager for the Ultimate Truth, for that Truth which will make us free. We must be willing to cleanse and prepare our body, mind and heart with great patience. We must make space in our daily routine for our spiritual pursuits, as every lover of learning creates hours for study. How many of our great scientists and scholars were forced in early years to maintain themselves by some uncongenial work, while they advanced along the line of their real vocation? We must feel that our spiritual practice is as vital to our life and health as our eating and bathing, and must be carried on with the same unquestioned regularity. We do not consider ourselves selfish or unmindful of the demands of others if we take time to cleanse and nourish the body; should the soul, too, not receive its share of care? When the yearning is keen enough, time and opportunity will not be lacking, for God is pressing on us from all sides. Every grief or failure is His call to turn from the unreal to the Real; every joy or triumph is a reminder that He is there. That Supreme Power which has driven us on from the earliest microorganisms to the human being is still impelling us, and will never let us rest until we realize our Godhood. Shall we hold back, clinging to our present unfinished state; or shall we yield ourselves up to that great, on-pushing Divine Energy? If we go with It, what is our reward? Supreme vision, Supreme bliss, and illumined comprehension of all things.

Actually we are all coveting the Real — real pleasure, real beauty, real strength, real love, but we seek it where it cannot be found, for every relative object, although seeming for the moment real in comparison with some lower and more fleeting one, proves unreal when placed beside a higher form of joy or beauty. Hence our constant change and search for something more satisfying, more enduring. Our present partial knowledge is like a twilight in which shadows appear realities, real things like shadows. At every step we seem to stand at dim crossroads, not knowing which to take. It is this perpetual uncertainty and indecision, that sense of unknowingness, which makes life so burdensome. Yet it cannot be otherwise so long as we walk in ignorance; for ignorance alone, not outward conditions, is the cause of all our misery, our doubt and discontent. As long as we look upon this great machine of the universe in ignorance, we shall be conscious of the noise, the danger, the toil and drudgery, the ceaseless revolution, the unsightliness of half-made objects, of disconnected parts, and we shall criticize, complain, and doubt. Let us, however, begin to understand the laws and principles operating beneath it all, soon our complaints and criticisms will turn to wondering admiration for the order and beauty manifesting everywhere. When, in the ultimate realization, we view the whole from the central point, the Final Cause, then we shall behold a new heaven and a new earth, in which the Real shines resplendent behind every form; and our one prayer will be: "O Thou Supreme Light of the Universe, lead all beings from the unreal to the

Real, from the darkness of ignorance to the effulgent light of knowledge, that they may behold Thy glory and enjoy lasting peace and happiness."

The Source of Power

If we would partake of the attributes of Divinity, we must connect ourselves with the Divine. There must be some point of contact, and we establish this through our thought. The more we think of ourselves, of our personal joys and sorrows, our selfish advantage or disadvantage, the less of our mind remains with which to think on God and the less of godliness shall we enjoy. Every thought of self puts out a thought of God and every thought of God puts out a thought of self. But the God-thoughts are full of sweetness and light and subtle power; while the thoughts of self are full of fear and disappointment and discontent. God-thought expands and liberates, self-thought contracts and enslaves. Why then do we think so much about ourselves? Have we found the companionship of our ego so satisfying that we should be reluctant to exchange it for the holier, sweeter companionship of God?

So long as we divide our attention, we shall be weak and undependable. Power comes only to the single-hearted. Christ has told us that the pure alone can gain access to the Divine; and purity means something more than mere cleanness of body, mind and heart. It means unmixed. If we take two perfectly pure chemical substances and put them together, the new substance produced is not pure; each of the constituent parts adulterates the other. Purity in the spiritual life, quite as much as in chemistry, demands uncompromising singleness — singleness of heart, singleness of mind, singleness of purpose.

Connection with the Source is all that should concern us, not what we shall get out of it. If we approach It devoutly and unquestioningly, we shall be filled to the full measure of our capacity; and as our capacity increases, so will our power. When we are in unbroken touch with God, we will always know what is needed to be known. We will render just the right service, we will speak just the right word, we will take just the right course. There will be no waste of energy anywhere, because we will have no steps to retrace, no mistakes to mend, and no wearing down on the bearings of life through friction. In all circumstances we will act in perfect conjunction with the one supreme cosmic power.

Planless Living

When great musicians embody their thought in symphonic form, they leave nothing to chance. They indicate with precision tonality and time-beat, bar and double bar, crescendo and diminuendo, note-sequences and rests. They realize that to leave it to the discretion of the orchestra when to come in and what to play would mean jangling confusion, and music would degenerate into noise. Creation is such a symphony — a mighty thought embodied in rhythm and harmony, with no haphazard, no ungoverned license, anywhere. Each note and phrase is clearly set down.

This exactitude and dependability constitute its chief value for us. We can know with certainty when the sun will rise and when it will set, at what hour tides will be high or low, what orbit a star or planet will follow, what course trees and plant-life will take. A creation without preconceived design and predetermined system would be a creation in anarchy. Imagine a universe in which stars and sun moved about at will, sometimes in this orbit, sometimes in that; where each ocean-drop had its own time for rising and falling; where a tree bore apples this season and figs next season. It would be a clashing, crashing universe and life in it would consist of disconnected fragments.

Someone said to the great Indian saint, Sri Ramakrishna, "God is free — He can do whatever He pleases. Can He make a mango grow on a peach tree?" Sri Ramakrishna answered: "Why should He? He has plenty of mango trees." Knowing the best possible way a universe should operate, a way that has stood the test of eternity, the Supreme Deity could ill resort to a variation that would represent a second-best way. This cosmic habit of doing everything in the best way is what we interpret as law. We ourselves follow the same course. When we find a better method of performing a task, we adopt it and discard the poorer one. If we learn that a certain way of lighting a fire is safe and another way may cause an explosion, spontaneously we choose the safer method. Repetition of this creates a habit, and reiterated habit constitutes the law of our being. We however, are variable, while the Divine is unwavering and absolute.

If all is designed and pre-determined, what have we to do in this great cosmic scheme? Cooperate with it. Every human being has an essential place in the universe. We are as necessary to the universe as the universe is to us. The part needs the whole and the whole needs the part — just as a machine needs the bolt to complete it, while the bolt needs the machine to fulfill its purpose. Each cosmic unit has its task in the general scheme of universal cooperation. A peach tree has the mission of being the finest peach tree possible and producing the best peaches. So with all forms of manifestation. It may be said: "How monotonous to always do the same thing!" Artists do not feel thus as they work at their easel. Their sole desire is to paint picture after picture until they have achieved a masterpiece.

Our natural vocation is the cosmic plan for us, it is the task we are best fitted to perform. A definite talent means a partial recognition of the plan of being, genius indicates a more complete grasp of it, the full glow of illumination tells us that the plan has been achieved. No one is happier than when they move along the line of greatest power. They ask for no variance save that of increasing power to let the fire of inspiration burn through.

Cooperation in the great cosmic plan is not possible for us, however, so long as we continue to make little plans of our own. So long as we persist in creating our own narrow world and in enthroning ourselves in the center of it, in supreme command, we cannot form a part of the great universe. We cannot follow our little way and the big way or "serve two masters" at the same time. If we try, one effort will neutralize the other. We are eager to plan, but do we make a success of our plans? We formulate an elaborate schedule for our day and at night it lies in broken fragments at our feet. Something unexpected has come up and shattered it. The unexpected was the cosmic plan, which fulfills itself in the face of our spurious independence and self-assertion.

There is but one mighty plan for the universe. When our individual plans conform with the universe's plan, they are accomplished; when they go contrary to it, they are frustrated. We may wish to force our peach tree to bear mangos, but the cosmos sees to it that it bears peaches just the same. This does not mean that there is a relentless tyrant driving us by the point of a sword. It means merely that the universe is well-organized.

There must be a system to ensure order and efficiency, there must be someone "in charge" to maintain the system and the system must be carried out. This becomes insistently true when the system is based on perfect wisdom and the leader possesses unlimited understanding and unlimited power. We may imagine sometimes that we could create a better universe or one that would function more smoothly, but that is only because we see it in parts, not as a whole. We take this part or that and magnify it until it seems to be the whole, this falsifies the values and spoils the picture. Our proportions are all wrong.

We must overcome our erroneous notion that if we entrusted ourselves wholly to the cosmic plan, we would be minimized to nothingness. Nature is not trying to suppress us. Her purpose is perfection. Her aim for each one of us is the most complete expression of being possible. She wishes to round us out on all sides. It cannot be denied that she disciplines us, but a tree would not be symmetrical without pruning and gold needs fire. When the cosmic power is allowed to work unhindered, it gives us the beauty of the sunset glow on the hilltops, the tender loveliness of the twilight, the extravagant plumage of tropical birds, the self-sacrifice of the honey bee, the industry of the ant, the gurgling note of song-sparrow or thrush. Still more it gives such towering radiant figures as a Jesus of Nazareth, a Gautama Buddha, a Pythagoras or a St. Francis of Assisi. Do they bear the mark of being minimized or suppressed?

We need not fear that we shall lose anything if we follow in their footsteps and break the bounds of our narrow personal world. The little plans we make do not sustain our life. The great universe is beneath us, above us and all about us. This it is which upholds us and carries us on to complete achievement in the face of the many hindrances we set up by our ceaseless planning. Our strength and our ultimate attainment lie in voluntarily unifying ourselves with it. We accomplish this by shifting our central point of interest. Now the petty details of existence absorb all our attention and the great things go by unnoticed. We fritter away our time and vital energy on nonessentials and the essentials we scarcely think of.

The habit must be reversed. We must pay more heed to the cosmic world and less to the little one we have made. We cannot study the greater one and live with it from day to day without our power, our vision, our efficiency gathering force and depth. An eminent physician of Boston standing in the high Sierras asked a forester of the region if he and his workers believed in God. The forester pointed to the lofty snow-capped peaks and replied: "We cannot look at those day after day and not believe in something bigger than ourselves."

To find and unite with "something bigger than ourselves" is the secret of all real happiness. To produce the desired result we must challenge every decision, every thought, every act of volition, with the question: "Is it in line with the cosmic plan?" The very asking will put us in harmony with the larger way. At first the practice may seem irksome and restricting, but little by little we shall form the habit of bigness and shall choose spontaneously to move in the broader spaces of the universe. When we have become wholly at one with the bigger plan and have ceased to fill our day with self-plotted engagements and tasks, there will be no danger of our life being empty, idle or lonely. Do we know anything more replete with activity and diligence than the cosmic universe? And have we found that our own calculating and planning have kept us from a sense of emptiness and loneliness?

No one who has not tasted it can know the exuberance and lightness of spirit that comes from living in perfect harmony with the Whole. Those who confine themselves in their own small self-created world "live without realizing life" — to borrow a phrase from François Fenelon's *Spiritual Letters*: "To shield ourselves from this self-imprisonment, let us lengthen our count and widen our area of vision. Let us take as our unit of measurement unlimited being. Let us travel with joyous hearts on the open road of the Infinite and the Eternal."

The Spirit of Contentment

Contentment is a vital spiritual principle, essential to higher attainment. In the Bhagavad Gita we read that those who are dear to the Lord are "content with everything," that those whose hearts are fixed on Him and whose lives are absorbed in Him are "contented and rejoiced." And the Buddhist scriptures declare: "Whosoever is desirous of doing good and of striving after the state of perfect peace, which is Nirvana, must be mild, content, of few wants; without care and of restful heart." The Chinese sacred books also make contentment the salient mark of the "sagely person." The contentment enjoined by the scriptures, however, is not a fitful mood changing with circumstance; it is a steadfast habit of mind, born of inner resources and wholly independent of all outer conditions. It does not lapse into discontent when hardships or misfortune darken the horizon. It supplies its own radiance and persists in the face of every trial.

Desire, not misfortune, is the cause of our discontent; and desire springs from a false conception of the universe. We look upon it as a store window in which are displayed countless objects for our choosing — objects which we imagine we can purchase or earn. The universe, however, is not made of marketable parts. No part may be broken off and owned privately. We may believe that we possess it but in reality it possesses us; and we pay tribute to it in freedom, peace, strength — sometimes even in our good name and our integrity. The universe is a unit, it cannot be subdivided and bought and sold. The only way we can enjoy it is to enter into it consciously and willingly and become one with it, obedient to its laws and regulations. When we see a blossoming tree by the wayside, we do not try to dig it up and take it home with us; we enjoy it where it is. When we look at a beautiful scene, we do not struggle to possess it. Joy does not come from possession but from knowledge and power of appreciation. The whole universe becomes ours when we learn to understand its true meaning and purpose.

Desire is not lessened by acquisition. It grows as we satisfy it. The only way we can overcome it is by rooting out from our nature that which generates it. Until this is done, we may change our surroundings, our occupation, all our conditions but the same covetous longing, the same discontent will confront us in the new environment. Environment and circumstance are the reflection of ourselves. Our discontented moods have their origin in our own attitude of mind; the outside world has little part in them. By running away, therefore, they cannot be conquered.

We cannot afford to indulge in discontent. It narrows and distorts our outlook and breeds pettiness and regard for trivialities. There is something purifying and sanctifying in a large grief but our petty passing grievances belittle and debase us. Rabindranath Tagore in one of his poems sends us this crying appeal: "Give me strength to raise my mind high above daily trifles."

A contented mind is the stabilizing power in the spiritual life. Without it there can be neither steadiness nor balance. Meditation, peace and serenity all rest upon it. It is vain to strive to meditate with our heart full of envy or a sense of injury, full of ambition and calculation. Our grievances and restless longings will dissolve our aspiration and our concentration will point downward rather than upward. Undeviating contentment is the basis of all spiritual practice and of all higher unfoldment.

The spirit of contentment and the spirit of surrender are one and inseparable. Each is essential to the other. Not until we surrender will our complaining cease. When however, we compare with seeing eyes our littleness with the vastness and grandeur of the universe, our weakness with its strength, our blundering effort with its intelligence and exactitude, it becomes easy to yield up our individual will to a mightier cosmic plan, willing and glad to let the universal Power and Wisdom manifest in and through us. Then our life will be glorified and our heart will be at peace.

God-Union

Our entire universe revolves, — moons around planets, planets around suns, suns around greater suns. Even a tiny electron has its orbit. This is true not only of the physical world, but of the world of human beings as well. Every human life circles round a center and the nature of that center determines the trend of the life. It also reveals the degree of its development. As we advance, we rise to higher and higher centers and our orbit widens.

A life, to be productive, cannot have several dominant aims. It must adhere to one definite center of effort. Our loftiest point of vision should be the center around which our life should revolve. If we choose a lesser center our outlook will darken and grow confused. We were not created to find pleasure in lesser things. We are of Divine origin — an origin that is infinite. We have sprung from Divinity, we inhere in Divinity; we live, move, think and act in the Divine. That which is fleeting will not content us. What can the little passing things of this world count against God?

Only when we make God the center of our life shall we cease to be restless and dissatisfied. He is the center now, but we are not conscious of it because we live at the circumference — on the outside of our being; we do not go within. Of this lack of inwardness the 17th century mystic, William Law, writes: "Your reason and senses, your heart and passions have turned all their attention to the poor concerns of this life, and therefore you are a stranger to this principle of Heaven, these riches of Eternity within you. For as God is not, cannot be, truly found by any worshipper but those who worship Him in spirit and in truth; so this Light and Spirit, though always within us, is not, cannot be found, felt or enjoyed but by those whose whole spirit is turned to it . . . . God, the source of all good, communicates Himself to the soul that longs to partake of Him, with even more certainty than the sun meets the flower bud that reaches for the light. He is our closest companion. He is nearer to us than we are to ourselves. He shares our pains and distresses. He carries our burden. If He does not take away pain and burden, it is because He would not impoverish us.

If we would attain conscious oneness with the Divine, we must lead an aspiring life. We cannot travel the level road. Our course must mount upward and upward — from peak to higher peak and on to the highest. There can be no compromise in our consecration or in our striving. We must "stand steadily and with perseverance." We may have many worldly duties, many claims upon our strength and time, but that will matter little, if we carry aspiration in our thought and God in our heart. Sri Ramakrishna counsels us, when we have work in the world to do, to do our work with one hand and hold the feet of the Lord with the other; when our work is done, to hold His feet to our heart with both our hands.

God-union is not the ultimate; there is a state beyond, that of conscious identity with Divine Being. To many this may seem sacrilege; to others, impossibility. In reality, however, it is the logical outcome of the oneness of life and consciousness existent throughout the universe. We are like vessels immersed in a boundless ocean. The water in the vessels is identical with the waters of the ocean, all that divides them is the thin wall of the vessel. Break that and the waters mingle and become one. The wall of the vessel is our sense of "I-ness" and "mine-ness." When by prayer and contemplation, by holy living and selfless service, this "I-ness" is broken down, the life and consciousness within and without us will merge and there will remain only the "Thou" and "Thine." Yet we are not obliterated. The waters of the river are not lost when they flow into the ocean. Each drop is still present, but it has taken on the nature and conditions of the ocean. So shall we become one with the Infinite Life, the Infinite Knowledge, and the Infinite Bliss of the Absolute, when we merge in that great ocean of Infinitude.

Oneness

The universe rests on oneness. Through the multiplicity and variety of created things runs a unity which binds them into a complete whole. In this visible variation there is no repetition; each object differs in some degree from every other. Every tree is an individual, each blossom has its special way of unfolding, and every human being possesses a distinguishing personality. Yet science is able to classify and tabulate. This is due to the underlying oneness of all things.

In the realm of mind and intellect the same law obtains. At the outset of study or intellectual research students are chiefly concerned with the many. They read many books, hold many arguments and discussions, use many words, see many differences. But as they go deeper they begin to relate and to coordinate. They read and talk less and think more. Finally their thought becomes wholly unified and they grow silent. The Chinese philosopher, Lao Tze, declares, "The sage instructs without uttering a word, remembering how all things in nature work silently together, fulfilling the purpose for which they are created without relying upon the help of others."

On the plane of spirit there can be no multiplicity. There must be oneness of ideal, oneness of purpose, oneness of method. The devotee must be steadfast and unified in both aim and effort. In a medieval manual of devotion the Lord gives this injunction: "You must make Me thy supreme and ultimate end if you truly desire to be blessed. Refer all things to Me in the first place for I am He who hath given all. Think of everything as flowing from the Highest Good, and to Me as their source, all must be brought back again."

We take up the spiritual life entangled in the many — many interests and many attachments. Our task is to disentangle ourselves, that we may reach the One. We accomplish this by the practice of renunciation. This practice does not demand of us rigid privation or retirement to a cloister. It does not ask us to go out of the world, it asks us to go out of ourselves. If we do this wholeheartedly we can remain in the world, love and serve, and yet attain the heights. Renunciation means simplifying, giving up the nonessentials, building our life on a larger plan. We must rise superior to our body, superior to our surroundings, superior to our circumstances, superior to the opinion of people and to their attitude toward us.

We must begin with our immediate environment — simplify the furnishing of our home, our dress, the food on our table. Wherever spaces can be made, we should make them. We need not fear that the result will be bareness or unsightliness. In simplicity there is greater beauty and distinction than in abundance. In our reading and study also we should be more one-pointed. We read too casually — a book recommended by a friend, a book found by chance, a book on the best seller list. This heterogeneous reading confuses the mind and disintegrates the deeper thought gained through meditation. We need not cease to read, but we must have a purpose in what we read. If we would advance toward oneness, we must unify our intellectual study and harmonize it with our spiritual practice. This is true of all media input. Thomas à Kempis tells us, "The more a man is at one within himself and becomes single in heart, the more and higher things is he able without labor to understand, for that he receives the light of understanding from above."

Passing from the many to the one, from multiplicity to unity, is the history of all religions. In their primitive stage they have many deities; every tree, every woodland, every mountain and valley has its presiding spirit; all the forces of nature are personified and deified. As the religious consciousness deepens, there arises a God of gods, and the first glimmering conception of oneness is born. A further awakening transforms the minor gods into aspects of the Divine. Oneness, however, is not yet attained; worshipper and worshipped are still separate. But in the virgin forests of India, in China, and Egypt, there arose great sages who proclaimed the union of worshipper and worshipped. The same truth is reiterated in the scriptural records of the time, as we see from such passages as this one, taken from the Bhagavad Gita:

> The Supreme alone exists, enveloping all.... Unattached, yet It sustains all.... It exists within and without all beings: It is unmoving as well as moving, incomprehensible because of Its subtlety; It is far and also near. Indivisible, yet It exists as if divided in beings; It is to be known as the Sustainer of beings; It destroys and also generates. It is the Light of light, and is said to be beyond darkness. It is knowledge, the One to be known, and the Goal of knowledge, dwelling in the hearts of all ... Those who see the separate existence of beings established in the One, and their expansion from That alone, becomes one with the Highest.

Whom the Self Chooses

Throughout the Vedic scriptures there is but one call — to know the higher Self, to know God, and it is significant that we are driven on to discover this Truth not by threats of punishment, but by promise of great strength, and supreme blessings. We read in the Chandogya Upanishad:

> The Infinite indeed is below, above, behind, before, right and left — It is indeed all this ... Those who see this do not see death, nor illness, nor pain, those who see this see everything, and obtain everything everywhere.

Another statement, in the Katha Upanishad, related to the sacred Word, the *AUM*:

> This Word is indeed Brahman (the Absolute), this Word is indeed the Supreme. Those who know this Word attain whatever they desire.

This is the best Support; this is the highest Support; those who know this Support are glorified in the world of Brahman.

Finally, again in the Chandogya Upanishad, we find a third statement that is explanatory of the other two:

> In It (Brahman) all desires are contained. It is the Self, free from sin, free from old age, from death and grief, from hunger and thirst, which desires nothing but what it ought to desire, and imagines nothing but what it ought to imagine . . . .
>
> Those who depart from hence without having discovered the Self and those true desires, for them there is no freedom in all the worlds. But those who depart from hence, after having discovered the Self and those true desires, for them there is freedom in all the worlds.

This means that those of illumination never have any desires contrary to the great cosmic Plan. If they did desire things apart from that Plan, they would not be illumined. The two conditions are contradictory. Those who have attained God-union have no interest apart from the interest of the whole. They do not differentiate or separate themselves from the whole. The cosmic Will is their will; the cosmic Law is their rule of action.

It is clear, therefore, that the only way that we can have all our desires satisfied is to make our will His Will. Then naturally we shall desire nothing but what is in accordance with the supreme, universal Plan, and that cannot fail of fulfillment.

We have been told that there are certain means by which we may attain that vision needful for union with the One. Of these, perhaps the greatest, is truthfulness. We have thought up to now that one tells the truth in order to be virtuous; but actually telling the truth is for the purpose of developing the sense of Truth within us. We possess faculties by which we perceive Truth, and by speaking the truth we cause these faculties to come into manifestation. That is why only the perfectly truthful can know the Truth. They alone have a developed Truth perception. Truthfulness in the spiritual life means absolute exactness in thought, word and action, with no distortion, deception or manipulation.

Most of us have been following the moral law, but our grasp of it has been largely intellectual; and we have accepted truth-telling as an intellectual necessity. It is, however, not enough to tell the truth; we must be truthful. In other words, every motion, the very expression of our face, each act, must be based on Truth. How often we avoid telling an absolute falsehood yet allow one to be inferred. How often we repeat things without knowing whether or not they are accurate; and how often we excuse ourselves and try to explain away our faults.

This is not practicing the Truth. If we are in the wrong we must be willing to stand up and say that we are wrong. If anyone accuses us and we realize that we are at fault, we must simply admit it, just as we admit that we are short or tall, stout or thin. We must feel always that the vital thing is to keep in line with the Truth, even if we are condemned or persecuted. "Blessed are they who are persecuted for righteousness' sake." Let us be upright, no matter how much we have to suffer for it. For until the Truth means more to us than comfort, honor, or happiness of any kind, we will not be able to perceive It. But when we have reached that point, no one can keep Truth from us. We will have earned It.

Discipline and Discipleship

Discipline is nothing but the shaping of crude material into more useful forms, the pruning and trimming to stimulate new life. But discipline presupposes one who disciplines. Self-discipline is practically impossible in the early stages of either physical or spiritual development. As in natural science it is recognized that any object will move indefinitely along the line of least resistance unless stopped or diverted by some stronger force, so we, if left to ourselves, revolve round and round in the same orbit. We do not rise or expand because we do not escape from our ego, from our own small standard of measurement. We need some propelling power from outside to force us to enlarge our orbit, to climb to a higher level.

The one way to make human beings better is to lift them out of their self-consciousness. We can broaden only by transcending the ego, for it is this little self that shuts us in and limits us. Yet so long as we have nothing to take the place of this ego, it must possess us. So this ego, although really a servant, lords over us; and there is only one who can make it subordinate — that is God. But He must come to us first in some concrete form. At present our own little self is the most definite thing we know. To put it in its subordinate place, there must be something equally definite. Vedanta declares that if we would attain the highest, religion and God must become as definite to us as our material life. Our spiritual education must be as systematic and precise as our secular education. We must have our classroom and teacher. We must have clearly defined duties, fixed lessons to learn, a higher authority to bow to, and a pure, mature and ripe ego to put in the place of our self-centered, immature, unripe ego, someone to serve and follow.

We cannot pass suddenly from the lowest to the highest. We cannot directly supplant the concrete by the abstract. We must move gradually up the scale from the gross to the subtle; and at every step a "mediator" between us and the Ultimate Ideal is such a help. Before we can form a true conception of Christ, we must see someone living the Christ-life. Before we can learn to define holiness, purity, consecration, we must find them embodied in some lofty character. That is what Christ meant when He said: "I am the Way." He did not mean that merely believing in Him would make a person holy. Don't we know people who have believed in Jesus for years and are as far as ever from the Christ ideal? No, He meant: "Walk as I have walked, resist temptation as I have resisted it, rise above the world as I have risen above it, then you will attain Truth".

In our spiritual childhood, however, it is almost impossible for us to do this alone. We reach out instinctively for a tangible example to follow, for someone who will give us an effective method and teach us its application by their own life and action. The finding of the Guru or teacher therefore becomes the most vital concern in the Soul's life, and for that reason in India it has from earliest times been made the foundation of all religious education. The great Vedic scriptures are indeed in large part nothing but a record of discipleship: Nachiketas learning the secret of death from Yama; Indra gaining, through long service, the knowledge of the Self from Prajapati; Maitreyi sitting at the feet of Yajnavalkya to be taught the lesson of immortality; or still further back, the unknown Rishi or Seer giving answer in the Rig Veda to the earnest seeker who sought him out and asked to "know that by knowing which all else can be known." Always in every line we catch the ring of the spoken word and see the picture of the loving teacher patiently dispelling the doubt in the questioning heart of the disciple who, through the years perhaps, of humble service — bringing water from the stream and firewood from the jungle — has become like a son or daughter in the household. From those Vedic days the Indian method has not varied for just as the system of apprenticeship invariably develops a high standard of excellence in the arts and crafts, so the system of discipleship as surely brings a lofty vision in the realm of spirit.

The disciple is an apprentice, learning the practice of religion through service and association. We too often imagine that taking up the spiritual life means reading many books about God, spending long hours in meditation, withdrawing from outer occupations. But, on the contrary, according to the Indian system, it means working with hands and feet, following the path of humble service. Why? To curb and quiet the ego. Unless there is silence within, God's voice cannot be heard. "Be still and know that I am God," the Bible tells us. But it is not possible for the beginner to attain this stillness all at once. We must work off our untamed energies, just as children must work off their exuberance and energy. We must purify our outer and inner nature by properly directed activity, as we purify our physical organism by wholesome exercise; for until we have purified the denser part of our nature which obscures the Divine, we cannot know the Truth.

We have this glimmering of knowledge that guides us from day to day only because it is a part, a ray, going out from that Infinite Knowledge. We only feel these little fleeting waves of joy because for an instant we have touched, though dimly, the great divine bliss of the Eternal. That is there, existing in our hearts now. We do not have to go anywhere outside to find it. We have only to learn where to go within ourselves. At present that light is covered over by the veils of impurity which we have drawn across it. It is because we have lived in ourselves; we have worked for ourselves and related only to ourselves. We have made ourselves so entirely commensurate with this little self that we cannot imagine anything bigger and so the great Self has been obscured and forgotten. Now what we must do from day to day is to clear away the impurities which cover it. This clearing away is what we call discipline. How can it be better accomplished than by serving one who has torn the veil and seen the Self? The easiest way to knowledge always is go live with one who knows. Associate with a holy, God-enlightened soul and God-knowledge must as surely come, although necessarily more slowly, since the faculties by which He may be apprehended must be unfolded.

But where can such teachers be found? In this busy commercial age saints and sages are not seated at every intersection. Yet have no doubt that the teacher and the teaching will come when we are ready. Never can we fail to know the Truth when we really hunger and thirst for it. If we do not know it today, it is because our hunger is so slight or because the hunger for worldly things is greater. We may say: "I do not hunger for them." Yes, we may not do so consciously; but the fact that we suffer when our desires are thwarted shows that we are hungering for them; the very fact that though our life seems empty, yet we do not turn to God to fill it, shows that we still want it to be filled by worldly things. Many think that they want God, but they actually haven't the least desire for Him. Our environment is unpleasant to us, we have many things to bear, and so we imagine that we are tired of the world and ready for higher things. But let God offer us a pleasant life, a little more money, a happy home, and we are perfectly satisfied. This shows that what we wanted was not God, or the religious life, it was a happy worldly life. So we must not deceive ourselves. We must prove that we want the Truth, and the only way we can prove it is by bearing cheerfully and bravely whatever discipline is given us, whether by the teacher or by life.

Quiet, steady, selfless service prepares us for the final victory. But service is not merely a positive thing. Negative service, the service of silent endurance for the sake of the ideal, also purifies. Those who have felt the call of Truth in their hearts turn away from no misfortune or hardship. When troubles and difficulties arise, they accept them cheerfully, thinking: "Another opportunity to wipe out a little more of myself," and so they embrace with appreciation the greatest trial. Such is the spirit of discipleship; and only when the spirit comes does self-discipline become possible. Each of us must literally work out our own salvation, just as we must acquire our own education. Someone must prepare the food, but we must eat it; so the teacher can only give the knowledge, the labor of digesting and assimilating must always rest with the disciple. A great sage in India once said to me: "The work of the Guru or spiritual teacher is like this: You are riding a bicycle in the wrong direction, someone comes and turns you round. You keep on pedaling just the same, but now you ride with new hope and confidence because you know you are headed towards your destination and have someone to guide you along the way."

The Three States of Consciousness

In and out through the duality of nature is woven a triplicity; the very two implies a third. There can be indeed not duality without a trinity, because where the two opposites meet is created a third thing born of the union of the two. Thus we have day and night and the point where they join called twilight. We have sound sleep and waking and the mingling of the two in dream. We have the knower and the object and the result of their union, knowledge. All manifestation falls inevitably into one of these three states, which are called in Sanskrit *tamas, rajas,* and *sattva*. The first is a state of darkness, heaviness, dullness, lethargy. *Rajas* is a state of unrest, activity, passion, ambition, self-assertion — the characteristics of the human plane; and the third is a state of calmness, lightness, illumination, serene joy — to be found only on the spiritual plane. In us these three states express themselves as the subconscious, the conscious and the superconscious; and according to the predominance of one or the other do we appear to be ignorant and brutish, an intellectual and moral being, or a saint and seer.

We are that which our consciousness dwells upon. If we fall short of our ideal, we have only to begin to lift our thought up the sliding scale of consciousness from that which we are to that which we long to be. To do this there are no chasms over which we have to leap. Our consciousness stretches in one unbroken line from the grossest to the subtlest stratum of our being; and on it we may climb steadily from subconscious through the conscious to the superconscious. These different states, however, haven't clearly defined borders. No milestone stands to tell us where subconscious ends and conscious begins. As certain thoughts and actions by constant repetition deepen into habits, they drop to the automatic plane; thus yesterday's conscious activity becomes today's subconscious; and in like manner the reasoned effort of the present moment will in time become instinctive. This is nature's method of releasing our will power from the dulling routine of our lower being, that we may push on to higher realms.

The upward process, however, must be a continuous one. We cannot jump suddenly from the state of *tamas* or heaviness to the state of *sattva* or illumination. And this rule applies not only to our general evolution, but also to our daily practice. When we feel overpowered by dullness or depression, it is futile to combat it by trying to meditate. We must first rouse our vital energies by some active exertion. Then when we have driven out *tamas* by *rajas*, we are ready to sit down and become reflective. To the great majority the third and highest state is practically unknown. Their life consists almost wholly in ceaseless reactions between *tamas* and *rajas*, that is, from over-activity to weariness and back to over-activity. This is true both in work and in play.

Usually when people feel the need to relax they go outside, they move towards the circumference; the wise turn inward and move towards the center.

To learn to control and direct these reactions is one of the primary lessons in our spiritual education. We must first eliminate all extremes. Elation and depression, feverish activity and lethargy, both represent unbalance, hence weakness. We must set our will firmly at the middle point and govern the swing of the pendulum into rest and action. Until we can do this we shall have no real strength or joy in living.

The body represents *tamas* or heaviness in us, that is why it weighs us down. Therefore when it begins to drag, we should learn to drop it from our consciousness as we do at the time of sleep. The same refreshment will follow. Naturally this cannot be done all at once. It will come only as the result of practice, through the cultivation of a higher state of consciousness. Now we live too much in the subconscious. Our chief concern is to make this body comfortable, to shelter, feed and clothe it. Yet so long as we make our physical existence the governing principle in all our activity, we are dwelling in the subconscious or brute state; not until we have ceased to identify ourselves with it and have discovered a loftier motive for action shall we rise fully to the human plane.

But here again little rest or peace will come to us. Our mind is a more wearying companion than our body. Desire for pleasure, many interests and ambitions, greed, jealousy, discontent, nameless longing, prod it on to ceaseless motion, making serene thought impossible. We are not as wholly absorbed in our own well-being and happiness as we were on the subconscious plane. We are ready to share up to a certain point, but beyond that we find ourselves at constant war with something or someone. The plane of *rajas* is the plane of struggle and conflict; it throws us back and forth between the contending dualities of pleasure and pain, honor and dishonor, success and failure, until worn and breathless we cry out for relief. As before, our only escape is into a higher state of consciousness; and we reach it, as in the previous upward step, by shifting the point of self-identity, by detaching ourselves from these mental conditions and realizing that our true Self is in no way touched by them. The ocean is always the same mighty ocean whether the surface is lashed to a fury or rolls in even swell; so down in the depths of our being the stream of our real life flows ever onward in steady quiet current, undisturbed by the waves and eddies that may stir its surface. The moment we have crossed into the superconscious or meditative realm all the noise of battle ceases and we are at peace.

The subconscious is the plane of sensuality; the conscious, of morality; the superconscious, of spirituality. In the subconscious, instinct guides us; in the conscious, reason; and in the superconscious, revelation or inspiration. The first and third seem unerring, the second full or error. Why? Because in the highest and lowest there is oneness or unity. The cosmic will works unimpeded through the other living non-human beings and through the saint. In ordinary people self-consciousness enters in and we are broken into two, hence every light brings a shadow which bewilders and misleads. Yet the very effort to distinguish between reality and unreality gradually develops the power of discrimination and converts the ignorant into a moral being. Then as we learn to efface ourselves for our neighbor and our neighbor's neighbor, the horizon of our self-consciousness gradually expands until it embraces the whole universe, we come "to see the Self in all beings and all beings in the Self," and we return to voluntary oneness with the whole. Our eye grows single, where we saw diversity we now see unity, and our being becomes full of light — the light of superconscious illumination.

Human beings were not meant to remain at the level of the animal, we were not meant to remain at the human level, we were meant to be divine. It is by our own choice that we grope our way along in our present state of unknowingness, seeing all things dimly. If we will but make the effort, we may in this very life gain the power of unerring vision. It must be done, however, by a gradual transformation not only of our inner nature, but of our outer environment. The process of purification must be both exterior and interior. Since through all nature there run these three qualities of *sattva*, *rajas* and *tamas*, we must strive to relate ourselves everywhere to the highest *sattvic* element of purity, goodness and light. Food is recognized as an effective factor in accomplishing this; but food in this case does not signify merely the nutriment we give to our body; it also includes that which we give to our mind, our heart, our whole organism. It is what we eat, what we read, the associations we seek, the desires we cherish.

As a good mechanic is careful to select an oil that doesn't clog the engine, so we should choose a physical diet that does not overweight our system. As much as possible animal food should be eliminated. Among vegetables, it is said that those which grow in the earth are the most *tamasic* in their nature and those that grow above ground are more *rajasic*, while fruits and foods which need not be cooked are the most *sattvic*. There can be no fixed rule of diet for all; it must be modified according to the individual constitution and circumstance. We must observe the effects of different foods upon us and take that which gives strength without destroying the sense of lightness. We must also consider what fits us best for our special task. We should not choose to induce a certain state in us merely because it is desirable, without regard to our responsibilities in the world. If we are free to devote our time to spiritual study and lead a retired life, we can safely cultivate more of the element of *sattva* in our system; but average persons, who are in close contact with the world, need some *tamas* or density just as a ship needs ballast. They should have a larger supply of *rajas* or vital energy; and if with these they can acquire by meditation and earnest study a predominance of *sattva*, they will do their work with a speed, efficiency and understanding impossible to the one weighted by *tamas* or rendered unsteady by an excess of *rajas*. They will also possess such poise and quietness that they will reduce waste to a minimum and suffer less from fatigue.

This superior state, however, is not gained by any method of exclusion or destruction. As nothing goes out of a dark room when a light is turned on, so no part of our nature is destroyed when we attain illumination. It is not a question of exchanging one kind of consciousness for another, but of extending our dominion over the whole area of consciousness. We must recover control over the subconscious, which now acts almost wholly independent of our volition; and we must lay hold of the superconscious. The subconscious mind is seated in all the nerve ganglia of the body and we govern it by regulating our sense-reactions. No impression can enter through our sense-gates except by our consent. It is we who record our sensations, they do not record themselves. A picture may form on our retina, but if we block the perceptive organ behind, we shall see nothing; or if we look at it, yet stop the reaction of the nerve, there will be no reflex motion. The same is true of sound. Usually when a noise disturbs us, we fix our attention upon it and increase its power tenfold. If, on the contrary, we withdrew our attention and turned it resolutely elsewhere, we would soon cease to hear it. By the same method we can rise above pain or any distracting sensation. We have a striking example of this when we are deeply absorbed in a book or swept by some strong emotion. Those who are complete masters of their subconscious minds see, hear, feel only what they choose. Every sensation and its corresponding reflex action are entirely under the command of their will.

The preliminary steps in meditation, such as the practice of posture and breath-control, have as their aim the release of the subconscious faculties. Until we are wholly free from distraction, we shall find it difficult to withdraw into the inner recesses of our being. The next step is the subjugation of the conscious mind. With nearly everyone this is now weak because it is used only in fragments. Very few can put the whole of it into any one mental or physical act. Hence the need of concentration. So long as one filament hangs loose, catching at chance objects, there cannot be an even, united flow of thought and no meditation is possible. When, however, perfect stillness of body and mind frees the entire stream of consciousness, the momentum gained is so great that it quickly carries us into *samadhi* or superconsciousness. Gradually with the increase of *sattva* in our nature, the meditative state will become habitual; then, however incessant the outer demands upon us, our thought will remain in unbroken contact with the Divine.

It is not by changing our life, but by infusing into it this quality of light and serenity that we shall become spiritual. Our inclinations, however, are not a safe guide in doing this. On the contrary they will unfailingly mislead us. When we are in a state of *tamas* or lethargy, through despondency or discouragement, our desire will be to lie down or sit idly brooding. What we should do is to keep steadily active until the heaviness is worked off. That is the secret of travel as a remedy for grief or melancholy. When, on the other hand, we are restive or keyed-up, our craving will be for excitement, change, a multiplication of engagements and duties. Persons of this temperament should seek in every way to simplify their life and leave many spaces in their daily routine. Whenever we find ourselves hurrying unduly, it is an excellent exercise to sit down, close the eyes, fold the hands, and swing to the central point of stillness, if only for a moment. No time will be lost; the poise gained will enable us to save that and many more minutes. The same remedy may be applied when we observe that we are moving noisily, overturning and breaking, or growing impatient and irritable. It indicates that there is too much *rajas* in our system and we should balance it by a voluntary exercise in quietness. The practice, advised in *Karma Yoga*, of pausing for a Godward thought before any undertaking is a great corrective for nervous over-activity.

The Path to Realization

Consciousness is one and universal; its modifications are limitless. In us they fall naturally into three classes — the subconscious, the self-conscious and the superconscious: the brute state, the human state, and the state of seership. There are no barriers between these groups. We can pass freely from one to the other; the only boundary line established is that of our own development. We cannot rise beyond our existing unfoldment.

Corresponding to these states are three aspects of thought — the dualistic, the qualified-monistic and the monistic. In the subconscious or dualistic state creation and Creator appear separate and matter seems a reality. In the self-conscious or human state a constant mingling of the higher and lower takes place. We ascend, but we bring with us our subconscious tendencies. Gradually, however, the radiation of the superconscious modifies these and we attain to a qualified-monistic outlook. As we move onward, the increasing flashes of the superconscious reveal to us little by little the underlying unity in all creation, we perceive oneness everywhere and become monistic in thought.

In qualified-monism the material universe possesses a relative reality; in pure monism it has only an illusory existence. We imagine that we can choose to which one of these three aspects of thought we shall adhere — whether we shall be dualists, qualified-monists or monists. It is not a question of choice, we must grow to the higher states. It requires a long and arduous ascent to reach the heights of monism and manifest oneness in all our thinking and living.

The point at which our consciousness is most active determines our habit of life. If that point is in the subconscious, we shall be prisoners of the body; and food, sleep, dress, pleasures of the senses, will dominate us. If we desire to acquire wealth, it will be in order to provide more luxurious surroundings, greater material comfort and convenience. If we seek admiration, it will be for our appearance rather than for any quality of the soul. This centering the mind in the material narrows and coarsens it. The early Taoist classic, the Yin-Fu-King, declares: "The mind is quickened to activity by external things and dies through excessive pursuit of them."

We may try to avoid this by mingling our material interests with spiritual practice, but we shall not succeed. When we sit down to meditate on some higher object, soon we shall find ourselves concentrating on a problem in our business, or on some difficulty in the household, or on a new garment. The material will overpower the spiritual. The only way we are able to reverse this is by first lifting the mind, fixing it on some higher point and holding it there steadfastly throughout the day. At first this may be difficult but after a time it will become a habit and we shall accomplish our daily tasks more efficiently through contact with our source of power.

The plane of human consciousness is a plane of noble striving. It is also the plane of attainment, because on it there is occasion for voluntary choice. We must choose to scale the summits of vision ourselves. No one can reach them for us. One of the minor Indian scriptures tells us, "Whoever shall be a lamp unto himself shall reach the uttermost heights." As human beings we stand midway between the brute state and the state of seer or saint; thus at every moment we must make a decision — whether we shall go upward or downward. If we go downward we shall revert to all our brute instincts. If we go upward we shall reach the Ultimate. Rabindranath Tagore says in one of his addresses:

> Ages and ages have passed, dominated by the life of what we call the self, which is intent upon seeking food and shelter, and upon the perpetuation of the race. But there is a mysterious region waiting for its full recognition, which does not entirely acknowledge loyalty to physical claims. Its mystery constantly troubles us and we are not yet fully at ease in this region. We call it 'spiritual.' That word is vague, only because we have not yet been able to realize its meaning completely.

This mysterious realm is the realm of realization. Realization is not the exchange of one point of view for another. It means limitless expansion of thought. The consciousness expands, expands, and expands, until the little personal self drops away and the individuality loses itself in vastness. All creation seems a mere point in an immeasurable ocean of Being, and the Absolute becomes known — not through vision, but through unification of the expanded consciousness with It. This is the state Lord Buddha reached when he attained enlightenment. He had not ceased to be; on the contrary, he had become more vividly living and his work for the world had just begun.

This final realization is of necessity monistic. The body has been left behind, so there is neither sight nor other senses to perceive with. Mind and intellect have become inactive, so it is not possible to know by reasoning or discrimination. One method alone remains, — to enter into the Ultimate and experience Its nature by union with It. "The knower of Brahman becomes Brahman."

Few attain this state of highest realization. "Among thousands only one strives for perfection and among thousands of faithful strivers only one knows Me in truth," the Bhagavad Gita tells us. How then do the great souls accomplish their mission? Sri Ramakrishna gives answer to this question thus: voluntarily they retain enough of the subconscious and conscious to anchor them to earth and enable them to do their work.

It is not that the outer world has ceased to be. It is still relatively real, but it has no existence in itself. It is the shadow of the Almighty. It lives and moves and has its being in Him. If it seem less real, we in contrast are more living and vibrant. We have been reborn in the realm of pure spirit, and no longer blunder or falter or fail. The universe reveals her innermost secrets to us and we perceive them by direct vision. Suffering there may be so long as we remain in the body, but even the pain will be radiant. Nothing can daunt or overcome us, for we live in daily, hourly communion with the Infinite and Eternal.

Holy Living

While I was living in India, there was a young Englishman, an Oxford graduate, who came to Kashmir. He carried with him a plain brown habit and a New Testament in Greek. He built a cabin under a tree near a stream. He prayed and meditated, read his Bible and lived his life. Little by little the simple folk of the neighborhood gathered around him, in reverence for him and veneration for the Ideal he served. He did not set up a foreign form of the Divine for them to worship, he did not offer them a new creed; he merely loved and tended them and lived a holy life. If he converted anyone, it was not to a doctrine or ritual, but to sweeter, saner living.

Centuries ago it was this expression Gautama Buddha enjoined on his disciples. When he sent them forth to enlighten humankind, he charged them to carry the Truth in their lives rather than on their lips; to express no condemnation on any religion they might meet in their journeyings, neither to impose their own, but to preach more by example than by sermon.

Holy living never offends, never antagonizes. It is alien to no race or land, to no creed or tradition. It is pliable and adaptable. It harmonizes itself with the custom and tradition of the people and place where it is lived. It does not try to impose its own special form of worship, its own aspect of the Divine, its own custom and tradition. If it remolds, it is done less by words and direct effort than by silent example. It is the only fitting vessel in which Truth may be carried from country to country, from people to people.

Religion falls naturally into two clearly defined parts — the essential teaching, and ritual, custom and tradition. The first is God-made, the second is man-made. The first is born of revelation, the second sprouts from the cultural soil of the special tribe or people; the first has world-value, the second is specific and cultural; the first is broadening and unifies, the second is narrowing and differentiates.

Saviors, when they come to earth, bring with them, not a ceremonial code or a formal creed, but a life and a few simple words of counsel. They let people worship as they will. They give them neither dogma nor creed. Why then should their followers stress their minor points? If we would move with the advancing world-current, we must go forth in the name of humanity; we must speak a universal language and worship a universal Deity. We must harmonize our thought with the cosmic law of unity in variety and feel a loving tolerance toward all faiths, all scriptures, all aspects of the Divine, all forms and rituals, recognizing that each one represents the fulfillment of a human need, the effort of human beings to draw near to God.

Psychic Power and Spiritual Vision

Human beings are not homogeneous entities. We are a composite of many layers of being. In the final analysis, however, our constitution may be reduced to a duality consisting of matter and spirit. But this does not imply a corresponding division into visible and invisible. We must not commit the error of inferring that whatever lies beyond the reach of the senses falls in the realm of spirit. There are many strata in the finer part of our organism which although entirely invisible are yet absolutely material, as material in fact as the ultra-violet rays which are imperceptible to the human eye. The first and most obvious in these coverings of matter is the gross body, a self-renewing garment which we wear, not for a season merely, but for a lifetime. Beyond that are the five external senses, made up of the outer instruments (eyes, ears, nose, tongue, tactile nerves) and the inner registering organs. Next to these comes the sixth sense, the perceiving mind or *manas*, from the same root as the English word "man." Beyond mind is the intellect or *buddhi*, comprising the discriminative faculty and reason, and still further behind lies the *ahamkara* or sense of "I."

When a vibration strikes on one of the sense instruments, it passes back to the corresponding organ and is registered as a sensation; the mind whose function is that of messenger only, carries it to the discriminative faculty; this, after analyzing and determining its character, whether hostile or beneficent, presents it to the ego; the ego in turn lays it before the real Self, that central power who is the final judge of all experience. Conjoined with the ego is the moral sense, the last and subtlest form of material manifestation, for even the loftiest height of ethics lies within the confines of matter. The whole of human manifestation indeed is only an ascending scale of material vibration, steadily increasing in rapidity and intensity until it transcends all ordinary idea of motion.

As inconceivable as this may be, a little thought will make it evident. Morality implies diversity, otherwise there could be no choice and on choice it rests; diversity presupposes form; and form, however subtle, necessitates matter. But, you may say, the objects on which the moral sense acts may be material, yet the ethical faculty itself is surely immaterial. That is impossible and contrary to the law of nature as we see it. The faculty always belongs to the plane on which it functions and is of similar constitution; otherwise there could be no point of contact between the object and the perceptive organ. The gross objects of the external universe are perceived by the gross senses; intellect is of the same fine substance as the thought forms with which it deals; while ego and the moral sense represent the same substance and energy in a still higher state of vibration, the reactions of which manifest themselves as emotions and ethical impulses. The quicker the vibration, the subtler the perception and the higher the nature of the activity; the grosser the vibration, the more dense and physical the experience or act. Thought vibration is incalculably swifter than light vibrations, and there is no instrument to measure the swiftness of the vibration manifested in a noble moral impulse.

Thus have we reached the boundary line of our nature as we know it, yet we have not even touched the real person — that formless Spirit out of which rise all these forms called body, mind and ego; that Unchanging Self over which these changes of thought and sensations play like shadows; that Invisible by the light of which all human activities become visible; the hidden Life-Force which animates and propels the living being. Now in the ascending scale of human manifestation, there lies the so-called psychic area, which is a curious region that so easily entices and entangles us. It begins just above the gross senses and passes into the manas or lower mind. From this we can see at once how material are the psychic powers and how inadequate and untrustworthy they are.

There are three states of consciousness recognized by all, — the waking state, the dream state and the sound sleep state. We call ourselves awake when we consciously direct our activities and identify ourselves with a definite environment. Then we fall asleep. At once our body and bodily association vanish and we enter into a finer state of consciousness, a purely mental state known as dream. Here our thought, freed from the restraining limitations of dense matter, moves with a startling ease and swiftness, performing feats abnormal to the waking being. Then all dream activity drops below the horizon and sound sleep comes. The psychic state, to use the term in its common application, corresponds to this dream state. It lies in that middle region where the strata of consciousness ordinarily manifesting as waking and sound sleep meet and mingle, creating a third condition which may best be defined as a twilight consciousness. This remains true even when, as we advance in understanding, we reverse our ideas of what sound sleep and waking are. To the spiritually enlightened, indeed, the state of alert physical consciousness which the sense-bound person calls waking, appears asleep; while that state where we draw inward to touch our Source, thereby gaining new life and refreshment, is more really a waking, even though, until we learn to do it consciously through meditation, it may seem asleep.

As everyone has power to dream, so have we access to the psychic realm. It becomes evident then that these powers, which are so greedily coveted by many, do not represent any exceptional gift or superior attainment. Nor have they any more value than our external senses. The world of psychic phenomena is in reality only a subtle sense world. If we know someone who can tell the hour by the town clock ten blocks away while it is still invisible to us, do we regard her as a more highly developed being? We merely recognize that she has a longer range of vision. So is it with one who can see something happening in another town or country or on another plane. The same may be said of clairaudience and all psychic manifestations. Hearing, seeing, tasting, smelling, remain the same however wide the area they cover. They never cease to be sense activities and in the sum-total of experience can count merely as human incidents along the way.

The possession of powers does not increase our value, it is the use we make of them which determines that. But we have not yet learned to use our ordinary senses wisely, constantly do they entrap and betray us. That is why every spiritual teacher and scripture so earnestly warn us to guard against the snare of the senses. In themselves the senses are not wrong. God did not give us a single power which was not meant to serve us. Their danger lies in our ignorance regarding their place and function. The intelligent person therefore is less concerned to acquire powers than to gain wisdom. We do not wish to multiply our difficulties by extending our sense territory. Already the struggle is great enough in conquering our gross physical senses, why double it by rousing a new set, which being finer and even more dangerous, just as a finely pointed blade is more dangerous in a child's hand than a stick. Psychic power is one of the readiest weapons at the command of the ego, because it fosters vanity, satisfies idle curiosity about the unseen, and produces phenomena which so cleverly counterfeit the spiritual as to delude even the thoughtful. Yet, when properly understood, it is not necessarily harmful, for the visions which sometimes come to the sincere-hearted along the way may serve to strengthen faith and to stimulate our desire to seek still higher things.

Ability to communicate with the departed, that most seductive form of psychic manifestation, also has its use insofar as it helps to demonstrate continuance of life after bodily death; but for the individual it can be no more wholesome or beneficial than promiscuous association with souls in the body. To be rushing here and there asking advice is always a sign of weakness. The strong person stays at home and seeks counsel of the soul. Why should it be any more justifiable to run to the disembodied for help? A person is no wiser for having dropped the body. The character and mind remain unchanged. They have merely put off an outer covering and are in the same mental state as when here in this life. If they were not an infallible guide then, they will not be now. It is also great selfishness to be constantly calling upon those on the other side, treating them like errand boys or girls with no independent life of their own. They are busy; they have as much to do as we; why should we interrupt them at our pleasure? The very fact of their leaving the earthly environment and associations in which we knew them, shows that they had finished with it and that their further development required some other condition. Should we hold them here for our consolation or satisfaction? In rare cases such communication may be carried on with benefit to both embodied and disembodied; but it is too rare to count upon.

The same may be said of all psychic practices on this plane. They are in most cases a form of indiscretion and meddling. Would we read the private mail of others? What more right have we to read their minds? Would we eavesdrop? Then why be proud that we have heard their conversation from a distant point? Let us not be content with such trifling manifestations of power. Let us no longer idle away our time in this realm of the near-invisible, dreaming dreams. Rather let us push on, saying: "If these little visions can so charm us, what must be the Ultimate Vision? So long as we remain under the spell of these subtler sense powers we cannot go forward. We are like jugglers performing tricks on the street for the wonderment of the crowd. Have we no larger ambition, no wider stretch of aspiration? We are children of the Infinite, what can this petty play of finite forces mean to us? It is true that these psychic experiences often seem to come of themselves without any apparent effort or desire on our part. If they come, it is because we give them access. Far down beneath the surface we are clinging to them. The moment we belittle them, instead of inflating their importance, they will begin to fade and vanish. This does not mean that we shall lose the subtle faculties which make them possible. They will merely sink into a dormant state like any unused organ, ready to wake when the whole person springs into new life under the quickening touch of Spirit.

In the night every object of a landscape is present, but forms and perspective are confused and out of scale. When the sun rises, each takes its proper place and discloses its own nature. So will it be with us when that first flash of spiritual illumination lights up our present obscurity. At once we shall perceive the purpose and value of every part of this human mechanism, and shall be able to use the whole freely without danger to ourselves or to others. Not one of us is wanting in any element necessary to ultimate attainment. Every being is equally equipped for the spiritual life. What is lacking is sufficient light to work by. Just as a fully equipped factory is useless without proper illumination, so are we.

The great question then becomes: How can we acquire this higher power of sight? The first condition is intense desire. All our outer senses were evolved through a persisting desire to pierce channels of communication with this objective world. The same steadfast longing to penetrate to the subjective or causal realm will develop the inner vision — the "third eye" spoken of in Vedic sacred literature. As those primitive forms of life grew aware of a universe of matter all about them and struggled to perceive it, so we must begin to realize that at this moment we are living in a mighty universe of Spirit to which we are blind and deaf. We sense it dimly, as did the jellyfish its world; we must strive with unwavering will to know it. That which obscures our sight is matter; we must remove it layer by layer. Not, however, by any objective process. The work is wholly subjective. It consists in gradually altering our point of view. We begin by ceasing to identify ourselves with the body, no longer believing that our happiness depends on its comfort or convenience. All this intricate system of living, with its multiplicity of attachments, occupations and possessions, rests on the belief that we are one with the body. Rid ourselves of that and at once our life will grow free and simple. So long as we devote the larger part of our energy to caring and providing for it, we cannot hope to transcend its limitations. Yet we must not neglect it. As we keep our clothes clean and well-mended, so must we treat this close garment; but having done that we should wear it unconsciously.

Next we must break the tyranny of the senses. We must free ourselves from the superstition that they are the surest channels of either happiness or knowledge. If it were not for the watchful censorship of the discriminative faculty, they would constantly deceive and we would never know. All they do is to admit raw material for observation; but only when their gateways are closed does the real process of knowing begin.

Let Your Light Shine

A lesson we must all learn in the spiritual life is that the law fulfills itself; we do not have to fulfill it. We imagine we must know nature's laws that we may apply them. The true reason for learning them, however, is that we may not interfere with them. They are operating incessantly and in perfect wisdom, but we block their free course. From this come our disappointments, our feverish unrest and bitter rebellions. When we permit nature to act without hindrance, our days move along in quiet strength and peace. That is why we are admonished to let our light shine. Actually the Great Light is perpetually shining; it lights everyone born into the world, we are told; but we do not let it shine through. It does not glow in our eyes or in our words and actions, because we veil it. Whenever a devotee attains the higher vision, the sign always noted in the Upanishads is that "their face shines as one who knows

God;" and when we no longer bar the inner light by wayward self-assertion, our whole being will radiate its effulgence. We have only to tear the veil of the finite and the Infinite will flash forth in all Its glory.

Knowledge gained by any lesser light is never enduring or dependable. A stronger lens in the microscope or telescope may overturn it. The interior soul light alone casts no shadows of uncertainty. Intellectual acumen, however keen, can never be a substitute for it. Christ implies this when He speaks of that which is hidden from the learned, but revealed to the childlike. The same idea prevails among Indian sages. They believe that intellectual attainments, far from being essential to higher vision, may even prove a barrier to it; because much study often sets the mind in a definite mold and makes it less receptive. All human powers, when used independently, represent not the manifestation, but the limitation of the universal Power. Only when we withdraw the obstructing action of our self-will, is It able to accomplish Its eternal purposes through us. "Hands off! Who are you to do God's business!" are Swami Vivekananda's warning words.

Nor is it difficult to make acquaintance with God's laws. They are operating all about us, as open to us as the law of gravity. Even the most hidden ways of nature become plain to the obedient and prayerful heart. But in our foolishness we recoil from the thought of complete surrender. We fear that we may be reduced to helpless parts of a grinding mechanism, driven we know not where or to what end. But such is not the way in which the Divine Power works. It does not drive or overwhelm. It cooperates and unites. The law in the universe allies itself with the law in us. We become a conscious part of it. We are not moved by it; we move with it. It does not act through us autocratically. It stimulates our own volition to go the higher way; and as we yield to the sweep of the larger will and energy, we feel a new and indescribable exhilaration.

We are inseparably one with the Supreme and have a share in all the joy of Divine manifestation, if we care to claim it. There can be no force in the universe hostile to us. God can have no interest apart from our interest, which would lead Him to thwart our sane impulses; nor can we have any interest apart from His, which would make it necessary for us to be on guard against the fulfilling of His plan. There can never be a wiser way to go than God's way. When we turn from Him and determine our own course, we deprive ourselves of every advantage and every chance of productiveness in our undertakings. We are all hungry for eternal life, for freedom, for lasting happiness, for boundless knowledge; but all these qualities are inherent properties of the soul. They are ours at this moment. The reason we long for them is because we ignorantly sense their presence within us, yet we are unable to express them. But we do not have to express them. They will express themselves, if we put no obstacle in their way.

We hinder the working of the Divine in us by our narrow conception of life. We think of ourselves as finite, and naturally we fall prey to finite desires and finite fears. So long as we believe that we have only a small detached fragment of human life, which can be snatched from us, we shall fight and perhaps even kill to protect it. Or if we are convinced that our present little horde of riches is all we can count upon for our sustenance, we shall be tormented constantly lest we lose it. In other words, so long as we hold the thought, whether defined or not, that God and His creation threaten our individual life and possessions, and that we must battle to defend them, we shall put ourselves at odds with all the providing and protecting forces of the universe.

One thing alone can set us right, — the sense of a common cause with the Infinite. As soon as we realize our indestructible nature and our true relationship with God, every thought of contention and fear will vanish from our mind. There can be no rivalry or enmity among the members of the cosmic body, any more than there can be rivalry or enmity between our hands and our feet. If one member of our organism is in pain, every member suffers; if any small part is cold, the whole body shivers. Life is one, and all living things are knit together by it. Knowledge also is one. Argument, dispute, whatever divides, closes the way to it. It reveals itself only in hearts which are washed clean of personal bias and assertive opinion. Joy, too, is one; it can never be had at the expense of any living creature. Those who feel the pains and pleasures of others as their own, they alone can taste it. Life, knowledge, bliss, these are universal indivisible attributes of God, and can be found in their fullness only when we throw off the bondage of the manifold and personal.

The aim of all spiritual striving is to make Reality real to us. That is what realization means. No one ever willingly pursues a shadow. It is because we believe the shadow has substance that we follow after it. We may think that God is real to us; but if He were, we would not be able to resist His superior charm and beauty. Our life shows that we still covet the shadow; otherwise why do we laugh and weep so easily over passing earthly joys and griefs? Why are we so deeply immersed in the petty details of mere living? We seem to forget that beneath the daily dramas, the mighty drama of Divinity is going on. The fasts and feasts of every religion have as their purpose to remind us of this profound fact. Of what use is a yearly Christmas, if it merely multiplies our outward activities and obligations? Christ might come a thousand times and leave us unsaved and unblessed, unless He lays His purifying touch on our individual life and heart. Spirituality means putting the accent on spirit; regarding spiritual advantage, spiritual obligations, spiritual relationships above worldly advantage and worldly claims. It is altogether a question of right values and whole-hearted consecration. External forms and observances play only a minor part in it.

The real things are big and simple. They demand no violent, distorting struggle. They do not entangle us, they free us. But they admit of no complexity or duplicity. They require us to be direct and uncalculating. Whenever our mind grows hot with anxiety or impatience, we may know it is because the unreal is closing in on us. If we will analyze, we shall find that nearly all our joys and sorrows spring from the crumbing of something which we believed was real, but which proved unreal.

We have formed the habit of giving our first service to the unreal. Now we must form the habit of serving the Real. It is the Real which makes life bearable. It is the yearning for a closer touch with Reality which pushes us on in our evolution. The Real will never fail us. From It come our joy and strength and light. God longs to share all the blessings of His universe with us. He would fill us with His Divine sweetness. If he asks us to become empty vessels, it is that He may give us more generously of Himself. Are those faint glimmerings of Divinity which we catch through matter worth more to us than the full light of God, unveiled and unrefracted? Have we grown so accustomed to the dimness of this world that we prefer to see Truth through a glass darkly? Apparently we like to grope our way in the darkness, only vaguely sensing the larger revelations. If it were not so, we would let God's light shine through us. We would answer the call: "Arise, shine, for thy light is come and the glory of the Lord is risen upon thee."

The Life We Find

"He who loses his life for My Sake shall find it," Christ declared. What life do we find? This is the crucial question we should all ask ourselves. Too often, however, it remains unasked and our thought turns with lingering reluctance to the life we are losing. It seems to gain in allure and value as it recedes.

More pleasing to many would be to take the pleasant out of the old life, join it to the pleasant in a new life, and have a composite life — a little of God and a little of the world. But a godly life and a worldly life cannot mingle. Their ideals and standards are altogether different and neutralize one another. The life rooted in the world is individualistic, the life rooted in God is universal; the one is outward, the other inward; one is acquisitive, competitive, calculating, ambitious for fame and power; the nature of the other is set forth in these instructions taken from an early book of devotions:

> Seek out a secret place for yourself; love to dwell alone with yourself, desire the conversation of none, but pour out devout prayers unto God that you may keep your heart humble and your conscience pure. Esteem the whole world as nothing. Prefer waiting upon God to all outward things; but know that you can not wait upon God and at the same time take delight in transitory things.

There are those who would barter with destiny. They consent to give up their present life if in exchange they receive a life of ease and pleasantness, with health, success, and prosperity as their reward. But nothing is more vapid and wearisome than a life of continuous ease and pleasantness. It robs us of the very power to enjoy it.

Suffering there will be in the life we find. But why recoil from suffering? It is a part of the rhythm of the universe. Nowhere in nature do we see a wave without a hollow, a sky without clouds, a landscape without shadows. Scattered clouds across the horizon make the beauty of the sunset, and shadows add to the loveliness of the landscape. Let us look upon our dark moments, not as evils, but as shadows adding to the loveliness of our character and to its strength. The new life must not make weaklings of us; on the contrary it calls to us to be heroic, noble, and enduring.

Pomp and importance have no place in the newfound life, rather it is a life of humility. Therein lies its greatness. Those who are leading it are known by their humility and their serenity. They do not delight in praise, in fame or honor; they do not boast; they do not resent affronts. They go their accustomed way in simplicity and quietness of spirit, exerting a silent power which nothing can resist. Gradually and imperceptibly they transform their surroundings and infuse them with the peace which they carry in their own hearts.

Actually we do not lose our old life, we transcend it. We pass from the little to the large, from the personal to the universal. The Whole becomes our unit of measurement — not a small individual part. We realize that we belong to the universe more than we belong to ourselves. Even our body is not ours. All its processes and requirements lie outside our jurisdiction. We cannot create air or food or sunshine for it. We live as tenants in creation, but we partake of all its advantages and gifts. The more entirely we submit to its decrees, the freer we are. On us alone rests the extent of our freedom and the measure of our blessing.

The life that grows out of the universal life is a life which wipes out all sense of difference, leaving only complete unity. Kinship with every living thing — with all living beings, with tree and flower, with the very rocks on the mountainside — awakens in our hearts. The highest and the lowest become equally dear to us. We take no account of merit or demerit, or worthiness or unworthiness. A mighty love is surging through us which unites and glorifies all things. It is not, however, a small personal love swayed by emotional reactions and impulses. It is a great love pervading all nature and flowing through every heart that is open to receive and convey it. It is a love that would lose countless lives for His sake.

The Value of Symbols

At the moment the first form sprang out of the great void of undifferentiated substance, the symbol was created. The heavens and the earth, the waters and all the elements came forth as signs and symbols of the Eternal. Each form rising out of the formless was a new God-symbol through which we might learn to worship. On and on through a multiplication of symbols creation moved, until even every word became a symbol. Thus we live in symbols, play with symbols, work with symbols, and strive for symbols. How can we utilize them to enrich our spiritual life?

Vedanta says: Take yourself just as you are, study the principles of your nature, see how analogous growth is on all planes; then follow the same natural method in spiritual training as you pursue in secular learning; that is, move with childlike simplicity from symbol to symbol until you are led spontaneously to That behind the symbol.

Whatever tends to awaken this spirit within us should be accepted with eagerness. The loving heart unconsciously gathers around it any object that reminds it of the beloved, and so the earnest devotee is quick to seize the smallest symbol or practice that makes God more real. Through this we cultivate the habit of seeing the Divine in all things, until at last we reach the point where, as Emerson said of Thoreau, "the whole universe is a symbol" — a glowing symbol of the Infinite and Eternal Lord.

Serve your present finite vision of the Infinite with faithful devotion and He will gradually unfold before you the fullness of His glory.

God's World and the Human World

The world we live in is wholly ours. Nothing can enter it unless we give it access. We believe that our life is shaped by the action of the outer world upon us; in reality it is wholly molded by our reaction on the world. This ceaseless play of external conditions is not what affects us; it is our attitude towards them. We have no actual acquaintance with the outside universe. All we know of it is the emotion or sensation it arouses in us. When some outer stimulus impinges on our consciousness, instead of studying it dispassionately and learning what it really is, we react immediately and judge its nature by the pleasure or pain, the strength or weakness, it produces in us. If its effect on us is pleasurable, we call it good; it if is painful, we call it evil. But in itself it may be quite the contrary; and what we are passing judgment on is our own mood, not that which strikes us from the outside. This is proved by the fact that we react differently towards the same circumstance at different times, turning pleasure into pain and pain into pleasure. Until we are able to curb these involuntary reflex thoughts, we can never escape from our present narrow self-made world. If, however, through the practice of non-attachment and fortitude, we learn to control these impulsive reactions, we shall pass naturally and automatically into a new and bigger world of thought and action.

At every moment we may live in one of two worlds. We may live in our own personal world, or we may live in God's world. Our little personal world is too small for God to live in. If we wish to live with Him, we must go and live in His world. His world is all harmony, order, peace and beauty. The dark ugly places we perceive in it are the shadows cast from our world by our limitations and lack of understanding. Whenever we have eyes to see the mighty cosmic power at work, unimpeded by fretful human hands, we are awestruck by the perfect adjustment of every part; the unfailing precision and dependability, the beauty and symmetry apparent everywhere. There could not be a pageant lovelier than the unfolding of spring, the sunset glow of the autumn, the white stillness of snow falling on winter fields and hills. Nature, when left to herself, is a constant lesson and upliftment; because nature lies quietly in God's hand. She is obedient to the cosmic will. She follows the cosmic plan. When we go out into a forest or on a mountain height, we say to ourselves: "How easy to be tranquil here!" But why is it easy? Because there we are in God's world; and whenever we are in God's world, we are at peace.

Nor is peace to be found elsewhere. We may search the furthermost corners of the earth, but we shall not be able to discover a single selfish, undisciplined person who is at rest. Always is there a prodding unrest in the heart, a nameless discomfort, bred of unsatisfied ambition, envy, rebellion, loneliness, and life-weariness. The only ones who seem to go on their way in silent content are the saints, the seers, the consecrated ones; those who live habitually in God's world. They, then, must have found our natural dwelling-place; for unrest is always a sign that the one who feels it is in an unnatural condition or environment. The state of "the fish out of water" is proverbial. If we are tormented, dissatisfied with the world we live in, may it not be because we are not where we belong?

We can go on as we are going life after life; we can continue to improve our mental reactions towards this world, making them finer, more unselfish; but always underneath there will be a gnawing dissatisfaction. If, however, for a time we give up working on this human world and begin even in a small way to seek entrance to the Divine world, we shall find our whole life transformed and our power of human helpfulness increased a hundredfold.

People who use their religion only to make this world a more comfortable place in which to live are misusing it. The essential purpose of religion is to rebind us to God; to lead us out of the finite into the infinite, away from the small and personal into the vast and universal. It seems strange that that which we cherish most ardently and which we are most reluctant to relinquish is just that which cheats us of this larger heritage — our personal point of view, our personal motive in action, our personal rights. These form the basis of our present limitation. There is no other. Within the circle of "me" and "mine" lie all our distresses and perplexities. The instant we emerge from it, we have a sense of liberation and expansion.

Nor is this confining personal outlook on life a difficult thing to eliminate. It does not penetrate deep into our nature. Even physically we get away from it quickly. When we pierce a little below the surface, we find ourselves with the same general constitution as every other human being. Our body is constructed like every other. It obeys the same laws and functions in the same way. The personal variation is wholly superficial. We go a little beneath the outer covering of our mind or of our heart and we come upon the same fundamental impulses of thought and feeling. Even selfishness, which is the cornerstone of personality, in the last analysis, is all the same. We cannot move away from the surface anywhere that we do not move away from the personal, from that which feels itself separate and at war with other separate entities. We are our own jailers. We have imprisoned ourselves and we guard ourselves with the greatest watchfulness lest by any change we escape from our prison-house of personality. Yet wherever we see people of heroic stature, leaders among peers, that which constitutes their bigness is the power to act from a universal motive in the service of a universal ideal. If we are a true scientist, we acclaim joyfully every new discovery without taking account of the channel through which it comes. If we are the messenger of spiritual Truth, we do not debase it by seeking our personal glory or honor. Christ deflected honor to Himself: "Why do you call Me good?"

When we can raise ourselves out of the narrowing circle of personality and begin to live according to the universal law, in harmony with the universal scheme of things, at once we transcend our little pains and troubles. They are born wholly of our attachment to the personal and our stubborn disregard of the universal. If our own small plan chances to be in line with the cosmic plan, we meet with what we call success. We gain our end and are happy. If, however, our personal ambition carries us contrary to the cosmic scheme, then we meet with what we call failure; but it does not mean that we have failed or succeeded in any ultimate or permanent sense. It means merely that in the one case we went with the Divine current and in the other we went against it.

At no time have we any rights to quarrel over, any interests to protect, anything to concern ourselves about except this — that we take our place in God's universe and fulfill our part in His mighty universal plan. This at once simplifies all our habits of thought. At present how many hours we spend in calculating what is best to do; then in calculating how to do it; again in calculating how to overcome the obstacles which prevent us from doing it; still again in contending with our fellow beings to beat down these obstacles. But when we have allied ourselves with the bigger life, we shall work with God in His vast world and shall accomplish spontaneously His good will and pleasure. There will be no more questioning or calculating. We shall not be watching with anxiety the course of the universe. We shall just be living and living with God. Then we shall have all the wisdom we need, all the love we need; we shall be sheltered and guided and watched over as the tender mother watches over and guides her little child.

How foolish then it is to cling to the little; to fight for it; to be wayward and defiant, or whining and complaining because of it! Let us rather adopt a new habit of mind. When we rise in the morning let our prayerful thought be: "Today God's universe will move according to a mighty, well-ordered plan — a plan that makes for beauty and harmony and loving-kindness. I am in it, I am a part of it. Grant, O Lord! That I may live at one with it." If we can put our life wholly back into it, we shall move less noisily, we shall talk less, we shall be less anxious and impulsive in our decisions and actions. A great rhythm will come in our thought, in our words, in our movements, even in our breathing.

When we cease to assert ourselves, God asserts Himself through us. When we turn towards Him, His light shines in us and through us and all about us. Now we break up that effulgence by the many-angled prism of our little self; but if we can yield ourselves joyfully and with one-pointed devotion to the larger Self within, then the light will shine unbroken. We cannot expand ourselves and continue to be ourselves in the smaller sense. Something must give way. It is not possible to take the infinite and eternal into this small finite being. We must, by complete surrender, go out into it. As the little light shines forth and mingles with the stronger light. It does not cease to be light, it does not become darkness; it only changes from a dim flickering flame off in a corner by itself into a radiant part of the great, far-reaching brightness.

Section Five

Spiritual Practice

Preparation. 342
   Patanjali's Yoga. 342
Wisdom and the Devotional Life 346
   The Path of Devotion 347
   The Need of A Chosen Ideal 353
Theory and Practice: Living the Life 356
   Living the Life 360
   The Secret of Right Activity. 362
   Wisdom through Service of the Ideal 364
   Karma Yoga: The Path of Work 367
Surrender and Obedience. 375
   Surrender 375
   The Laws of Life 377
   The Planless Life 379
   Strength Through Surrender 382
   Obedience 383
Detachment & Renunciation 387
   Concentration 387
   Detachment 388
   The True Meaning of Renunciation 390
   Renunciation and Achievement. 393
   Vedanta and Renunciation 394
   Desirelessness 400
Self-Discipline/Self-Mastery 403
   Discipline 404
   Self-Control 405

Love and the Great Love. 407
Truthfulness. 409
Trust. 410
Generosity and Greed. 411
Gladness of Heart, Joy and Thanksgiving 413
    Obstacles to Joy. 414
    The Seat of Happiness 416
The Spiritual Value of Appreciation 419
Mind, Concentration, Meditation and Worship. . .421
    The Power to Think 421
Concentration and Single-Mindedness 422
Meditation. 427
    Meditation as Habit Builder. 429
    The Practical Value of Meditation 431
    Fill Your Mind With Me 433
What is True Worship? 437
Silence 440
Transcendence and Union. 442
Atmosphere. 443
The Power of Music. 444
Right Breathing 445
Food. 448
    The Value of Food in Spiritual Training. 448
Health and Healing. 450

There are many methods and spiritual practices which help us to prepare, to sustain and to deepen our inner life. Many are universal and found in the majority of faith traditions around the world and go back thousands of years. As always, Sister Devamata provides clear and practical instruction.

Preparation

Patanjali's Yoga

Just as a certain amount of preliminary work is necessary in order to construct a strong building, so also in order to practice Yoga or to gain the highest spiritual vision, we need ample preparation. Unless we are willing to pay heed to it, our efforts will all be in vain and we will not succeed in our spiritual strivings. The preliminary work must be well done. As Christ said, unless the house is well-founded on a rock it does not stand; the wind may blow it down and ruin it. So we cannot withstand the difficulties we find in practical life unless we have increased our power of perception, until we have prepared the foundation of our building.

Patanjali gives some practical methods by which we can eliminate the pain-bearing obstructions that stand in the way of our wisdom, the things which cause ignorance; for ignorance is the cause of all bondage.

Through constant practice we must shape new habits, new impressions — in fact a new life – so that the past has no more influence upon us. It is not very easy to break past impressions and the influence of past associations made in this life or previous lives. We have to practice repeatedly; we have to make new impressions on the mind again and again. The mind retains every imprint, and perhaps past impressions are stronger than the present impulses. That is the reason why, when subtle spiritual truths are first declared by a lofty soul, they have very little effect on the ordinary mind. The experience and message are not in accord with the ordinary happenings of human life, and consequently take a little longer to make any impression. Thus Patanjali suggests constant, habitual practice.

The first time we sit down and try to concentrate our thoughts, try to create an atmosphere by following certain rules, it may not have much effect on the mind, nor give as much as is promised in the books or by the teacher. But as we go on faithfully, as we practice discrimination, we will find that gradually these new impressions become stronger and more dominant, and the past impressions become weaker and weaker until they fade away entirely.

An ancient Hindu scripture says that there is only one way of ascertaining what is good and what is bad, what is virtue and what is vice: that whenever we help anyone by thought, word, or action, it is called virtue; and whenever, whether consciously or unconsciously, we injure anyone, it is called vice, the only sin that exists. That is the foundation of Indian teaching. The same teaching declares, all that has been taught in thousands and thousands of scriptures can be told in half a verse — not even a whole verse: not doing harm to another, is indeed the basis of spiritual life; to directly or indirectly injure anyone, is vice.

Now the eight-fold practices which Patanjali gives are called the limbs, or branches, of Yoga. They are the practice of non-injury, truthfulness, non-stealing, continence, non-receiving of gifts, purity, cheerfulness, surrender to God.

Ahimsa is a Sanskrit word for non-injury or the non-injuring of anyone by thought, word, or action. This is the foundation of many spiritual philosophies. The whole teaching of the Lord Buddha is based upon this one principle. Non-injury is the highest of all virtues. Those who practice that, attain to the Highest.

The idea of non-injury also gives rise to vegetarianism. People who follow this practice are not willing to take life for their own sustenance. The motive which has led humankind to live on food which does not require killing, is the highest motive of all. At the same time we must remember one thing: the ideal of vegetarian living is not merely to live on food that is not animal; it means also the purifying of one's own heart. We must be very careful that we do not bear unkind thoughts in our mind. If we do, then our mind is not fit for a holy life, a contemplative life. The condition of purity is absolutely essential for Yoga practices.

Whenever anyone has practiced *ahimsa* even for a short time in their words and action, they create an atmosphere of non-injury. Take for example Lord Buddha, when he was giving his message to all, without distinction of caste or creed; some men plotted to attack him in the forest where he was absolutely helpless and unprotected, except for his own loving heart, but he knew no fear. When they approached the Buddha, they were overpowered by the influence which radiated from him — the feeling of love, charity, and forgiveness — and they could not strike him.

When we are incapable of saying or doing anything that is unkind or harmful, when our heart is absolutely free from envy, jealousy, hatred, and all such propensities, there arises the real spirit of non-killing, non-injuring; then we have gained one step which forms the very foundation, the very cornerstone, of the structure we are building in order to gain the superconscious state.

"You cannot serve God and Mammon." We cannot compromise. Whenever we take a high principle, a lofty ideal, and try to compromise with our physical desires, with our lower propensities, there will always be a clash.

Our spiritual practices must first be well established, then we may strive to gain that supreme vision which is described as the superconscious state, beyond all limitations of the senses, for without this foundation such vision will be impossible.

Next to non-injury comes the practice of **truthfulness** — truthfulness in what we say and in what we do. We must be true to the principle of our life, not betray anyone in thought, word, or action. Truthfulness has a tremendous effect and it means that we are able to become absolutely free from all hypocrisy.

Next is the practice of **non-stealing**. That means, of course, that we should not take possession of what does not belong to us, but also we should not take more than what we need; we should not try to deceive anyone; we should not be false, untrue; and this is also to be practiced in our thought, word, and action.

The practice of **purity** means purification of the body, mind, and heart. Purification of the body is, perhaps, the easiest. It can be attained by cleanliness, which is very important. We can succeed in keeping our surroundings, our clothes, and our body clean. Those who do not keep the body pure and spotless are undoubtedly sinking in *tamas* — dullness, heaviness. The very fact that they indulge in such low propensities will impede their spiritual growth.

But inner cleanliness is more important. We cannot achieve it except by discipline of mind and thought. We must not allow any low or unclean thought to be harbored in our mind; we must not dwell on things which are unwholesome, for whatever we think we assimilate.

The practice of **continence** also means purity — purity of heart. The Soul is pure, spotless; the Soul is sexless and genderless. The idea of sex, and such limited feelings, rise from bodily consciousness. So long as we confine ourselves to that, we can never know what continence is. It is the idea of the pure life, and in the pure life we find the manifestation of God.

The practice of **non-receiving of gifts** is not always understood. What has it to do with the spiritual life? Very much, because receiving means dependence; it also means exchange. Always it means bondage, for according to Indian teaching, when we receive a gift we take not only the gift but also the quality of the giver. A relationship is established between the two.

Of course the exchange of gifts can sometimes be very helpful if the source is pure. Then the dependence does no harm. But now we are talking about striving for spiritual consciousness — aspirants who are trying to balance our minds, our thoughts, our consciousness. Therefore we must be independent. For this reason, in India aspirants who are striving for spiritual life never accept anything. We want no attachment to anything that is worldly, so that we can give our whole heart and soul to God. Then when we attain our Ideal — when we become masters — we find that we desire no possessions; we accept whatever comes.

People often ask how it is that a holy person accepts anything. Their idea of acceptance is quite different. They may accept in order to bless another soul, although they have no desire in their own heart; they have risen above all limitation, above all duality; they are not touched by any bodily action. Those who have attained consciousness of the Supreme have severed themselves permanently from the little self, and giving to them is almost like giving directly to God.

Cheerfulness: this is another virtue we must develop if we want to advance spiritually. We must never let our spirit sink into despair. We must keep faith in our ultimate achievement of the spiritual goal.

Finally, we must practice **discipline**. There are certain rules as to the hour when we rise, when we bathe, when we do various things, and this routine is followed automatically, voluntarily and involuntarily. We follow it without question, because we say we need it for our physical health and well-being. Similarly, there are definite rules and exercises which we must follow if we are equally interested in our Soul's welfare, in the cultivation of Soul-consciousness. If we say, as many people do, "I cannot bind myself by such routine," then we are not being true to ourselves. We do bind ourselves to sleeping, to eating, to our physical comforts and habits, and we feel unrest unless we have them.

In the same way, a teacher, a seer, will tell us we need to cultivate spiritual habits and practices for the health of our Soul. The teacher will ask how we are to acquire a healthy Soul-life, a wholesome spiritual life, if we are not willing to follow the prescribed rules. So we must learn to discipline our appetites, make our body less attached to comfort and luxury, and prepare it in such a way that it will become a helpful instrument for spiritual conquest.

We need to **study** in order to train our mind. The mind jumps from one thing to another, but we learn to hold it, and to send it in certain directions, teach it to associate with holiness, train it with purity and worship of God. We surrender all to Him — everything— without reserve.

These are the methods by which we can prepare our foundation for a spiritual life. Patanjali, the philosopher, says they should be practiced without any break, without interruption, and that these rules are universal and for everyone. As we follow these rules of the spiritual life uninterruptedly and without distraction, our doubts disappear and we see things as they are. Our lower nature cannot deceive us, cannot distort the truth, for as we practice, our vision becomes more and more clarified.

Spiritual growth is not a matter of accident, an act of chance; it is the effect of systematic work, work with understanding, work to make the right foundation. Then our life and character become well established, and nothing can shake or move or overthrow us. As Lord Krishna says in the Gita, even the greatest sorrow cannot overcome those who have found themselves, their true Self, their true being.

How can we fully understand these principles? Let us think of it this way; once we have united our heart with the Divine, no longer can we feel any delusion, no longer do we bring in that sense of ego — "I and mine." Those who have consecrated their lives, whose actions are guided by God, their thoughts, words, and actions — are really done by the Supreme Being, for He is Truth itself.

Wisdom and the Devotional Life

Two aspects of the spiritual life are stressed in the Bhagavad Gita with equal insistence. One is devotion, the other is wisdom. They are represented not as rival paths to attainment but as complements, completing each other. Devotion, with its fervor of spirit, carries forward to the goal; wisdom lights the way. The Lord declares in the Gita: "To these ever steadfast devotees I give that Yoga of wisdom by which they come unto me. Out of pure compassion for them, I, dwelling in their hearts, destroy the darkness born of ignorance by the effulgent light of wisdom."

Those who seek to follow the spiritual path without this effulgent light stray into by-paths and miss the goal. The tempering influence of wisdom in the devotional life is essential. Without it there is danger of the life of devotion growing emotional and unsteady. By its nature, devotion tends to extremes. It places great importance on outward observances, it multiplies rituals and ceremonies, it multiples symbols and sacred images. There is need of the restraining influence of wisdom to keep the devotee to the middle path.

The Path of Devotion

Nothing sweetens the daily life more than the practice of devotion. An interval spent in quiet communion with the Ideal at dawn and at the evening hour fills the entire day with fragrance. Also nothing kindles greater ardor in the heart than the worship and selfless service of a lofty Ideal. It awakens a sense of Divine companionship and brings God closer than any other method of approach. The Gita tells us: "That Supreme One in whom all beings abide and by whom all this is pervaded can be attained by wholehearted and exclusive devotion to Him." But the devotion must be steadfast and focused. There can be no scattering of interest or effort. Neither can there be any rival thought or feeling in the consciousness. The offering of devotion must be unmingled and made with complete surrender. The promise is a rich one. The Lord declares, "Those who worship Me and meditate on Me without any other thought, to these ever steadfast devotees I secure safety and supply all their needs."

On the path of devotion we must learn to make everything definite. We can think about an abstraction but we cannot feel about it. This is true even when we contemplate such lofty qualities as purity or truth, or love itself; but when we see these embodied in some life or character, then the heart begins to glow. This gives us definite elements with which to work. We must have a definite aspect of God to think upon, by means of which we may approach Him. We must have definite tasks or ways of serving Him. We must have definite symbols. Also we should have a special place for our daily meditations, and if possible, a little altar or table on which to place those things that awaken holy associations. Finally we should have a definite subject of meditation. No one can kindle the fire in the heart merely by going into the silence. That is a lazy kind of meditation. There should be set hours for spiritual practice, and all through the day we should have before us the clear concept of our Ideal. We must remember this especially during the first stages of the devotional life, while we are in the process of developing the higher feelings. Above all, we must be careful not to allow ourselves to wander into a sense of haziness. That is why we must keep to specific tasks, otherwise, sooner or later, we grow sentimental and visionary.

Another thing against which we must guard ourselves in our devotional practice is the tendency to imagine that this practice can be made a substitute for our active duties. People often feel justified in neglecting some duty on the ground that they wish to meditate or to read a holy book or to pray, or sit in front of their altar; but that is not what the devotional life means. The real devotional life means doing all the outer things with greater feeling. It is not concerned with the isolated practices of devotion, but with its living application.

So long as we are in the world we are forced to follow the way of Karma Yoga, or dedicated action. The difference between the true Karma yogins and devotees is that Karma yogins are seeking to disengage their minds from the fruits of their action, which mentally they lay before the feet of the Lord; whereas devotees look upon their action as a vessel which they are to fill with His love. Therefore they are impelled to fill it to the brim. If we were to neglect our household duties under the pretense of devotion, we would be like a child who climbs into our mother's lap and tells her again and again how much we love her, all the while hoping she will forget the work she had given us to do.

We must guard ourselves very carefully lest we make our devotional life an emotional life. It must not become in any way an indulgence. Our purpose in following this path is not merely to experience flights of ecstasy; nor is it in any way an escape from the responsibilities of life. The true purpose is to develop our heart faculties, or highest mental faculties, and our feeling. It is not a question of developing more feeling; we have all we need. It is a question of disentangling our feelings from our sensations and from our intellectual processes, so that we may give them a perfectly pure flight toward God. There must be no internal boiling or seething of any kind, because these deeper movements of the soul belong to the *sattvic* state, a state of perfect clarity, with not even a single bubble rising to mar the complete transparency. That is what serenity means.

Usually that which is called devotion is a mixed condition, made up of sensation and feeling. Sensation is a quality of nerves; feeling is a quality of the heart. The two should never be entangled. That would only lead into the emotional state, with its swing between elation and depression. Moments of extreme elation are always followed by moments of depression. The Bhagavad

Gita speaks of being free from elation and its opposite. When we approach God with true devotional spirit there is a great calmness, serenity and stillness, akin to the feeling we sometimes have on entering a great cathedral where all is quiet. This calmness should be ours not only when we approach the altar, but as we approach each task of the day. Every one of these tasks should be looked upon as an altar on which we are going to lay a sacrifice — a sacrifice of some part of our little self. We literally perform an oblation. The nature of the task does not matter in the least. It may be dusting a room; it may be adding a column of figures; it may be writing a page; it may be sewing a seam; it may be cooking a meal; it may be some literary work or scientific pursuit. It makes no difference what it is so long as we look upon it as an altar. The Lord does not care what an altar is made of: it is the dedication, the spirit of consecration that goes into it that counts. Therefore when we give ourselves to each task in the same way as we would make an offering to God, then we are truly practicing the devotional life.

How often we hear it said: "I don't like this work! The spiritual life would be easy for me if only I could have something else to do." When we spend our time in this way, complaining, and looking about for some work that would be more pleasing to us, then we have missed a great opportunity. A person manifesting such a spirit might stay quietly at home praying all day and all night for fifty years and not have even a glimpse of what spirituality means. A complaining spirit means an absolute halt to all devotional endeavor. Not any amount of praying, not any amount of reading scriptures will, of themselves, take us one step onward. They would have no effect at all without living the life. It would be like leaving poison in the bottom of the glass and changing the water on top.

We must feel the joy of devotion; we must have eagerness to serve. When a child goes along the road with its mother, how it runs to her with every little thing it sees along the way, and how happy it is to have some treasure of stick or stone or flower to put in her hand. That is the attitude of the devotee — we are perfectly happy just so long as we have something to give to God, just to have the feeling of giving, giving, giving. There must not be, however, any grasping element intermingled with the longing to give; that would impede our devotional expression.

You can see from all this that the devotional life is not at all what people think it is — prayers and the singing of hymns and going to church and spending hours in meditation, or trying to meditate. It is the outpouring of the spirit to God through our every thought, word and deed. But if we have to have some special condition for that outpouring, then it is of a very poor kind. A fair-weather friend is a poor friend, so are fair-weather devotees poor devotees. Those who remember to turn to the Lord only when everything is going their way, very rarely get to the Lord at all. Spiritual giving cannot be a partial giving. The whole of us must go to God or nothing of us can go. You cannot move toward knowledge in one lobe of your brain and not in the other. The whole of you has to move toward knowledge. This is equally true in the life of the Spirit. We may try to create substitutes for uttermost giving; but there are no substitutes.

The time is come when we should define our terms very carefully. Whatever we do that is not in direct line with our higher development is an escape and the Lord will not accept it. From the time we rise in the morning until we go to bed at night, every single act, every part of our being must tend towards the Ideal, that is, if we are truly following the path of devotion. Our very heart must beat in rhythm with God's heart. We must pray that every breath may pulsate with the great Divine inbreathing and outbreathing. If our job is to be a salesperson, our thought must not be, "How can I persuade people to buy things whether they want them or not, so that I may have a big profit?" Rather it should be, "Here is a child of God. I also am a child of God. Let God determine the entire matter between us." No one ever lost by following this method. If you work at home, think of your home as the temple of your Ideal. Therefore keep it spotless and pure — not merely outside: the very atmosphere must be washed clean of every impurity.

In dealing with human beings, always, even before you speak a word or come in actual contact with someone, have a moment of becoming indrawn, in order to sense the presence of God, so that through Him a true relationship may be established.

These everyday actions make up the true factors in our spiritual experience. The altar, the candles, the flowers and the pictures are like toys — beautiful, spiritual toys — which, like all true toys, have an educational value. We have, however, no more right to play with them all the time than a child has to play with their toys constantly.

We must not ask to have circumstances and times created for our spiritual convenience. We must make every circumstance and every time an opportunity for our practice. The result will be that when leisure moments do come and we are free to go to our shrine or our quiet corner, our meditation will be fruitful. It will take no time at all to concentrate the mind, because we shall not have to wait to establish a prayerful attitude. Our thoughts throughout the day will have done it; the preparation will be already completed, so that at once our whole heart and mind and being can flow out to the Divine. Even if we have only five minutes those five minutes may lift us toward the superconscious. As soon as we close our eyes our mind will be concentrated and we shall have a true communion with our Ideal. One minute of genuine meditation is sufficient to carry us through many hours. Just one touch and we are filled full of power and light.

In the *Narada Bhakti Sutras*, (perhaps India's most ancient and authoritative commentary on the life of devotion) we find it written: "Love cannot be made to fulfill desires, for its nature is renunciation." That love that leads us to God because of what we can get out of God is not love at all. We can measure the amount of our devotion by the unmindfulness we have of the outer things that we are letting slip from our grasp. Another measure is indicated in the Gita where it is said that one of the signs of spiritual growth is aversion to gatherings. Whenever the average person wants to be distracted, they rush here and there, but the person who is truly following the devotional way of living covets every moment of solitude and leisure for contact with the Ideal.

So it is that as we genuinely dedicate our life, we shall find that outside things have less and less value for us. Our life — our thought life, our heart life and our physical life — instead of accumulating, will have greater simplicity, therefore there will be larger spaces within us to fill with God. Simplicity also is a measure of the life. The least coveting for outer things shows that that part of our being is not filled with true love for the Lord. Remember — the very nature of true love is renunciation. That is real love — the renouncing of the self and everything connected with the self. That is the unfailing measure.

Desire and aversion spring from the same root. Little discontents, little dislikes, little complaints, little grievances, all of these indicate to us that we are not really practicing devotion. If we were growing in love for God we would not be thinking of anything else. In seeking to appraise any love, ask yourself, "How much are the people concerned willing to give up for it?The same is infinitely truer when it comes to the love of God. Renunciation is really a by-product. It is the result of our love. But never imagine that by giving up you will become loving. You will merely be creating a void that will gradually be filled in with some form of selfishness. The giving should not be calculated. It will come as the natural result of intense love. If you are moving toward God how can you help but love Him?

As a matter of fact, we cannot touch any part of the universe without touching God. But we are touching Him only through His dress of nature, His disguise. When we contact Him inwardly it is so much more wonderful, so much more satisfying, so much more inspiring, that the outside contact seems very dull compared with it.

If we really love God, we shall love our spiritual practice, our times of communion and prayer. Now how often we go reluctantly to the hour set apart for worship. We wait till the very last moment, and then rush in two minutes before the time is up. It shows that we get more from our external contact with God's universe than we do from God. If that were not so, we would be watching for a chance to come earlier rather than later, in order to have a longer time alone with the Beloved, and we would come away reluctant to bring our meditation to a close.

Renunciation is of two kinds. In the beginning of the devotional life there is always great love of ritual. During the first stages it is of real help. It is a means of holding the attention and stimulating the feeling for God. As we go on, however, and the inner communion grows more and more real, the outer forms will become less needful for us. Very soon we shall forget about them and go deeper within. So we need not be troubled when the forms and symbols begin to mean less to us, provided that something within is beginning to mean more.

The other thing we find is that we have to renounce involvement with worldly affairs. People are apt to draw back from this renunciation. They persuade themselves that their main obligations are on the outside; but nine-tenths of these outer activities are self-created. We must begin to discriminate between the essential and the non-essential. As we grow covetous of time to give to God, we shall find that most of the present demand on our time and strength will drop away from us. When we are freed from the old conditions, however, let us see to it that we do not create new ones.

Sometimes God seems to leave us alone. Then instead of seeking human companionship, let us go into the very depths of solitude and wait for God to join us there. Let us feel that He has made a tryst with us and we shall not move until He comes and keeps that tryst. If we are given duties that perhaps take us away from things we long to do, let us make that the occasion also for a meeting time with Him. Let us wait and watch. Perhaps the reason we are kept at these tasks is to break our attachment to something else, to free us in a negative way from something within that is binding us. The minute that bond breaks we shall be freed from these duties.

Always wait for God to join you in the place where you are. If the task allotted you is to free you from something within yourself, then if you approach it with willing heart, God will be there to cut the knot. We may be sure that whatever conditions surround us in life, we shall not be kept in them one minute longer than is necessary to teach us the lesson they contain. That is what it means to pray to God that our tasks may become less and less. We may think that this means having fewer and fewer things to do. It means praying to God that our self-chosen tasks may become less and less, but it does not mean ceasing to serve. In the eighty years of Lord Buddha's life he went insistently from place to place. He was constantly teaching. Sri Ramakrishna used to teach twenty hours out of the twenty-four. God does not allow His children to be lazy; and He does not give them too much time to pray. It is a question of reducing our self-chosen, often unwisely chosen, tasks, in order that God may use us ever more and more for the fulfilling of His tasks. When we hold that in our mind, our whole life will be transformed.

The Need of A Chosen Ideal

When children begin to write, they are given a copybook with a line at the top of each page to copy. If they wish to draw, some simple object is put before them as model. If they take up music, the teacher places a hand in the right position on the keys to show them how they must hold theirs. Imitation of something lies at the bottom of all education and growth. The baby learns to walk and talk by watching or listening to others. Their elders serve as a constant suggestion and stimulus to their unfolding powers and their chief ambition is to imitate them. Within them undoubtedly there is an impelling desire for self-expression, but the form which such expression takes is largely determined by the outer environment and associations. One of the first conscious acts of the growing child is the choice of some example to follow — a bigger brother or sister, some hero of the hour, a character in history, or perhaps a champion athlete. Whatever the bent of mind or age, we are always measuring ourselves against some abstract or concrete ideal that towers above the level of our own capacity. We cannot be our own god, however we may try. Behind every created form we sense the presence of a faultless pattern, the archetype or prototype, as Plato called it, which nature is striving to make manifest. Everywhere the Absolute Ideal beckons and evades us, luring us on to the final perfection.

In target practice, we know, the bull's eye must be clearly defined, otherwise our aim will be wavering and the shot ineffective. So in life and especially in the spiritual life. We must have some definite, concrete Ideal to follow, in the beginning at least. As we advance, it will spontaneously grow more subtle and abstract. But we are children in the spiritual world and everything must be made distinct for the child mind. An oral definition or a sign of the hand is not enough; the letter or figure must be drawn large on a whiteboard. The object-lesson is vital in early training. It was the recognition of this need which led in India for the system of discipleship as the best means of attaining spiritual efficiency, just as apprenticeship is considered essential to secular efficiency. When the Soul-consciousness awakens, the first step, according to Indian teaching, is to find the Guru or Master who embodies the Ideal and who will thus produce a model which the disciple may copy. Close daily association with a holy life is regarded as the surest means of gaining holiness; and no instruction imparted through precepts is believed to be as potent as that of a living example held constantly before the eyes. We know how sometimes even to read of a saintly character will kindle a new fire of devotion in our hearts.

It was to give us definite ideals of godliness that all the saviors came to earth; and one of the chief marks of their greatness is the precision and definiteness of their teaching. Nothing is left vague or hazy. To Jesus, the Father in Heaven was not a subtle metaphysical abstraction. He was more real than any earthly father and the relation Jesus bore to Him was as familiar and intimate. This is one of the fundamental lessons of His life, — that God must be to us a living, pulsing reality. We cannot love air or fire or water, even though we recognize that they are necessary to our physical existence, because they are without outline and evasive; so as long as the Supreme remains to us a vague, undefined principle, we shall never feel true love for Him and by love alone can we gain union with Him. We must bring Him near to our hearts by entering into some natural relation with Him.

To many it may seem a superstition to conceive of the Divine in so human and so familiar an aspect. But this prejudice is based wholly on a misconception of the reason and purpose of a clearly defined Ideal in the spiritual life. It is not meant to represent or describe the Infinite. A sum-total of all conceivable names and relationships could not do that; the Infinite would still remain undefined and indescribable. Its purpose is to create a point of contact with God. We can never by any effort of ours gain knowledge of the Absolute. The lesser can never encompass the greater. It is He who must reveal Himself to us. "He whom the Divine Self chooses, by him the Self can be gained," the Vedic scriptures declare; and that one is chosen who is seeking knowledge of the Higher Self. Only those who hunger and thirst after righteousness shall be filled. Our heart must be turned towards God. In ordinary life we do not attempt to explain anything to a person whose attention is wholly fixed in another direction; so God knows that it is useless to try to reach us so long as our thought is absorbed in other things. It is not easy, however, even for the earnest seeker to fix attention upon a formless abstraction; there is nothing upon which to fasten and the heart wanders. Let the Supreme Being, on the contrary, become to us a definite conception, — a real mother, a real father, a real friend and companion; at once it grows easy to think of Him and live with Him, a point of contact is established, and He can gradually reveal to us all aspects of His Divine Being.

If it is less difficult for us to acquire this sense of unbroken association with the Divine through some visible form — a God-illumined character or an Incarnation – then we should take that one which makes the strongest appeal to our spiritual nature and follow with steadfast devotion. It doesn't matter through what channel we gain contact with God; it is enough to touch Him at any point and salvation is ours. Those who purify themselves by unfaltering service to their Ideal "easily attain the infinite bliss born of contact with the Supreme;" such is the promise of the Bhagavad Gita. We must never forget, however, whatever the lesser example we hold before us, that God is the supreme goal. The Gita lays insistent stress on this. All our life and effort must be directed towards Him alone, and only those interests and associations should be cultivated which strengthen our relation with Him.

But it is not enough to possess an Ideal. We must make it a working model after which our whole life is patterned. It would be no help to children to carry a copybook around under their arm, they must fill its pages with letters. An Ideal is equally useless to us unless we are striving to follow it day by day and hour by hour. We must meditate on the character, the life, the words, all that the Ideal represents and try to reproduce that in ourselves. If we desire to match a color, we go from shop to shop always laying our sample against each piece of cloth shown us; in the same way we should refer each act and thought and word to our Ideal. This will keep us open to its purifying influence and gradually we shall form the habit of constant communion with it. We do not realize that spirituality is a habit; courage and steadfastness and singleness of heart are habits; and the easiest method of forming these habits is by association, either in thought or in outer life, with one who possesses them. When we live with people, unconsciously we grow to talk and walk and act like them; and when we live every moment with a pure Ideal, we quickly grow to resemble it. We must always imitate something. We must strive for something. Let us take whatever seems holiest and highest to us, keep that before us, copy it, think of it, serve it, love it; little by little it will fade away and in its place will stand the Supreme Ideal, God Himself.

Whatever obscures His Face and weakens our yearning for His companionship must be eliminated, no matter at what sacrifice of worldly advantage. We must seek out those who stimulate us on the God-side, and gradually withdraw from those who foster the thoughts and habits that smother our higher impulses.

Theory and Practice: Living the Life

In all activity we find two factors — will and deed, faith and works, theory and practice; and we recognize that a life is useful and happy only in proportion as the will takes shape in deed, or as the theory is made a fact in practice. We can never be happy so long as we make pretensions which our daily living does not substantiate. And nowhere is this as true as in religion. Yet strangely enough in religion more than anywhere, theory is an accepted substitute for practice. We would not consider a person travelled who sat at home and informed himself of foreign countries through books; nor would we expect anyone to become a good artist merely by reading about painting, but that person quite commonly passes for religious who listens to sermons or reads in the scriptures about God without seeking to know Him, and who admits the possibility of realization but makes no effort to gain it.

People go from place to place. They listen constantly to teaching. They have an idea that they are universal if they hear a Christian sermon in the morning and some Buddhist teaching in the afternoon and another kind at night. They think that by running here and there they have a great interest in spiritual things; that the more things they can sympathize with and not understand, the broader they are. Their life is so full of theory that there is no room or time for practice. As a matter of fact, religion begins the day we stop running about, the day we stop talking, the moment we begin doing.

Freedom of thought and action, however, must not be confused with dissipation of energy. It does not consist in going here and there, hearing different forms of teaching but declaring allegiance to none. The law of spiritual growth allows us choice in method, but exacts faithful adherence to the method chosen. Each of us, Vedanta declares, must determine our own path but having once entered upon it, we must not deviate from it. It is no more rational to mix methods in religion than in music or art. A student in any line, who is continually shifting from one school to another, never becomes proficient. We develop proficiency only as we select the form of teaching best adapted to our requirements and follow it with steadfast regularity, until we have so far mastered the technique of our calling that we need not think of method at all, but can give free play to the spirit within. Nor should we fear that we may become narrow by adopting this course in our religious life. So long as we remember that our faith is only a means to an end, we are safe. Devotion to a form unquestionably contracts, but one-pointed devotion to an Ideal expands. When God is truly the goal, any road by which we seek Him must inevitably broaden and broaden until it loses itself in infinity. Restless curiosity is not catholicity, nor is multiplicity of interest a sign of universality. One does not become universal by running back and forth on the circumference, but by moving steadily down one radius to the center where all radii meet. We must take up one method and follow it until it is proved to be either good or bad. We must take up one systematic training, exactly as a child does in school. It is the only way we can advance.

Religious reading is mere theory. The only practice is when we begin to read our own heart and our own mind. That is the only book for the earnest person who is seeking to know God. We must discover that within ourselves which responds to that which is in the book. Never can we read above our own understanding. A frog living in a well cannot imagine anything larger than its well. This is literally true of every living being. We can only interpret a thought according to our own experience; truth is the measure of our understanding. We think we read books to enlarge our mind, and we merely contract the books to the size of our mind. The only thing we can get out of a book is to take what little we understand and begin to practice it. What does the practice do? If we take the thing we read today, practice it for a week, and then read it again, we will find out. It is not enough merely to think about what we have read. It must be practiced.

Yet we still must have the theory from day to day. We must listen to it constantly. We must read it in the scriptures, in the place where it is stated with realization; that is the difference. Ordinary literature is all theory. Sacred literature, the scriptures alone, give the virtue of practice and realization.

Many people today prefer to read books on science. Why? Because the scientists are telling something they have seen, experienced, practiced. That is the secret of the whole reaction against scholasticism, against theology. "I have a theory and you have a theory. Now you come and hear my theory and see if you won't like it better." Each one has what they think is a more intelligent theory to take the place of your less intelligent one. But the scientist says: "I have cut this up and I know that it is so. I have watched this grow and I know that it is so." People want to get the absolute fact.

Now true scripture, if we know how to read it, is just as scientific. As much of Christ as we get in the Bible, so much of the truth we have. When He says a thing, He knows it; He has seen it; just as the geologist has seen the structure of the earth.

So it is with the Vedic writings. The ancient rishis saw those things. They have taken the geologist's hammers, as it were, and broken up the structure of God's universe and discovered the cosmic secret. That is the reason why, if we want to read, we are told to go and read the scriptures — because we are reading of practice; we are not reading theories. So we must go to the place where the scriptures are expounded and hear them, and then begin to practice them.

In Vedanta we are told there are three stages in the religious life. The first one is to hear the truth. The second one is to ponder upon it; and the third, which comes of itself, is the realization of it. We find exactly the same thing is true in science of any kind. One who has not studied, will not know. We do not need to know everything that Christ said, nor is it necessary to know the Bhagavad Gita by heart, from beginning to end. But we do need to take one theory, one proposition, no matter what it is, and begin to ponder upon it; think it out; work it out as if it were a geometrical figure in our own mind, and see what we get out of it.

There is one more thing to learn in this spiritual practice: that is not to take all the propositions at once. When we learn to read, we don't read the first, second, and third readers all at the same time. We begin with the first. So it is in spiritual practice.

It is the same with religion. That is why when we are not sure in our faith we are open to doubt at any moment. We do not really know whether God exists. Doubt is at the bottom of all weakness, and doubt is the misery of a theoretical life. Our jealousy, our discontent, all spring from doubt. All of the evil passions spring from doubt. The Bhagavad Gita says, "He who has doubt in his soul perishes." And doubt is always the misery of theory.

How can we be sure of a thing if we haven't experienced it? In spiritual practice we must take each thing and prove it. We don't spend our time in making empty statements about something we haven't proved to be true. When once we have had even a little bit of spiritual experience, nothing can shake us.

Many people say they believe in God. They think they do, but their whole life proves that they do not. If they heard that someone they loved more than anybody else in the world was in town, wouldn't they go quickly to that person? They say they love and believe in God, but they do not make the least effort to go and find Him. It is proof they do not believe in God, for what is God? They say He is all-beauty, all-power, all-glory, all-life. Now if anyone actually believed that, would they rest one moment until they had found Him? When we really come to the awakening that God exists and that He is the thing that we say He is, we shall not rest night or day until we find Him. We will not say He is this or that, immanent or extra-cosmic. What do we care what He is? We want to go and see Him for ourselves.

If I am looking for the source of great beauty, and if you cannot tell me how to get to Him, I will look elsewhere. Swami Vivekananda was in this state when he was a boy of eighteen. There had risen in him a determination that if God was anywhere he would find Him. He went from one holy man to another and asked, "Do you believe in God and pray to Him? Have you seen Him?"

In Calcutta he was looked upon as a skeptic because he would go to this place and that, wherever they were singing the praises of the Lord, and ask, "Why are you singing the praises of somebody you have never seen?" He came to Sri Ramakrishna and said to him, "Do you believe in God?" "Yes." "Have you seen Him?" "Yes." "Can you show Him to me?" "Yes." That was enough. From that moment he followed Sri Ramakrishna. Nothing ever turned him aside. Here was a man who had seen God, to whom God was reality.

But people say, "How can you see Him? You cannot. That is all nonsense." Do you suppose that God, who has made Himself visible in all of His universe, in all of these myriad forms, in all this play of power and glory and wonder, cannot make Himself visible to us in just the form that we can best comprehend? Since He is omnipotent He has the power to come to us in any dress, to show Himself to us in any form. That was what happened in that wonderful chapter on transfiguration in the Gita. Arjuna said, "Show me Thy Lordly form. I have thought of Thee as friend and teacher; now I desire to see Thee as Thou art." Krishna replied, "Thou canst not see Me with these eyes of thine. Do not try. It is of no use. But, behold, I give thee the divine eye."

When we long for God, not in mere words, not by reading books about Him, not by going to a church or a temple to worship Him, but long for Him enough to travel night and day to reach Him, to make every activity of our life, every effort of our heart carry us towards God until our whole being is one quivering call for the divine, God never refuses to manifest Himself to us. He will come whether we are highly educated or not. Nothing matters. God will show Himself to us in the way we can comprehend Him; and having seen Him in that form, there will come into our mind and heart such realization, such understanding that we can comprehend God in all forms.

Give up all this intellectual seeking for God. Be earnest. Never for a moment forget your purpose and longing for God. You need not have a scripture, you need not even have a theory, you need not have a name for God. You need have only your own soul and its earnest longing for Truth, then you will flourish and bear fruit. That is all you need; just such earnestness, longing, and determination to embody in your life as much of Truth as you know today, with a firm belief that out of that practice will come each day a larger and greater knowledge of the absolute Truth.

Living the Life

Religion is not an end in itself. It is a method — a method, as the word signifies, by which we may rebind ourselves to God; and like all methods it has no value unless applied. As a method, however, it need not be fixed or exclusive; for in all departments of knowledge the greatest elasticity in method is observable. How many methods there are in music! How many schools in painting! How many systems in science! In every case the end is the same and the elements to be dealt with are similar, but the manner in which the means are handled to gain the end is capable of infinite variation. Each of us, indeed, introduces our own modifications. Likewise in the spiritual life, as each of us works out our own salvation we evolve our own religion. We may seem to follow in the general plan of action the broad lines of some accepted creed; but if we could place our thought under a psychological microscope, we should see how we interpret and bend the familiar injunctions according to our own mental constitution. It is this individual variation which makes our faith living. Forbid or strangle it and our spiritual nature hardens and withers. We see it wherever bigotry seeks to cast all spiritual aspiration and observance in some sternly defined mold. Freedom is the primary condition of growth for how can we expand unless there is room for expansion. As soon as all latitude for self-expression is denied, practice degenerates into routine and the letter smothers the spirit.

In living, each new vision calls for a fresh effort and readjustment, which will again lead to a further vision. If we do not make full use of the light which has already come to us, our life will remain in a static condition; we shall receive no new material to work upon. Until we are faithful in lesser things, we cannot expect to be made ruler over greater. Too often we wait for some impelling revelation before devoting ourselves to the spiritual life; but only as we utilize our present opportunity will we create a new and larger one. The first task for us is to put into practice what we now recognize as true, to make our lives obedient to the higher laws we already know.

Take, for example, the ordinary problem of anger. We are all struggling to control our temper, but how many are making a fundamental effort to conquer anger itself? We wait until we feel ourselves growing angry, then we try to suppress it by a sudden act of will, as one would push down the cover on a kettle which is boiling over. But the method does not prove effective; the waves of temper still rise. What we should do is to focus our energy on the inside at the point where anger begins, not on the outside where it ends. We should go deep down within, find that thing which reacts in anger, and deal with that. The only way to permanently eliminate the tendency to anger is by altering our sense of values, by increasing our measure of things through discrimination so that that which made us angry will appear too trifling to disturb us. When Arjuna complains to Sri Krishna in the Bhagavad Gita that he sees no chance of acquiring serenity and self-control because of the extreme restlessness of the mind, Sri Krishna replies: "Undoubtedly the mind is restless and difficult to curb, but through practice and dispassion it can be conquered." Do not work on anger today and discontent tomorrow and the love of riches the next day. No, work on the question of anger until you have solved it. It is a very curious thing that when you have solved one problem you have solved them all, because when you have found in yourself that thing which gets angry and that thing which nothing can touch, you have found that which will solve all your problems. Then your work is done. In no other way can you possibly have a stable religious life. So long as you are working only from theory, at any moment you can be confounded.

It is this element of dispassion in our practice which makes it fruitful. There is a natural upward tendency in every living thing which asserts itself the moment the clinging to the lower level is removed. Thus every growth implies an act of detachment. The child outgrows its toys and drops them; the treasures that tempt the youth fall unheeded from the hands of the riper adult. We practice indeed in order that we may outgrow, just as one repeats day after day an exercise in music, only to put it aside the moment it is learned and take up another.

The Secret of Right Activity

The seers of old, seated in seeming inaction on the heights of the Himalayas, evolved the practical system of Karma Yoga or the science of right activity. How can we make each action bring its full equivalent? How can we perform each task with a minimum loss of energy? These were the questions for which they sought and found answers.

There can be no such thing as inactivity on the plane of manifestation, they taught. Activity may become gross or fine, it may be outer or inner; but living itself means action. The heart never stops, or the lungs; all the subconscious forces of our body are ceaselessly active. It is evident then that as human beings we have no choice between action and inaction, we may only determine the nature of our activity. Proper direction and conservation of energy become therefore the two primary lessons of life.

At present we live in the comparative degree: — Is this better or wiser or higher? We should go a step further and live in the superlative: — Is this best, wisest, highest? There is a "best" at every moment: — a best way to wake and to fall asleep, a best way to work, a best way to play, a best way to expend each hour of living. If we wake heavy, drowsy, longing for more sleep, we are starting the day with the subconscious or lower self uppermost. We should train ourselves, by holding the proper thought as we fall asleep at night, to waken with the feeling of the privilege of life, the privilege of work, the wealth of the hours before us. As soon as we form the habit of waking in this attitude of mind, we shall rise alert, strong, rested. So with each act of life; it must seem a privilege, rich in opportunity for higher attainment and service. Then there will be no division in our thought, hence no friction or waste.

We must learn to have a single purpose in our mind throughout the entire day. Perfect single-mindedness implies a dominant aim in life; but it also means that we should try to hold our entire thought on the task in hand, never letting it wander to what has gone before or to what is coming after. This is the secret of all efficiency — one thing at a time, our energy absolutely centered on what we are doing, an immersion into which it is almost impossible to divert our attention. The average thought is seldom fixed; it runs back and forth across the main line of activity. Is the task pleasant or unpleasant? Will it succeed or fail? Is it worthwhile? So it calculates and measures the questions and wastes energy; for every useless thought means leakage and decrease of power. The wise care little about the nature of their work; for them there is no difference between task and task, one is not irksome and another agreeable; they are wholly concerned with the force which works — that it may be used to the greatest possible advantage and the largest end.

The quickest way to arrive at this point of view, Vedanta says, is to detach our mind from all anxiety regarding the results of our action. In nothing do we spend so much futile energy as in calculating, while we work, the outcome of our effort. By that divided line of thought we inevitably reduce the result; and the more we waste energy in calculating, the smaller must it be. If we stop every little while to measure the amount of ground we have covered, it will take us a long time to make our journey. We should put the whole of ourselves into our work and let the result take care of itself. It is not possible for any effort to be fruitless, for there can be no action without a reaction of equal strength and similar nature. The more centered the act, therefore, the stronger and more productive must be the reaction. Even should it fall short of our hopes, we shall spare ourselves needless suffering and regret if we keep our attention fixed on what we put into each act rather than on what we get out of it. Every disappointment borne cheerfully means so much energy saved for a future and more effective action. Life is like any other game; if we play, not to play well, but to win, we nearly always grow irritable and lose both our temper and the game. Good players maintains their poise under all circumstances and are intent only on the perfection of each stroke. The Gita teaches us that when it tells us that the first lesson in Yoga or spiritual practice is even-mindedness; and the second is skillfulness in action.

What differentiates one person from another then? Our own will. And what makes the difference between one person's will and another will? The Ideal and the trust with which it is served. That is all. Get a high ideal and relate yourself to it, and then your will will grow stronger. If we try to run our little machine as an isolated mechanism, it will run down every few moments; but if we keep it connected with the power center, it becomes inexhaustible; and it is by our thought that we connect ourselves.

Wherever and whatever we may be, let us set out from this day to be the finest sort of person we can be and lead the highest kind of life. Nobility of character needs no external name or condition to ennoble it. Let the humblest person serve a lofty ideal with steadfast devotion and they glorify themselves and their condition. The secret is less in what we do or what we are, than in what we serve. Is God the pivot of every action? Then we are safe. We cannot work to small ends. The Power which keeps the earth moving round the sun, will keep us swinging in our proper orbit in harmony with the universal plan.

Discontent, envy, doubt, selfish ambition, these are the causes of all friction and waste; and they can be eradicated only by broadening our vision. We must regard ourselves not as isolated entities living a little life of our own, but as parts of a great whole with a universal mission.

Wisdom through Service of the Ideal

"The wise who have realized the Truth, will teach the supreme wisdom. Learn it by reverence, by enquiry and by humble service." The service referred to in these words of the Bhagavad Gita is very different from what is understood as service in the world. In the world we think of service as doing something for another. But the service which leads to wisdom is being something for the sake of the Ideal. The doing is wholly secondary and follows spontaneously. It is what we are from moment to moment which determines whether we are serving God or not. The merit of spiritual service is measured by the interior state, not by the outer activity. One person may be constantly busy in performing acts of righteousness and another may appear to be inactive; but if the first person's good works are interwoven with the thought of self, and the mind of the second is completely surrendered to the Divine, the apparently inactive one is the truer servant; "waiting on the Lord," listening for the word of command. If we are truly serving, our concern is to keep in perfect rhythm with the cosmic motion and to work or wait as it impels us. We unite ourselves with God and let God unite us with the world. Our contact with outer things may be intermittent, but our connection with God is never broken. As Sri Ramakrishna tells us: "Do your work in the world with one hand and hold the feet of the Lord with the other. When your work in the world is done, hold the feet of the Lord to your heart with both your hands."

However sincere may be our desire to serve God, we have too little penetration to discern where or when or how. What do we know of His plan or of our part in it? What assurance have we when to speak or when to remain silent, when to act or when to stand with folded hands? Yet there is no need of uncertainty or discouragement because of this. If we will but join ourselves with the great cosmic power, it will carry us with unerring precision to the right task at the right moment. That power is constantly in motion, ordering and fulfilling all things according to a divinely appointed plan. When we move with it, we fall naturally into our proper place and find our special work. One thing only is asked of us, — that we keep our mind single and fixed on God; for when the eye is single, we are told, then is the whole organism full of light, the light of wisdom.

In the spiritual path every act of service must be preceded by an act of purification. This was the meaning of Christ's injunction that before we lay our offering on the altar, we must go and make peace with our brother or sister. If there is anything in our heart which agitates it or chills its fervor, if there is in our mind anything which clouds or distracts it, if there is any element of selfishness in our motive, then our service will not be acceptable, however great may be our outer effort or offering. Unless we serve with a tranquil heart, a single mind, a joyous spirit, and wholly without calculation or self-mindfulness, we cannot be drawn in closer to the Ideal.

Another vital requisite in this higher form of service is — it must be done with our entire self. In ordinary life, when we are serving anyone, we do not feel bound to empty our mind of every other thought. But this does not pass as service in the spiritual life. There can be no division of thought or energy or love. They must all go into each act of service. We must serve "with all our heart and with all our soul and with all our strength and with all our mind." If we give the whole of ourselves, it is a large gift, no matter how small it may seem to be. If on the other hand we have a great deal to offer, but keep something in reserve for ourselves, then our offering in God's eyes appears miserly and insignificant. It is by this that spiritual service is measured — not how much we give or how much we have to give, but whether we give the whole.

God covets the whole of our heart because He knows that with less than that we cannot receive His gifts. They are so abundant that He wishes us to come with the very largest vessel we possess, in order that He may fill it to the brim.

There is still another essential element which must enter into all service of the Ideal. We must not serve for the joy it brings to us, but for the joy it gives to Him. This is especially true when we serve the Ideal through some living teacher. His desire must govern us, not our own. The least thought of self-gratification destroys at once the value of our service. We must seek through it, not increase of happiness, but increase in power of denial. We may covet the privilege of serving the teacher directly, but the teacher may wish us rather to serve him or her indirectly by rendering service to others. We may wish to do what keeps us near; the teacher may set for us a task which takes us far away. Thus it is told of Nityananda, the beloved disciple of the great teacher, Lord Gauranga, that one day the Master called him and said: "You must go to Bengal." Nityananda replied in sorrow: "How can I leave you? The body cannot live without the soul and you are my soul." Lord Gauranga rebuked him, saying: "Because you love me, you do not wish to go away; but we are not in this world to please ourselves." "Yet it breaks my heart to leave you," Nityananda protested weeping. The Lord embraced him with ineffable tenderness and said: "When you suffer in my absence, remember that I too am suffering for you."

To be willing to be "the servant of the servant of the Lord" is regarded in India as the final test of the spirit of service. "Inasmuch as you have done it unto the least of these my brethren you have done it unto Me" were Christ's words. When we seek to make terms with our Ideal, we lose the power to serve truly and also we deprive ourselves of the blessing which otherwise would inevitably follow. Vedic sacred writings are full of instances of illumination gained through unquestioning and uncalculating service. When Satyakama came to the sage Haridrumata Gautama and asked to be taught by him, the lad was given "four hundred weak, lean cows" and told to lead them forth to pasture and to return when the herd numbered a thousand. He sought out the high mountain slopes where the grazing was richest and in patient solitude he kept the herd until there were a thousand. When he returned, the Chandogya Upanishad tells us, his face shone as one who had seen God.

Service of an Ideal is a holy and sacred calling, which requires earnest and single-hearted consecration. There is no higher duty. It glorifies even the lowliest life. It makes easy the roughest path. Those of us who undertake it must feel as ones set apart, as no longer belonging to ourselves. We have become the servant of the Most High. Ever mindful of this, we move prayerfully through the activities of the day, asking: "Lord, what will You have me do?" Never will the answer fail to come if we ask in sincerity of spirit. It may not take shape in words, but we may be sure that the duty which presents itself is the one for us; and the Gita says: "Better one's own duty, though devoid of merit, than the duty of another, well performed. Better is death in following one's own duty, the duty of another is full of danger."

Let us go forth then to our daily tasks with new courage, new resolution, new love and joyous gratitude that we have a place in the Divine's household and may prove a little useful to His children. Let us never in our ignorance try to impede the working of His perfect plan, but let us strive to make ourselves eager channels through which He may act and speak and help. If we can learn to serve Him in patience and complete surrender, within our hearts will come from day to day a deeper peace, a larger joy and a growing light of wisdom.

Karma Yoga: The Path of Work

Every moment we are passing through bodily, mental or moral states, but every moment our condition is changing. We cannot stop the state of experience, but we can shift our point of relationship to it; we can make it relate us to God instead of relating us to ourselves. We might occasionally forget ourselves if we were not so busy relating this state or that to our little ego. So long as we do this, how can we forget? Yet it is the only way the ego lives in us, by attaching us to the states through which we pass. That is why the path of devotion, or any spiritual path, offers such freedom, such liberation, because little by little we begin to relate those states to something high instead of something low, to something big instead of something little. Then these very states which have bound us, begin to free us.

Whenever any experience comes to us and we relate it to the inner Self and through that to God, then the sense of oneness rises, which means that we have moved up along the three lines of self-knowledge, God-knowledge, and the union between them, we have gone one step farther towards illumination. This is equally true regarding the three processes, of work, discrimination leading to wisdom and renunciation. It is not that we work until we are purified and that then, with our purified mind, we begin to discriminate; and after a long process of discrimination we learn to renounce certain things that hold us back. Every act, every momentary experience, contains these three processes.

Of course work does not mean just washing or book-keeping, it means activity. Whenever work is mentioned in the Bhagavad Gita, it means that. Every moment we are active in some way. We cannot be static any more than we can avoid action. Every act we do necessitates discrimination, and the very moment we discriminate we necessarily drop the unreal, the less valuable, and move toward the Real. No one ever willingly or knowingly holds on to the less valuable and throws away the more valuable. Thus as we discriminate we begin to perceive the Real.

That is what renunciation means. It simply means letting go of the things we do not want. This renunciation takes place every moment. If these three elements of activity, wisdom, and renunciation are not present in our life, we may know that it has not fulfilled its true purpose. Actually they should form a part of every phase of life, and they do form a part of every phase of the thoughtful person's life. When we merely follow the path of activity without the other two elements, we are moving steadily towards disintegration. By attaching to our action the process of discrimination, however, we cultivate the habit of thoughtfulness.

Unfortunately most of us forget to discriminate. How many acts of our day are impulsive acts? We think we can go on and do the act, and after we have done it and the result comes, then we can discriminate. But the very smallest act should be accompanied by discrimination. Is this piece of work vital or nonvital? Is this something that can be left out, or is it essential? The spiritually-minded are always seeking to know where they can eliminate, simplify. If we are going to buy something we should ask ourselves, "Can't I manage a little longer without it?"

All life at the present time is organized to defeat our discriminative faculty. We go into a store, and everything put there is to catch our eye and lead us to buy impulsively. It is arranged so as to make a quick impression on our minds, in order that we won't discriminate concerning it. This is like life! We must keep ourselves on guard against this. We should be constantly watchful that we do not perform the slightest act without the process of discrimination, which means dropping the unreal. The moment we succeed in doing this, we shall be astonished at how simply our life flows.

Take, for instance, what we believe are our obligations. Many of them are based upon the illusion of our own importance. We think we can bring so much to this person, or that person cares so greatly for us that we cannot disappoint her. All these acts are based on the belief in our own value. Yet these may not be our real obligations. They are real only for those who cannot see beyond them. The real obligations lie always behind these in another set of relationships. While we are busy running around, God is waiting patiently. We picture ourselves as going around and giving pleasure and joy, but do we stop and ask ourselves what we have within us with which we can give this joy and delight? We get into a whirl and imagine that we are essential in so many things that it is needful for us to keep on doing and going. But if we learn to discriminate we shall find that we have deeper tasks to fulfill, tasks that are far more vital.

The rule of action, or the rule of procedure, is exactly the same for all the different paths. In the Bhagavad Gita there is one little verse that gives the rule for fighting the battle of existence. "Regarding alike pleasure and pain, gain and loss, victory and defeat, fight the battle. Thus sin will not stain you." It is significant that the moment the Lord takes up the question of work, the very first thing He tells us is to refrain from attachment and, looking with equal eye upon success and failure, to perform Yoga.

Until we learn to act without attachment we have not begun our effort toward Self-knowledge. When the whole of us wants that Self, we can attain It, but if we are attached to anything else and have desire for anything else, we are destined to failure right from the beginning. We cannot move to the north and to the south at the same moment. We cannot move outward and inward at the same moment, and the only way we can gain Self-knowledge is by moving inward. That does not mean that we have to sit in meditation all day. Moving inward means inward desire. When the wise speak of living inwardly, they never mean that we are to shut ourselves away from everybody. They mean that all our desires must move inward all the time, even during the performance of our outward duties. It is this constant in-moving thought, in-moving desire, in-moving aspiration that is meant when they speak of turning inward. If we have one attachment, one desire on the outside, we are bound there, we will not be able to move toward our center. So it is when we start the spiritual life. In order to avoid pain we stay near that thing to which we are bound. We must realize this. We cannot compromise in the life of the Spirit. Either we want it or we do not want it.

The great mistake is to think that spirituality is a commodity. Spirituality is a mighty vocation. This means that we are not just to bring a little spirituality into our life, it means taking our life and putting it into spirituality, in the same way that we take our life and energy and thought and put them into law, or medicine, or art, or music. We take the whole of ourselves and put it into the object of our choice. The extent to which this is done determines the difference. So it is in the spiritual life; we have to put the whole of ourselves into it. But we cannot do this so long as we try to calculate results, because some part of us will have to stay outside in order to receive the results and measure and weigh them.

Anyone who goes into the spiritual life with an idea of even gaining illumination, will not get it. All personal desire ultimately has to be renounced. Of course we may begin, just as a child does who is starting school, with a personal, self-centered motive and gradually gain a higher incentive; but until we reach the point where we are living the spiritual life because any other life would be perfectly unbearable to us, we may know that we have not yet really put our foot upon the path, or tasted of the life divine. When we go out into the world with a longing to see the movies or to enjoy other distractions, thinking we need these things to recreate us, we may know that we do not yet want the spiritual life. When, however, we experience these diversions and all the time keep wishing we could have stayed at home and read some uplifting book, or gone out and walked in the woods where we could have thought about higher things, when we feel restless and filled with a longing for something bigger and deeper and holier, then we may have hope that we are actually advancing spiritually.

We have the idea that struggle is the sign of spirituality and that therefore we are more spiritual when we are struggling. In the East they say that as long as we are struggling we have not become spiritual. We must constantly cultivate a taste for higher things — not struggle against lower needs, but just look forward and upward and cultivate a taste for God, as we now cultivate a taste for good literature by reading good books. There is something in us that responds. Every time we open a holy book, every time we sit in meditation, every time we say a prayer, we develop a little more feeling for divine Reality, and never again can we have quite the same feeling for the outer changing things of this world. It is not by shutting ourselves off from the world, it is by opening ourselves to God that we attain Him. Then the way becomes very easy. Do not try to measure growth. Someone asked Sri Ramakrishna once: "What can I do to attain illumination?" He said: "Stop thinking about it. Think of your Ideal."

The next condition we must consider is even-mindedness. This comes necessarily the very moment we have thrown off the idea of weighing and measuring success and failure. The Lord says in the Gita that "work with the desire for results is far inferior to work with understanding." We all know that those who work for what they are going to get out of it are very seldom the best workers. Become a master in your work. Learn that in the spiritual life there is nothing trivial. The smallest task is as vital as the biggest. Absolute care in even the most humble or most minute task is what marks the Path of Work in the Indian Yoga system. If we have a room it should be kept in perfect order; it should be immaculately clean. If we have a glass to wipe, we wipe it until it shines. That is why the next condition of this Yoga is skillfulness. It requires a great deal of conviction and steadfastness to practice it. Also when we really get into the swing of it, there rises in us a great exhilaration as we do our work, because when we are working we are thinking of the One for whom we are doing it. When we pray, we pray to come into communion with that Higher Spirit, and when we work, we must work to come into communion with that same Spirit. Therefore there must be skillfulness. There must not be the least shirking. That Spirit is perfect and only as we work perfectly can we move towards perfection.

All this holds good not only in relation to positive activity, but also in regard to rest. That is, if we are resting, we must rest with that same realization. We must feel the same consciousness in resting that we have felt while doing everything else.

We should be as lighthearted as possible. There should always be joy. There is no perfection without joyfulness, and real joyfulness itself leads to perfection. So every act must be a joyful act.

We have two obligations every moment of our life; one is to the lower self and to the world, with which the lower self is related, and the other is to the

Higher Self and to God, with whom the Higher Self is related. So long as we hold to the lower demands and feel that they are primary, so long as we feel that we must give our whole thought to our worldly concerns even though it means letting our higher interests go, we shall never be free from action. Though we should sit perfectly still and not move our hands or feet, still our minds would go on surging. In fact it would be most difficult for us to sit still at all, because we would be thinking of so many things waiting to be done. If, on the contrary, we make the inner our first consideration, a sense of quiet will arise within us, while outwardly there will be less and less for us to do. Others will feel that they do not have so much claim upon us. They will begin to realize that we are living for something greater than the small issues of life. When we learn to live our life at that higher level, we shall be shielded by our own consciousness from the trivial and the unimportant, and it is in this way that we gradually gain freedom from action; it is by reversing our sense of values and always considering the divine obligations first.

Always the Divine first, let that be our attitude of mind. "God, what will You have me do?" It is not that the Lord would have us fail in our worldly duties. So we need never fear that if we take this course the Lord will lead us away from our genuine obligations.

Actually no one can ever, even for an instant, remain inactive, "for all are impelled by their nature to act incessantly." There is nothing more foolish than to suppose that we can ever stop acting. The very conditions in the human body mean that we have to act in order to maintain its existence. Since that is the case, it is useless to wait for a less active life before taking up our spiritual practice. Such an idea is one of the tricks of maya, or illusion. We always think that when we get through our immediate task then we shall have a little leisure; but before we have finished the work in hand, another task has arisen, and still another. We say: "When this is done I shall have time for prayer and meditation or some more serious occupation." Thus we go on and on, finding excuses for our inertia. We are always seeking some reason to justify our doing the worldly thing and giving our strength and energy to worldly concerns.

Now all this does not imply that we have to abandon what is needful to our bodily existence. I think if we should make a study of our actions, we should find that three-fourths of them are not in connection with the necessities of life at all: they are for indulgences. If we were only willing to reduce our life to a simple basis; if we could only get a true idea of the real nature of riches and of poverty, we should begin to realize that poverty of the soul is far more terrible than poverty of the body.

We now come to a definition in the Gita of what it means to be active in the spiritual sense and what it means to be active in the physical: "The one who, restraining the organs of action,..." In other words, those who sit down and say, "I am now going to live a life of meditation!" "Those who, restraining the organs of action, sit holding thoughts of sense-objects in their mind, that self-deluded one is called a hypocrite." This refers to those who imagine that just by sitting still and meditating and reading holy books they are living the spiritual life. But that is not the way at all. The spiritual life means living with the consciousness of the Spirit. Your hands and feet may be busy every minute and yet you may be spiritually centered in your thoughts and feelings.

"People, walk with the consciousness of the Spirit within you!" said Pythagoras. What a wonderful text to carry with us! That is what it means to be spiritual; not sitting down and doing nothing and being aware some of the time of God and some of the time of our senses, and most of the time of ourselves. Meditation, in that sense, has nothing to do with it. A meditative life means a continuous flow of thought toward God. It can flow through every task, through every action, through every condition of life. That is being spiritual. The Gita tells us that that those who, drawing inward and restraining their mind and senses, "follow, without attachment, the path of action with their organs of action, they are esteemed."

You may say, "How can I draw inward when I have to be giving my thought to my task?" If you examine yourself I think you will discover how very little of your thought actually goes into your task at any time. While you are doing it, you will find that you are generally thinking of other things, or of what benefit it will be to you, or of what pleasure it will give to someone else. Spiritual practice does not mean withdrawing our mind from the task to God, it means withdrawing our mind from all these things unrelated to the task itself, and then, having done that, offering up the task to God.

It is exactly the same process of mind that a lover goes through. Everything the lover does is done in relation to the beloved; everything is shared with the beloved; and that must be the attitude of one following the path of action or work. Constantly the mind and senses must be restrained from non-essential things and fixed on the work in hand that it may be done as perfectly as possible, in order that it may be worthy to offer to the One Beloved.

Anything that does not move toward perfection cannot possibly draw us toward God. But in order to do our work as perfectly as possible the whole of our energy and attention must be given to it. When we realize this, concentration at once becomes natural. There is not the smallest task that we can do for the Beloved One that does not need the whole of us to do it; otherwise it does not move toward God — it cannot. It cannot carry us to the Ideal.

Every movement of the mind should be as precise as possible. The very way we walk is an indication. When we have this feeling we will never bump into things; we will never knock over things; we will never break things. As we pick up something we will remember that it is not ours, that it belongs to God. It is just as much a sacramental vessel as one that is used on the altar. For us, everything is sacred, everything is holy. "Take off the shoes from your feet, the ground that you stand on is holy ground!" — that should be the attitude of mind. It is a wonderful attitude to have. Nothing so quickly wipes out the consciousness of "me" and "mine," which more than anything else betrays us into carelessness in relation to our individual thoughts and deeds. We say, "I am doing this for myself, so it does not matter how I do it."

"This world is bound by actions, except when they are performed for the sake of sacrifice. Therefore perform action without attachment." That is the measure which divides spiritual action from worldly action. The action is the same; it is thought that determines its nature. A holy thought transforms an ordinary act into something totally different.

We never need to try and change our action, we need only do it as a sacrifice to God. Turn it into a sacrament and it becomes a great opportunity. For the spiritual there is no such thing as a hindrance. Everything is an opportunity in their lives. That is what doing things as a sacrifice means; it means a sacrifice to God. Therefore go on and perform any action, no matter what it may be, but do it without selfish attachment, then "there is no possibility of evil results." The spiritually minded ones, however, do not think of the results. They have no preconceived ideas of any kind. They only know that a task has been set before them and that they must do it as well as they can and as an offering to the Supreme. This is the lesson we are given to learn, and in the learning of it a disagreeable task may be given to us again and again, until we come to feel that it is a special thing that God asks us to do, but for His sake instead of ours. When we know that, then we turn to it with love and do it with our whole heart. No matter how insignificant it may be, we would not want any other assignment. The Lord is always giving us things that we do not know how to do, because He wants us to learn how to do them, and we are always trying to escape, trying to avoid doing those very things, and so the lesson has to be repeated and repeated. Therefore Sri Krishna states: "The world is bound by actions except when they are performed for the sake of sacrifice."

The true devotee never takes the first fruits of anything. The first is offered to the Lord; what is left to the sacrificer is looked upon as the remnant of the sacrifice. Sri Krishna refers to this when He says: "The righteous, eating the remnant of sacrifice, becomes free from all sins; but the unrighteous who cook for themselves eat sin." Whatever we do for ourselves alone, no matter how high the results may seem to be, partake of sin, in the sense that self-centered action forms the basis for all degradation; it tends to lower rather than elevate. Thus once more we see that it is the attitude of mind not the bigness or smallness of an action that marks its spiritual value. For example, how many people prepare food with the thought that they are not doing it for themselves but as an offering to God?

One of the subtle tricks that our ego plays upon us along the way is to persuade us to measure our progress. When it is not able to draw us back into the world, or to desire worldly things, then it tries this deception, and we begin to pull ourselves up by the roots, as it were, to see how much we have grown. But that is not the way to walk the path of sacrifice. We should leave it entirely to God. We have nothing to do with our progress at all; we should even be willing not to progress. Whatever God gives back to us as "the remnant," we should take with perfect content, whether it be growth or non-growth. That is to say, we have given all to God and we accept without question whatever God gives to us in return. If He gives us nothing, that too is as it should be.

Surrender and Obedience

Surrender

Surrender is not a sudden act of will. It is a process of development. It means transcending one by one the different strata of our being. In the ancient writings of China a story is told of a seeker after Truth who came to a sage and asked to learn of the Tao (God). The sage hesitated, but at last consented "with deliberation." The pupil proved so apt that in three days he was able to banish from his mind all worldly matters. Instruction continued and after seven days he was able to banish all thought of fellow beings and things. This accomplished, in nine days more he was able to count his life as foreign to himself. This attained, his mind became as clear as the morning and he was able to see his own individuality. That individuality perceived, he was able to banish all thought of past and present. Freed from this he penetrated to the Truth that there is no difference between life and death. From this by meditation and detachment he was able to acquire an understanding of the unity of all things in the Tao.

To reach thus the heights of spirit the surrender must be continuous and complete. Body, mind, intellect, and moral sense must be made a sacramental offering. The body must be schooled to obedience and restraint. It must serve, not as a toy to play with, but as a tool to work with, for higher attainment. Our attitude of mind also must be reversed. We must no longer look upon ourselves as the center of a little world of our own, with our benefit as the measure of advantage; the universe must become our world and the benefit of the whole our measure of advantage. We must rise above personal likes and dislikes, personal prejudices and antagonisms. Our love must become a habit, not a fluctuating emotion. It must flow out to all people, to all living and growing things, equally. Nature gives us this lesson; — the tree shades even the one who prepares to fell it, the sun shines on the saint and the sinner, the rain falls on the ploughed field and the neglected one.

Even from the scriptures also we learn the same lesson. In the Bhagavad Gita the Lord says: "Alike am I to all beings: hated or beloved there is none to me." The Bible tells us that God is no respecter of persons. In the *Yin-Fu-King* or *Book of Harmony of the Seen and the Unseen*, it is said: "Heaven has no special feeling of kindness, so it is that the greater kindness comes from it." And Chuang-Tzu writes: "Be large-minded like space, whose four points are illimitable, and form no particular enclosures. Hold all in love, favoring and supporting none specially." By this universal love and by the practice of gentleness and holiness all inharmony within us is transformed into harmony and we enter into conscious harmonious union with the Whole. When this union is attained, we seek no longer to direct our own life, or to change our nature. We put ourselves back into the universe and leave it to the Supreme Power to mold and lead us, knowing that the One who heals the wound of the broken branch and swings mighty suns in their orbits, will not fail to strengthen in us that which is weak, to turn to beauty that which is unlovely, and to bring to fruition the deeper yearning of our hearts.

The Laws of Life

No one can be truly happy who does not obey the laws of life. By life is not meant the narrow personal daily round regulated by individual advantage and individual needs, but the great cosmic life revolving in a wide circumference round an inalterable center. Obedience to the laws of this larger life does not curtail our freedom, it sustains and reinforces it. The more we conform with these, the freer we grow; and freedom is an essential condition of happiness.

These cosmic laws are not arbitrary decrees made without regard to the well-being of those whom they govern. Their purpose is to safeguard us from error or weakness. They are like road signs put up to mark the way to highest attainment. They bring a sense of bondage only when we run counter to them. Swimmers pay little heed to a river's current until they try to swim against it, then it blocks their progress; when they go with it, it picks them up and carries them forward. The bondage we feel, when we oppose the cosmic laws, does not spring from any restricting force exercised by them; it is due to the fact that we fall under the sway of a lesser power — our own self will. This contracts our sphere of free action at once, because it operates in a narrow area.

But how can we fulfill laws with which we have no acquaintance? And how many are the laws of which we are ignorant! We do not have to fulfill them; they fulfill themselves with reiterated persistence and exactitude. This world would be in chaos if the law depended on individual knowledge and impulsion. The order is reversed, — we depend on the law. If it were at any time inoperable or variable, we would have nothing to tie to. Our ignorance or infringement of it does not affect it; it affects us. We are the ones who are checked and shattered. The law continues to operate unhindered.

Mere knowledge, however, is not an antidote for our suffering, when through ignorance we strike out against the cosmic course of action. Knowledge brings greater responsibility and calls for a wider vision, a more pliable will. Knowledge without obedience terminates in catastrophe. It is the knowledge of the law which makes the sin, St. Paul declares. If we keep a flexible open mind and try whole-heartedly to move with the cosmic current, we shall obey the laws of life spontaneously — even if we are unaware of their existence.

Law — observance is more an attitude of mind than an act. It does not consist in isolated efforts to unify our will with the cosmic will, as we would steer a car in a moving procession. We let go of the lesser and the larger claims us. We are swept up into the mid-stream of cosmic activity and become an integral part of it. The practice of obedience is a vital factor in this process of unification. We cannot bring our little will suddenly in line with the great will. If we did it with conscious effort, we would do it haltingly and ineffectively. It must be done automatically. Our obedience to the laws of life must be swift and spontaneous. It cannot be laborious or calculated.

Obedience must be practiced as we practice scales and arpeggios in music. We must seek opportunities to obey. If we could realize with what danger are fraught the high places of authority and command, we would cease to covet them. They breed self-importance, vanity, arrogance, all the harsher traits which are subversive of happiness. We must be humble to be happy. Life is enriched for us just in proportion as we are humble. Humility does not mean lowliness only; it means receptivity, the power to absorb and assimilate. Those who are loud and unremitting in their demands on life are never content, and without contentment there can be no joy. Contentment creates an atmosphere of serenity and peacefulness which are signally favorable to the growth of glad-heartedness.

The law of love is the highest law of life. When it finds free expression it creates a cosmic contact which in time awakens a consciousness of common interest, a sense of unity. The love, however, is more than a spasmodic emotion which warms and cools, waxes and wanes, expands and contracts. This love is a profound universal expression of feeling, steadfast and all-inclusive by its very nature. It is not possible to love the law without loving its Source and its object. The love must cover the Divine and humanity as well. Creator and creation rise and fall together. We cannot love one without loving the other equally. Nor can there be any variability in the outflow of feeling. It must not change according to the object to which it goes. It must pour forth from one's heart in an unvarying stream, whether or not anything lies in its path, just as the rain falls with the same refreshment on all alike.

The Planless Life

We are told in the Bhagavad Gita that the wise life is a planless life, and we readily interpret this to mean an aimless, unordered life. But this is not what is meant. There is a mighty plan always. The universe moves according to the most perfect plan that can be conceived and everything in it has its place and purpose. Order and system reign everywhere. The individual plan disturbs this system. If we could imagine an army in which the whole campaign is thought out, every officer has his instructions, the command is given, but each soldier sets out to fight the adversary according to a scheme of his own; what kind of a battle would it be? Yet that is what we do in life.

We consider it a sign of strength and superiority when we elaborate a personal aim and hold to it in the face of every obstacle. But if we can follow to the end those who insist on moving in their own direction without regard to the universal plan, we shall find that they inevitably end in disappointment and collapse. They may carry their own way on through years, perhaps through an entire lifetime, but if their way is contrary to the cosmic way, the crash must come sooner or later.

Those of small vision rise in the morning with minds full of self-created projects. At this hour they will go here; at that hour they will go there; they will see this person or perform that task. Rarely do these plans accomplish themselves strictly according to schedule and the mind grows irritated by the constant thwarting of its efforts. The far-seeing, on the contrary, do not lay themselves open to these unnecessary causes for anger and discomfort. When they rise, they remind themselves that the day is already planned out, not only for them and for the other ones whom they wish to see, but for every living thing, great or small. Each tiny root fiber, every bud and leaf, has its work to do. The whole universe, they know, is a great workshop in which every unit of existence is allotted its particular task. Therefore instead of mapping out the use of their time and energies according to a limited personal standard, they send up an earnest prayer from their hearts that they may take their place in the scheme of things and fulfill each hour in God's way the duty which God appoints. A universe in which everyone followed this rule of action would be a universe without friction, without disappointment, without all the abortive effort and loss of energy from which it now suffers.

True planlessness, however goes much further. Every preconceived idea regarding the outcome of our activity is a plan. We do our work expecting a certain definite result, but that may not be the result that the universe has in view. Hence we fail of our purpose, grow angry and rebel against the injustices of life. To avoid this, Vedanta tells us that in all our activity we must hold ourselves free from attachments to the fruits of our actions, both for our own sake and for the sake of humankind. To attach ourselves to any special outcome may force a result which will throw out of order that portion of the universe where we are working. Our energy will be wasted and nothing will be accomplished. Granted a momentary achievement, it will soon be obliterated by the inevitable adjustment of the cosmic order of things. If, on the contrary, we offer up all our activity to God as a free will offering, then even if our effort be a mistaken one, the Great Divine Wisdom will be able to swing that misdirected energy into the cosmic current and make it count despite our weakness and lack of understanding.

We must carry our practice of planlessness further still. In our spiritual life nearly all of us expect to grow at a certain pace and attain certain clearly defined ends. We look upon our daily practice as if it were an investment committed to bring us a fixed dividend. We imagine that if we sit and meditate faithfully each day we should begin before long to have visions or some glimmering of illumination. How many of us battle at frequent intervals with a sense of disappointment because our spiritual practice has not transformed us as we expected it to do; or we have not made the progress or acquired the wisdom which we counted upon when we began. But this very element of calculating expectancy bars the way to progress. It divides the attention and energy, making it impossible for us to put the whole of ourselves into our effort.

We should make no terms with God when we set out to know Him. We are ignorant of what spiritual growth involves. It may be good for us to gain no outer results from our practice during a long interval. When plants are first repotted it is better for them to remain for a season in the dark until they are thoroughly rooted. So we too may need to put down deeper, stouter roots into the spiritual soil before there is any apparent growth on the surface. To try to force a visible growth might wholly defeat the working of the higher principle within us. There are times also when we seem rather to go back than forward. We are more irritable, less in harmony with our surroundings, less lovable, less useful than formerly. But even this must not betray us into a premature judgment regarding the workings of the Spirit. If we are doing our best, we must be patient and long-suffering towards these failings of our little self, remaining firm in our trust in Divine Wisdom and not asking to interfere with the ways of God by substituting some way of our own. This period of apparent deterioration is probably the first step, and a necessary one, in the process of purification. When the inner spiritual fire is kindled by regular practice, it sets the whole system to seething and throws to the surface all the sediment of old habits and tendencies. Only by this means can they be permanently eliminated.

To lead a planless life means to set no goal except the goal of unswerving conformity with the cosmic plan; to ask nothing of God except that we never fail in surrender and obedience to Him. Until we have developed the habit of planlessness, we can never attain complete surrender. Before that there will always lurk an element of bargaining in our submission. We have an end to gain — power or illumination or freedom, so we yield ourselves up to God as we would to a physician or a teacher or a higher official. We even take it for granted that surrender must bring escape from suffering; and when it does not, we quickly take ourselves back and begin once more to direct our own life.

We shall never know the joy or the power of the spiritual life, until we are ready to let God fill every hour of every day as He may choose; to create any condition which He may see fit to create; to use our energy as He will. We must be ready to go here and there, to succeed or fail, to meet honor or dishonor, to live in solitude or on the noisy thoroughfare. In other words, we must have no plan apart from His plan. Nor need we fear, if we reach this point, that our life will lack direction. For the first time it will have a definite course. Now it starts in one direction, then it is pushed into another, and continues to be swayed by circumstances until through a happy chance it falls into line with the cosmic current. Only when it moves habitually with that current, will it become consistent and continuous in its aim.

In striving to cultivate a habit of planlessness, however, we must guard ourselves against the error of beginning on the outside. What we must seek to change is not our outer mode of living, but our attitude of mind. As we persevere in our daily spiritual practice, we shall grow naturally into a more vivid sense of God's guiding wisdom and learn to turn more and more to Him for counsel. Thus gradually His way will take the place of our way and we may not even realize the change. There will be no sense of blankness or lack of routine in our day. Events and duties will follow one another normally. We shall always see clearly what is to be done; but we shall live more wholly in the present, and the future will not stretch out in so long a perspective as it does now, confusing our thought and dividing our attention.

This is what planlessness means — to merge our many little plans into the one great plan; to exchange our countless shifting aims for the one great cosmic aim; to live a larger life in union with a mighty scheme; in other words, to be an integral part of God's great world instead of living in a narrow imprisoning world of our own making.

The illumined never have any desires contrary to the great cosmic plan. If they did desire things apart from that plan, they would not be one of illumination. The two conditions are contradictory. Those who have attained God-union have no interest apart from the interest of the whole. They do not differentiate or separate themselves from the whole. The cosmic will is their will; the cosmic law is their rule of action.

It is clear, therefore, that the only way that we can have all our desires satisfied is to make our will His will. Then naturally we shall desire nothing but what is in accordance with the supreme, universal plan, and that cannot fail of fulfillment.

Strength Through Surrender

By the inherent law of our being, we move steadily toward perfection. All creation impels us. The perfection to which we are predestined, however, does not consist merely in a multiplication of virtues, in being good or even saintly. It consists in expanding from the little to the large, from the personal to the universal, from the finite to the infinite. The human must be transmuted into the Divine. This can be accomplished only through the complete submission of the lower to the higher. In no other way can the inherent perfection of our nature find expression. Thus self-surrender becomes a cosmic obligation.

This surrender to the universal does not make us captives or slaves. On the contrary, it frees us; because through it we attain a state of oneness — not only oneness with God, but oneness in ourselves. We cease to sway between the dualities, -— like and dislike, desire and aversion, joy and sorrow, pleasure and pain. It is this fluctuation in thought and emotion that is the real cause of our slavery. Slavery is unknown to those who have yielded themselves up to the Highest and thus become unified. We walk by one light only, —the light of Divine wisdom; we hold but one aim, — to move in perfect harmony with God and His universe; we cherish but one feeling, that of love — a love that flows out equally to enemy and friend, as the sun shines and the rain falls on all people without regard to their merit or demerit. Thus united in spirit and will with cosmic Being, we are no longer subject to the tyranny of enslaving reactions.

When we cannot understand or operate the whole mechanism, how can we expect to manipulate any part of it? If we cannot direct the great universe swinging in endless space at breathless speed, we should not ask the direction of that part of it we call our life or our work. So long as we isolate ourselves from cosmic Being, we cannot be strong.

To be united with cosmic Being, however, does not mean being caught in a relentless machine; rather it consists in establishing connection with the Source of love and wisdom, of peace, joy and strength. It means entering into conscious relationship with an all-tender Mother, who watches over us and directs us more wisely and more lovingly than we could do it for ourselves. Our quarrel with Her is that She is not immediate enough. We utter a prayer or put forth an effort and expect an instantaneous result. But prayer and effort are seeds planted in the cosmic garden; they have their season of blossoming and fruit-bearing as every tree or plant has. We should not ask that they bloom and bear at our bidding.

Obedience

Obedience is a quality essential to spiritual progress. But the practice of it is not easy, especially if we have the habit of independent thinking, because it suggests always a curtailment of our rightful liberty. We even imagine that if we obey constantly, our own will, will be weakened and we shall fall into a state of passive bondage. But if we look deep into our experience, we shall find that that in us which makes it difficult to obey is far more enslaving than any outside authority possibly could be. Rebellion and disobedience are signs of immaturity and childishness. It requires wisdom and bigness to be truly obedient.

We see it in military discipline. The best private makes the best general, they say. Why? Because the power of command springs from the same root as the power of obedience. Both require well-grounded self-control, quick intelligence and absence of selfish calculation. Thomas à Kempis lays insistent emphasis on the spiritual value of being subservient to a higher command. "It is a very great matter to stand in obedience," he writes, "to live under a superior; and not to be at our own disposing. It is much safer to stand in subjection than in authority. Those that endeavor to withdraw themselves from obedience, withdraw themselves from grace. Those that do not cheerfully and freely submit themselves to their superiors, it is a sign that their flesh is not as yet perfectly obedient unto them."

In India the place of the disciple is regarded as the most favorable of all for higher attainment. To have occasion to serve, to efface the individual will, to be in the rank and file rather than in the lead, to suffer rebuke: — these are the conditions best adapted to spiritual growth and most eagerly sought by the sincere devotee. The immature, when they are corrected, rise at once in self-justification. They are eager to prove that they are not and cannot be wrong; but the true disciple salutes and stands silent. What strength of will lies beneath that silence! We need never fear that we shall be put upon by following this course. Nature and God invariably justify the right; we do not have to vindicate it. The one who is right is justified by that fact alone and sooner or later it will become evident, either in some outward turn of events or in her character. A new power will appear in her which will more than offset the moment of abasement.

It is one of the most purifying of spiritual practices to listen tranquilly to counsel or reproach. Whatever humbles us will in the end as surely exalt us, if we meet it with quiet submission. Humility is an invariable accompaniment of spiritual maturity. No truly great person was ever boisterous, rebellious or self-assertive. The larger virtues are inconsistent with the quality of mind and cannot be acquired so long as it persists. We must have openness of heart, receptivity, eagerness to learn, if we would gain the vision; and when we have these, the whole universe becomes our teacher. No Truth can be hidden from us. "Unto the humble God reveals His secrets and invites him to Himself."

Obedience, in the ultimate sense, is a subjective rather than an objective habit. We cannot obey any outer voice efficiently until we have learned to follow the Voice within. We must live in strict harmony with the larger law so far as we have made acquaintance with it. There must be no compromise with our furthest vision. As much as we know, that we must do. "It is the knowledge of the law which makes the sin," St. Paul declares; in other words, we are held responsible so far as our knowledge reaches. Our actions must be shaped not by self-conceived plan, but by a vital principle. Public opinion, material benefit, personal importance, these must not be admitted as data in the solution of any problem. We must be obedient to the highest revelation granted us even in the most trifling question. By this habit of thought alone we shall make ourselves perfect in concentration and meditation, for it will keep our attention constantly focused. Now our forces are scattered because we are obeying so many gods — the gods of health and prosperity, the gods of tribe and family, the gods of success or power; in the confusion we forget almost to obey the God of Truth. When we learn to obey the Supreme from the time we wake in the morning until we lie down at night, all the lesser acts of obedience in our daily round will become easy and automatic.

Christ, you remember, said: "Whosoever will be chief among you, let him be your servant." India's teaching with equal emphasis tells us that if we would be perfect in devotion, we must be willing to be the servant of the servant of the Lord. Why should we be so eager to exalt our little self, to justify it, to hold it up for admiration, when it is the cause of all our discomfort and misery? The one who humbles or silences it is our truest friend, not the one who puffs it up by trivial praise.

Obedience is a stauncher material to build into character than self-will. St. Francis of Assisi, at times a stern disciplinarian, recognized its value so avowedly that when he travelled through Italy, preaching as he went, he always made one of his brother monks leader of the band, while he himself took the place of obedience. All greatness is born of humility and submissiveness. Only those who can give obedience are able to govern.

Not until we learn to obey the laws of the universe will they cease to hamper and restrict us. We need not fear it will weaken our will. On the contrary, voluntary obedience strengthens and gives new power to command. The universe demands submission of us. If we do not obey its laws, it disciplines us until we do. The greater portion of our discipline comes in this way, — as a reaction caused by our infringement, voluntary or involuntary, of cosmic law.

Every act of self-will increases our discipline, but the discipline does not come as a cosmic punishment. It is not the action of the universe upon us; it is the result of our rebellious pressure against it. The pressure and rebellion may be unconscious and due to ignorance, but the effect is the same. We cannot "kick against the pricks," as St. Paul puts it, without being wounded, and the wound we receive is what we call discipline. It is the rebound of our own mistakes. No other form of correction makes for character.

Those who are in a position to govern their fellow-beings should remember this. Any discipline that is based upon the leader's self-will or upon an artificial, not a cosmic, cause will dwarf the character of the one disciplined. The outcome cannot fail to weaken and induce further rebellion. True discipline can be given only out of a perfectly surrendered heart. In administering it, the first impulse should be toward the Divine. Before we chasten or rebuke another, we must unite ourselves with the governing Power of all others. This act of submission will eliminate our self-will and throw us into rhythm with the universe. Then alone are we able to deal effectively with the self-will of the one we seek to correct.

Three cardinal vows characterize the vocation of religion everywhere: — chastity, poverty and obedience. The most vital is obedience. Chastity commits the neophyte to perfect purity and singleness of aim; poverty demands of us detachment from material things and freedom from the sense of ownership; but obedience lifts us out of the finite into association with the Eternal and Universal, for true submission inevitably leads to union. If we can remain faithful to the one vow of obedience or surrender, then wherever or however we may be living, we shall be as truly consecrated and cloistered as any monk or nun. But how can we know the Divine command, you may ask. It is always sounding in our heart. If we do not hear it, it is because we do not listen. God is trying incessantly to make His voice heard, but our own mind drowns it. The daily acts of outward obedience create the needful silences in which He may speak. This is their chief value.

The spiritual life is a very easy life when we have learned the secret of obedience, just as a child's life is an easy one when it is naturally obedient. When we have become submissive to the Great Mother of the universe, Her Divine wisdom will direct us, Her Divine inspiration will impel us, Her Divine love will envelop us. We shall never walk in darkness or lack for definite guidance. There will be no convulsions of uncertainty, no torments of indecision. Our days will flow along normally and happily in a broader, deeper channel. We shall be swept into the cosmic current and shall pass naturally into a holier, sweeter, serener life, free from the disquieting sense of self-importance and authority.

Detachment and Renunciation

Concentration

Dispassion is an essential factor in developing the power of concentration. Until we are completely detached and free, we cannot have full use of all our faculties and forces. Let us be tied by the finest thread, and that thread may pull and set the whole mind in motion just when we have succeeded in bringing it to a state of stillness. Clear judgment, balance, resolution, moral rectitude, genuine love, all these fruits of concentrated thought are possible only in a state of freedom; and freedom implies detachment. Unless we have entire possession of our forces, how can we focus them? They must be wholly at our command to give or withhold, to loose or restrain. The method by which this is accomplished, we are told again in the Gita, is by governing our desires and aversions. "Let none come under the sway of these two," it says, "for they are their enemies." Most of us attach ourselves to our desires and detach ourselves from our aversions, but the wise reverse the process. They move away from their desires and towards their aversions and in this way keep to a firm middle path. Whenever we recoil from any condition or experience, we turn and face it with firm determination until it ceases to cause any reaction in our minds. If a desire arises, in the same way, we look it over and over with calm dispassion until its power dwindles and dies. Very few of our desires can bear close scrutiny, except those which are better classed as aspirations.

Unless these multiple reactions of our mind which we call likes and dislikes are controlled, absolute concentration is out of the question. Nor is it possible to have a fixed purpose and serve it. This is why the practice of dispassion is so important. It is also an incalculable aid in removing the numberless non-essential concerns which now distract our thought and consume our strength. True concentration cannot be had in fragments; it must cover the whole of life. In order to develop it, we must first determine our center and then move towards it with unswerving resolution. Our reading and study, our associates, our work and our play, must all carry us to that specific end. So long as the goal set is a material one, however, there cannot be complete one-pointedness; for the aim cannot be steady when the mark is shifting. And no created thing can be wholly stable. It is for this profound reason that the Vedic teachers reiterate their yearning appeal to make God the final aim of all our effort; for in Him alone shall we reach a state of perfect unity.

"The one who works for Me, has Me for his supreme goal, is devoted to Me, is free from attachment and bears enmity towards no creature;" in this short rule lies the whole secret of concentration. When our life flows in undivided current towards that ultimate Center, then not only will our individual forces be unified, but they will enter into union with the supreme cosmic force and act in harmony with it.

Detachment

Western minds recoil automatically from the idea of detachment. They conceive it as a reluctant act of will, through which one is stripped bare and left naked, shorn of all that is dear and pleasant. That is a wholly erroneous conception. It is not a process of impoverishment, or a corrective for the love of acquisition; it is a method by which one acquires more wisely and more abundantly — the method which St. Paul presses upon his followers when he admonishes them to "prove all things; hold fast to that which is good".

This brief admonition reveals the two fundamental practices to all development. They are discrimination and detachment – inseparable companions in the process of unfoldment. One represents the act of investigation, the other the act of choice. First scrutiny then volition. The Katha Upanishad describes it thus: "The good and the pleasant approach a man; the wise one examines both and discriminates between them; the wise one prefers the good to the pleasant, but the foolish man chooses the pleasant through love of bodily pleasure." Both the wise and the foolish practice detachment; but the wise detach themselves from that which has only fleeting value and hence cannot give lasting satisfaction, while the unthinking detach themselves from things of vital importance and attach themselves to small secondary factors of experience.

We are doing this constantly. Not an hour of the day passes that we do not cheat ourselves of Reality and sell our heritage for a trifle. Why is this? We don't deprive ourselves of the good willfully, or take by preference a lesser good. When we do it, it is because we believe the wrong thing to be good; that is, we makes our act of choice without prefacing it by an act of discrimination. We do not examine the consequences of our course of action before we set out to attain it. Goodness, beauty, enduring happiness, permanent advantage, these elements of life expression do not need to be advertised with extraneous inducements. To see them in plain relief against the more somber background of humanity is to covet them. If we do not reach out for them it is because we are looking somewhere else. We do not see them. Let us begin to cultivate the habit of discrimination and learn to scrutinize all things dispassionately before we close our hand upon them and judicious detachment will take place of itself spontaneously.

A fundamental reason why our practice of detachment is so abortive and apparently fruitless lies in the fact that it is only partial. Our real desire is to detach ourselves from the unpleasant and hold fast to the pleasant. We wish to take one side of the coin and leave the other; but the moment we split a coin, we debase it and it has no further current value. In the same way we adulterate our experience and in place of accepting the full, rounded lessons life would give us, we ask for a diluted synthetic substance we label experience, for which we ourselves would provide a formula.

The dualities which make creation possible and which form the basis of all sense perception are even more inseparable. They are but interchanging aspects of the same thing, sometimes appearing to us as pleasant, sometimes as unpleasant. If we would discard one aspect we must discard both.

Detachment is a cosmic process that lies at the base of all evolution. Without it there could not be any survival of the fittest. It alone makes possible the sifting of the tares from the wheat. It means weeding out what is destructive or what is unproductive or what has lost its usefulness. The swelling seed-pod casts off its blossom petals, the tree casts off its ripened seed, the seed in turn breaks its sheathing. This is not a mere negative procession of events. It has a lofty creative purpose.

Nature teaches a deeper lesson than that of negative detachment. For her, detachment is a mere by-product of a higher attachment. It has no causal value, it is only an effect — the automatic effect of fastening one's interest and desire to something more worthwhile; and that which is most worthwhile is that which is most permanent and enduring — the Ultimate. Life is a continuous chain of attachment and detachment, of grasping and letting go. But the process is of secondary importance in nature's scale of values. The petals of the blossom drop off casually, the fruit in its turn falls off naturally, leaves come and go — these passing facts concern her little. Nature's concern is for the tree — to foster its life, to preserve its beauty, to increase its stature and strength. Falling leaves, decaying fruit, fading petals are all to enrich the soil around its roots; heat and cold are to keep its sap in circulation; rain and sunshine are to freshen and to vitalize it. The tree is everything — the storm or sunshine that toss or brighten it are passing incidents.

The same is true of us. Pleasure and pain, honor and dishonor, victory and defeat, gain and loss, are but incidental factors. Let us suffer or enjoy, let us gain or lose, let us fall or succeed, but let us be human. Let us face the dual conditions of life bravely, knowing that as we try to eliminate a single phase of experience, we will betray our personhood and cheat ourselves of a rare opportunity for growth. We are told in the Bhagavad Gita that those who are not afflicted by these changing moods of life are fitted for immortality; in other words, those who can meet with lofty serenity and gladness of heart all that may befall them are fitted for higher and higher expressions of being.

The True Meaning of Renunciation

True renunciation has nothing to do with giving up in the material sense. Renunciation, according to Vedanta, is merely overcoming the sense of ownership. Christ tells us that we cannot serve God and Mammon; that is, we cannot have two standards of measurement, two varying ideals, two conflicting aims in life. It is not more possible than it is to follow simultaneously two different methods in music. Yet in choosing one standard or ideal we are not called upon to blot every other from our consciousness. The law of the universe is not a law of exclusion. In order to make way for one thing, it is not necessary to push out something else. There is a place for everything in God's creation, and so should it be in our life.

Serving God does not mean rejecting the world. It means changing our point of view regarding it. Now the world exists for us in relation to ourselves. When we make God's service our first thought, it will still exist for us, but related to Him. Our attitude will be like that of a person who is consumed by an absorbing ambition. She refers whatever arises in her daily round not to herself, to her personal comfort and pleasure, but to her ambition. If it hinders that, she puts it aside, however it may tempt her; if it furthers that, she makes gladly any sacrifice it may entail. In the same manner must we measure the importance or value of every experience, not by its effect on our material condition, but by its bearing on our relationship with the Divine.

We need not fear that this will make us indifferent towards our human duties and obligations. In trying to overcome the feeling of ownership we are not forced to give less care to our outer possessions or to ourselves. On the contrary, we take better care of both, because we look upon them as God's. In ordinary life when anything is left with us in trust, we do not dare misuse it; because some day, we know, we shall have to return it and we would be ashamed to have it marred or hurt. We should have the same feeling towards our external belongings and our physical organism. They are a part of the universe and we are answerable for their use. Realizing this does not lessen our satisfaction in them. Rather we have more, because we enjoy them — not the fact that we possess them, as is too often the case now. They are dearer, more lovely to us because they belong to God. If we are deeply devoted to someone, how happy we are to have a book or a picture or anything that was theirs. So will the world gain new value for us when we disassociate it from ourselves and associate it with God. The most insignificant thing then will seem to us a sacred relic. We shall catch the fragrance of His divine being in every passing object or person. The whole material universe will be a reminder of Him.

Renunciation really means casting our burden on the Lord. At present, life weighs heavily on us because we are trying to hold on to something which does not belong to us. We are struggling to pull a little part of the universe away from the whole and the universe pulls against us. No wonder that we tire and lose heart! The instant we let go, the weight will disappear; and we shall be none the poorer. As members of the cosmic body we partake of its universal life and power and riches. Can any small personal possession offset that? The sense of ownership merely builds a fence around a minute corner of creation and shuts us away from all the rest. We cannot take our little portion out of the universe and do what we will with it. We can only stay inside the enclosure and ensure a self-enforced imprisonment, fighting all the while nature's efforts to free us. The ones who do not resist, when life's varying fortunes batter down the fence, are truly the rich ones; because the whole universe lies open before them.

Our feeling of poverty and misfortune springs from a sense of separateness. We picture ourselves standing alone in space surrounded by things we call our own, which we are forced to protect against numberless enemies intent on making them their own. Actually they can be neither theirs nor ours. Individual ownership in the light of cosmic economics is a chimera. We may keep a thing from another human being for a season, but we can never keep it from the forces of nature or from God. In a night all that we possess may be swept harshly from our grasp. Then what are we to do with all these things we call ours? Leave them where they are and look after them diligently; but hold them so lightly that should they be moved elsewhere, we shall feel no wrench. We should be as faithful in poverty as in abundance. "The superior ones," declares a Confucian text, "can find themselves in no position in which they are not themselves. In a position of wealth and honor, they do what is proper to a position of wealth and honor. In a position of poverty and lowliness they do what is proper to a position of poverty and lowliness." They know that it is the Lord who gives and takes away and that true blessedness is to be found in the Giver, not in His gift.

So long as our chief satisfaction in worldly things comes from the consciousness of possessing them, we shall be driven by a feverish unrest to get more and more; and we shall be cheated of any real joy in what we have. The sense of mine-ness is the destructive element in all our happiness, because it sets us against the cosmic law. God's creation is open and free to everyone. Not one corner of His vast universe is shut away. His every truth is waiting to be discovered. His wonder and glory are flashing before us. His revelation is incessant. It is we who will not hear or see. The barriers against which we push are within ourselves; they are the barriers of I-ness and mine-ness. All our limitations are self-created; and were our possessions a thousand-fold greater than they are, we should still feel restricted, unless our sense of values is altered fundamentally. We could label the whole external universe ours and still the hunger of more would be there. The sense of lack will never go, so long as we lend all reality to these temporary worldly contacts and fail to give reality to the one vital contact — with God.

> In the Infinite alone is bliss. There can be no lasting joy in the finite. The Infinite is immortal, the finite is mortal . . . In the world they call cows and horses, elephants and gold, fields and houses, greatness. I do not mean this, for in this case one thing rests in something else, but the Infinite rests in its own being. It is below, above, behind, before, right and left — the Infinite is all this. Those who see, perceive and understand this, love the Infinite, delight in the Infinite, revel in the Infinite, rejoice in the Infinite. They are the masters of themselves and lords of all worlds. But they who think differently from this, live in perishable worlds and have other beings for their rulers. — Chandogya Upanishad

Renunciation and Achievement

Renunciation lies at the root of all achievement. It concentrates our forces and charges us with moral energy. It removes from life all obstructing elements and unifies thought and habit. Without the cooperation of every power and faculty nothing great can be achieved.

The practice of renunciation is universal. It is not possible to acquire without giving up. To receive we must have empty hands. The mere act of renouncing, however, does not possess any unique merit; it is the purpose for which we renounce that measures its value. If the goal is base and selfish, the renunciation will be degrading rather than uplifting and will deserve condemnation, not admiration. If, on the contrary, the end is noble and free of self-seeking, the renunciation cannot fail to elevate and prove rich in fruition. Those who renounce for worldly ends will achieve only small and fleeting results, however mighty they may seem to be. Those who renounce for the sake of a lofty ideal attain permanent spiritual riches which cannot be counted.

No act of renunciation involves a loss. As we cannot acquire without giving up, so we cannot give up without acquiring. The balance must be kept. Nature abhors a vacuum and she fills it according to the size and pattern of the void. The reason why the majority of us shrink from the idea of renunciation is because we do not perceive its benefits. The benefits gained are more often interior and hidden, while the sacrifices made are exterior and visible; and it is our tendency to attribute more reality to the seen than to the unseen. All power, however, has its source in the unseen. Life and consciousness are both invisible, yet whatever is visible rests upon them.

In the eyes of many, renunciation as a pursuit or vocation makes a life idle and barren of practical fruitfulness. History, however, does not bear this out. Great things have never been achieved in any age without great sacrifices and denials. Christ knew not where to lay his head; Buddha renounced a kingdom; Saint Francis, a rich inheritance.

True renunciation is always productive. It gives strength to overcome the dread enemies of all constructive effort, self-pity, self-importance and self-love. Nothing stultifies our achievement so much as self-pity. When we yield to it, we forget our Divine power, forget that the Divine is our close companion, and that disappointments and defeats are but incidents of a day in an eternal life which we are living now, at this moment. We whimper and whine like beggars, asking for a penny when the whole universe is ours. "You are a distinct portion of the essence of God," Epictetus tells us, "and contain a certain part of Him in yourself. Why then, are you ignorant of your noble birth? Why do you not consider whence you came? You carry a God with you and know nothing of it. It is within yourself that you carry Him."

Self-importance and self-love falsify our values even more than self-pity. When we are swayed by them, ambition becomes the motive power of our action instead of principle. We reduce the universe to a personal world and substitute the part for the Whole. With such a distorted sense of proportion it is not possible to accomplish anything of enduring worth. "Complete self-abandonment" is the definition of renunciation given by a great Indian teacher. Going forth wholly from one's self does not mean the practice of asceticism or morbid self-torture; it means exchanging the little for the large, the part for the whole, gaining a more universal outlook. We can curb our desires and appetites, cultivate simplicity, be more discerning in our reading and amusement, less trivial in our conversation, more steadfast in our aims. We can revive the discarded virtues — temperance, justice, tranquility, gentleness, dignity, generosity, fortitude. Above all, we can consecrate ourselves to nobler living, to loftier aspiration and to the renunciation that means complete self-abandonment.

Vedanta and Renunciation

We must keep very constantly and clearly in our mind what renunciation means in the Vedanta philosophy. It is perhaps the one aspect of the teaching which is most often misunderstood, thereby causing confusion in a certain part of our nature. As a basis for comprehension we must grasp the idea, first, that there is an outer universe which is always the same, is constructed on a basis of perfect law, harmony, beauty and rhythm, and moves with the majesty and glory of the Infinite.

Second, that there is also our world, which is created out of our reactions against the outer world. That is to say, the outer world impinges upon us, upon our sense faculties, our sense organs, and as a result, our senses react upon the world, and in this way we create a sense-world of our own. In the same way, the world-thought impinges upon our thought or intellect and we react in our opinions, in our judgments, prejudices and ideas, thus creating a thought-world of our own. The great moral universe outside acts upon us and again we react in our ethical conceptions of duty and of service, and so create a moral world of our own.

Now this self-created world of ours is not a dream or an illusion. It actually exists, in the sense that it is made up from the materials of the outer world, hence it is real in the same way that the great cosmic universe is real. But this little world of ours, unlike the great universe, does not move in majesty; it is not changeless; it is not built on law and harmony and rhythm; because our reactions are not always uniform, they do not always repeat themselves in the same way, and the reason for this is that there is a third world inside of us.

Actually, we never see the great cosmic universe as it is. God's world is really unknown to us, because we behold it only as it is refracted by our likes or dislikes. Always we see it colored or distorted by our opinion of it. There is, however, as I have said, a third world within us, and that is the thing in us which reacts. Inside of us there is this world of feeling, opinion and sensation which causes these outer reactions.

Now when Vedanta talks about renunciation, it never talks about renouncing the great cosmic universe and going and living somewhere outside of it; it talks about renouncing this self-created world which blocks our true vision of the real world. Until we have renounced this world of our own creation we never can get at reality. Therefore renunciation is a renunciation of our own little world, in order that we may see the great world, or the cosmic universe as it really is, and hence have a direct vision of Truth. That explains to us why the Sanskrit term *vairagya* is used, meaning dispassion. All our play of feeling and of passional life comes from this little world of ours. In order, therefore, to stop that play, we must detach ourselves from its origin; for this reason the terms renunciation and non-attachment are practically synonymous in the Vedanta terminology. The only way we can renounce the outer world is to detach ourselves from that within us which reacts. We cannot renounce the outer reactional world of ours until we have detached ourselves from the third and inner world where action and reaction have their origin. Thus it is that all renunciation in Vedanta is a subjective renunciation.

In the Bhagavad Gita, the Lord Sri Krishna tells his disciple, Arjuna, that the path of wisdom and the path of action are entirely the same, — that they both lead to liberation. Why? Because we are not trying to get away from action, we are trying to get away from reaction. There is a great difference. The supremely wise act wholly without reaction; that is the reason their vision is so clear, their mind so steady. They are not seeing the universe through their own opinion about it. They are not carrying on this collateral line of thought or feeling while they are acting. In other words, they are not reacting. The whole of their attention is fixed on the action. Hence action and reaction with them are the same.

Also contemplation and action are the same. The very moment we can carry on a continuous action with the ideal of perfection in relation to it, we are living the life of contemplation or meditation, because meditation means an unbroken flow of thought towards an object. If we have the power to place in that object the Divine Presence (which is already there) and then let our thought flow towards it, we will have a perfect meditation. That is why Sri Krishna says that the person who sees these two paths of action and meditation as different does not see truly. They have no idea of the relation of these two to each other or of their relative value and the place they must take in our spiritual life.

The true renouncer is not the one who tries to give up the outer world, but rather the one who does not react in these dual conditions which we call pleasure and pain, honor and dishonor, heat and cold. Why? Because the only thing from which we have to detach ourselves is this thing inside of us which produces the reaction. That is all. So it becomes wholly a question of how to detach ourselves from this inner world.

The outside world, the cosmic universe, we can never renounce. It is actually impossible to renounce it because we are an inherent part of it. This does not mean that we have always to live absorbed in gross matter or thought; it means that as long as our development requires us to manifest in a body or live here on the physical plane, we shall have to take the materials from the great universe suitable for that purpose.

There is, however, never any sorrow or trouble from staying in God's universe. Our troubles come from living in our self-created world. The truly spiritual are not trying to get out of the universe; they are trying to get into it, away from their own little world. They desire to find God's world. God's world is always beautiful, because it is an expression of perfect wisdom, perfect love and pure light. So we need never be afraid that it will lead us astray. It is our reaction to it that does that.

The first thing that we must do is to lose this idea that "I am the doer." As a part of this great marvelous mechanism, this wonderful manifestation of God, which the cosmic universe is, as a part of that, we are to take joy in action, just as a musician who belongs to a great orchestra takes joy in playing in the orchestra. We never want to give that up. What we must give up is trying to play a solo in it. Musicians who feel the joy which comes from merging themselves with the orchestra and with a great musical composition, such as a symphony, and who are wholly absorbed in its expression and in following the conductor, have not the slightest desire to give up the joy of playing or to renounce their part in the performance. On the contrary, the thing they want most to do is to keep right on; not that they may express their own thought or idea, but that they may be instrumental in expressing something far greater that can come only from the orchestra as a whole.

That is exactly what we shall have to do as we move along — not try to escape from action, but feel instead more joyful every day as we realize that our action is part of a very mighty action, expressing infinite wisdom. Some day that will be our attitude of mind. We shall stand constantly in awe and wonder before this great drama that is being enacted on the stage of the universe and in which we have the good fortune to play a part. We shall try to play it as perfectly as possible. We shall have all the joy of a supreme artist engaged in a wonderful creation of art. We shall not want to renounce; we shall be free of any reaction that would cause us to renounce. It is only when in the midst of activity we learn to control our reactions that we enter the path of renunciation. That is why it is impossible to follow this higher path without performing action. We should look upon each duty in life that comes to us, upon everything we have to do, as an exercise in eliminating reaction.

There is one thing that marks the action of the one who is rising above reactions. "They do nothing at all, whether eating, sleeping, breathing, walking, talking, letting go and holding on, even opening and closing the eyes." They have ceased to think, "I am the doer!" therefore actually they are not acting. As long as we identify ourselves with our actions we cannot possibly get over our reactions. If we identify ourselves with the things we are doing, then we create a world of our own, and live on in that small, self-created world, and keep on doing.

We come ultimately to realize that there is an omnipotent power on which we must draw even to take a little breath. We could not breathe at all if it were not for the great breath of the universe; we could not move a finger if it were not for the mighty action which impels us. Without this central source of power we would be absolutely motionless, just like a device which has not been turned on. The power is not there. Through our breath we gain life and without life we could have no power. Where is it then that our action begins, where do we come in? When we start to analyze, it is just like peeling layers off an onion; we get to the center and there isn't anything there. Sooner or later we begin to realize that this body is a part of the great cosmic body and that we are related to that cosmic body the same way some small cell in our body is related to us. It may think that it is living in a world all by itself, but it is particularly sensitive to bodily changes. If we take the body to a cold place that cell is going to feel cold. If the body is hot, the cell also will be hot. Similarly we are related to the great cosmic body. Our mind is nothing but a wave in the vast ocean of mind-stuff. If there were not this universal mind-stuff or thinking substance, what would we think with? Therefore where does our thought begin? The answer is: nowhere at all. When we take up the question of the moral sense, if there were not a great cosmic universe we would not have any choice between good and evil. Our morality is based on choice, and it is only in relation to the cosmic universe that this very deep question of moral choice is possible.

So it is that taking these things one by one, we find that it is really true that this little individual self, this personal self, is not doing anything at all. As part of the great cosmic universe it is doing a wonderful thing, but by itself it is doing nothing. It is the mighty Power within that acts. That is why Vedanta emphasizes again and again this one thought of renunciation — this letting go of the idea, "I am the doer," this sense of an isolated entity. The whole renunciation lies in that.

When we are able to go about in the world with this feeling of detachment, aware that there is a divine Power working through our instrumentality, making it useful in a way that it never could be useful by itself, then we will begin to know our real greatness and that it is possible to go through life freed from this imprisoning world of self. That is what freedom means. This is what it means to act without creating bondage. We can move in the great universe as an inherent part of it, feeling all the thrill and throb of it, yet forgetting ourselves. The Bhagavad Gita says that those who act thus, surrendering all actions to Brahman, the Supreme, and abandoning all attachment, are not touched by evil, as a lotus leaf is not wet by water. A lotus leaf does not have to get out of the water to keep dry. The water never stays on a lotus leaf; it rolls right off and does not cling to it at all.

The Karma yogins, that is, those who worship God through action, continue to act, but for purification alone. They seek to wash themselves clean by ridding themselves of the little self. This does not mean holding on to the ego and polishing it off every day in order to make it a nice, clean, shining ego, although that is how most people interpret it. They want to keep this "I" by making it a nice, moral I. I am loving; I am generous, charitable, etc. — that is their idea of self-purification. But that is not what it means in this teaching. It means purifying ourselves by getting rid of the idea of self, washing it off each time it comes up. The Karma yogins perform actions with the body, with the mind, with the intellect, even with the senses, but without the feeling of I-ness.

There is no harm when we eat food to have it taste good to us; there is no harm in listening to beautiful sound; there is no harm in smelling delicious fragrance. There is no harm in any of these things; but they must be done without the sense of ego. Ego must be purged out of every bit of action, whether of mind, body or senses. That is why we are told to abandon all attachment. It is our little self that is attached to things. We do not have to be attached once we lose the sense of I, me and mine. When we realize that the whole universe is ours, and that we belong to the universe, then there is no reason to cling to any part of it. When we are afraid that somebody is going to take from us the little things which we desire, then we are attached. As the Gita declares: "The steady-minded, by giving up all attachment to the fruits of action, obtains peace."

Our spiritual practice must bring a continuous result; it must be continuous in itself before we really taste the fruit of our effort. We must wait until steadfastness becomes a quality of our mind. Then we are sure to have peace.

Sri Krishna states that the "unsteady, being attached to fruits through desire, is ever bound by action." That is, we may detach ourselves at intervals. Some things are very easy to let go. We can detach ourselves very easily from those things for which we do not care. Lots of people think that they would like to renounce. We have a vision of not working any more, of retiring to the forest and doing nothing. We can very easily detach ourselves from associations that irritate us. We can very easily detach ourselves from the unpleasant things. Also we can detach themselves from the things that are neutral; then later, perhaps, we can detach ourselves from the things we like. There are always three or four things, however, way down at the root of our being — our pet indulgences, pet prejudices — which are very difficult to abandon. Thus we will be fickle until we have pulled up these basic attachments and made the supreme sacrifice. So long as we have not rooted up self we will always be changeful in our practice of renunciation. We renounce with great determination for a while, until we begin to pull on that deep root; then we go back. The point of stress is the point where our growth is measured. By the amount of pull we can make on that deep root without cringing and giving up, our growth in renunciation will be determined.

Desirelessness

Give up all desire and become desireless. When we hear such words, there is something in us that rises in rebellion because we identify achievement with desire. We imagine that if we give up desiring we become passive and lifeless, doing nothing. But the truth is that giving up desire, as we have been asked to do, does not mean giving up the power which now expresses itself through desire. That power is inherent within us, pressing upon us and impelling us toward achievement. Our desire segregates a small part of this power, cuts it off from the Source and uses it to some small end. Whenever an ordinary desire, bred of our smaller vision rises in us, it is like a barrier which rises and checks the flow of power. Soon stagnation sets in because that in us which desires is something which is apart from the Infinite.

Desire is bred of the sense of lack; of the feeling of imperfection. If we believed that we possessed everything, we would not desire. We would have no anxiety as to the full provision for each day's needs, for every emergency of life, or for anything necessary for our existence. We do not believe it however, and feeling lack, we begin to desire.

To the one who longs for a higher way of life, there can be but one desire. We cannot get over desiring. We have been desiring ever since we were amoebas. Therefore, we must transmute desiring into the highest kind of desire. This is the only cure for all our countless little desires. Such is the work of the spiritually minded person. One may desire, as long as it is directed in the right way. A great teacher once said, it is all right to have a selfish desire, only be so selfish that you desire the biggest and the most wonderful thing in the world — God. Do not stop short of anything lesser. Be so selfish that you want the Highest. Always in life the selfish are those who grab for the most, so reach out and demand the very best, and that is God. Know that nothing will ever satisfy you short of the Infinite.

We have in the depth of our consciousness, remembrance of having been divine, one with the Whole; we possess the remnant of Eternity, of the

Limitless, and that is why we quickly outgrow all that is finite and fleeting. It is not because the Lord meant us to do it. He did not watch and see somebody interested in the finite and say I will cast a shadow over them and keep them from enjoying it. God likes us to enjoy the finite world. He has made it so beautiful, so wonderful in order that we may gain some pleasure from it for as long as we are attached to it. But still something within ourselves keeps us from enjoying the finite in full. It lies in that memory of something bigger. The Soul in us lives in that memory, the memory of oneness with the Infinite. You may ask, "Why did we ever leave it?" This question lies at the base of all metaphysics and all philosophy — the problem of the origin of evil. Asking the question presupposes the inability to understand the answer because the question rises out of an obscured mind. When the mind becomes clear the question never rises. Our only refuge lies in listening to the voice of the Soul asking. "Do you want something bigger, something of longer duration, that which you now only vaguely remember?" Listen to it. Do not be frightened. Do not turn away thinking it to be only an imaginary voice, a voice that is leading you away from all human desires and relations. No, it is guiding you to more vital friends, more vital relationships with your fellow beings. Let your one desire be to be guided by your higher Self, to be united with That, to let it manifest itself through you. Have the attitude of mind, "Lord, what wilt Thou have me to do?"

We must cultivate the taste for God, even as we cultivate a taste for art or for music. We cannot expect to love Him until we know Him. We don't love a stranger. We may hear of some great hero or a wonderful humanitarian in a faraway place and feel great admiration, but that glow of the heart that comes from personal acquaintance is not there. We may praise, but personal love is missing. Therefore, as long as we live a life apart from God, wholly alienated from Him, how can we expect to love Him? We must go to Him, get acquainted with Him. How do we do this? He will come to us in whatever aspect we choose, in the guise that will appeal most strongly to us.

When we learn to live with God, God becomes just as real as an earthly father and mother. If we think of God as the Divine Mother, She comes in that form and fills the heart with light and joy. It is the same consciousness of the presence, the same sense of someone who soothes and consoles when we grieve as that which comes from earthly parents only in a magnified degree. Often it seems that the heart is like a little home where a fire burns on the hearth, and the great loving Mother is seated there by the fireside waiting for us to come to Her, to sit beside Her and live with Her. When we do this we have no other desires left, only the desire to be close to Her.

God is more lovely than all the loveliness of the earth put together. He satisfies our taste for sweetness, because there is none as sweet as God. He satisfies our longing for companionship, because all earthly companionships, however close, must sometimes be at a distance and then there is heartache; but when God is our companion He is never far away. He is always right there, so we can have no loneliness. Rather our times of solitude become the times of greatest companionship and sweetest communion. Also, God does not let us lack for anything. Those who depend on themselves and on the world can never be truly rich because there is always anxiety in their minds, anxiety that they will not have enough, anxiety lest they lose what they have. God does not like to see His children impoverished or in lack any more than does an earthly parent. I have seen people leaving wealthy homes to become wandering monks with not a cent to their names and will somehow survive because everything that is necessary was provided for them. Sri Ramakrishna owned absolutely nothing. People continuously bought him many things, and he continually refused them. He had absolutely no desire for material objects.

We feel our earthly lack but that does not mean that we should give up work which provides for our needs. Only we should not be greedy. We need simply to feel that we will be led to do the right thing and thus gain what is necessary for our highest development. Our desire must fall in line with the cosmic will. Can you imagine an ocean wherein a drop of water refuses to be in the hollow, wanting always to be on the wave? It is the same with us. When we give up foolish, selfish desires and throw ourselves into the universal current, we may fall into the lesser or rise into the greater and not even know it. We merely know that we are in rhythm and harmony, and are moving in union with the universe and the Eternal.

When we give ourselves to Him, gathering up all desires into that one great desire, in order to be wholly united with Him, there comes such a feeling of security, joyousness and peace that there is no longer room in our heart for any small desire. The key to that desireless state is in our hands. The door is not bolted but we keep it locked because we are always turning outward, seeking external things, trying to enrich ourselves with baubles and counterfeit riches, altogether unmindful that within are the real jewels, the genuine riches that endure through all eternity.

Self-Discipline/Self-Mastery

We become self-disciplined through right knowledge and through abstinence. Self-discipline means wiping out wrong habits of the past and gradually effacing all careless ways of living. It means growing fundamental in our thought and character — reaching down to the root of everything.

Abstinence means keeping ourselves from forming detrimental new habits, abstaining from whatever leads us away from true vision. We must abstain not merely from things that are wrong, but from things that will not take us to the goal toward which we are traveling. For example, if we really desire vision of Truth, then we should abstain from all reading that diverts our mind from that end; we should abstain from associations that will turn us from our path; because we cannot be too careful, especially at the beginning.

Those who form desires in their minds are born again according to those desires. As long as we have desire for anything but God, we are led aside from the straight road that leads to divine realization. There are many kinds of desires and the world attracts us from many angles. You may say, "Other people, perhaps, are drawn aside, but I am not." Question yourself. Study yourself and note how directly you are moving in a straight line toward God. Daily watch your desires and see how many of them carry your mind away, even when they do not actually turn you from your chosen course. Those desires are seeds which some time must come up and bear fruit.

How are we going to know what is right and what is wrong? There is an easy rule. Always there are two things facing us, a higher and a lower; when we choose the higher, it is right; when we take the lower, that is wrong.

Desire God with your whole heart and soul and every desire you could possibly imagine will be satisfied forever; for God is the ultimate superlative of all things; therefore it stands to reason that when we find Him we find all. Remember that Christ said, "Love the Lord your God with all your heart, and with all your mind, and with all your soul."

When desires rise, therefore, instead of doing violence to them, turn them into prayer. By doing that you turn their intensity to the attainment of your Ideal. If it is success that you want, say, "There is only one way to be successful, only one place where true success can be found; That is in God. I will seek it there. O Lord, lead me to it." If there comes into your heart a deep longing for companionship say, "There is no companion or playmate equal to God. Lord, I am lonely; satisfy this hunger in my soul!"

When the mind is not clear it is foolish to try to discriminate. First turn to God. The very moment you drop yourself and direct your whole thought toward Him, you come into the light. It is the difference between trying to thread a needle by candlelight and doing it in broad daylight. By seeking God you change your whole vibration. Your very first cry to Him starts a down flow of His power into your troubled heart and crowded mind. If you keep on crying out to Him, victory cannot fail to be yours.

That is why we must cease to resist His power, and we do resist every time we desire something from the world and rebel because we cannot have it. Each time we allow those lower desires to rise within us, we are resisting that effort of the Soul to make Itself felt and known, and it is because of this that we are not illumined. Illumination lies in our own hands, but it cannot be brought about all of a sudden; we must bring it about little by little, and we do this by transmuting our desires of the world into desire for God.

The Soul or the Self is not to be gained by one who is destitute of strength — who is faltering and wavering. It becomes very evident why that is not possible. If, for instance, on one day you are all enthusiasm and invoke the great Self within you and on the next day you move in the opposite direction, you create a terrible confusion in the mind. You allow the higher forces in your nature to begin to work in you, you open yourself to those spiritual influences, and then you turn back to the world. The result is that you are rent and torn, like a battleground.

You must be absolutely strong, if not strong in your own strength, then in the knowledge of God's strength. Of all lives, the spiritual life is the one in which you can least afford to waver, because when you have had revealed to you even a small amount of higher Truth, your responsibility is very great. We should pray day after day and hour after hour that we shall not lack in strength or firmness. We cannot always be steadfast in knowledge, for our knowledge is limited, but we have to be steadfast in heart — the heart should be fixed on God.

Discipline

Discipline is the condition of growth and of productivity. It exists everywhere in nature. The field is disciplined when the plow furrows it or when the harrow combs it. The tree is disciplined when its branches are pruned. Discipline means molding crude material into useful form, or pruning and trimming to stimulate new life.

We need some propelling power from without to force us to climb to a higher level and enlarge our sphere. Direction and stimulus are necessary in the early stages of development. Yet we shrink from bending to authority. It offends our self-will and we hear it will endanger our individuality. Musicians are not less musicians because they play in an orchestra and obey the beat of the conductor's baton. They follow the score and leader unquestioningly, and the more they subordinate themselves to both, the better musicians they are.

Discipline is an inevitable fact of living. The wise, recognizing this, cooperate with it and begin to discipline themselves. They organize their lives in such a way that every part of their being is exercised and stimulated to new productivity. They leave no spaces for slipshod, haphazard habits or methods. They strengthen their will by following a well-charted routine with persevering regularity. They feed their higher nature by devoting fixed hours each day to inward reflection and study. They cultivate a deeper moral sense by loving service to their fellow-beings. They stimulate their mind by serious thoughtful reading. They fortify their body by wholesome manual labor. They curb their desires and through inward practice transform them into aspirations. Thus daily regulating and disciplining their entire nature, they build a strong, well-rounded character and become a more vital, sustaining element in human society.

Self-denial is an essential of self-discipline. One implies the other and both lie at the root of all successful achievement. No vocation, trade or profession, no occupation of any kind, can succeed if there is not single-minded effort behind it, and we put ourselves in harmony with it by subordinating ourselves to it. This act of submission takes the form of self-denial. We achieve and grow strong by renunciation and discipline.

Self-Control

Self-control has little to do with restraint. It springs from a state of mind, not from an act of will. It concerns less our relation with the outer world than our relation with ourselves. The unthinking look upon themselves as independent units, bearing a purely external relation with the universe; and when they fail in dealing with it, they try to improve their behavior, not their character. If anger rises, they struggle to keep it down; if someone irritates them, they make an effort not to show it. Their practice in control is directed wholly toward a specific event or person at the moment of test.

The thoughtful, on the contrary, do not wait for the hour of stress, nor do they devote their attention to their behavior. The control they exercise rests, not on isolated acts of will, but upon a continuous striving to build up a strong inner force which will sustain them under attack. A control that is based on suppression or concealment is not control. It merely delays the outburst of impatience or resentment. Calmness of manner can be counted on only when behind it stands calmness of mind, and behind calmness of mind must stand an enduring moral force. Behavior is admirable and dependable only when it rests on character, and character in turn must be upheld by a clear vision of fundamental values.

If we would cultivate self-control, we must develop character. We must devote our effort to the basic springs of action within, and pay little heed to the outer irritations which stir the surface of our being; that is, we must work on that inner something which makes the disturbance possible, instead of on the disturbance itself. Our practice must not be to hold back, but to go forward in nobility of spirit and convert our enemy into an ally by our fairness and friendliness. Generosity of heart and a willingness to yield do away with all need of control. We transcend the situation.

Two causes lie at the root of nearly all our impatience and irritability. They are egotism and a distorted sense of proportion. We create a world of our own and put ourselves at the center of it. This throws everything out of focus. Our outlook on life becomes falsified. Until we can break this little world of our own making and learn to live in the great universe, we shall not be able to overcome our self-importance and maintain steadiness in temper and demeanor. The sense of ownership and of personal rights will stand as a constant menace to our composure. Yet nothing could be more illusory. The mark of possessing anything is freedom to do with it as we choose; but is that possible in a creation based on fixed law? At every turn things happen despite us. Drought withers our crops, fire consumes our forests, floods ravage our towns. Values drop and our fortune is gone. Can we call our own what we are able neither to govern nor to hold?

The universe is an indivisible unit. It cannot be subdivided and parceled out in sections. The beauty and bounty of it belong to all equally. We partake of them according to our capacity. If we would enjoy the universe more fully, we must increase our capacity; but at no time can we possess any part of it.

When we seize upon a portion of it and call it ours, it is taken from us. If life does not snatch it from our grasp, death does. Cosmic benefits, it is true, may not seem to belong to all equally, but that is because our scale of measurement is not a correct one. We compare in different lives year with year or decade with decade, instead of lifetime with lifetime. Also we take account of outer conditions only. Inner conditions are not laid on the scale when we weigh advantages and disadvantages. Outer conditions may give to a king glory and wealth, and to a pauper want and misery; but from the viewpoint of the inner, the king may be a pauper and the pauper may be bountifully rich. The law of compensation, the law of karma, works unfailingly. The equilibrium of the universe demands it. Why then do we wrangle and quarrel and sacrifice our composure for the sake of belongings which are not ours and for rights that we do not possess?

As we learn that the laws which govern our welfare are identical with cosmic law, we rebel no longer and the chief cause of our turbulence is removed. The trained mathematicians do not try to work out their problem contrary to the rules of mathematics; chemists in their experiments do not petulantly disobey the laws of chemistry. No true scientist puts himself in rivalry with the universe, nor does he defy it; he cooperates with it. If we will make the universe our ally and conform to its larger law, instead of living and acting in obedience to the lesser law of our individual will, the whole universe will sustain us and we shall develop a habit of serenity which cannot be broken.

Higher understanding alone is a permanent corrective for loss of temper, envy, jealousy, resentment; and a higher understanding is gained by a constant readjustment of values. When, through experience and discrimination, we perceive how petty and nonvital are the things which disturb us, we cease to trouble over them and our nature grows still. It is always the surface wounds which trouble us; the mighty experiences of life awe us to calmness. If we will lengthen our unit of measure, lift our standard, and live in harmony with our farthest vision, we shall reduce to a minimum the occasions of agitation.

Love and the Great Love

The law of love is the highest law of life. When it finds free expression it creates a cosmic contact which in time awakens a consciousness of common interest, a sense of unity.

Those who love another for what they can get out of another have a very poor kind of love. To love just for the joy of loving, however — that is true love. Therefore, if we love God because we cannot imagine anything sweeter or more adorable, then we are truly beginning to love.

The power to love grows with our growth. A narrow heart cannot hold a large love. Only one of expanded nature and lofty spirit is able to love truly. When the first flickering spark of love kindles in the heart, we begin to love by loving ourselves. As the spark becomes a flame and mounts, the area of our feeling widens; we love our family, our home, the animals in our care; then our neighbors, our town, our country; but always that which is directly related to ourselves.

In the second stage of love, we love more generously, but we expect an equally generous return. The element of exchange enters in. Love, however, as it grows, purges and purifies. Little by little it wipes out the self and we are content to give more and more and receive less and less, until at last we give all and ask nothing.

Now for the first time are we able to love God worthily. So long as we divide our heart between God and the world, our love for both will be unstable and our life will be confused. Only when we love God with our whole heart, and humankind and the world as a part of Him, are we in harmony with the universe and all it contains. Our contact with others is more full of loving-kindness and understanding when we reach them through the Divine. The Divine Presence blots out all rivalry; all envy and jealousy; all hatred, harshness and anger; leaving only consciousness of the beauty, the nobility and perfection hidden in the soul of every living being.

A strong love for God alters completely our outlook and transforms our nature. Mystic, Jan Van Ruysbroeck, declares: "The God-seeing person, who has forsaken self and all things, and no longer possesses anything as his own, but stands empty of all . . . feels himself to be an eternal life of love, which craves above all else to be one with God."

This is the loftiest height the human heart can attain, but it is not the highest form of love. It is still personal and dualistic. In all expressions of it there are two, — the one who loves and the one who is loved. The highest love is impersonal and monistic. It does not calculate personal merit or demerit, worthiness or unworthiness; free from emotional impulsiveness, it feels no reactions of hatred or resentment. It does not grow cool and withdraw when rebuffed. It has no thoughts of return or exchange, does not mete out its bounty. It is universal and all-embracing. No one is denied it, those partake of it who open themselves to it.

This highest love is known as Divine Compassion. It is an attribute of the Divine and like all Divine attributes, — consciousness, life, intelligence, wisdom — it is infinite and all-pervading. Its nature is made plain by this story from the Upanishads:— A father instructs his son to bring a cup of water and a lump of salt. The boy is told to put the salt in the water and after a moment to taste the water from the top. "How is it?" the father asks. "Salty," the boy replies. "Taste it in the middle." The boy tastes it in the middle, and the father asks again: "How is it? Once more the boy replies: "Salty." "Taste it at the bottom." The boy tastes it at the bottom and finds it salty. Then the father declares: "As the salt is present everywhere in the water so is the Absolute Brahman everywhere present in the universe." In like manner also is love permeating everywhere.

The love we give and receive is not an individual love, it is part of the Great Love filling all creation. As it filters through the human heart, it appears divided and individual, but it never ceases to be indivisible and one. Manifesting as cosmic attraction, it holds the stars in their orbits and revolves the earth round the sun. Countless are the channels through which it finds expression, countless are the ways in which it enriches and sweetens our lives.

With this mighty Divine Love permeating all things, we have no cause to feel unloved or lonely and desolate. That love presses upon us more insistently than the atmosphere about us; if we do not feel it, it is because we are intent on seeking a small personal love all our own, unshared with any other. When, however, our vision broadens and the Great Love kindles in our heart and glows in our life, we shall become radiant centers of that greater love — a love that knows no boundaries. Then whatever life we contact will be stronger and sweeter because of our touch. And we shall walk through the world fearlessly, knowing that we are shielded and guided by a love that never changes or fails.

Truthfulness

We have been told that there are certain means by which we may attain that vision needful for union with the One. Of these perhaps the greatest is truthfulness. We have thought up to now that we tell the truth in order to be virtuous; but actually telling the truth is for the purpose of developing the sense of Truth within us. We possess faculties by which we perceive Truth, and by speaking the truth we cause these faculties to come into manifestation. That is why only the perfectly truthful can know the Truth. They alone have a developed Truth perception. Truthfulness in the spiritual life means absolute exactness in thought, word and action, with no evading anywhere.

All of us, so far as we are able, have been following the moral law, but our grasp of it has been largely intellectual; and we have accepted truth-telling as an intellectual necessity. It is, however, not enough to tell the truth; we must be truthful. In other words, every motion, the very expression of our face, each act, must be based on Truth. How often we avoid telling an absolute falsehood yet allow one to be inferred. How often we repeat things without knowing whether or not they are accurate; and how often we excuse ourselves and try to explain away our faults.

This is not practicing the Truth. If we are in the wrong we must be willing to stand up and say that we are wrong. If anyone accuses us and we realize that we are at fault, we must readily admit it, just as we admit that we are short or tall, stout or thin. We must feel always that the vital thing is to keep in line with the Truth, even if we are condemned, or persecuted. "Blessed are they who are persecuted for righteousness' sake." Be upright, no matter how much you have to suffer for it. For until the Truth means more to us than comfort or honor, or happiness of any kind, we will not be able to perceive It. But when we have reached that point, no one can keep It from us. We will have earned It.

Trust

Trust and vision are inter-locked and inter-dependent. They unfold in alternating rhythm. As vision widens, trust deepens, and deepened trust brings larger vision. Coordinated, they carry to ultimate illumination. Both are essential elements in our being. They form part of the framework of our higher nature. Every act of life is an act of trust and a proof of vision — not the vision of these outer eyes, but a vision born of a deeper, more penetrative inner sight.

When we breathe, we exercise trust — that there will be air to fill our lungs; when we walk, we practice trust — that the earth will hold and not engulf us. When we cultivate and plant, we have trust— that a harvest will follow. Nor do we doubt that planets will turn in their orbits, that the sun will rise and set, tides ebb and flow, at the appointed hour.

Trust is the warp on which we weave the pattern of our daily living. Experience of created things it is claimed, rests upon sense perception; but if there were not a more stable foundation beneath the variable perceptions of our senses, our experience would contribute little toward our knowledge or toward our development. Sights, sounds, tastes, and smells in themselves deceive. Objects register on the retina reversed and must be turned right side up in our brain. Sounds reach us undefined until they are interpreted by our brain. So with touch, taste, smell.

"Intellect takes us along in the battle of life to a certain limit," Mahatma Gandhi states, "but at the crucial moment it fails us." Trust transcends reason. It is when the horizon is darkest, and human reason is beaten down to the ground, that trust shines brightest and comes to our rescue.

Trust, among all spiritual gifts, is the most fundamental. Even love without it would not endure. Its power is limitless. Joined with vision, it makes the invisible, visible; the inaudible, audible; the intangible, tangible. It strikes deep into the essence of things, and sheds light where there was darkness. It reveals God to us, and us to ourselves.

Generosity and Greed

We make ourselves beggars of circumstance. We measure life's benefits by what we receive, rather than by what we give. But giving alone enriches. Receiving impoverishes. It lays a heavy weight upon the life, which only giving can lift. Our giving, however, must not be from the residue of our resources and our interest. It must not be thrown like reluctant alms. It must be fresh and fragrant and free from all grudging and calculation.

There is no store so scant that it cannot be drawn upon, no one so poor we may refuse to give. We may not have outward wealth, but we can share ourselves, our sympathy, our good will, our appreciation, our forbearance, our cheerfulness. Nature does not wait until she has gathered an abundance before she bestows a benefit. She gives, according to the season, of what she has at hand.

It is not lack of resources that checks our more generous impulses; it is fear, fear that we shall not have enough left to meet our own needs and satisfy our own ambitions and desires. Out of this fear grows the most insidious foe of giving, — greed. Whenever we enter into competition with the cosmic will and seek to wrest from it more than belongs to us in the universal order, we are guilty of greed. Whenever we desire to have more than others — more honor, more praise, more importance, greater material advantages — if we are envious or jealous or discontented, we are guilty of greed.

The seed of greed lies hidden in every desire and if we allow it to germinate, it will destroy our sense of proportion and stifle all our finer feelings. Nothing is more futile than to give place to desire. The desire that is in harmony with the cosmic will must come to fruition naturally and inevitably. There is no need to formulate it. The desire which is contrary to the cosmic order will be frustrated, however we may try to force its fulfillment.

The bounty of nature surrounds us on every side. It flows through us and over us in perpetual benediction, bringing with it no sense of obligation. The tree gives its shade and its protection, the flower its beauty and its fragrance; the sky spreads before us the splendor of a sunset or the loveliness of a dawn; rain waters our fields, sun ripens our harvests, wind sweeps clean the air we breathe. Could we have a more salient lesson in unasked giving?

Cosmic generosity acts silently, deliberately, organically, more by natural growth than by sudden mechanical adjustments. It plants the seed of a benefit in our life and lets it come to fruition in its own season. Sir James Jeans, the distinguished English scientist, writes in his volume, *The Mysterious Universe*: "To my mind, the laws which nature obeys are less suggestive of those which a machine obeys in its motion than of those which a musician obeys in writing a fugue, or a poet in composing a sonnet."

The great cosmic power is ever seeking new avenues through which to pour His benefits and His blessings. As all nature tells of His glory, so would He have every human life tell of His bounty. But no life may serve as a channel to convey it that strives to hold what is given. The effort to keep blocks the channels and shrinks to a minimum the capacity to receive.

Hoarding is always destructive. If we close up a room and cut off all ventilation, the air will grow stale and sicken us. If we put our food under lock and key and refuse to share it, it will decay and sicken us. If we hide away our material possessions, we impede the free circulation of cosmic resources and impoverish the whole human family, ourselves with it. The one who hoards is the most poverty-stricken among us, — our nature is shrunken, our vision distorted, and our existence one of loneliness.

Circulation is the condition of life on all planes. The Cosmos exacts free interchange and intermingling of its resources. We are not meant to be insulated units with a little store of our own, kept under lock and key and doled out at our convenience. We are chosen to be purveyors of God's bounty — open channels through which He pours His riches.

The abundance of the universe lies at our hand. Why should we close off a portion of it and limit our giving to that small supply? As much as we give, so much shall we receive. Nature permits no vacuum, neither does she consent to undue accumulation. When it occurs, an explosion — social or physical — will surely follow. It may come tardily and it may take various forms, but it is inevitable.

The currency of cosmic generosity does not consist of mere monetary coinage. That forms a part of it, but it is the least part. Culture, education, mental stimulus, knowledge, encouragement, kindliness, courtesy — these are a more vital part. But highest of all are the gifts of heart and spirit, — spiritual understanding, love exalted aspiration, holiness, purity, steadfastness. Those who are equipped to convey these gifts from the Divine to humanity are the truest benefactors of humankind. They are companions of God, and because of their closeness to Him, they are able to transmit His beauty in fullness. They keep back nothing, they seek nothing, they ask nothing, except to give themselves wholly to the service of God and the blessing of all beings.

Gladness of Heart, Joy and Thanksgiving

Glad-heartedness is not a quality we acquire; it is the spontaneous outgrowth of being. It does not depend on temperament or mood. It is not the property of a chosen few. It is an inherent attribute of all nature – cosmic and individual. "Out of bliss the worlds are born; in bliss they live, and to bliss they go!" the Vedic scriptures declare.

This cosmic gladness inheres in the heart of every human being as fragrance in a flower or flavor in a fruit. It is continuous and habitual — like a lamp placed in a windless spot, it does not flicker. It cannot be fitful or changing, for it is not a reflex of some other feeling or condition. Steadiness and unbroken continuity are its fundamental attributes. It is a light which shines by its own nature, — self-luminous. It lies deeper than happiness. Cosmic joy is profound, serene, inward and unalterable. It is the "joy within" of which the Bhagavad

Gita speaks. When we awaken to its presence, despair, despondency, all sense of injury vanish. This inner fire of gladness may be covered, hidden for a short time, but it cannot be smothered. Soon it begins to glow through its covering and bursts once more into flame. If we do not feel it always, it is because we have blanketed it with the outer. We need to uncover it.

True glad-heartedness cannot rest on anything variable, for the cornerstone of all joy is certitude — the certainty of continuance. As soon as the element of uncertainty enters, our joy falls to a lower level and breaks into two — joy and sorrow — pleasure and pain. We must detach ourselves also from our own changing moods and tempers. These are the most deluding media of reflection. They seem more real because they are more inward, more a part of us.

All true joy is in the Unbounded, the Upanishads proclaim. "The Infinite is bliss. There is no bliss in the finite. In the Infinite alone is bliss." That joy which rests on the Unbounded is itself unbounded. It is the eternal flame rising from the fire struck by the meeting of God's divinity with our humanity. It is a purging, purifying flame which burns away all grief and doubt and fear and leaves the heart aglow with divine gladness.

Obstacles to Joy

There are no outward obstacles to happiness. All obstacles that block the way to joy are within us. One of the greatest barriers to our brighter moods is vanity. The vain person is a slave of public opinion. They are beggars of praise. They battle to prove themselves right, even when they know they are in the wrong, to maintain their standing among others. These conditions are all subversive of peace; and if the mind is not peaceful, the heart surely cannot be happy. Vanity acts like a corrosive, it eats out the core of joy and leaves an empty shell, the hollow of which a vain person tries to fill with flattery and the plaudits of the world.

How can we eliminate this joy-killing trait from our character? Cease to feed it. Cease to run away from rebuke and criticism. Cease to reach out for recognition and commendation. Sweet words are as dangerous for the vain as sweet food for the diabetic. We should avoid them as rigidly. The craving for praise is as deleterious as the craving for an intoxicant. Now we move eagerly towards what pleases us and as eagerly away from what is unpleasing to us. We should reverse the process for a time, until we have worn down our vanity. Praise and recognition of effort are not unwholesome in themselves, it is only when they nurture the ego that they become harmful. When we accept them in a modest spirit, they stimulate our nobler impulses, give us new courage and make us more humble.

Vanity has many correlates — self-consciousness, self-pity, self-justification, sensitiveness, resentment, impatience, suspiciousness. It is useless to name them all or try to correct them individually. They all spring from one root, for which I shall coin the term "selfness," to distinguish it from selfishness. It is a state of consciousness which runs beneath and parallel to all our activity — a mental accompaniment to the melody of action, as in a song. It evidences its presence by such unspoken thoughts as "I am doing it," "I am being unselfish." More of our unhappiness is traceable to this undercurrent of thought than to surface events. It is in this subway of consciousness that take place all the reactions that we call pain, suffering, anger, self-commiseration. Like air-bubbles they start here and rise to the surface, gaining in magnitude as they rise.

We cannot suppress this underlying thought-stream. As long as we think of ourselves as a detached entity in a dual creation, our consciousness will also be dual. We cannot stop the flow of the stream, but we can change its character. If we fill the outer current of our thinking with something bigger than ourselves, we shall transform the companion current as well. This is the value of having an exalted ideal, a strong love for a noble person, a lofty purpose which translates itself into service, an absorbing devotion to a holy cause. Such larger interest crowds out the little self and make for happiness.

It would be an unending task to try to overcome all the inner and outer obstacles to joy; but when we climb out of our self, we surmount them all in an instant. To do this, we need to put ourselves back into the universe. Now we live as an isolated unit. We think of ourselves as a big person, on a big earth, in a big solar system, part of a big universe; and all this bigness reflects back on us. But when we consider that in astronomical calculation this earth is counted as a point without length or breadth or magnitude; and that each of us is only one of many billion on that unidimensional point; our scale of values receives a dramatic readjustment.

I would not belittle the sacredness and grandeur of human life. It is a gift we should treasure and use reverently; but it is great only when it is lived as part of a great Whole. Then all obstacles to happiness go down and nothing can darken the brightness of joy that shines through and through us.

The Seat of Happiness

Happiness can never be the direct purpose of life. Real happiness may be said to be a by-product. It is something that comes when we are striving for something else. The very moment we make happiness the goal of our striving, we fail to attain it, because such striving has always an element of self-seeking and wherever the self, or ego, is present, there real happiness cannot be. Thus we are told in the Bhagavad Gita, at the end of the second chapter: "As the ocean remains calm and unaltered though the waters flow into it, similarly a self-controlled saint remains unmoved when desires enter into him; such a saint alone attains peace, but not those who crave the objects of desire."

We are always happy when we are in rhythm with the cosmic plan; that is, when we are in the right place at the right time and moving in the right direction; and for this "right" there is only one gauge: the Supreme. When we are coveting anything, be it a place or a person or a condition, if we could but realize that one thing and one thing alone can bring real and abiding happiness, and that is to move in accordance with the Divine will, we should save ourselves the misery of reaction and disillusionment. There is, however, one exception to this general rule. If we are fortunate enough to come in contact with one who is a pure channel for the Divine, we may experience a taste of genuine happiness, because their nearness to the Divine gives them power to lift other people to a higher level and to reflect into their hearts the light that is in their own. But even then those hearts must be open to receive it.

The plan of the universe is so carefully worked out, so uninterruptedly compact, that there is for each one of us at every moment, just one place to be. When we are in that place, we are with God. If we are not there, then God is not with us: He is in our place, doing our work. This is true for the whole scheme of things in nature. We see that every object has its own niche to fill — in the spring, in the summer, in the autumn. Every little insect has its task. Take the earthworms, for example; we give them no thought, yet there is work for them to do each day. Likewise we have special tasks in the universe every instant of our lives, and only when we are accomplishing these are we united with God, the source of joy or bliss. When we realize this, instead of spending all our energies in trying to find happiness, we shall direct them toward Him; for once being united with Him, all joy shall be ours and we shall be kept in the right place at all times and in all conditions.

We should try to prevent personal or individual desires from rising in our mind, because they bring a dividing influence. Those who have really set out on this higher path have but one thought: "Where do I belong at this moment? At this very instant there is some special place, some special task for me, there is only one thing for me to do, only one word for me to say, only one way for me to breathe in order to be in rhythm with the great cosmic breath."

Those who are in their proper place and working according to the universal scheme of things, in harmony with the divine will, are invariably happy. Nothing counts except the unification of our little will with the great will.

Thus in the Bhagavad Gita it is said that one who acts without any sense of I, me, or mine, obtains bliss. This is dwelling in God. Those who attain this state are never again deluded. What does it mean, that we will never again be deluded? It means that we will never again be deluded by any foolish desires. We simply say that we would like to be as God and with God, and move with the will of God, that is all. No glamour of the world can possibly cloud our mind. Those who attain this state, even at the end of their lives, enter into union with God. They have not tried to be happy, they have not tried to escape from any pain or any discipline, or any difficult karma; they have not tried for anything except just to give up the little self and let God take them.

Joy demands continuance. When the sense of impermanence enters, it ceases to be pure joy. Fear and unrest adulterate it. It is evident then that the seat of happiness cannot be in the outer world, where sunshine and storm, light and darkness, heat and cold, play in unceasing sequence. Variation is the law of nature. There is no form or manifestation that is immutable. Creation is a procession constantly on the march; but it is not a dismal procession. On the contrary, it is full of beauty and delight. If it saddens us, it is because we demand of it what it is not equipped to give.

The external universe was not designed to give us permanent happiness. Its purpose is to prepare us for joy. It is a gymnasium which develops our capacity for gladness by exercising us in happiness and sorrow. One acquaints us with it by its presence, the other by its absence. Pain has no positive existence; it is merely the absence of happiness, as darkness means absence of light, or as a hollow is only the measure of the displacement of water in a wave. Neither can be regarded as a definite unit of being. Both stand as a negation of something else. Strike a match and darkness is gone; kindle happiness and grief has vanished.

The way to meet grief and gloom is to call up their opposites. We cannot drive darkness out of a room, leaving vacancy; we eliminate it by bringing in the light. Nor can we drive grief from the heart, leaving emptiness behind. It is overcome by a counteracting feeling. Depression is never conquered by brooding over it or by struggling with it. That but deepens the shadow. The weight is lifted by dwelling on some thought-picture that will induce cheerfulness. Learn and repeat a vitalizing poem, read a helpful book, or say over and over some strength-giving word, move briskly: these simple practices will clarify the mind. Do not let the mood soak in and saturate. Do not let it settle back, when it has been dissipated. Keep up the thought-exercise until all danger is past.

In the same circumstance and environment, sadness and happiness play over the mind, altering its color, sometimes even without apparent reason. This shows that the outer condition is secondary, even negligible. It is we who lend it importance by our attitude towards it. We blame it, not ourselves. We give it power to overwhelm us; it has none of itself. The mistake we make, when we are assailed by a destructive darkening mood, is to move outward. Soreness of heart or soul is cured only by inwardness.

This universe is like a series of concentric circles, graduating in size and turning round the same fixed center. When we are struck by misfortune or grief, nearly all of us rush out to the circumference and seek respite in distraction. We try to forget. The wise run towards the center and seek solace in vision. They try to understand. It is not difficult to perceive which course is productive of the most lasting benefit. One scatters and weakens, the other focuses and fortifies.

We imagine that if we had a little more bodily comfort, a little more diversion, a little more importance, better health, we would be happier, but when environment and circumstance provide these; joy does not come with them. Something else is lacking. A fleeting pleasure may flash across the consciousness, but it is as quickly gone. One of the most salient errors made by the world in all ages is to confound pleasure with joy. They are not synonymous. Pleasure is objective, joy is subjective. Pleasure is a reaction from some impinging object. It is wholly dependent and variable. Joy is a fixed state of mind and heart, independent of all action and reaction. The chief conditions for its presence are stability and unlimited power of expansion. That which gives real joy must touch the Infinite.

Our physical organism and our senses do not meet any of these requirements. The body's capacity for enjoyment is very restricted. If we try to stretch it through greed of pleasure or indulgence, something snaps. Intensive use or strain of any part of our physical organism results inevitably in deterioration or total loss of use.

The senses contribute generously to our happiness. They are the avenues through which we contact the beauty and wonder of nature; yet with all their cultural and educational value they do not offer a stable foundation for joy. They do not coordinate. They cannot work in perfect unison, because they depend on different outer stimuli.

The mind is as changeful as the senses. The moral sense too is alterable. It grows with our growth. The standards of today are not the standards of tomorrow. As our ethical vision becomes keener, we see finer and finer distinctions, new capacity for joy develops and the old sources of satisfaction no longer content us. Permanence in such conditions is impossible.

Only when we reach the universal Center of our being do we find a dependable base on which to rest our happiness. There is no doubt that we are many times happy along the way, but the happiness is fluctuating and lacks some of the vital elements of true joy. Not until we touch the point where we are in unbroken contact with eternal certitude do we feel the confidence and peace essential to genuine joy.

The Spiritual Value of Appreciation

The critical attitude defeats itself. It closes the avenues of discernment and deadens the perceptive faculties. As it grows through practice, we look by habit for imperfections and cease to see the merits. We listen for the false note in music or search for the wrong color-value in art. The intelligence seems at stake, if some defect or demerit is not discovered. Criticism becomes habitual fault-finding, and judgment the reaction of mood or prejudice.

Unreasoning admiration is as harmful as unthinking depreciation. Whether we admire or condemn, if we do it without understanding, we desecrate that which we judge. What we need to practice is discrimination. Discrimination is the servant of appreciation. It provides a balanced and impartial method of weighing all the elements in a judgment, while appreciation completes the task by laying stress on the qualities. It does not ignore the defects, but it leaves them in the shadow.

The habit of appreciation is not difficult to cultivate when we remember that no work of human hand is a finished product. We ourselves are not finished. We are still in the making, and our achievement cannot reach beyond our furthest limit of power. Humanity, individually, is moving toward perfection; but we must not apply the standard of perfection to it or to its accomplishment before it has attained its goal. Along the way there is need of courage and of hope. The least word, or gesture even, which cools the ardor or breaks the confidence of any member of the human family, does injury to all humankind and delays its onward march.

Appreciation spiritualizes social relations wherever it finds expression. It pacifies and makes us mindful of our points of contact rather than of our points of difference. The appreciation of another's creed or custom, ideal or aspiration, reconciles and unites. There is always some truth in every doctrine, some merit in every effort, something fine in every character. If we will hold to this nobler side of life, we shall lift the standard of living and doing, not only for ourselves but for all people. Also we shall soothe and silence the grievances and antagonisms which rise so readily in the group consciousness.

Nothing is more subversive of appreciation than gossip. When we find how far at times it reaches, we realize its danger. Gossip feeds on failures and shortcomings, on slander and denunciation. It delights in criticizing and finding fault. It tears down and refuses to rebuild. A proverb declares: "He is void of wisdom who despises his neighbor." Little intelligence is required to destroy or condemn, but to create or to appreciate calls for power and wisdom.

Appreciation is the lubricant of life. It makes the mechanism of daily life run smoothly. Out of it grows courtesy and graciousness. Both are essentials in the interactions of human beings. Our interactions should not be made a matter of social convention. They belong to a higher, nobler realm. We are all children of one Supreme Parent. Shall we make of life a battlefield? Or shall we live in kindliness and generosity of spirit? Let us rather silence the harsh tones in our voice, check the sharp word on our lips, and go forth into the world, not to wound and sadden, but to bring new hope, stauncher courage and loftier vision.

Mind, Concentration, Meditation and Worship

The Power to Think

The power to think is a gift, and like all talents it can be developed only through intensive practice. We would not expect to paint or to model or to play an instrument without training. Thinking also must be acquired by exercise. Taking the thoughts of others will not help us. Our thoughts are the outgrowth of our whole being, not merely of our brain. They are the product of our individual experience.

The first step toward independent thinking is to learn to direct our own mind. Now, words, sights, sounds, the behavior of our neighbor, shape our thoughts. They are reactions of the outside world upon us rather than our reaction upon it, — a rebound of the senses, not an inward act of intellection. Wisdom and true knowledge do not come in this way.

As we give daily exercise to the body, so each day we should set apart fixed times for exercising the mind. Plato claimed that, since thinking was our supreme gift, we should devote at least five years of our early adulthood to the practice and study of abstract thought. This was possible for those who walked with their Master along shaded paths in the garden of the Academeia in Athens; but for the hurrying people of today, the utmost that can be asked is fifteen minutes in the morning and again in the evening.

During these two quarter hours the practice should be to choose an elevating thought, which makes strong appeal to the mind, analyze it, dismember it, delve into its deeper meaning; then put it together again and apply it. Those who do this cannot fail to gain from their practice a new and illuminating conception of the thought chosen. Also they will have increased their power of reflection, which is the channel through which all true knowledge comes to us.

Intelligent observation of nature is another helpful practice. The scientists bending over their microscopes, or scanning the heavens through their telescopes, or studying their test-tubes, are alive and alert — the very embodiment of thought. We may lack microscope and test-tube, but we cannot find a better laboratory than the garden, the woodland, the open field or winding lane. Flowers, trees, birds, and the countless living things of forest and meadow are full of suggestions for deeper thinking.

As we think, we are freed from bondage to self and to the world. We care less to read, and even more we care less to talk. The cry is for freedom of speech and freedom of thought; but what will they profit so long as we lack the power to think? The best we can offer is an opinion born of habit or prejudice. We have not thought out into the wider spaces of life and acquired a broader scale of values.

The mind has no attributes of its own. The use we make of it determines its nature, — whether it be clear or clouded, strong or faltering, sluggish or alert. If we use it wisely and to noble ends, it will become a dynamo of power and carry us to the heights of thought. If we use it lazily and to small ends, it will weaken and fade into ineptitude. It rests with us.

Concentration and Single-Mindedness

Our thought is the material out of which we build our character. A character can be strong only when the thought is focused. If we wish to achieve in any direction, we must gather up our scattered forces and turn them as one unit on the task at hand. Concentration, therefore, becomes a vital element in character-building. To be effective, however, concentration must be preventive in its practice, not corrective. It should consist in not scattering, rather than in gathering up. We should never wait until our energies are dissipated before we bring our will into play. We must penetrate deeper and base our practice on a habit of life. The whole course of our daily living must be centered. Every thought and action, every task and interest, must have a centripetal motion.

Without a center this is not possible; consequently, the need in every life of a clearly defined and unwavering purpose. If this purpose is stable and ennobling, it will act as a strong magnet and draw round it all our wandering forces. If we haven't a fixed goal for our effort we never unify our energies. An occasional impulsive interest may focus them for a moment; but as long as there is an ebb and flow in purpose, all attempts at concentration will be abortive. Unless the daily life is upheld by a continuous, vital aim, we cannot fail to be fitful.

Nearly everyone waits until we have need to fix our attention, then we make a hasty call upon our scattered thoughts. The suddenness of the appeal jars the mind and scatters it even more. Dormant impressions and irrelevant memories are shaken to the surface and begin a war on our struggling faculties.

It is because we have not created a habit of attention that this happens. If we would do each task before us with one-pointed interest, very soon we would gain unified attention and consequent strength of mind. No special equipment, no special time or place, is required for this practice. Every form of occupation, every occasion, offers opportunity for it.

It may not be possible to hold the same thought all the time. We are forced to think of many different things in the course of the day; but there must be no overlapping. Our thoughts must move in single file. We must train ourselves to turn off one line of thought before we admit another. The best way to do this is to make it our custom to mark off each change of thought by a pause. This can be merely a brief moment of silence, or it can be a remembrance of our purpose of life. If the second way is chosen, it will serve as a shining thread running through all our thoughts and actions, and knitting them into close union.

Singleness of aim demands simplification in our living and thinking. We must eliminate all nonessentials, keeping only things of primary importance. We must cease to multiply our engagements and our interests. We must read less and more vitally. We must pay fewer visits and have fewer ornaments and articles of furniture in our house, fewer garments in our closets, fewer occasions for envying and coveting in our hearts. We must avoid whatever distracts or divides our attention. We must leave wide spaces in our thought for higher consecrated thinking. This may not seem easy; but if we will form the habit of questioning the importance of each demand upon our time and strength, and discard the nonvital, we shall have little difficulty in focusing our energies and simplifying our life.

True concentration cannot be attained in fragments, it must cover the whole of life. We must determine our center, then move toward it with unswerving resolution. Our study, our affiliations and relationships, our work and our play, all must carry us to this end. So long, however, as that center is on the material plane, we shall not achieve perfect one-pointedness. The aim cannot be steady when the target is shifting, and no created thing is wholly stable. Only when we make the Divine the center to which our purpose holds, can we hope to reach complete unity of forces and faculties. As our life flows in undivided current toward that ultimate Center, the irresistible attraction of the mighty force within it will draw all our energies to a focus and we shall see with one-pointed vision, act with unified power, and think with an unscattered mind.

Concentration is a question of character. Its true practice is preventive, not corrective. It consists in gathering up. So long as the method employed is merely corrective, we shall make little progress in attaining it. It is of small use to learn to collect our energies, if at every hour we dissipate them again. We must push farther back in our nature and deal with that which creates all this ceaseless labor for us. Our search will lead us quickly beyond the surface process of mental control with which the idea of concentration usually is associated. It will carry us to the very taproot of our being.

Nor will periodical exercises develop the power of concentration in us. It will come only through a habit of life. The whole course of our daily living must be centered. Every thought and action, every task and interest must lead to our center. Without a center, however, this is not possible. Hence the need of a clearly defined and unwavering purpose. When the true vocation is found, concentration becomes an easy matter. But it is even more important for the one who is without a special calling. The purpose set must be a sound and ennobling one.

Those who haven't a fixed goal for their effort never unify their forces wholly. An occasional impulsive interest may help them to do so temporarily, and in that moment they accomplish something worthwhile; but so long as there is an ebb and flow in their purpose, all attempts at real concentration will be abortive. Unless the life beneath rests on a stable basis, the thought control will always be fitful. Dormant thoughts and sensations are shaken to the surface and begin a ruthless war on their straining minds. All sorts of irrelevant impressions stored up in their memory — a headline, an irritating word, a forgotten obligation — rise and mock them, until the object of their concentration is wholly forgotten in the struggle to concentrate. This is the experience of nearly everyone during the initial stages of meditation; and it springs in large part from the mistake of waiting until the hour of practice before turning the thought on the subject of meditation. As we prepare for our practice, we should start our mind flowing towards it. Then there will be no sudden jarring adjustment of the thought current, as all our energy, now exhausted in drawing our attention from previous concerns, may be used in meditating.

Students in concentration should train themselves to shut off one line of thought and turn on another, as they would turn off and on electric lights; although in reality the turning on, if done whole-heartedly, will turn off also. In recent times it has come to be regarded as a mark of cleverness for someone to carry on several lines of work simultaneously; but if we observe carefully, we shall find the stamp of mediocrity on all that they do. The efficient worker permits no division of interest, either within the mind or outside. They need not think or do the same thing always, but their thoughts move in single file.

The practice of unified attention is one which needs no special time, place or equipment. Any form of occupation offers abundant opportunity. An excellent specific exercise, however, is to memorize a verse or text; then, as we walk along the street or ride in the car, to fix a certain distance during which the mind shall not be allowed to wander from the passage chosen, analyzing and reflecting on it with resolute intentness. Or, if we are reading, it is good to read over and over the same paragraph until we have read our whole attention into it. Another useful exercise is to refuse to respond for a brief interval to the teasing call of the senses. Now our sense gates hang loosely open and at the slightest disturbance the mind rushes out through one or the other, dragging the body after it to see or hear or taste or touch. The ones who wish to advance in concentration, however, learn to open and close these gates at will.

There are two essential steps in every act of concentration. The one is consecration; the other simplification. Unless we can give ourselves wholly to the object of our attention, we cannot focus all our energies upon it; but, when we have unified our interest, it follows naturally that we shall seek to eliminate whatever is not related to it. Behind the sense of consecration there must be a strong desire. No one can devote sustained thought to what does not seem worthwhile. This is one of the weakest points in the ordinary effort at concentration. We try to concentrate without conviction. We undertake a task or read any book which happens to come our way, then we wonder why we do it so listlessly, with our thoughts flying to the four points of the compass. We lack the sense of consecration without discrimination. We should never expend the least thought, strength or time without first determining by careful analysis and reasoning whether the object or act deserves our attention. Every hour of life, every ounce of energy, is given us in trust. We are answerable for its use to the great cosmic Being. What right have we then to use it thoughtlessly and to small ends? If we have a desire to do so, our values are false and we must begin our practice of concentration here. It is impossible for us to give ourselves fully to what is not vital, for the real part of us will lag behind, dragging on our wayward energies. Only as we move towards the vital and eternal shall we go as a unit, because then our Soul goes with us.

The primary lessons in concentration, therefore, are lessons in right analysis, which will cultivate in us a correct sense of values. As soon as we have persuaded ourselves by a preliminary act of discrimination that a certain line of conduct will bring us the highest return, we shall have little difficulty in focusing our energy on it. No one cares for the false and unreal. What person will labor to amass a fortune of counterfeit currency? It is because our conviction is vague and faltering as to what is or is not of value that our forces are so scattered. We are a house divided against itself — one part seeking the real, the other coveting the unreal. But let our desire for the real be stimulated sufficiently, at once our interest and effort will gather to a point around it. All extraneous concerns will be cast aside; our mode of living will grow simpler, a large amount of energy will thus be released to focus on the central aim; and we shall find ourselves possessed of a power far greater than we imagine possible. The properly trained mind is always concentrated; it has only to shift at need its point of attention. Nor does this mean an abnormal, strained condition. Concentration is its normal state, as it is natural for the muscles of an athlete to be always firm and strong. This comes, however, only after long and steadfast effort. Yet it can be attained even by the most turbulent "through practice and dispassion," Sri Krishna declares in the Bhagavad Gita.

Dispassion is an essential factor in developing the power of concentration. Until we are completely detached and free, we cannot have full use of all our faculties and forces. Let us be tied by the finest thread, and that thread may pull and set the whole mind in motion just when we have succeeded in bringing it to a state of stillness. Clear judgment, balance, resolution, moral rectitude, genuine love, all these fruits of concentrated thought are possible only in a state of freedom; and freedom implies detachment. Unless we have entire possession of our forces, how can we focus them? They must be wholly at our command to give or withhold, to loose or restrain. The method by which this is accomplished, we are told again in the Gita, is by governing our desires and aversions. "Let none come under the sway of these two," it says, "for they are their enemies." As a frightened horse is led up to traffic again and again until its fear is conquered, so whenever our systems recoil from any condition or experience, we turn and face it with firm determination until it ceases to cause any reaction in our minds. If a desire arises, in the same way we look it over and over with calm dispassion until its power dwindles and dies. Very few of our desires can bear close scrutiny, except those which are better classed as aspirations.

Meditation

The aim of meditation is to enable us to make spiritual ideals a reality. The mind is constantly distracted by the world. We do not know how to listen to the Voice which would answer all our questions, remove all our doubts, and soothe our hearts. We must learn in some way to drown out the distractions of our mind. This is done through meditation, when our mind's faculty is whole, one-pointed, when our senses are not engaged in following unrealities but are withdrawn and turned with conscious effort to that which is Real.

We must learn to look within. We must control the outgoing forces and make our mind single-pointed. Until we do that, we can never reach our deeper nature, our innermost being. Meditation opens the channel whereby we enter into the inner realm. When we enter into deep meditation we feel nourished; we feel joy — a sign that we have tasted the real meaning of meditation. It must come to us for this is the aim of spiritual living.

We must feel that the spiritual life is as real as our present one. We can do this by cultivating a habit of meditation on the Supreme Being day after day, keeping a fixed hour. If we neglect this and are carried away by hunger of the senses, we are starved and our heart remains unsatisfied. The feeling of the reality of the spiritual life, the realization of God, comes rapidly to those who strive with earnestness, faith, purity, and cheerfulness of heart. Steadfastness, discrimination and will power are needed in order to pull out of the doubts and fears which, in the beginning, often hold us back. We must give up all littleness and cultivate selflessness. The more we disentangle ourselves from the little self, the more quickly we can progress and unfold our spiritual nature.

Unless we touch the base of our life, the great inner Principle of wisdom and strength, before each outer effort, our endeavor will be sadly ineffective. This cannot be done at random, however. There must be firmly established contact with the center to be able to swing there quickly at the moment of need. If God remains a stranger to us, we shall forget Him in the rush of living. We must develop the habit of association with Him. This can be done only through regular practice of meditation.

The nervous unrest we feel now when we sit down and try to meditate proves how far we have moved away from the central point of strength and stillness in us. We are like a boat with hoisted sail tugging at its moorings. We can scarcely wait to plunge into the activities of our usual round. The only way that we shall overcome this scattered state is by setting apart certain definite hours for silent meditation and observing them with unwavering determination. It does not occur to us to skip the brushing of our teeth or the combing of our hair, however hurried we may be, and such should be our attitude towards this daily exercise of interior communion. The time devoted to it may be short, but it must be kept with rigid exactitude. Otherwise we shall falsify our values and persuade ourselves that the outer is more important than the inner.

Regularity and persistence are vital elements in our spiritual practice. A brief meditation at a fixed hour in the early morning is more effective in its results than a long meditation snatched by chance in the course of a busy day. We debase our practice when we make it a question of chance. Our habit of life must conform with our aspiration. We cannot be world-conscious hour after crowded hour, then suddenly at our convenience become God-conscious. At all times our thought must rest in the high places of our consciousness. We make this possible by repeating silently a sacred name or a holy text as we go about our daily tasks. It will not lessen our efficiency. On the contrary, we shall be more efficient; because our mind will be focused and we shall have full command over it.

There is no reason at all for us to bemoan the fact that we have very little time for meditation. Probably we have the time if we want to take it, although we always claim that we have not; we do not have time and opportunity, however, for spiritual practice, because the first practice on the path of wisdom is the right performance of action. So the Lord tells Arjuna: "A person does not obtain freedom from action by giving up or abstaining from action." That is only laziness. There is but one way that we shall ever reach a more serene life and that is to keep right on with the outer things that we are doing and begin to change from within. When we cease to rush less on the inside we shall not have to rush so much on the outside.

Time does not exist except in the mind. There is no such thing as time as an objective realty. Time exists in us and it is measured by the interval between two thoughts. That is all that gives us any idea of time. A slow succession of thoughts gives us the idea that time is moving slowly. When we begin to have larger ideas of life, a greater sense of obligation toward the real things of existence, time for us will move in a more measured tempo and our sense of rush will go. We create it for ourselves. Even in the busiest hour we have leisure for spiritual practice, because we can turn that very occupation into practice. It is not by ceasing from action that we are freed from action, it is by a growing awareness of something within us which readjusts our sense of values. In other words, we have to realize that our actions are springing not from external conditions and obligations but from that in us which responds to those obligations.

Meditation as Habit Builder

Although the source of happiness lies in the depth of our being, it requires no far journey to reach it. A single lofty thought will carry us immediately to it, while a right habit of thinking will enable us to live in unbroken contact with it. The question becomes — not "how can we create happiness out of the materials at hand?" But, "how can we reach the central supply of happiness, where it exists in perpetual and unvarying abundance?" The gift of joy is unvarying and impartial. It is bestowed on every heart in equal measure.

One of the most effective is meditation. It is not an alien or unaccustomed practice, as may be supposed. All humanity is meditating on something; for what is meditation? It is a continuous flow of thought in a fixed direction. A miser meditates on her money, a merchant on her business, an artist on her art, a mother on her child, a devotee on God. Meditation is a universal practice, but the flow of thought too often is not directed in channels that are productive or conducive to happiness. We must choose the channel of our thinking.

We may not have to learn to meditate, but we must learn to organize and direct our thought so that it will move naturally along constructive paths. To do this we must make meditation a regular practice. This is difficult unless we set a fixed hour for it. To keep the same hour every day creates a helpful rhythm.

Our practice again must be systematic and inclusive. No part of our being should be left out. Meditation deals with the whole person. It calls into play all faculties and organs. Tuning them in perfect unison, it draws them more and more inward, until they reach a point of silence, held spell-bound and awe-struck by the exalted calm of that inner center of being.

In the practice of inwardness, our first concern should be to find the right posture. Spine, neck and head must be erect and free; chest up, body relaxed and at ease. There is no mystic advantage in sitting cross-legged on the floor; but it gives a firmer posture and releases the subconscious mind from the task of holding the body on a chair against the pull of gravitation. If one must use a chair, it should be of such a height that the thigh is perfectly horizontal, the leg below the knee perpendicular and the feet firmly on the ground. One must not lean back — that destroys the erectness. Some imagine they meditate better lying down; but that position impedes the free flow of the nerve currents and also one can fall asleep easily or drift into a state of mere musing, which Charles Dudley Warner defines as "sitting in the sun and thinking of nothing."

The next step must be to make the breath rhythmic. The in-breath and the out-breath should be even. Nearly always with everyone the out-breath is shorter than the in-breath. One must find the count of the out-breath and breathe in and out on that — not more than eight times to begin with. The number of breaths can be increased little by little. This will help to establish rhythm in the physical organism. Care must be taken, however, that this exercise or in any part of the practice the body does not stiffen. It is better not to clasp the hands — they are sure to tighten. Rather lay the back of the right hand in the palm of the left hand.

To make meditation an effective habit-builder we must keep a subject of meditation for a long period until we are saturated with it. We must build it into our thought-life. What that subject should be depends upon our individual need. It must fill in some lack in our character. We become what we think on. For one who is quick to resentment and self-justification a helpful thought-picture to hold is that of Christ in the audience-chamber before Pilate hearing bitter accusation yet giving answer only in these undefending words: "Thou has said." His judge was eternal justice, why should He speak in His own defense?

At the outset we should not try to fix the mind on a single focal point, we should follow out a line of thought, but not wandering from the main subject. First we think about it in general, then we think on it deeply and lastly we become identified with it. The thought process becomes less and less diffuse, until thinker and object attain perfect union. Then the thinker partakes of the thought and the purpose of the meditation has been accomplished. It may take days or weeks, but the time-element should not enter into it. To build the thought into the life is the aim of the practice, not to do it on a time schedule. One thing is important — the object of meditation must be sympathetic, one that makes appeal to the mind and heart.

All this technique is vitally helpful in habit-building, but it is only secondary. The salient thought is to have a fervent sincere desire to acquire the habit. That desire will make the daily practice easy and rich in results.

The Practical Value of Meditation

To approach each task of the day, we should draw inward, collect our scattered energies, pause for a moment of uplifted thought, then go forward to our work. This moment given to higher thought is the first exercise in meditation. It is the seed of the meditative life.

The power to meditate is less a question of practice than of growth. It depends more on character than on the mind. So long as all our tendencies are outgoing and our interests scattered, we shall not be able to meditate, however often and long we may try. We must reorganize our habit of life and become more inward, more thoughtful, more silent. St. John of the Cross, in a letter to the Carmelite nuns of Beas, declares that those who are over eager to converse with others are little eager to commune with God. "To contemplate is to receive," he writes elsewhere, "and it is impossible to receive the highest wisdom otherwise than in a silent, receptive spirit." The mind must be "like the atmosphere which the sun illumines and warms in proportion to its calmness and purity . . . It is in profound peace and tranquility that the soul is to listen to God."

Meditation has been defined as a continuous flow of thought like oil poured from one vessel into another. It is a flow of thought, not fixity of thought. Beginners make the mistake of choosing an abstract subject, then struggling to hold the mind on it as on a point. This is not possible in the early stages of meditation. It requires long training to be able to fix the thought at will. In the beginning we must be content to carry on a line of thought, keeping always to the central subject. The mind will wander from it at first; but as the interest deepens, it will approach closer and closer, until subject and mind become one.

In determining our subject of meditation, we must be careful to choose one that makes strong appeal to the interest and to the aspiration; also that lends itself to analysis and application, — an incident in a holy life, the spoken word of a great teacher, some sacred text. A more concrete, yet inward subject is a radiant flame burning in the heart. We may think of it as kindled by God's hand, to reveal His presence; or as a pervading light flooding our whole being. This thought can be developed indefinitely until mind and heart glow with radiance. Whatever the subject chosen, it should not be changed until we have exhausted all the benefit to be derived from it. To make our daily meditation a matter of chance or whim is to neutralize all its advantage. In Yoga training the same subject is carried through many exercises.

The mind is not the only part of our being active in meditation. Body, intellect and moral sense all come into play. Through the necessary practice of posture, through breath-control and the regulation of the nerve currents, the body does its part and receives its share of training. The senses do their part by withdrawing and remaining inactive. Intellect carries on the process of discrimination and analysis; and the moral sense applies the lesson gathered from the study of the subject on which we are meditating. Thus the whole nature is exercised.

As character provided the foundation for meditation at the outset, so in return meditation remolds the character. Erect posture, necessary to concentrated higher thought, induces a nobler bearing; rhythmic breath creates rhythm throughout the system; and the more even flow of the nerve currents eliminates gradually the nervous irritability which overtakes us at times apparently without reason; dwelling on a holy thought elevates and strengthens mind and intellect, and the character, nurtured on daily meditation, grows mellow and full of grace. In a word, the practice of meditation transforms our whole being and is vital both to our spiritual life and to our life in the world. No one can safely begin the day without spending some time in quiet contemplation; nor should we let the night fall without going apart to lift the thought away from outer concerns and turn it Godward.

A frequent error is to mistake concentration for meditation. Many acquire the power of concentration yet know nothing of meditation. Both represent a continuous flow of thought; the one, however, is wholly mental, the other is spiritual. In concentration the thought may be directed either upward or downward. In meditation it is up-reaching only. A strong desire, or an absorbing ambition will develop the power to concentrate, but neither desire nor ambition will induce the lofty serenity of mind essential to meditation. Concentration, it is true, is vital to meditation but it is only a preparatory practice and cannot be substituted for it.

Meditation with active thought is a primary form. There is a higher meditation in which the thought is receptive rather than active. It consists in "listening to God" — opening ourselves to the inflow of the Divine. Divinity surrounds and pervades us, yet we live our life unconscious of Its presence; in receptive meditation we become aware of It. When the door of our heart is open and Godward at all times, the mind becomes habitually meditative. This does not mean that it grows dreamy and inept. On the contrary, it is more alert, more effective, because it thinks as a coordinated whole, undisturbed by the noise of conflicting thoughts or the confusion of conjecture. It has acquired the power to pierce through the deceptive surface of things and penetrate to the deeper essence below.

The ultimate form of meditation carries us beyond thought and words. It cannot be defined or described, it can be known by individual experience only. When Sri Ramakrishna was asked what samadhi or super-consciousness was like, his reply was, "If anyone should ask you what is the taste of ghee, what could you answer? It is like the taste of ghee (clarified butter)." So is the highest meditation undefinable. It holds within its silence all knowledge, all power, all peace. Those who attain it have reached their journey's end. They need return no more to the world of birth and death. They have come to the realm of the Immortal One.

Fill Your Mind With Me

Of the four paths of Yoga two are, in one sense, subjective. That is, they are paths which we must follow by ourselves. The other two are paths in which we find great assistance in having a teacher. The two paths which we must follow for ourselves are the path of *Karma* — or work — and *Jnana* — or discrimination. No one else can discriminate for us on this path of *Jnana*. We ourselves must seek Reality, day after day, saying "Not this, not this." Necessarily we can gain a right sense of values from the teaching, but the practice is essentially a subjective and individual one. The same is true of the path of *Karma*, or an active life. Certain principles are given, and we must follow them for ourselves.

But on the path of *Bhakti Yoga* or the path of devotion — and the path of *Raja Yoga* — or the path of concentration and meditation — in India a teacher is considered essential; and of the two paths the path of devotion must precede the path of concentration and meditation. That is to say, unless we have an intense yearning for Truth, and seek out, and have devotion for, the teacher, we do not gain very much in the real study of concentration and meditation. When the desire arises to set out on the path of *Bhakti Yoga*, in the development of the devotional nature, great emphasis is laid upon finding the teacher; that is always the first act.

Then the disciple, or the Truth-seeker, is initiated; that is, the Holy Word, the mantra, is given — but the Word is merely a vehicle by means of which actual power is transmitted from the teacher to the disciple. Soul aliveness, or soul awakening, comes through the touch of another soul. Those who find the teacher are always regarded as very fortunate, but that touch may also come to the yearning heart through the mere reading of one sentence. Sometimes it comes through a dream. Even if we have not found the living teacher, no one who is earnest will be without that touch. God can give the word in the silence of the heart.

The first step in the spiritual life is called *Brahmacharya*. This means not only the practice of perfect purity, but also of service. In the West it is often thought that the spiritual life means that a person sits cross-legged all day long, meditating, or spends hours in not being active. As a matter of fact, a disciple cannot enter the spiritual life without a long period of very active service. This is symbolized by the first act of the novice in seeking the guru, or spiritual teacher. The novice always approaches the guru with the sacrificial wood in her arms. It signifies that she is coming to be the hewer of wood and the drawer of water for the teacher. This is literally the beginning. The disciple cuts wood, brings water, and does the menial tasks.

In reality there are no menial tasks. The reason is that in order to gain a superconscious state, we must rise above our bodily conditions. By lowly service we rise above the gross body. When people talk about purification, they almost always have rather a distorted, or perhaps a partial, idea of what it means. They have an idea that they clean things out, just as they would a bureau drawer. If the body is dense, they think they can get it a little lighter and then go on living their bodily life. But purification means this: that the normal place for every Soul is in divine consciousness, just as the normal place for water is at its source and it is always trying to find it. So the normal place for the Soul is in contact with the Divine. Just as a fish taken out of water is perfectly miserable until it struggles back, so the Soul struggles and struggles to reach its source. The only thing that prevents it is the density of our two bodies, our gross body and our subtle body. Purification means that we remove some of the density of our body so that it can rise. The actual purpose of all purification is not to make a lighter body to live in, or a pleasanter one, but to remove the ballast or the weight, so that the consciousness rises. The way to transcend bodily lethargy is by very active service — a service in which we submit our bodily tendencies to another will.

It is extremely difficult to make way for that teacher, but if we cannot do it, how can we make way for God? God means the whole universe. We must have the willingness to let everything in the universe come in before us, and the only way we can do it is by standing aside. When we can serve an Ideal, or one who represents an Ideal, and will stand by, we shall be constantly uplifted through that service. Whether we have the living Ideal or not, we must keep constantly in mind that service towards God and His children. It is the first step in this path of devotion.

When we take up the spiritual life, it is not enough merely to do the routine tasks. They can quickly become automatic, and the old selfish habits can be growing underneath. Thus when we have a day that is free, we do not indulge the body by staying in bed a little longer, eating a little more, and doing a little less. Even as, on ordinary days, we make an effort to get up early in the morning for the sake of our business, so on a day that is free we have a chance to do it for God. We get up at the same hour, and we take our holiday in giving a little joy to our Soul, by spending a little more time in prayer and meditation, and in reading holy books. In this way a holiday really becomes a Holy Day. We are refreshed. Why? Because it is not our work that tires us. It is a state of heaviness or denseness; it is lethargy into which we have fallen by thinking our power is limited, our strength is limited, we are a body; and all this means *tamas*.

If, on the contrary, we bring ourselves into a state of *sattva*, of lightness and serenity, through more meditation and holy thought and holy study, then that heaviness is counteracted and fatigue is cured.

This element of service — of rising above the body — is absolutely essential. It must be practiced continuously. We must constantly be looking for opportunities for service.

There comes a time in our spiritual life when we think we no longer need bodily training and bodily discipline, and that great intellectual activity will take their place. It does not, any more than reading a book takes the place of eating a meal. We have to carry these three elements all through life with us. We have a gross body to deal with as well as a subtle body, and the training of the subtle body is not a substitute for training the gross body. Both must be trained.

We will always be called upon to keep the balance. The more earnest we are, the most sincere, the more we will be forced to maintain this balance of life. Every living being who starts out on the spiritual life, and above all on this life of devotion, must be very careful that the body is given so much activity every day, that the mind is given so much practice, and also the Soul; there must be this perfect balance.

Wherever we find lethargy seizing us, at that point we must work. Whenever we resent any call upon our energy, it means we need that call and should answer it even though we have to do violence to ourselves. Lethargy is the willingness to leave things as they are, rather than make an effort to put them right. Therefore the practice of having perfect order is not merely for the sake of order, but to overcome that lethargy within us.

Service to the guru, or spiritual teacher, is one of the best ways to overcome lethargy. A true teacher awakens in us a great love and a great eagerness for service, and that keeps alive our activities and stimulates our energies; also the example is before us all the time.

To keep the balance we must realize how these three elements must be constantly in our mind and put into practice: service, in order to rise above the gross body; concentration, which helps us to rise above the subtle body; love, which takes us to God.

We must use our discriminative faculty. As we advance we learn to say, this thing is good, but has it anything to do with what I am striving for? If not, I will leave it out. We are perfectly frank and simple. When we take up that habit of life, that resolution, we begin to know what concentration is. When we do not allow the trivialities of life to ripple the surface of our mind, concentration becomes easier. The deeper thoughts of life quickly unify. The nearer we get to the depths of our being, the less differentiation there is, the more unity. The conservation of our energies becomes greater.

It is not that we are going to give up all recreation. At times recreation is more vital than work, but we learn to discriminate and always look at it in relation to our spiritual life. When recreation leaves us spent and with a sense of having drifted away from our spiritual ideals, it is something that can be left out. There are other times when we have a joyful, mirthful time and we come home like children. That is good recreation.

What is True Worship?

Worship may be defined as the process by which we seek to unite ourselves with the Divine. It is universal…not limited to particular people, faith tradition or state of development.

All living beings feel the All and when they feel It, instinctively bow before It. The only question is where and when and how. People of a certain temperament believe that the more form is heaped on form, sound on sound, beauty on beauty, litany on litany, the greater the worship; while others of differing nature claim that the barer the walls, the emptier the altar, the simpler the music, the more extemporaneous the prayer, the surer is our approach to God. Individual bias in religious practice is as natural as in bodily habit and those are wise who, conserving their energy by moving along the path of least resistance, choose that form which makes strongest appeal to their particular temperament. The wrong consists in denouncing all other forms, not seeing their equal for people of different constitution.

Since the earliest Vedic times, sages have acknowledged this need of endless variety in expression, while proclaiming absolute unity in essence. For that reason their activities have never been directed towards conversion. Believing that each person's religious consciousness is evolved from within, its effort has not been to superimpose some alien form of faith, but to infuse new life into the existing ideal; in other words, "not to destroy, but to fulfill" (or infill) as Christ and every other savior has said.

No one need be taught to worship. It is a spontaneous act of the human mind. Every being is pouring out thought and energy in oblation at the feet of something. What that object is determines our character even more than our creed, for "whatever a person constantly thinks upon, that they become" and worship means the unbroken flow of mind and will towards a fixed end. If it is money or fame or power, then we are as truly an idolater as if we melted up all the valuables in the safe and recast them into a graven image. The same may be said of those who serve God for some return, who expect as the wage of their adoration immunity from misfortune and affliction on this earth or an eternity of enjoyment in heaven. "Four kinds of the virtuous worship Me," the Lord tells us in the Bhagavad Gita, "the distressed, the seekers after knowledge, the seekers after material prosperity and the wise. Among them the wise, ever steadfast, devoted to the One, excel; for I am supremely dear to the wise and they are dear to Me. Noble indeed are all these, but I regard the wise as My very Self; for with soul ever steadfast they are established in Me alone as their supreme goal."

To worship God for any material, personal benefit is regarded in India as "worship of the gods" or the minor aspects of the Divine. Those who direct all their thought towards prosperity are said to worship the god of success, those whose whole desire moves towards intellectual attainment are worshippers of the goddess of learning, and so through all the Vedic pantheon. Yet not even the most ignorant Hindu worshippers bowing before the crudest image ever believe that what they invoke is other than some personified aspect of the Eternal and Supreme Lord. To the precise and clear-seeing Hindu mind all people remain polytheists so long as they are swayed and governed by worldly cravings, for each new ambition is a god they worship until it grants them their desire. Only that one becomes a worshipper of the One God who desires God alone.

Yet these lower forms of worship are not condemned as wrong. They merely represent the childhood of religion, the baby stage of stretching out the hand towards whatever amuses or attracts. We must grow up to realize that it is more blessed to give than to be in want. There is nothing we cannot gain from the Supreme if we only importune long and fervently enough. He even bestows on us the faith and perseverance necessary to attain our end; but He sorrows that we ask so little of Him, for "limited and perishable is the fruit acquired by these ones of small understanding," it is said in the Gita.

God yearns with all His heart to give us the true and the eternal, but we continue to implore of Him the false and fleeting. And He gives it because in the infinitude of His love He cannot resist our cry. But through each new disappointment He strives to teach us that no gift of the world can be equal to Himself; that not the greatest thing which we may ask of Him can be so wonderful as that which He will freely bestow on us when we come to Him in love, asking nothing. Only when we have learned to fold our hands in humble surrender instead of lifting them in eager supplication will the spirit of true worship stir within us. We must worship for the joy of worship, for the sweetness of turning our thought to the Beloved and uniting our soul with His. Can it matter how that is done? When the child runs to the mother, or the loving wife to the husband, is there need of any fixed form to express the outpourings of the heart? Rites and ceremonies have their value as amalgamating influences in collective worship or as focal points to center the attention; they count little as means of winning divine favor. They are for us, not for God. Their purpose is to fan the dulling fire of devotion in our hearts, to rouse our lagging thought; but as the faith grows deeper, the knowledge of spirit broader, the love stronger, simpler and simpler will become the method taken to reach the Lord.

Nowhere do we read of the great teachers training their disciples in intricate rituals. One child-like prayer was all that Jesus left; while Sri Krishna tells us: He who offers to the Lord a leaf or flower, a fruit or water with devotion and a single heart, that is to God a welcome oblation "Fill thy mind with God alone, work for Him, be to Him devoted, worship Him and adore Him, steadfastly uniting thy heart with Him alone and regarding Him as the Supreme Goal, thus shalt thou come unto Him" — such is the rule of life He gives.

Sri Ramakrishna tells the story of a saint who one day was absent from the hermitage when a devotee in distress of mind sought counsel. His son anxious that he should not have come in vain sought to help him. "If you will but repeat God's Name three times, you will find peace," he said. When the saint heard of it, he turned reprovingly on his son, saying: "My child, how little is your faith! Do you not know that if you utter the Lord's Name only once with all your heart, you will gain peace throughout eternity?" The secret lies in gathering up the whole of our being and laying it with unquestioning devotion at the feet of the Supreme: not trying to reach Him through calls for health and prosperity or through bigoted insistence on dogma and doctrine; not feeling that we are nearer to Him because we recite a special creed, worship a special savior, follow a special form.

God knows not higher or lower, greater or less. Those who have ever stood face to face with the Lord or truly perceived His divine presence in a Christ or Buddha, realize that the Divine, incarnate or discarnate, is beyond weight and measurement. Whatever the form He wears, always within shines the same resplendent glory; and time, place and country have no power to limit Him. Is it imaginable that the Supreme could calculate that in a special moment among a special people He would come to earth once and once only to bless His children? Only the finite human mind could conceive such a plan. The Divine Mind is universal. It is alike to all beings, never a "respecter of persons." It knows no chosen people. It recognizes no chosen time. When it is spoken in your language, it seems highest to you; when in mine, it seems highest to me; because each can then best comprehend its spirit. But always it is the same message uttered in endless forms and tongues to countless peoples. Truth must always be one, whatever the name we give it.

Should it, however, at this moment fall upon our ears in its full might, it would daze and deafen us. We must grow into the Universal, and along the way we fashion anew each day the God before whom we bow. Every expansion of our consciousness brings a fresh conception of the Divine and a readjustment of our ideals. As much of the Absolute as our understanding can cover, so much becomes our God, personal or impersonal according as we have transcended our own small personality. But only when we have laid aside the last remnant of "I" and "mine" will our consciousness overflow the final barrier and cover the whole. Then for the first time shall we worship the One God, Who bears all Names, Who hears all prayers, Who receives all sacrifices, and Who loves with unmeasuring tenderness all living beings.

Silence

One of the first requisites of spiritual practice is silence. The soul accomplishes its tasks under cover of a great stillness. As we mount upward in the scale of evolution, our emotions draw inward and our thought grows quiet.

Wisdom is born of silence, seldom does it spring from speech. Language veils the thought. It misinterprets rather than interprets. The more we talk, the less we shall know. "By the one whom the Self chooses, by that one alone is It attained." This may seem like partiality, but whom does the Self choose? That great Self chooses the one who is pure in heart, watchful and always on guard. To that one It grants great treasures of knowledge. "The wise and purely mystical one never speaks except when he cannot help it," the Spanish mystic, Michael de Molinos, writes. "Rare are the ones who set a higher price on hearing than on speaking."

Nothing is more wasteful than continuous talking. It squanders the vital energies and creates an exhausting molecular activity in the brain, which drains the whole nervous system. Tongue, brain, nerves and mind are not constructed for perpetual motion. They need pauses in which to recharge their forces. If we would learn to practice silence at intervals through the day and lessen our period of talking, we would avoid needless argument, misunderstanding, and consequent depletion of vitality.

Power and authority rest with the silent ones. Both are cumulative. They cannot be acquired suddenly, nor can they be called forth at will. They are built up gradually out of what is saved from our normal supply of energy.

Our forcefulness and our power to command are measured by the amount of our reserve. Nature supplies us with an overflow of strength for emergencies. If we do not conserve this and use it wisely, we shall always remain weaklings, without force or authority.

It is the petty things of life that make us noisy and talkative. The great moments awe us to stillness. We move toward them with mute lips and noiseless step. As the great moments are silent moments, so the little moments are made great by silence. Silence lends dignity to the most trivial task.

The practice of silence is irksome to us because our silences are empty. We must fill them from within. We must garner in our mind a bountiful store of lofty thoughts. We do this either by memorizing helpful passages we find in our reading, or by thinking deeper into life for ourselves. Our habit too often is to express a thought the moment it comes to us. This robs it of its force and wastes it. Thought gathers strength through silent reflection and becomes a part of our reserve. In this riper form it is of much greater value to us than as a mere topic of conversation.

Outer silence, to be effective, must be reinforced by an inner silence. If the mind is full of a multiplicity of thoughts, outer stillness will be of little avail. Inner silence does not demand absence of thought, it calls for oneness of thought. As long as there are even two thoughts in the mind, there will be a certain play between them and that will disturb the inward quietness. Through the practice of concentration we simplify our thought-processes until we attain one-pointedness. When this is reached, a great peace settles on heart and mind and we grow silent within and without.

Concentration is the instrument of inner silence. It quiets the over-active senses; it stills the mind and intellect; it spreads a silent calm over the struggling moral nature; then when it reaches the realm of spirit, automatically it passes the task to meditation, which carries the whole being into the depths of silence.

Deep meditation is the silence of the Soul. In this silence the Soul reveals itself. Its language is wordless. It perceives and expresses through the medium of pure consciousness — a consciousness which is self-luminous and which illumines whatever it falls upon. The Bhagavad Gita declares: "Those whose ignorance is destroyed by Soul-knowledge, their knowledge of the Soul, like the sun illumines the Supreme." Soul-consciousness goes far beneath the outer covering of creation and touches the essence. It discloses the ultimate mystery of the universe, — that every living thing, every tree and rock and clod of earth, is vibrant with the Divine.

Wisdom is the fruit of assimilated experience. It is nurtured in the silence of solitude, in the stillness of meditation. Noisy argument or intellectual reasoning will not give it, nor will the study of books. An unlettered recluse in a mountain fastness far from schools and libraries may possess more wisdom than a learned scholar in a university. Independent thought and superior living are the foundation on which it rests. The marks of its presence as set down in the Bhagavad Gita are these:

> Humility, unostentatiousness, non-injuring, forgiveness, simplicity, service to the spiritual teacher, purity, steadfastness, self-control, absence of egoism.... One-pointed and unwavering devotion to Me, resort to secluded places, distaste for assemblies; constant devotion to spiritual knowledge, realization of the essence of Truth, this is declared to be wisdom.

The truly wise are more inward than outward in their methods. They are never assertive or dogmatic. Their judgments and attitudes toward life are always sane and tolerant. In the Bhagavad Gita they are called chosen ones of God. The Gita declares, speaking for the Lord: "I am supremely dear to the wise and he is dear to me .... I regard the wise as my very self; for with soul ever steadfast, he is established in Me alone as his Supreme Goal."

Transcendence and Union

There is only one way to meet any problem, even the most practical, and that is to rise above it. We cannot deal with anything so long as we are on the same level. For instance, we try to improve our human nature, but we cannot do it beyond a certain point. To transcend human imperfection we have to rise to a new plane of consciousness. Now this can be done by a sudden realization of our divine Self or by an appeal to that Supreme One with whom the divine Self is united. That is, by Self-realization or by realization of our oneness with God.

We are always one with God, but we do not know that we are. We could not exist if we were not one with existence, and God is existence. The fact that we know even one thing in this universe shows that we are united with

God, because we cannot know anything apart from the principle of knowledge, and God is infinite knowledge. Every time we know the least fact it is a demonstration of our union with Him. If we are one with Him in one thing, we are one with Him in all, because infinity cannot be divided. If we experience one moment of happiness, one flash of joy, that proves our oneness, because there is no joy outside of God. God has the monopoly on all happiness and all knowledge and all light, and when we wish to possess these we have to go to God for them.

The unfoldment of the consciousness of our oneness with God constitutes the whole work that we are called upon to do. That is why we must awaken to the realization of our true being. For so long as we do not know that we are one with the Supreme Spirit, we continue to be painfully human. We may have an unlimited fortune in the bank, but if we are not aware of that fact we are just as poor as the one who has no money there at all. If we do not know it, we cannot draw upon it, and if we do not know, are not vividly conscious of our oneness with God, we are the same as if we were separated from Him. The proof of this lies in the fact that whenever we are in trouble, we run from one human being to another, we exhaust all the human possibilities for help, and when they fail we kneel down and pray, but we do it only as a last resort with a little, foolish sense that it is weak to do so. This shows that we do not believe either in the efficacy of God or in His power, and that, therefore, we are not actually drawing upon that one source of unfailing help, strength and wisdom. It is very different with those who have realized the meaning of the sentence, "Thou art That." They begin at the God-end. They don't try the human until it fails, they say, "I will try the Divine until It fails." But it never fails, and they do not have to go anywhere else.

Atmosphere

An individual atmosphere surrounds all living beings. It is the product of their thought and feeling and their mode of life. It tempers their contacts with the world as the earth's atmosphere tempers the fierceness of the sun's rays. It softens the blows and quiets the joys. No impression from the outside reaches them unaltered. As it penetrates their atmosphere, it mingles with something of themselves and becomes a part of them before it is registered by their perceptive faculties.

We should not disregard our body, neither should we place its care before all else. The more we center our interest in the physical, the denser our atmosphere becomes, and the more impervious we are to finer impressions. If we will but lift our interest and effort to a loftier level, it will become transparent and shining. We must never forget that our atmosphere is the product of our own manner of living, the result of our own thought and feeling. It is we who create it. We make it dull or radiant.

How can we clarify our atmosphere? We do it by spiritualizing our life. When we make Spirit the ruling principle of our daily living, the atmosphere around us no longer obstructs and distorts; it transmits and illumines.

The Power of Music

The German poet, Heinrich Heine, asks the question: "What is music?" and he gives his own answer in these words: "Like a twilight mediator it hovers between spirit and matter, related to both, yet differing from both. It is spirit, but spirit subject to the measurement of time; it is matter, but matter that can dispense with space."

Confucius, it is said, began his teaching always by playing softly on a stringed instrument; and he declared that music brought the mind in right accord with the will of Heaven.

To exert power, music need not be purely classical. The deeper forms of tonal expression, — religious music and the works of the master-composers, exercise undoubtedly a stronger, more enduring influence on the hearts of people; but the lighter forms also have their place. Whatever is born of the heart as well as of the head, and is the product of inspiration and efficient training serves as a channel for bettering humankind.

A province which has been scarcely invaded by music, yet which seems peculiarly to belong to it, is that of healing. Personal experience has taught me that acute pain can be transcended by hearing a symphony or some other exalting composition. Why should it not be so? Matter is in constant vibration. When the vibration is disturbed, the rhythm of the body becomes jangled and illness ensues. The regular beat of music restores the troubled vibration and the pain or malady is relieved.

Right Breathing

In every created being are two elements, called in Vedic science *akasha* and *prana*, *akasha* being primordial substance and *prana* primordial creative energy. This *prana* is the life principle. Without it nothing can live. If we wish to be truly alive, therefore, we must acquaint ourselves with the nature of this *prana* and learn its control and use. In our own system its most evident form is to be seen in the motion of the lungs, commonly known as breathing. Breathing, however, is not the cause of this motion, but its effect. In each physical organism is a tireless pumping system, driven by the power of *prana*, which inflates and empties the lungs. The capacity of this pumping engine determines our health and strength; yet the average person, it is said, uses only one-sixth of our power, that is, we take in only one-sixth of the oxygen which we might have to cleanse and renew our system.

There are three planes of consciousness latent in every being — the subconscious, the conscious and the superconscious. The superconscious is a wholly unknown realm to the ordinary human being; and even those who recognize its existence are powerless to reach it by any calculating effort of their own, however zealous and sincere. It unveils itself when mastery of the two lower planes are gained. In accomplishing this, the control of breath becomes a valuable factor. Breath stands at the meeting point of the subconscious and the conscious. It is, as it were, the handle by which we may seize and govern the activities of both planes. In our daily experience we demonstrate this constantly. When the breath becomes short or irregular, at once the mind grows confused. That is why people under a sudden shock or provocation which "takes their breath away," lose their presence of mind.

The nerve currents also are regulated through the breath. It is, indeed, the breath which propels these currents through the hollow passages of the spinal vertebrae. When the breathing is irregular, the nerve force is driven in jerks, the whole system is jarred and loss of energy follows. This explains our exhaustion after a fit of weeping or of anger. We have squandered our vital energies. Taking long deep breaths before an open window will help us restore the rhythm of the system and repair our wasted forces. By a resolute practice of rhythmic breathing we can also prevent rising temper or rising despondency.

The science of *pranayama* or breath-control is a comprehensive one and deals with breathing exercises of many different varieties. Some have for their aim to regulate the circulation and temperature of the body; others to purify and regulate the nerve currents; still others to stimulate the different nerve centers and their accompanying centers. Some have great healing efficacy, sending the *prana* or life-force to depleted parts or withdrawing it from congested ones; others keep the vital energy equally distributed, thus maintaining general health. It is impossible to enumerate all the many kinds of exercises contained in this branch of Yoga; but as the larger part of them have as their purpose to rouse the finer forces of our being and set in motion subtler activities, they must be practiced with great caution and only under the guidance of a teacher. Each individual temperament calls for some modifications of the general exercises. For that reason it is not safe to take them from a book and begin practicing the exercises by ourselves. But it is perfectly safe to cultivate the habit of deep rhythmic breathing and through this alone we can bring up the standard of efficiency in all our work.

Chronic inertia is one of the worst forms of infection, no drug could be more harmful. It is a kind of moral sleeping sickness, which little by little deadens all our faculties and kills our higher aspirations. There is but one remedy for it, — to quicken and focus our present store of *prana* and increase the supply. It has a vital influence on our spiritual development also. Meditation and higher vision are impossible in the state of *tamas* (density and heaviness). Before we can make any progress in these, we must quicken all the life currents of the body by expanding and regulating the lung action. That is why breath-control is given so important a place in all preparatory Yoga training. We must deepen and lengthen our normal breath. A good way to do this is to bring it into rhythm with our step, especially when we are walking in the open air. If our natural breath today covers six steps, next week we must try to increase it to seven and later, if possible, to eight. But we must exercise great discretion and not strain the lungs. In the beginning this practice may make us feel breathless; for that reason it should not be continued for more than a minute or two; then for an interval we should turn our attention entirely away from our breathing.

In bringing our breath into rhythm with our step, we must be careful also to keep it in rhythm with itself; that is, the in-breath and out-breath must be of equal length, both must cover the same number of steps. If one is naturally shorter than the other, it is better to reduce the longer to the count of the shorter one; then gradually increase both together. This exercise in time will make our breath as regular as the swing of a pendulum; and the parts of the system will be brought into rhythm; our scattered forces will be harnessed; and not only will our strength be increased, but the wear and tear of the system will be reduced enormously.

The engine which has a jerky, irregular motion wears out quickly; and any break in the rhythmic action of our body or mind weakens our organism and opens it to attack from disintegrating outside forces. Nature is working ceaselessly to keep us strong and well and active. Our system is constituted to withstand every kind of attack, but we do not cooperate with it. We do not take advantage of the simplest, most obvious means provided. We are content to pant our way through life, to live and move breathlessly. We take in only *prana* enough for our immediate use and have no reserve with which to meet unexpected demands. That is why we are unnerved and overcome so easily.

Endurance, steadiness, precision, are essential to efficiency and all these hang upon the breath. It determines the amount of life-force we take into the system and how evenly and continuously we distribute it. So long, however, as we make rhythmic breathing a purely mechanical exercise related only to our own little organism, the results must be small. Our real power will come when we bring ourselves into unison with a larger rhythm and unify our breath with the great cosmic breath which pulses through the universe. We all know how the force of every soldier is increased when the regiment falls into step, and further power comes when the breath of all of them is unified by singing or whistling. A new strength is generated which is more than the sum total of the individual units of strength in the company. We see the same thing in a tug of war, or in hoisting a sail, when they expel their breath simultaneously by uttering some word or sound.

If this is true of a small group, how much more must it be true when we join with the universal cosmic forces. There is an in-breathing and out-breathing of God, a great breath wave of involution and evolution down the cycles. There is an in-breath of summer and an out-breath of winter; an in-breath of day, an out-breath of night; an in-breath called birth and an out-breath called death. Everywhere there is this swing of the pendulum of the life-breath between the dualities which make up creation. What power must be ours when we join ourselves with it! But how may we do it? By what means may we gain this union? By our thought.

Thought serves as the connecting link between ourselves and the universe, both inward and outward. When we think of anything, we are joined with that thing for the duration of our thought and partake of its qualities.

If we fix our mind on a holy person, holier feelings begin to rise in us. If our thought dwells on one who is hateful or unholy, a certain perversity seizes upon us too. But since we cannot encompass the whole cosmic universe by our thought, how then shall we become united with it? By training our thought to flow in habitual current towards that One in Whom the universe lives, moves and has its being; that One Who "breathes the breath of life" into every living thing. When we are unbrokenly God-mindful, we enter into the Divine being and fall spontaneously into rhythm with its rhythm. Our breath, our thought, our every motion, our whole life will pulse in harmony with the pulse of creation; we shall stand no longer as isolated units possessing a limited store of strength and ability, but we shall have the full strength and intelligence and skill of the Infinite behind us.

This is the secret of the power of the saint or the devotee. They may appear to be physically more frail than the worldling, but in the moment of need they will manifest a superhuman strength against which the sturdiest muscles cannot prevail. They may be without schooling, yet their intuitional knowledge will confound the learning of the greatest scholar. The smallest wheel or piston shares in the mightiness of the engine when it moves in harmony with it; so do we share in the power of God and His universe when we live in perfect unison with His life, our heartbeat at one with His great heart, our breath in rhythm with His never-ceasing cosmic breath.

Food

The Value of Food in Spiritual Training

In all Vedic teaching the term food has a much more extended meaning than in Western usage. It refers not merely to the food which we give our body; but in a far greater degree to the food with which we nourish our mind, our heart, our Soul-life. The great Indian sages realized the fact that food determines our constitution on every plane of our being. It affects in equal degree our character and our bodily condition. Diet, indeed, has become an acknowledged branch of social science; but too much stress is laid on the purely physical aspect of it, and too little on its value in developing the higher nature.

The words of the Bhagavad Gita that "Creatures come forth from food" are literally and insistently true. As created beings we are coming forth from food at every moment; and those who are striving for spiritual consciousness cannot be too watchful as to what we feed our bodies, our minds, our hearts and our moral sense. If our body is not properly fed and properly disciplined we have a very poor foundation to work upon. The larger part of our bodily weaknesses and disabilities is due to the misuse of food. The first error which we nearly all make is to regard pleasure as the chief purpose of eating, and to judge the value of food by our personal likes and dislikes. This is a very misleading standard on which to base our diet. Our appetite can rarely be our guide. We must first cultivate a right taste and a right understanding as to the true purpose of life. It is not necessary to adopt an austere diet, nor is it wrong to enjoy our food; but we must teach ourselves to enjoy what is most beneficial for us. The physical organism can be trained to respond to any demand of the mind, and nothing is more easily cultivated than a taste for the proper foods, when we go about it intelligently.

Our diet must be regulated by our mode of life. There can be no universal rule regarding the foods to be eaten or eliminated from the diet. Our activity level and work, our constitution, and the deeper aim of the heart must determine this question; but whatever the diet adopted, two factors must be held constantly in mind — to keep the inner nature so far as possible pure, unweighted and pliant; and to fortify the outer nature against the effect of external conditions.

If we are physically very active, we need the ballast of some heavier foods, just as a ship needs ballast when it sets sail on the high seas. The quality and amount of our food should be changed also whenever our daily routine changes. In India when devotees retire to the forest to practice Yoga, they may reduce their diet to wild herbs, wild honey and a few chappattis (unleavened whole wheat bread) baked on a hot stone in the sun; but when they return to populated regions, they gradually alter the quantity and character of their food; otherwise their organism will be too sensitive to stand the jarring change.

Foods, Vedanta teaches, fall naturally into three classes and produce corresponding effects upon the system. Some foods are full of *tamas* or heaviness and weight the body; others are *rajasic* in their nature and create excessive activity, unrest, nervous energy; and there are still others which nourish, yet leave the body light and responsive to higher stimuli. The ordinary diet should contain a mixture of these three kinds of food, with emphasis laid on that one which corresponds with the nature of the life.

Among vegetables, those which grow in the ground are most *tamasic*; those which grow above the ground and are ripened in the sun are more *rajasic*; while those which not only grow in the sunlight, but which do not have to be cooked, such as salads and fruits are most *sattvic*. For example, among cereals, oatmeal is more *tamasic*, wheat products more *rajasic*; rice and corn more *sattvic*. These three elements should be present in the daily diet. We should have some article of food which provides the necessary density or bulk, others which renew our active forces, and still others which nourish the finer parts of our nature. All three need to be sustained in us, but in proper proportion. It takes very much less *tamasic* food, because of its greater density; and much more *sattvic*, because of its lightness.

Meat is not a necessary article of food. Cereals, nuts, cheese, the various pulses, will give all that meat gives, without the added impurities inseparable from animal food. Yet too sudden a change from the habit of long years is not advisable. First we should cut out the heavier meats, being content with fish and chicken, and should eat these less and less frequently.

We must guard ourselves from overeating. Too much food depletes the system quite as much as too little. When we oversupply the body with nutrition, it is forced to exhaust its vital energies in taking care of the surplus. We should keep ourselves in the lithe, sinewy condition of a runner or an oarsman. Any reduction in diet, however, must begin with the nonessentials — those foods which pamper the appetite rather than strengthen bone and tissue. Above all we must eliminate eating between meals. Like any other mechanism the digestive system needs rest. But there is a deeper reason. When food is put into the stomach, the greater part of the *prana* or life-force is drawn to that point to digest it, leaving the brain and other organs temporarily impoverished. This explains why after a hearty meal one finds it so difficult to do any serious work.

Health and Healing

Health means wholeness, and it resides permanently at that point of our nature where we are in unveiled contact with the Whole. It is not something which we gain or lose. It is an inherent quality of our being. Therefore somewhere within us we must be whole today. The schools of teaching which recognize this and tell their followers to affirm "I am perfect," "I am divine," are defective in their results because they do not make plain what is divine and perfect. They fail to define the "I" for which this may be claimed. Such statements to be effective cannot be mere theoretical affirmations. They must be based on a clear conviction rooted in our own experience.

When we set out to discover the seat of sickness or ill-health, soon we find ourselves baffled and bewildered. In our physical organism there is not one fixed point on which we can fasten. We see matter rushing round and out as in a whirlpool. Forty-five seconds suffice for the blood to make the circuit of the system, depositing new material and carrying away the old; each breath takes in and casts out; food is consumed, assimilated and eliminated. The change of material particles is incessant.

The idea that "mind governs matter" carries us little further; for what is mind? A finer form of matter, and more mobile because it is finer; just as gas is more evasive and volatile than earth or water. The incalculably subtle material of thought moves and changes with a velocity which we cannot measure. Our states of mind are far more difficult to maintain than our bodily states. They vary from moment to moment. Of itself, also, mind has no operative force; it is only an instrument. Behind it stands the thinking agent. And here we lay our hand upon the seat of some of our various ailments.

The sense of I-ness is the matrix which gives form to all the inflowing matter. "I am weak," "I am ill," "I am miserable" — these are the thought-molds which perpetuate much of our discomfort and suffering. If we can break our identification with these bodily conditions, nature will be left free to work. She converts even decay and death into new forms of life. It is we who defeat her efforts by this habit of false identification. When our sense of I-ness is vigorously diverted, we forget our aches and pains; and if the impression is strong enough, the physical disability may be healed.

Herein lies the secret of all so-called miraculous cures. In those cases, intense faith snaps the thought connection with the physical affliction and establishes a new association, through which the system is opened to a surging current of restorative energy. A Christ charged with an inexhaustible store of vital energy and able to sweep away lethargy or doubt by the power of His God-filled personality has no need to heal by installments. One touch, one word, one moment's contact suffices.

The efficacy of certain affirmations finds its explanation in this same principle of shifting the thought association. So long as the attention is fixed on the constructive idea embodied in the affirmation, we cooperate with nature and the suffering or discomfort may be relieved.

The wise method is to understand that there are different planes of being, and that we do not escape from the conditions of a lower plane by remaining there and denying them; or by trying to apply the principle belonging to a higher plane. We escape from them only by lifting our self-identity to the plane where that higher principle acts spontaneously without any coercion on our part. Thus, to assert "I am divine and perfect" in order to make our human nature and imperfections more comfortable cannot bring a lasting result, because our method has no foundation in Truth. If, on the contrary by our daily living we strive to manifest the latent Divinity within us, the Divine power, as it acquires full expression, will accomplish its own ends.

The ones who have done the mightiest work in the world have not always been physically the strongest. How many have had to push against serious bodily disabilities, yet they have rendered heroic service to humankind. Haven't we all endured strains which seemed far beyond our strength to bear? All the power, the health and the strength we have come from the Soul; and they will flow through a frail body with as great a force as through the strongest, if we will but open ourselves with unwavering faith. And as they flow they will heal. We block the channel by the ready attention we pay to every little ache and pain. This destroys our sense of proportion and lends reality to conditions which, if left to themselves, would disappear. The best way to deal with them is to think about something else; if they will not be forgotten, then they must be handled in a way which appeals most strongly to our reason and individual conviction.

Nature meant us to live a balanced life. Every part of the organism should be brought into daily activity. A properly regulated routine for each day should include a certain amount of manual labor, a certain amount of intellectual work and an equal amount of spiritual work. Upon this last we should lay special stress, because our Soul-life has had the least place in our past routine and has greatest need of being fostered. It is because it has been allowed to starve may be contributing to our unhealthy condition. Yet whenever any disorder appears in the system, immediately we swing our whole attention back on the body and begin to pamper it. We lie in bed, abandon our usual routine and cut ourselves off from the things which would keep alive our Soul consciousness. By degrees we induce a spiritual anemia, which undermines both our health and our morale. If, on the contrary, we were more fervent and regular in our spiritual practices, more eager to remain in contact with those who sustain our spiritual rather than our bodily consciousness, very soon we should discover that there is no limit to the supply of strength and power and life at our command, granted that we make ourselves receptive to it.

We should give all necessary care to our body, but only that it may be a more efficient vehicle to carry us to our goal and to be able to serve. Our primary aim must be to reach God. When we behold His face and feel the benediction of His Presence, the body and the things of the body will be forgotten. And this is the main purpose of health.

Steady muscles, well-functioning organs, quiet nerves are not the full measure of our strength. Only when our entire being is gathered up and brought in union with God shall we be made truly whole; and only as that unity persists, shall we continue whole. Christ offered the basic cure for all ills, whether of flesh or thought, when He told us that we must love the Lord our God with all our heart and all our mind and all our strength and all our Soul; because love alone will bind us close to the Source of life. More than a thousand years before, Sri Krishna prescribed a like remedy in these words: "The one who works for Me (the Lord), has Me for his highest goal; is devoted to Me, is free from selfish attachment and bears enmity towards no creature, that one enters into Me." Those attain the full realization of wholeness and perfection.

Appendix A

Notes on Research

Chapter One:

The identity of the Swedenborgian minister that hosted Laura and her mother in 1893 was not identified by author, Marie Louise Burke, in *Swami Vivekananda in the West, New Discoveries*. Burke simply wrote that Laura and her mother were the guests of a Swedenborgian minister in a small town in Ohio.

Urbana was a small town in Ohio of 6,000 in 1890s and did have a Swedenborgian community. The minister Louis H. Tafel had attended the Parliament of Religions. It would not have been an event of general interest to Swedenborgian ministers of the time.

Reverend Tafel was also head of the language department at Urbana College since he was fluent in Latin and German; Swedenborg wrote everything in Latin.

Our thanks to Reverend James F. Lawrence, Dean of the Center for Swedenborgian Studies at the Pacific School of Religion in Berkeley, California for our information about Reverend Tafel. In an email dated November 11, 2020 he wrote, "Rev. Tafel was the sort of person who would have loved the Parliament and he had big arguments with the tendency among Swedenborgian members to be exclusive or clannish. He believed in a broad approach to the religious quest. My own feeling is that you can with confidence identify Rev. Tafel as the minister [in question]."

Chapter Two:

In many books referencing Laura Glenn or Devamata, it is stated that her family is related to the statesman, Benjamin Franklin, through her mother, Elizabeth Franklin Glenn. According to a journal kept by Sister Amala, Devamata's secretary, Devamata herself stated this as a family-held conviction. Effort was therefore made to establish the family lineage.

Benjamin Franklin's lineage has been carefully documented by Y-DNA testing and no male relatives of Benjamin's father or grandfather have been found in the United States. The search for a distant male relative of Benjamin Franklin is now happening in England. Women descendants do not carry the DNA marker. Lisa R. Franklin, administrator of the Franklin Y-DNA Project wrote in an email, "Thus far no Franklin families in the U.S. are documented as kin to statesman Benjamin Franklin though nearly every Franklin has a 'family' story about being kin."

Two options were researched for further clarification.

Case 1: Laura's grandfather, Nelson D. Franklin, was listed in the will of Major Anthony Franklin (1778–1859) as his son. Anthony's lineage was stated in an application of his great grandson to the Sons of the American Revolution (1880–1970) (SAR) on ancestry.com. The application listed Captain Joel Franklin married to Susanna Lewis as Anthony's father and therefore Nelson's grandfather.

Case 2: Other documents submitted on ancestry.com give Nelson's paternal grandfather as Henry Franklin Jr, (1747–1782) who was the son of Reuben (Long) Franklin. Reuben and his brother were both adopted by their uncle Lawrence Franklin upon the death of their parents (Henry Long and Ana Franklin Long). Reuben and his brother changed their last name from Long to Franklin while under their uncle's care.

CONCLUSION: Whether Joel Franklin (case 1) or Henry Franklin Jr. (case 2) is the paternal grandfather of Nelson Franklin, the lineage is the same for they are cousins (their fathers were brothers). Anthony Franklin and his descendants, which includes son Nelson Franklin, are in the Long family (DNA analysis confirms it).

Additionally: The lineage of Ana Franklin Long (mother of Rueben and his brother) traces back to England. Ana's grandfather, Edward Franklin (1638-1694) was born in Norfolk, England and migrated to Virginia. Ana is the great-great grandmother of Nelson Franklin.

If Laura's family is indeed related to Benjamin Franklin, the relationship had to be established in England along female lines.

Chapter Three:

Laura's age differs in present-day literature, ranging from 1861–67. Ohio did not require birth certificates until 1867; this might account for the variety of dates.

One of the earliest recordings of birth-dates is the U.S. Census of 1870 (State of Ohio, County of Hamilton, city of Cincinnati), as enumerated on the 3rd of June, with Laura as seven and Cora as nine. This places Cora's birth in the year 1861 (birthday in June) and Laura in 1862 (birthday in September). Cora is approximately fifteen months ahead of Laura.

According to the Vassar transcripts of both girls, they entered College in 1878. Laura's age was stated as 16; Cora entered at 17. The birth-years were therefore 1862 and 1861 respectively.

The NY Passenger and Crew Manifest (1820–1959) lists both sisters Laura and Helen returning to New York City from Europe on September 27, 1890. The ages were given as: Laura 28 and Helen 20. This confirms a birth-date of 1862 for Laura and 1870 for Helen. This same manifest has Laura returning from India to the U.S. on October 25, 1909 with birth-date given as "abt. 1862."

Stephanie Burgevin's online family tree has given the birth-dates of each Glenn child—Laura born September 16, 1862 and Cora born June 14, 1861. Her information was derived from the Spring Grove Cemetery in Cincinnati and passport applications. Stephanie's great-great-great uncle is James Glenn and she states that Laura is her "first cousin, three times removed."

In 1889, Laura and Helen stayed at the Baudy Hotel in Giverny, France. The registration book gives Laura's age as 27 and Helen's as 19. This would place birth-years as 1862 and 1870 respectively.

An Outlier:

In the U.S. Census of 1900 enumerated on the 18th day of June, Cora was 38 and Laura was 36 (turned 37 in September). That would put their birth-years at 1862 and 1863 respectively.

Chapter Three

In many books referencing Laura Glenn or Devamata, it is stated that she tried her vocation in some Anglican religious community. In an attempt to verify that claim several communities in existence on the East Coast at the time were contacted. Those four were: The Community of St. Mary (NYC, 1865); The Community of St. John the Baptist (NYC, 1874); The Sisterhood of the Holy Nativity (Boston, 1882); and The Society of Saint Margaret (Boston, 1873).

Though contacted, none of them were able to verify that Laura was a guest or expressed interest in joining, for even a short period of time. Some only recorded the names of ordained sisters and not those simply trying out their vocation. For others, their records didn't date back as far as 1900.

According to Cora's diary, Laura went to Boston for the winter of 1900, staying at the Berkeley Hotel—now the Revolution Hotel. The Society of St. Margaret was located in Boston at the time. The Mother House was in Louisburg Square on Beacon Hill. With their novitiate surging around the end of the 19th century, they purchased three adjoining houses at #15, #17 and #19 Louisburg Square. All three buildings were connected.

There are two other facts that point to the Society of St. Margaret as the likeliest community in which Laura had an interest. In the box of family memorabilia, a brochure describing the Society was found, though no information as to why, when, or by whom this information was obtained. The Society is also the only group of women mentioned by Devamata in her writings. In the article entitled "The Way of Humility and Gentleness", Devamata writes,

> It is said that the Sisters of St. Margaret at midnight walk unharmed through the most degraded quarters of Whitechapel in London, and even the most besotted drunkard staggers out of their way. It is not the veil which calls forth this sudden reverence; it is the love in the heart of those gentle ones who move so quietly and fearlessly through the teaming crowd bent on evil.

Conclusion: If Laura did show interest in an order, it was most likely the Community of St. Margaret in Boston.

Appendix B

Foreword written by Devamata to *Days in An Indian Monastery*

The Monastery around which cluster the larger part of the memories recorded in these pages is at Mylapore, a beautiful suburb of Madras, in South India. Day after day I sat in the dim monastery hall at the evening hour listening to the swaying voice of a great soul. What I heard was simply spoken, but it engraved itself so indelibly on my mind that often when I crossed the road to my dwelling at nine, eleven o'clock still found me beside my flickering candle writing out what had been told me.

After I had filled several notebooks I let Swami Ramakrishnananda know of them and he asked me to bring them to him. The following afternoon he met me with the question: "Sister, how did you do it? As I read your notes I felt that I was speaking."

This commendation planted the seed of a new thought—to interweave this teaching with my other Indian experience and call the volume "*Days in an Indian Monastery.*" As we were driving into the city where the Swami was to lecture, I revealed my plan. He turned to me in the carriage, his face lighted by a radiant smile, and said: "That will be splendid, Sister, and you are just the one to do it."

By these words he laid a sacred task in my hands. I accepted it humbly. Now it attains fulfillment. With grateful heart has it been accomplished.

My life in India brought me in close daily association with some of India's mightiest spiritual Teachers. It was lived under the protection and guidance of one of her greatest religious organizations. These blessing seem too rich to garner and hide away in one small memory. I therefore offer these reminiscences to the world with the prayerful hope that what I have set down in devout reverence and gratitude may create a wider understanding and a deeper sense of kinship between East and West.

Devamata.
Ananda-Ashrama,
La Crescenta, California,
July, 1927

Preface written by Devamata to the first edition of *Inspired Talks*

All who had the blessing of personal contact with Swami Vivekananda are of one accord that those who knew him on the lecture platform only, had but a small measure of his true power and greatness. It was in familiar conversation with chosen friends and disciples that came his most brilliant flashes of illumination, his loftiest flights of eloquence, his utterances of profoundest wisdom. Unfortunately, however, his printed works so far have shown us only Vivekananda the lecturer; Vivekananda the friend, the teacher, the loving master, was known only to the happy few who had the rare privilege of sitting at his feet. Glimpses of this side of the great spiritual genius are revealed to us, it is true, in his published letters; but the present volume is the first to give us words spoken by him in the intimacy of an inner circle.

They were taken down by Miss S.E. Waldo of New York, who from the early days of the Swami's American mission served him with unremitting devotion. It was to her that he dictated his translations and explanations of *Pantanjali's Aphorisms*, published in his *Raja Yoga*, and often has she told me how she would sit for long periods of time watching always to see that the ink on her pen was kept wet, ready to write down the first word that would come as the Swami would emerge from the depths of self-contemplation into which he had plunged, to discover the true meaning of the terse Sanskrit phrases. It was she also who prepared all his American publications for the press; and so great was Swami Vivekananda's confidence in her ability, that he would pass the type-written transcriptions of his lectures over to her with the instruction to do with them what she thought best, for his own indifference to the fruits of his work was so extreme, that he could not be induced to give even a cursory glance at his recorded words.

Through this constant faithful service with heart and brain, the disciple's mind became so at one with the master's that, even without the aid of shorthand, she was able to transcribe his teaching with wonderful fullness and accuracy. As she herself said, it was as if the thought of Swami Vivekananda flowed through her and wrote itself upon the pages. Once when she was reading a portion of these same notes to some tardy arrivals in the Thousand Island Park home, the Swami paced up and down the floor, apparently unconscious of what was going on, until the travellers had left the room; then he turned to her and said: "How could you have caught my thought and words so perfectly? It was as if I heard myself speaking." What need of other commendation?

The Ramakrishna Mission of Madras is highly gratified in having been entrusted with the task of presenting these truly *Inspired Talks* to the public, and it wishes to express its heartfelt gratitude to each one of those who have aided in making this rich treasure, so long hidden, the property of all mankind.

Devamata
Madras,
November, 1908

Foreword written by Devamata to *Spiritual Teachings of Swami Brahmananda*

Swami Brahmananda was one of the most eminent and one of the most beloved of the disciples of Sri Ramakrishna—the first also to come to Him. Sri Ramakrishna regarded him as His own son and admitted him to the utmost intimacy. In this familiar daily intercourse the disciple caught the glint of the Master's effulgence. It shone through all he said, all he did, all he was. It gave him unlimited power and insight, and an authority no one thought to dispute. This last he used sparingly. He led rather by quiet appeal than by more insistent methods, but so mighty was his spiritual force that his gentlest suggestion was to those who heard it, a word of command.

It was my blessed privilege to be closely associated with the Swami during the six months of his first visit to Madras. When the present book of counsel was put into my hands to revise, edit and prepare for publication, there arose before my mind once again the picture of that majestic, yet childlike, figure moving in the twilight shadow up and down the dim monastery hall at Mylapore; once again his gentle voice sounded in my ears; once again the benediction of his loving presence fell in refreshing shower over my spirit. I have striven to let that voice sound unmuted through these pages; to leave unbarred the benediction of that presence.

The spiritual instructions which follow were spoken in largest measure at Benares, Kankhal, Belur, or elsewhere, in informal conversations. Some were written in personal letters. In the earlier days of the Swami's administration as President of the Ramakrishna Mission he remained nearly always in retirement at Puri, or at the Head Monastery of the Order on the Ganges above Calcutta. At that time he was reluctant to assume the place of teacher. At Madras, if any one asked him a question he would answer: "Go and ask Sasi Maharaj. He knows everything. I know nothing."

Later he emerged from his seclusion and became an active and stimulating visitor at the various Centres of the Mission. The teaching set down in the present volume belongs to this second period. It was preserved by devout disciple and published in the *Vedanta Kesari*, The Official Magazine of the Mission's work at Madras. Carefully and reverently revised, it appears now in more permanent form.

The counsels given are pre-eminently practical. They are the spontaneous expression of the Swami's own wide vision and profound spiritual experience.

Their power is irresistible. They transform and redeem. They kindle fresh ardor in the heart. They transmute life into living. Charged with a holy message they go forth now, bearing to world and cloister alike, the promise of spiritual achievement.

Devamata
Ananda-Ashrama,
La Crescenta, California, U.S.A.
June, 1931

Address given by Sister Devamata at the opening of the Bangalore monastery in 1909

The opening of a Math in India is a common occurrence, and perhaps on that account, makes little impression on the unthinking mind. But as for myself, I am not accustomed to that mode of thought. I believe that when the key turns on that door and the door opens, a new era begins for Bangalore and for all the world. Swami Vivekananda was the sole living word of Sri Ramakrishna sounding about the whole world, and though he was alone in his work, yet today we are hearing from the very heart of Africa, from the farther islands of the Pacific and from the very northern parts of Europe, the appreciation of Ramakrishna Mission as the living word of Swami Vivekananda. In it he has embodied all his plans, all his hopes and all his methods of work for India and the rest of the world. If you read his rules and ideas as he formulated them, you will find in them the summary of all his lectures, the incarnation of the very life and soul of humanity. This epitome marks, as it were, the very embodiment of Swami Vivekananda.

When that simple unknown sannyasin came down from the North with his kamandalu in his hands, did any of you know that a new dawn was appearing in the spiritual world; did any of you know him throughout all those years of wandering in the North before he came to the South? Did you know then that there was a smoldering fire in him which was destined to grow into a flash in Chicago and bring new light to the world, of which you never dreamt before?

You know that in the physical world, the period of parturition is great just in proportion as the manifestation of life is high. In the physical world we get quick results. But in social and political movements the forces are high and the results are very slow. So also, in the spiritual world where the growth is organic, that growth is necessarily slower still, just as a tree that has to bear the brunt of the strong wind must necessarily have its roots deep into the earth to resist it. And so this Math stands today as the result of silent and unknown work on the part of some of Swami Vivekananda's children, who have lived here amongst you, almost unperceived by you, and yet today, you have this sign of visible spiritual development. Silent as it is, you might hope to obtain mighty results therefrom.

I know that there are some amongst you who would have wished, that before the Math was built there could have been a workshop or an Industrial school. But, my friends, I have had more experience perhaps in the world about the practicality of such things than you, and I have found that the good works in the world are divided into two ways like this. Suppose one works in a prison-house, concerned to make prisoners comfortable, to give them soft beds, wholesome food and proper recreation; while another says what does it matter what people say, or what the prisoners eat; these people in prison, come let us break it open and take the prisoners out. This course alone will give them happiness. The fact is, we never even dream that we are in prison, and that is why today so many Industrial schools, asylums for the aged and the widows are established. But it was the glory of the sons of India that they said, they would rather sleep on the ground and go semi-naked about the streets and face starvation than think of obtaining spiritual freedom by any other means but renunciation. That is the reason why although India is so low, she yet stands high on the spiritual platform, and although she is weak, she has yet a spiritual power that is supremely worthy of her.

I have lived two-thirds of my life in a country where people eat three hearty meals a day and yet go hungry, sleep on soft beds and yet find no rest; they live in palaces and yet feel themselves homeless. Why? Because they are becoming more and more slaves to Mammon, and that spirit is driving them day and night by false deception, bringing them no happiness. But you, here in India, are given to spirituality, a spirituality which gives food to feed the soul and a place where the soul can rest in peace. You are therefore quite at home with it, and can you give it away for Mammon? No.

Do not lose this opportunity. Certainly, there was no one in our times who ever understood the message of God but Swami Vivekananda. There was never any one who knew the needs of modern India better than he. There was never a greater spiritual teacher and a lover of mankind than he. And this is his work. Do not say that it is hard for any one to understand the mission of Vivekananda, and that on this account you cannot work with him. Swami Vivekananda was no doubt so mighty that one man cannot understand him. But one man may have grasped something of Vivekananda, and another may have understood something of him also. So let us stand together and work together; and if you all thus stand together striving shoulder to shoulder to realize those ideals which he has set before us, then, I say, the result of our conjoint labor here will be prodigious, and Bangalore will be rendered a very great city. You may not just quite realize the effect of this work, because it is only the dawn that is before your eyes. But I can tell you that when the first shining rays of divine light dispel the long night of the foolish imitation of European habits and awaken you to a sense of your own self-consciousness and strength, then you will arise and realize what has really been achieved by you and what you are capable of doing.

Glory yourselves on the fact that you have made a home for the children of Swami Vivekananda and Sri Ramakrishna, not only for the children who speak your language and are used to your ways and customs, but the children of all the world. And then truly will it be a new day when the people from the West, North and South will gather together here and joining hands with you will sing, perhaps in different languages and in different ways, the glory of the one God, and will work together for the united common family of humanity. When this stage is reached and only then, the spirit of Swami Vivekananda will be a perfect rest and will live in the eternal abode of that divine Guru Sri Ramakrishna, and you yourselves will be sharing in the labors, the glory and the joy that is his in his eternal rest.

From: *A Spiritual Centre Blossoms: Ramakrishna Math, Bangalore First 100 years—1904-2004*

Devamata's foreword to *Book of Daily Thoughts and Prayers* by Swami Paramananda

There are moments when the spirit is mute and powerless to give utterance to its interior yearning. It feels the need of a vibrant word to rouse it from its numbness and voice the voiceless aspiration. Hence attempts to provide, in one form or another, daily thoughts for the day's round are coincident with the rising of the religious consciousness. The ancient Forest-Books or Upanishads of the Vedic period were but the accumulated effort of great sages to help those who surrounded them in their woodland hermitage, to meet the daily problem with triumphant heart. The medieval breviaries and manuals of devotion were written or compiled to the same end. The present volume is another contribution to this daily sacrament of prayer and holy thought.

The idea of preparing it is not of recent conception. As far back as 1912 Swami Paramananda wrote me from Switzerland: "Other day I was thinking a little of the next book—(from your letters). Can't we call it 'A Book of Daily Thoughts and Prayers'? what do you think of it?" I had written to him that the idea had come to me to gather from his later letters and certain notes of his teaching material for a companion volume to the *Path of Devotion*, made up from earlier letters. It was not possible, at the time, to carry out his new suggestion, as the book under preparation was practically ready for press when the suggestion came; but the intention remained with me and at last has assumed definite form.

The present volume has lost nothing through the delay, for now it has a much richer store to draw upon. From year to year, I have garnered stray thoughts jotted down on scraps of paper lying on the Swami's desk or work table, or tucked in some book. I have noted vital sayings and set aside countless passages from letters. All the material used, except the lines taken from the Swami's poems, has been drawn from unpublished sources; chiefly from familiar instructions given to his household at the morning or evening meal; or from fragments of conversations, written down with groping hand and unseeing eye on the terrace of the Ashrama in the moonlight, or by the flicker of a hearth-fire, or by the dim flame of a far-away candle. The prayers were caught with the same stealthy silent pencil at the moment of their utterance.

They sound in consequence the more living note of spoken supplication. The quotations from the Scriptures are from the Swami's translations.

Coming from such intimate sources, the words which follow possess special helpfulness in the intimate inward strivings of each day. They have been classified and arranged in consecutive and cumulative sequence. The thought is carried forward from day to day, so that at the end of a month a new and defined impression will be made on the character. Each day brings its salient thought to be held through the waking hours in continuous mindfulness; a brief lesson amplifies this and imbeds it more deeply in the consciousness; a prayer feeds and strengthens the natural upward-reaching devotional aspirations of the heart.

A few lines from the Swami's sacred and illumined poems are given as a daily exercise in memorizing. Memorizing is one of the most productive of spiritual practices. It provides a rich inner library to which one can turn in the moment of emptiness or distress. A single line called up in memory will sometimes turn the thought into an entirely fresh and wholesome channel. Thus on each page will be found food for all the faculties of the aspiring spirit.

The Swami's words lend themselves with peculiar aptitude to a work of this nature. His sentences have the focused, shining quality of a finely-cut gem which requires no embellishment or ornate setting. They stir the higher, holier impulses of the soul and impel to consecrated living. They carry forward by their inherent vitality and strength. The book calls for no other introduction than itself. With its tender counsel and ringing appeal it will find its way, by the force of its spiritual power, into the heart and sanctuary of every seeker whose hand it reaches.

Devamata
Ananda-Ashrama,
April, 1926.

Appendix C

END NOTES

Chapter One Endnotes
Vivekananda and New York Vedanta Society

1. Marie Louise Burke, *Swami Vivekananda in the West, New Discoveries* (ND) (Mayavati, India: Advaita Ashrama, 1985), 3rd ed., 3:12.

2. Swami Tathagatananda, *Vedanta Society of New York, A Brief Survey* (VSNY) (New York: The Vedanta Society of New York, 2000), 99.

3. Marie Louise Burke, ND, 3rd ed., 1985, 3:63.

4. Sister Devamata, "Memories of India and Indians," *Prabuddha Bharata* (PB) 37, May 1932, No. 5, 242. Source: *Prabuddha Bharata or Awakened India*, 1896-2009, Archival Disc.

5. Sister Devamata, "Memories of India and Indians," PB, April 1932, No. 4, 190. Archival Disc.

6. Ibid.

7. Ibid.

8. Ibid., 190–191.

9. Ibid., 191.

10. Ibid.

11. "Society News," *Cincinnati Commercial Gazette*, June 26, 1895, 4. https://newspaperarchive.com/other-articles-clipping-jun-26-1895-2188109/

12. Marie Louise Burke, ND, 3:341–342.

13. Marie Louise Burke, ND, 3: 458.

14. *Reminiscences of Swami Vivekananda, By His Eastern and Western Admirers* (REM) (Mayavati: Advaita Ashrama, 1983), 3rd ed., 126–127.

15. REM, 3rd ed., 123–124.

16. Marie Louise Burke, ND, 3:528.

17. Sister Devamata, PB, April 1932, No. 4, 192.

18. Ibid.

19. Gopal Stavig, *Western Admirers of Ramakrishna and His Disciples* (WA) (Mayavati: Advaita Ashrama, 2010), 719.

20. Sister Devamata, "Memories of India and Indians," PB, No. 6, June 1932, 304. Archival Disc.

21. The *Brahmavadin* 7, December 7, 1901, No. 2, 113–114. Source: Brahmavadin Digitalized Archives, 1895–1914.

22. Marie Louise Burke, ND, 3:529.

23. Swami Tathagatananda, VSNY, 161.

Chapter Two Endnotes
Laura's Family Background

1. "William Glenn, A Widely-Known Business Man of Cincinnati," *The Indianapolis Journal*, July 18, 1887, 2.

2. Cincinnati History Library and Archives of the Cincinnati Museum Center, WILLIAM GLENN WILL_MSS1071, Box 1, Ebersole Family Papers, Folder 6. pdf.

3. Mrs. T. L. Tomkinson, *Twenty Years' History of the Woman's Home Missionary Society of the Methodist Episcopal Church, 1880–1900* (Cincinnati: Missionary Society of the Methodist Episcopal Church, 1903), 244.

4. Source Citation: Year: 1860; Census Place; Cincinnati, Hamilton, Ohio; Roll: M653_1023; Page: 192; Family History Liberty Film: 805023. Source Information: Ancestry.com. 1860 U.S. Federal Census [database on line]. Provo, UT, USA.

5. Source Citation: Year: 1870; Census Place: Cincinnati, Hamilton, Ohio; Roll: M590_1207; Page: 37A; Family History Library Film: 552706. Source Information: Ancestry.com. 1870 U.S. Federal Census [database on line]. Provo, UT, USA.

6. "A Great Fire Causes a Loss of Over $300,000," *Xenia Daily Gazette*, January 27, 1890, 1.

7. "Tells Why His Buildings Soar Skyward," *Commercial Gazette*, May 24, 1892, 6.

8. "Fortunes of Vast Proportions Possessed by many Cincinnatians: The Queen City Has Two Score of Millionaires," *Cincinnati Enquirer*, May 5, 1895, 13.

9. "After Costing Its Backers Half a Million Dollars," *Cincinnati Enquirer*, June 16, 1896, 4.

10. "James Glenn Falls Victim to Paralysis," *Cincinnati Enquirer*, November 27,1911.

11. Source Citation: Will Records 1792-1918: Probate Place: Hamilton, Ohio Wills Vol 117-119, 1911-1912. Source Info: Ancestry.com. Ohio, Wills and Probate Records, 1786-1998 [database on line]. Provo, UT, USA: Ancestry.com Operation, Inc., 2015.

12. "Wesleyan's Daughters," *Cincinnati Enquirer*, November 20, 1882, 4.

13. Ibid.

14. "Mr. and Mrs. J. M. Glenn Entertain," In Society, *Cincinnati Enquirer*, December 12, 1890, 4. Also *Cincinnati Enquirer*, December 14, 1890, 21.

15. "Yacht 'Mystery' of New Haven Yacht Club," *New Haven Daily Morning Journal and Courier*, New Haven, Connecticut, August 24, 1882, 8.

16. Letters of Elizabeth Glenn, found in a box containing Glenn family memorabilia, in the care of Laura's great-great niece, S.M. Newell.

17. Ibid.

18. National Archives and Records Administration (NARA); Washington D.C., Roll#: 35; Volume#: Volume 064: Germany. Source Information: Ancestry.com. U.S. Passport Application, 1795-1925 [database on-line], Lehi, UT, USA: Ancestry.com, Operation, Inc., 2007.

19. "FOUR Working Girls' Clubs Already in Cincinnati and a Fifth to be Formed," *Cincinnati Enquirer*, March 14, 1895, 8.

20. Barbara Welter, *Dimity Convictions: The American Women of the Nineteenth Century* (Athens: Ohio University Press, 1976), 16.

21. Susan Harris Smith and Melanie Dawson, ed., *The American 1890s: A Cultural Reader* (Durham and London: Duke University Press, 2000), 192.

22. Source Citation: Year: 1860; Census Place: Circleville, Pickaway, Ohio; Roll: M653_1023; Page: 192; Family History Library Film 805023. Source Information: Ancestry.com 1860 U.S. Federal Census [database on line] Provo, UT, USA.

23. "State Assembly," *The Cleveland Daily Leader*, July 28, 1859, 2.

24. Source Citation: Year: 1880; Census Place: Carthage, Jasper, Missouri; Roll: 694; Page: 480D; Enumeration District: 060. Source Information: Ancestry and the Church of Jesus Christ of Latter-day Saints.com, 1880 U.S. Federal Census [database on line] Lehi, UT, USA.

25. "A Credit Sale," *The Circleville Democrat*, February 26, 1864. Information provided by the Pickaway County Historical Society and Genealogical Library.

26. Ancestry.com. New York, New York, *Extracted Death Index* 1862–1948 [database on line], Provo , UT, USA: Ancestry.com. Original Source: Index to New York City Deaths 1862–1948. Indices prepared by the Italian Genealogical Group and the German Genealogy Group, and used with permission of the New York City Department of Records/Municipal Archives.

Chapter Three Endnotes
Laura's Formal Education

1. *Bartholomew English and Classical School, First Annual Catalogue* (Cincinnati: Aldine Printing Works, 1876), 7–14.

2. John Brough Shotwell, *A History of the Schools of Cincinnati* (Cincinnati: The School Life Company, 1902), 432–433.

3. Vassar College, *Letters Home: Social Life at Vassar* 1845–1880. http://digitallibrary.vassar.edu/collections/newspaper-archives, Click Browse Digital Library Collections, By Creator.

4. Vassar College, *Sixteenth Annual Catalogue of the Officers and Students of Vassar College* [SAC](Poughkeepsie: Vassar College, 1881), 44. http://digitallibrary.vassar.edu/collections/newspaper-archives. Choose view all and Vassar Miscellany.

5. Vassar College, *First Annual Catalogue of Officers and Students at Vassar Female College from 1865–1866* [FAC], 1. http://vcencyclopedia.vassar.edu/curriculum encyclopedia.vassar.edu/curriculum

6. Vassar, SAC, 16.

7. Vassar, FAC, 3–4.

8. Ibid., 7–8.

9. Maria Mitchell, *Life Letters and Journals* [LLJ] (United States, 1896), 99–100.

10. Ibid., 98.

11. Ibid., 102.

12. Ibid., 106.

13. Dorothy A. Plum and George B Dowell, *The Great Experiment, A Chronicle of Vassar* (Poughkeepsie, NY: Vassar College, 1961), 19.

14. Ann Wyman (Southward) Diary 1878–1880, Evan James transcriber, Vassar College, 65–67. Select student scrap books. http://digitallibrary.vassar.edu/islandora/season/Laura%20glenn?type=dismax Choose Browse Digital Library, by Title, Wyman.

15. Ibid., 65–67.

16. Ibid., 66.

17. Ibid., 71.

18. Vassar College, "Home Matters," *Vassar Miscellany* 10, No. 5, February 1, 1881, 251. http://digitallibrary.vassar.edu/collections/newspaper-archives Choose: Vassar Miscellany.

19. Vassar College, "Home Matters," *Vassar Miscellany* 10, No. 7, April 1, 1881, 352. http://digitallibrary.vassar.edu/collections/newspaper-archives Choose: Vassar Miscellany

20. "Beauty High Up: Vassar Girls on Summit Mountain", *The Kingston Daily Freeman*, May 20, 1881. http://www.Fultonhistory.com

21. Vassar College, "Personals," *Vassar Miscellany* 11, July 1, 1882, 533. http://digitallibrary.vassar.edu/collections/newspaper-archives

22. Vassar College, Vassar College Encyclopedia. http://vcencyclopedia.vassar.edu/faculty/original-faculty. Choose Marie Mitchell

23. "Vine Street Opera House," *Cincinnati Enquirer*, July 9, 1882, 12.

24. Alumni Association of Vassar College, Biographical File Box #5.

Chapter Four Endnotes
Laura's Family: Travels Abroad

1. Christopher Endy, "Travel and World Power: Americans in Europe 1890-1917," as an article in *Diplomatic History 22* (Oxford: Oxford University Press, Fall 1998), 565–594. http://www.jstor.org/staple/24913627

2. Cora Hamilton Bell, personal journal entry, from Family Memorabilia Box held by S.M. Newell, Cora's great-great-niece.

3. Sister Devamata, *Days in An Indian Monastery* (Cohasset, MA: Vedanta Centre, 1975), 3rd ed., 83.

4. Sister Devamata, "The Living Presence," *Vedanta Kesari - Sri Ramakrisna Centenary* Issue 22, No.10 and 11, February-March 1936, 404. Source: Digitized Archives, 1914–2014.

5. Vassar College, "Personals," *The Vassar Miscellany* 17, No. 1, October 1, 1887. www.newspaperarchives.vassar.edu. Choose Vassar Miscellany, 39.

6. Sister Devamata, introduction to *Sri Ramakrishna and Saint Francis of Assisi* (La Crescenta, California: Ananda Ashrama, 1935), 9–10.

7. Sister Devamata, "Memories of India and Indians," *Prabuddha Bharata* 37, No. 12, December 1932, 607. Source: Digitized Archives 1896–2009.

8. Mary Smart and E. Adina Gordon, *Flight of Fame, The Life and Art of Frederick MacMonnies 1863–1937* (Madison, Connecticut: Sound View Press, 1996), 96.

9. Nina Lubbren, Kathleen Pyne, Margaret Werth, *Impressionistic Giverny; A Colony of Artists, 1885–1915*, Katherine Bourguignon, ed. (Chicago: Terra Foundation for American Arts, 2007), 207.

10. Mary Smart and El Adina Gordon, *Flight of Fame, The Life and Art of Frederick MacMonnies, 1863–1937*, 104–105.

11. "Chicago Letter," *The Critic*, April 22, 1893, 261.

12. Mary Smart and E. Adina Gordon, *Flight of Fame*, introduction.

13. *The Life of Swami Vivekananda by his Eastern and Western Disciples* (Mayavati, India: Advaita Ashram, 1979), 5th ed., 400.

14. "Stained-Glass for Cincinnati," Fine Arts, *The Critic* 19, No. 582, April 15, 1893, 243. www.google.com/books/edition/

15. "Women Translators and Their Meager Rewards," *Saturday Evening Mail*, Terra Haute, Indiana, September 17, 1898, 2.

16. Christopher Endy, "Travel and World Power: Americans in Europe 1890–1917," 578. http://www.jstor.org/staple/24913627.

17. Helen Glenn Ward Marx, personal journal entry, from Family Memorabilia Box held by S.M. Newell, the great-great grandchild of Helen.

18. Mary Smart, *Flight of Fame*, 191.

19. Sister Devamata, "Robert Browning and the Vedanta," *The Message of the East* 5, No. 2, February 1916, 25.

20. "Longcroft: A House and Garden at Mamaroneck, N.Y.," *House and Garden* 4, No. 5, November 1903, 222–226.

21. Barr Ferree, ed., *Yearbook of the Art Societies of New York, 1898–1899* (New York: Leonard Scott Publication, Co., 1899). Googlebooks.

22. "The New Theater and What It Means to Dramatic Arts," *Brooklyn Daily Eagle*, November 27, 1910, 6.

Chapter Five Endnotes
Spiritual Training under Swami Abhedananda

1. Swami Tathagatananda, *The Vedanta Society of New York, A Brief Survey* (VSNY) (New York City: Vedanta Society, 2000), 142.

2. "Vedanta Work," *Brahmavadin* 7, No. 2, December 1901, 115. Source: Digitized Archives, 1895–1914.

3. Sister Devamata, "The Living Presence," *Vedanta Kesari – Sri Ramakrishna Centenary Issue 22*, No. 10 and 11, February and March 1936, 399. Source: Digitized Archives 1914–2014.

4. Ibid., 400.

5. Sister Devamata, "The Living Presence," *Vedanta Kesari*, February-March 1936, 400.

6. "Vedanta Works," *Brahmavadin* 8, No. 3, March 1903, p.188. Source: Digital Archives.

7. Tathagatananda, VSNY, 146.

8. Mary LePage (Sister Shivani), *Swami Abhedananda in America* (SAA) (Calcutta, India: Ramakrishna Vedanta Math, 1958), 2nd ed., 108. First edition title: *The Apostle of Monism*.

9. Mary Le Page, SAA, 112.

10. Sister Devamata, "The Living Presence," *Vedanta Kesari*, February-March 1936, 399–402.

11. Ibid., 401.

12. Ibid.

13. Ibid., 401–402.

14. Ibid., 407.

15. Ibid., 402.

16. Ibid.

17. Ibid., 399–400.

18. Swami Saradananda, *Sri Ramakrishna and His Divine Play*, translated by Swami Chetanananda (St. Louis, MO: Vedanta Society of St. Louis, 2003), 411.

19. Sister Devamata, "Memories of India and Indians," *Prabuddha Bharata* (PB) 37, No. 5, May 1932, 244.

20. Tathagatananda, VSNY, 168

21. Mary LePage, SAA, 234.

22. "Prabuddha Bharata—100 Years Ago," *Prabuddha Bharata* 109, No. 2, February 2004, 17.

23. "Vedanta and the Swami in Manhatten," *Brahmavadin* 10, No. 6, June 1905, 344–348.

24. Mary LePage, SAA, 115.

25. Gopal Stavig, *Western Admirers of Ramakrishna and His Disciples* (WA) (Kolkata: Advaita Ashrama, 2010), 737.

26. Sarah Ann Levinsky, *A Bridge of Dreams* (BD) (West Stockbridge, MA: The Lindisfarne Press, 1984), 89–90.

27. Ibid.

28. Tathagatananda, VSNY, 162.

29. Stavig, WA, 318.

30. Swami Abhedananda, Preface of *Memoirs of Ramakrishna* (Calcutta, India: Ramakrishna Vedanta Math, 1967), 3rd ed.

31. *Vedanta Monthly Bulletin*, Vol 3, April 1907–1908, 208.

32. Mary LePage, SAA, 175.

33. *Vedanta Monthly Bulletin*, Vol. 3, April 1907–March 1908, 15.

34. Mary LePage, SAA, 176.

35. Swami Chetanananda, *God Lived With Them* (GLT) (St. Louis, MO: Vedanta Society of St. Louis, 1997), 470.

36. Tathagatananda, VSNY, 276.

37. "Prabuddha Bharata—100 Years Ago," *Prabuddha Bharata* 109, No. 2, February 2004, 17.

38. Sarah Ann Levinsky, BD, 104.

39. Ibid., 107-109

40. Ibid., 109.

41. Amrita M Salm and July Howe Hayes, *The Inspired Life of Sarah Ellen Waldo* (Kolkata, India: Advaita Ashrama, 2019), 356-357.

42. Ibid.

43. Abhedananda, CWSA, Vol. 10, 133.

44. "News and Notes," *Vedanta Monthly Bulletin* 3, No. 8, November 1907, 145-146. Google Books, free read.

45. Ibid.

46. Sister Devamata, *Swami Paramananda and His Work* (La Crescenta, CA: Ananda Ashrama, 1926), 89-90.

47. Ibid.

48. Sara Ann Levinsky, BD, 259.

49. Sister Devamata, "Memories of India and Indians," *Prabuddha Bharata* (PB) 37, No.6, June 1932, 302.

50. Ibid.

51. Ibid.

52. Ibid., 303.

53. Swami Paramananda, Foreword to *Path of Devotion* (Mylapore, India: Sri Ramakrishna Math, 1974).

54. Ibid.

55. "The Path of Devotion," *Vedanta Monthly Bulletin* 3, No. 11, February 1908, 193.

56. Sarah Ann Levinsky, BD, 139.

57. Swami Paramananda, *The Way of Peace and Blessedness*, 3rd ed. (Cohasset, MA: Vedanta Centre, 1961), Dedication of the book.

58. Sister Devamata, PB, June 1932, 303.

59. *Complete Works of Swami Ramakrishnananda* (CWSR), Vol.3 (Mylapore, Chennai, India: Sri Ramakrishna Math, 2012), 32.

60. Sarah Ann Levinsky, BD, 140

Chapter Six Endnotes
Madras

1. Sister Devamata, *Days in an Indian Monastery* (*Days*), 3rd ed. (Cohasset, MA: Vedanta Centre, 1975), 38.

2. Ibid., 211.

3. Ibid., 148.

4. Srimata Sudha Puri, compiler and editor, *Swami Paramananda's Life and Work: A Chronology 1884–1940*, (Cohasset MA: Vedanta Centre, 2019), 71. Unpublished, Cohasset Archives.

5. Swami Tapasyananda, *Swami Ramakrishnananda, The Apostle of Sri Ramakrishna in the South* (ARS) (Madras, India: Sri Ramakrishna Math, Madras, 1972), 111.

6. *Swami Ramakrishnananda As We Saw Him, Reminiscences of Monastic and Lay Devotees* (RMD) (Mylapore, Chennai: Sri Ramakrishna Math, 2012), 213.

7. Sister Devamata, *Days*, 65.

8. *Swami Ramakrishnananda As We Saw Him* (RMD), 21.

9. Sister Devamata, *Days*, 97.

10. Ibid., 42

11. Ibid., 51–52.

12. Ibid., 61–68.

13. Sister Devamata, In Foreword to *Days in an Indian Monastery*

14. Sister Devamata, *Days*, 146.

15. *Complete Works of Swami Ramakrisnananda* (CWSR) (Mylapore, Chennai: Sri Ramakrishna Math, 2012), Vol. 3, 110.

16. Srimata Sudha Puri, compiler, and editor, *Swami Paramananda's Life and Work: A Chronology 1884–1940* (SPC) (Cohasset, MA: Vedanta Centre, 2019), 75. Unpublished.

17. Sister Devamata, *Days*, 150.

18. Sister Devamata, "Memories of India and Indians," *Prabuddha Bharata* 6, Vol. 37, June 1932, 303. Source: *Prabuddha Bharata (Awakened India) 1896–2009*, Digitized disc.

19. Sister Devamata, *Days*, 152.

20. Ibid.

21. Ibid., 159.

22. Ibid., 161.

23. Ibid., 175.

24. Primary source: Swami Chetanananda translator, *Swami Brahmananda Smritikatha*, Ubodhan Karyalaya, 2003, 29. Secondary Source: H. Mukerjee, "Sister Devamata," *Bulletin of the Ramakrishna Mission Institute of Culture*, September 2018.

25. Foreword of *Spiritual Teachings of Swami Brahmananda*, 2nd ed. (Mylapore, Madras: Sri Ramakrishna Math, 1933).

26. *A Spiritual Centre Blossoms: Ramakrishna Math Bangalore First 100 years—1904-2004* (SCB) (Bangalore, India: Sri Ramakrishna Math, 2014), 42.

27. Ibid., 46.

28. Ibid., 49.

29. Sarah Ann Levinsky, *Bridge of Dreams*, 113.

Chapter Seven Endnotes
Calcutta, India 1908

1. Sister Devamata, *Days In An Indian Monastery*, 3rd ed., 274.

2. Sankari Prasad Basu editor, *Letters of Sister Nivedita* (LSN) (Calcutta, India: Nababharat Publishers, 1982), Volume 2, 987.

3. Sister Devamata, *Days*, 213-14.

4. Ibid.

5. Ibid., 215.

6. Swami Chetanananda, *Sri Sarada Devi and Her Divine Play* (SSD) (St. Louis, MO: Vedanta Society of St. Louis, 2015), 225.

7. Sister Devamata, *Days*, 225-26.

8. Sister Devamata, "Memories of India and Indians (Yogin Ma)," *Prabuddha Bharata* 37, No. 12, December 1932, 457-58. Source: *Prabuddha Bharata, 1896-2009*, Archival Disc.

9. Ibid.

10. Pravrajika Prabuddhaprana, *Saint Sara, The Life of Sara Chapman Bull* (Dakshineswar, Calcutta: Sri Sarada Math, 2002), 1st ed., 477.

11. Amrita Salm and Judy Howe Hayes, *The Inspired Life of Sarah Ellen Waldo* (Kolkata, India: Advaita Ashrama, 2019), 357.

12. Sara Ann Levinsky, *A Bridge of Dreams* (BD) (West Stockbridge, MA: The Lindisfarne Press, 1984), 141.

13. Sister Devamata, *Days*, 227.

14. Ibid., 228–29.

15. Sister Devamata, Dedication of *The Open Portal* (La Crescenta, CA: Ananda Ashrama, 1929).

16. Sister Devamata, Introduction to *Sri Ramakrishna and Saint Francis of Assisi* (RSF) (La Crescenta, CA: Ananda Ashrama, 1935), 9–10.

17. Sister Nivedita, *Kali the Mother* (Calcutta, India: Nabajiban Press, 1992), 6th ed., 58–59.

18. Sister Devamata, *Days*, 245.

19. Sister Devamata, "Memories of India and Indians (Latu Maharaj)," *Prabuddha Bharata* 37, No. 11, November 1932, 506. Source: *Prabuddha Bharata, 1896-2009*, Archival Disc.

20. Sister Devamata, *Days*, 262.

21. Shankara Prasad Basu, LSN, Vol. 2, 1003.

22. Sister Devamata, *Days*, 215.

23. Ibid., 162.

24. Sara Ann Levinsky, BD, 141.

25. Sister Devamata, *Days*, 72.

26. Ibid., 76.

27. Shankara Prasad Basu, LSN, Vol. 2, 988.

28. "Sister Devamata (1867–1942)," Written material on Devamata from the Cohasset Archives.

29. Sister Devamata, *Swami Ramakrishnananda As We Saw Him* (RMD) (Mylapore, Chennai: Sri Ramakrishna Math, 2012), 197.

30. "Sister Devamata (1867–1941)," Written material on Devamata from the Cohasset Archives.

31. Sister Devamata, Foreword to *Sri Ramakrishna and His Disciples* (Cohasset, MA: Vedanta Centre, 2005), 2nd ed.

32. *Complete Works of Swami Ramakrishnananda* (CWSR) (Mylapore, Chennai: Sri Ramakrishna Math, 2012), Vol. 3, 36.

33. Ibid., 35.

34. Sister Devamata, Introduction to *Sri Ramakrishna and Saint Francis of Assisi* (RSF) (La Crescenta, CA: Ananda Ashrama, 1935), 9–10.

Chapter Eight Endnotes
The First Centers

1. Holy Mother Sarada Devi, letter to Devamata, November 3, 1909. Archives of Cohasset Vedanta Centre, MA, File: Letters of Holy Mother to Devamata.

2. Srimata Sudha Puri, compiler and editor, *Swami Paramananda's Life and Work: A Chronology 1884–1940* (SPC) (Cohasset, MA: Vedanta Centre, 2019), 109. Cohasset Archives.

3. "Indian Swami in Washington Teaching Universal Brotherhood of Man," *Washington Sunday Star*, June 16, 1910, 56.

4. "The Heathen Invasion," *The Hampton-Columbian Magazine*, October 1911, 400–411.

5. Sara Ann Levinsky, *A Bridge of Dreams* (West Stockbridge, MA: Lindisfarne Press, 1984), 162.

6. Srimata Sudha Puri, SPC, 128.

7. Ibid., 111.

8. "Sanitation Needs of India," *Washington Times*, April 17, 1915, 8.

9. "Real Estate Market," *The Christian Science Monitor*, January 20, 1914, 19. Fultonhistory.com

10. "Real Estate Market," *The Christian Science Monitor*, June 23, 1914, 19. Fultonhistory.com

11. Sister Devamata, *Swami Paramananda and His Work* (SPW) (La Crescenta, CA: Ananda Ashrama, 1926), 184.

12. *Message of the East*, Vedanta Centre, Boston, MA, Vol. 5, January to December 1916.

13. Sara Ann Levinsky, *A Bridge of Dreams*, 211.

14. Sister Devamata, SPW, 200.

15. Ibid., 188.

16. Srimata Sudha Puri, SPC, 312.

17. Sara Ann Levinsky, *A Bridge of Dreams*, 184.

18. Letter of Sister Christine, Cohasset Vedanta Centre Archives, Cohasset, MA.

19. Srimata Sudha Puri, SPC, 266-308.

20. Sister Daya, *The Guru and the Disciple* (TGD) (Cohasset MA: Vedanta Centre, 1976), 32.

21. Ibid., 120.

22. Ibid., 13-14.

23. Ibid.

24. Ibid.

25. Sarah Ann Levinsky, *A Bridge of Dreams*, 256.

26. Ibid., 239.

27. Swami Paramananda, Letter to Sister Devamata. September 13th, 1920. Archives of Cohasset Vedanta Centre, MA, File: Paramananda letters to Devamata.

28. Sarah Ann Levinsky, *A Bridge of Dreams*, 223.

29. Ibid., 230-231.

Chapter Nine Endnotes
Years of Rapid Growth

1. Sara Ann Levinsky, *A Bridge of Dreams* (BD) (West Stockbridge, MA: Lindisfarne Press, 1984), 258.

2. Ibid., 265.

3. Ibid., 266.

4. Sister Devamata, *Swami Paramananda and His Work* (SPW1) (La Crescenta, CA: Ananda Ashrama, 1926), Vol 1, 19.

5. Srimata Sudha Puri, compiler and editor, *Swami Paramananda's Life and Work: A Chronology 1884-1940* (SPC) (Cohasset, MA: Vedanta Centre, 2019), 324. (unpublished).

6. Sister Devamata, SPW1, 19–20.

7. Srimata Sudha Puri, SPC, 318.

8. Swami Shivananda, Letter to Devamata dated March 20, 1924 from the Ramakrishna Mission, Belur. Cohasset Archives, File: Letters from India.

9. "Report," *The Message of the East*, May 1923, No. 5, Vol 12, 116–17. Kessinger's Legacy Reprints.

10. Sister Devamata, SPW1, Vol 1, 264.

11. Ibid., 268.

12. Sara Ann Levinsky, BD, 281.

13. "Ananda Ashrama," *The Message of the East,* May 1923, No.5, Vol 12, 116-17. Kessinger's Legacy Reprints.

14. Sara Ann Levinsky, BD, 291.

15. Ibid., 297.

16. Ibid., 308.

17. Swami Paramananda, *Book of Daily Thoughts and Prayers* (Foreword) (Cohasset, MA: Vedanta Centre, 2016), 6th edition.

18. Sister Devamata, SPW1, 320.

19. Sister Devamata, *Swami Paramananda: Mystic, Poet and Teacher* (Cohasset, MA: Vedanta Centre Publishers, 2016), 2nd ed., Dedication page.

20. Sister Devamata, *Swami Paramananda and His Work* (SPW2) (La Crescenta, CA: Ananda Ashrama, 1941), Vol. 2, 57.

21. Ibid., 60.

22. Sara Ann Levinsky, BD, 327.

23. Srimata Sudha Puri, SPC, 447.

24. *Tree of Shelter*, Commemorative Issue (Cohasset, MA: Vedanta Centre, 1979), 42.

25. Ibid., 44.

26. Sister Devamata, SPW2, Vol 2, 140.

27. Sara Ann Levinsky, BD, 430.

28. Ibid., 435.

29. Srimata Sudha Puri, SPC, 545.

30. Ibid., 568.

31. Sister Devamata, *The Open Portal* (La Crescenta, CA: Ananda Ashrama, 1929), 45.

Chapter Ten Endnotes
Author

1. Editorial comment, "Consciousness and Character," *Vedanta Kesari*, August 1931, Vol. 18, No. 4, 136.

2. S.T. Clover, Press Notice found in appendix of *The Habit of Happiness* (La Crescenta, CA; Ananda Ashrama, 1930).

3. Sister Devamata, *The Habit of Happiness*, 20.

4. Sister Devamata, *My Song Garden* (La Crescenta, CA; Ananda Ashrama, 1930), in foreword of book.

5. Sara Ann Levensky, *Bridge of Dreams*, 203.

6. Sister Devamata, "The Power of a Holy Life," *Message of the East Monthly*, October 1934, Vol. 23, No. 8, 238.

7. Sister Devamata, "Path to Realization," *Message of the East Quarterly*, July, August, September 1939, Vol 28, No. 3, 150.

8. Swami Shivananda, letter to Sister Devamata, May 30,1931, in box labeled 'Letters from Abroad to Sister Devamata,' Cohasset Archives.

9. Sister Devamata, "The Living Presence," (TLP) *Vedanta Kesari* (Sri Ramakrishna Centenary Issue), Vol 22, February and March 1936, 400.

10. Ibid., 403.

11. Ibid., 404.

12. Sister Devamata, *The Companionship of Pain* (La Crescenta, CA; Ananda Ashrama, 1934), available through Cohasset Archives.

13. Sister Devamata, "Power of Music," Lecture of Devamata available through Cohasset Archives.

14. Maud Keck, author of foreword to *The Companionship of Pain*.

15. Sister Devamata, Letter to Sister Daya, Correspondence File, Cohasset Archives.

16. Sara Ann Levensky, BD, p. 493–494.

17. Editorial comment to article, "The Living Presence," *Vedanta Kesari*, Volume 22, February and March 1936, 398.

18. Sister Devamata, TLP, 405.

19. Paramananda, letter to Devamata in Sister Daya's journal found in the Cohasset Archives in box of 'Sisters' Journals.

20. Letter to Devamata in box labeled 'Letters from Abroad to Devamata,' Cohasset Archives.

21. A letter from Madras to Devamata found in a box labeled 'Devamata memorabilia,' at Cohasset Archives.

22. Letter from Ramu (Madras) to Devamata found in box labeled 'Devamata memorabilia,' at Cohasset Archives.

23. Srimata Sudha Puri, compiler and editor, *Swami Paramananda's Life and Work: A Chronology 1884–1940* (SPC), (unpublished), Cohasset Archives, 679.

24. Ibid., 688.

25. Sister Lillian, personal journal found in box labeled 'Sisters' Journals at Cohasset Archives.

26. Proctor Adelaide (1825–1864), "A Lost Chord," information from Google.

27. Devamata, "The Guru Song," *Handbook of Daily Worship*.

28. Sister Amala, personal journal found in box labeled 'Sisters' Journals at Cohasset Archives.

29. Glory Raye, "In Memory of Sister Devamata," *Message of the East Quarterly*, 1943.

30. Marie Louis Burke, *Swami Vivekananda in the West, New Discoveries*, 3:458.

Acknowledgments

Chapter One:

Betty Robinson offered encouragement and information about Devamata throughout the years.

Rev. James F. Lawrence, D. min., Ph.D. Dean of the Center for Swedenborgian Studies at Pacific School of Religion in Berkeley California.

Swami Chetanananda of the St. Louis Vedanta Center for permission to replicate the picture of the emblem of the Ramakrishna Order as envisioned by Vivekananda, given in his pictorial biography entitled *Vivekananda: East meets West*.

Chapter Two:

Rosemary Osterhus was an invaluable online researcher and fellow traveler on the road.

Lisa Raney: Archivist at the Cincinnati Historical Library and Archives of the Cincinnati Museum Center.

Lisa R. Franklin: Administrator for the Franklin Y-DNA Project.

The Pickaway County Historical Society and Genealogical Library sent information on Nelson Franklin. (210 N Court St. Circleville, Ohio 43113)

Steffanie Hanor Burgevin: Burgevin family tree on ancestry.com includes the Glenns. She is the niece, three times removed, of James Glenn.

Manuscripts and Special Collections (MSCC) of New York State Library.

Chapter Three:

Dean Rogers, Special Collections Assistant, in Archives and Special Collections, Vassar College Library. Dean Rogers assisted in research on Vassar's extensive online offerings.

Kathleen Giblin, Associate Registrar, provided Vassar transcripts.

Biographical files from AAVC (Alumnae and Alumni of Vassar College)

Sister Monica Clare, CSJB, Sister Superior of The Community of St. John Baptist.

Adele Marie Ryan, SSM, Sister Superior of the Society of St. Margaret.

Ellie Miller, Archivist Assistant for Archives of the Episcopal Church in Austin, Texas

Chapter Four:
Stuart Smart and Sarah Campbell, son and daughter of Mary Smart, author of *Flight of Fame, the Life of Frederick MacMonnies*. Contacted by phone.

Linda Guest: Historian at the Lyons Public Library, Lyons, New York. Contacted by phone.

S.M. Newell: The great-great granddaughter of James and Elizabeth Glenn and caretaker of the Glenn family memorabilia. To her, we owe a debt of gratitude for her hospitality and help.

Chapters Five through Ten
Srimata Sudha Puri, Compiler and Editor of *Swami Paramananda's Life and Work: A Chronology 1884–1940* an invaluable source of information (unpublished).

M.S. Nanjundiah, author of *A Spiritual Centre Blossoms: Ramakrishna Math, Bangalore First 100 Years—1904-2004*. Permission obtained for the reproduction of Devamata's speech.

Swami Devabhaktananda, Vedanta Centre Cohasset, MA, typed all of Sister Devamata's lectures from the *Message of the East* in preparation for this book. He also supplied the scores of Sister Devamata's music compositions.

Deborah Lang (Devija), archivist at the Vedanta Centre Cohasset, exceedingly helpful in locating information.

Other mentions
Manuscript readers:
  Anna Hourihan, and editor
  Janet Walker, and editor
  Pamela Hoye (Jayanti)
Retouched Photos:
  James Woodward, CA
  Mary Jane Zanelli, Albany, NY
Book and Cover Designer:
  Carolyn Vaughan (Kalyani), St. Louis, MO

Index

Numbers in italics are photographs.
LG=Laura Glenn, DM=Devamata, SP=Paramananda, VK=Vivekananda,
RK=Ramakrishna, AA=Ananda Ashrama

A

Abhedananda, Swami: time with VK, 25–26; LG training, 69–86; foundation stone for Bangalore Monastery, 96; move to country retreat, 98
Achala, Sister (Edna Massman): secretary to SP, 125; journal, 128; 135, hiking at AA, *139;* 140, at AA, *149*
Afsprung, Alice (see Vimala, Sister)
Akhilananda, Swami: assistant to SP, 144; started center in Rhode Island, 145
Amala, Sister (Camilla Victoria Christians): DM's secretary and aide, 125; hiking at AA, *139;* assisted with SP biography, 173; last days of DM, 174
Ananda Ashrama: relics at AA, 114; beginning of, 138–151; hiking the grounds, *139;* Temple of the Universal Spirit, *146;* SP at AA, *148;* sisters & DM at AA, *149;* DM and SP at AA, multiple views *150;* fire and trouble, 155–156; DM outside cloister, *169*
Arnold, Sir Edwin, *The Light of Asia:* 17
Ashokananda, Swami: fire sacrifice for SP, 171

B

Bangalore Math/Monastery: 96–98; at the time of its inauguration, *97, 98*
Bartholomew English and Classical School: LG formal schooling, 41
Belur Monastery: DM visited, 106
Bhagavad Gita: 17, 24, 84
Bodhananda, Swami: assigned to head NY center, 98
Book of Daily Thoughts and Prayers: 9, DM compiled, 143; 144, 160
Bose, Dr. Jagadish Chandra: botanist, 99, 100
Boston Vedanta Centre: established, 119–120; Queensbury St., *122;* photos of Boston centre altars, *134*
Brahmananda, Swami: 83, letter of welcome, 88; visit to Mylapore, 91–95; dedication of new monastery, 96–98; group photo with DM, *97;* 160, DM book about, 170
Brahmavadin: journal of Ramakrishna Order, 9, 22; DM article, 25; 69, 71, 75, 76
Bridge of Dreams, A: SP biography, 136
Broadway Magazine: article about Vedanta in NY, 76

Browning, Robert: DM in Florence, 66; 124, 159
Bull, Sara Chapman: disciple of VK, 17; 22, 98, 100, 103, 106
Burke, Marie Louise: author of *Swami Vivekananda in the West, New Discoveries*, 20, 176

C

Calcutta (Kolkata): 99–108, 111
Carnegie Lyceum Hall: service in memory of VK, 26; lectures at, 71
Chatterji, Mohini M.: translator of Bhagavad Gita, 17
Chicago: VK spoke at Parliament of Religions, 15, 18
Christians, Camilla Victoria (see Amala, Sister)
Christine, Sister: in India with DM, 99; visit to Dakshineswar with DM, 106; visit to Boston VC, 128
Cohasset Vedanta Centre Ashrama: 9, 123, 152–154, SP service on the grounds, and House on the Rock, *153*; dedicated as Ananda Ashrama or little ashrama, 153; construction of community house, *154*; first altar on the mantel, *154*
Columbian Exposition (World's Fair): with Parliament of Religions, 15, 60
Companionship of Pain: DM's last booklet, 159, 165–167

D

Dakshineswar: DM's visits, 104–106, memories of, 131
Daya, Sister (Georgina Frances Walton): platform speaker, 125; wrote *The Guru and the Disciple*, 131–132; at AA, 139–140; took services at Boston, 147; at AA *149*; DM letter to, 167; 171, care of DM, 173–175
Days in an Indian Monastery: written by DM, 9, 11; accounts of DM's time in India, 88; 90, visit to Holy Mother, 101; reminences of Ramakrishnananda, 110; 160
Devamata, Sister: important to Vedanta in the west, 9; meaning of name, 10; first vision, 72; second vision, 74; initiated by SP, 81; 81–84, compiled notes for *Inspired Talks*, 84–85; India, 87; Mother's blessing, 88; teaching of Ramakrishnananda, 89–91; *Inspired Talks* published in India, 92, Bramananda visit to Bangalore, 94–96; spoke at inauguration of the Bangalore Math, 97–99; in Calcutta, 99–108; first visit to Holy Mother, 100; Ramakrishnananda beloved teacher, 109–111; return from India, 113–114; lectures in DC, *116*–118; photo in 1912, *119*; purchase of Queensberry St., 120, *121*, 122; at Boston Centre, *124*, 125, 126, 127, at the piano, *129*; two music scores by DM, *130*; photo with her mother and at Nantucket, *131*; on Revere Beach, *133*; contracted encephalitis, vigil held, 136; long recovery, 137–138; compiled *Book of Daily Thoughts and Prayers* and wrote first volume of *Swami Paramananda and His Work*, 143–144, described Temple, *145–148*; images at AA, *149–151*; first book of poetry, 156; as author, 159–163; 30th anniversary of work in Vedanta, 163–164; spiritual visions, 164–165; accident and pain, 165–167; photo 1938, *169*; correspondences, 169–170; tribute to SP, 171–172; passed from this life, 173–175; "In Memory of Sister

Devamata," 175; exemplar of VK's vision for modern people, 176
Development of the Will: early booklet by DM, 159
Devi, Sri Sarada (see Holy Mother)

E

Emblem of the Ramakrishna Order: *24*

F

Festival of the Divine Mother: AA temple dedicated, 148
Four yogas: VK taught in New York, 16, 20, 21; depicted in emblem of the Ramakrishna Order, *24*; new vision of spiritual life, 79

G

Gayatri Devi, Rev. Mother: minister at Cohasset Vedanta Centre, 9; SP brought her to U.S., 144; conducted classes, 147; services for SP, 171–172
Girish Chandra Ghosh: Bengali playwright and actor, 107
Gladwell, Rhoda May (see Seva, Sister)
Glenn, Laura Franklin: first introduction to VK, 17–19; becomes member of Vedanta Society, 25; early life in Cincinnati, 27–41; formal education, 42–55; travels abroad, 57–68; first mystical experiences, 70–71; head of publishing at NY Vedanta Center, 71–73; compiled the sayings of RK, 73–75; met Paramananda, 77; initiated by SP and given the name Devamata, 81
Goodwin, Josiah John: took notes of SV talks, helped initiate *Brahmavadin*, 21–22
Gospel of Sri Ramakrishna: Adhedananda edited and published in U.S., 78; 110
Greenacre Religious Conference: 16
Guru and the Disciple, The: 131
Guru Song, The: composed by DM, 172

H

Habit of Happiness: DM wrote, 160; 161
Hall of the Universal Brotherhood, New York 17, 18
Holy Mother (Devi, Sri Sarada) DM met, 100–104; Holy Mother in her shrine *100*
"Hymn of Adoration" (poem by DM): 156–157

I

India and Her People: lectures by Abhedananda, 76
"India and Hinduism": first lecture by VK in U.S., 15
Inspired Talks: from notes by Miss Waldo, 17; notes transformed into book by DM, 84–86; 92, 110
Iyengar, C. Ramaswami: right-hand helper to Ramakrishnananda, 88

K

Kali: 105
Kissam, Eliza (see Satya Prana, Sister)

L

La Crescenta, California: 114, 123, purchase of land for AA, 138; 145, 156
Latu Maharaj: disciple of RK, 107; 163
Landsberg, Leon: right-hand man to VK, 16, 17
Letters from India to Devamata: 169

M

MacLeod, Josephine: 24, 100, 106, 109
Madras Publishing House: 95
Mahendranath Gupta (known as "M" and Master Mahasaya): 77, 105, 106
Massman, Edna (see Achala, Sister)
Message of the East: DM editor, 119; 120, 123, 124, 130, 140, 159, 162, 175
Miller, Brother Jack: 126
Mitchell, Maria: 46, 47, 49
Morgan, Marguerite (Mangala): 139
Muller, Professor F. Max: translated Upanishads, 17, 75
My Creed: poems of SP, 137
Mylapore Monastery: 82, 86, 87, 89, 91, 94, 95, 96, 108, 109, 110, 170
My Song Garden: children's poems of DM, 160, 161

N

Nantucket: Glenn family summer home, 35–37, 58; DM in Nantucket, *131*
New York Vedanta Society: 7, 15-26, 67, 69, 80, 92, 114, 115, 168, 175
Nikhilananda, Swami: 171, 175
Nivedita: 99, 100, 103, 106, 108, 109

O

Open Portal: Poems by DM, 104, 156, 160, 161

P

Paramananda, Swami: DM's first meeting with, 77–83; *81*, first books, 85–86; 88, 98, to Boston, 108–109; work in Boston, 113–132; *121, 127*, new work in CA, 138–156; *139, 148, 150, 153*, care for child, 162; 164, 167, 168, correspondence with DM, 169; final tributes, 170–173

Path of Devotion, The: 85, 86, 143
Prabuddha Bharata: DM wrote for, 9; 24, 72, 75, 160, 163
Premananda, Swami: 94, 106, 107, 113, 114, 169, 177
Proctor, Adelaide Anne (poet): 172

Q

Queensberry Street Centre: 120, DM in front of, *121;* original building, *122; 123,* 125, *127,* 140

R

Ramakrishna, His Life and Sayings: compiled by DM, 74–75
Ramakrishna Mission: 10, 100, 119
Ramakrishnananda, Swami: 82, 83, 86, beloved teacher, 87–*97; 89,* 103, *108, 109,* 110, 111, 115, 117, 120, 163, DM correspondence with, 169–171
Ramakrishna Order: 22, emblem of the order, *24;* 71, in Madras, 87–88; 110
Ramakrishna, Sri: 22–24, DM visions of, 72–74; gospel by "M", 78; 83, DM love for, 84; living presence, 89; 91, 93, 94, 103, in his presence, 104–108; 110; St. Francis of Assisi, 111; lock of hair, 113–114; 124, 146, vision of at AA, 164–165; hundredth anniversary of birth, 167–168; 173, 174
Rhythm of Life, The: poems of SP, 137
Ridgely Manor, NY: 23, 114

S

Sabatier, Paul: scholar of St. Francis of Assisi, 59
Sarada Devi (see Holy Mother)
Saradananda, Swami: 103, 104, 105, 107, 120, 137, 163
Satya Prana, Sister (Eliza Kissam): 114, 117, 119, *121, 149,* 172
Seva, Sister (Rhoda May Gladwell): 125, 136, 139, *149,* 172
Shanta, Sister (Mary Lacy Staib): 125, 140
Sherwood, Katharine: 113, 114, 117, *121,* 147
Shivananda, Swami: 106, president of RK Math, 137; 145, 147, 148, 163, 164, 169
Soul's Secret Door: poems of SP 137
Song of the Sannyasin, The: 170
Spiritual Teachings of Swami Brahmananda: 11, 95, 170
Sri Ramakrishna and His Disciples: 9, 110, 160
Sri Ramakrishna and Saint Francis of Assisi: 59, 111, 160
Staib, Mary Lacy (see Shanta, Sister)
St. Francis of Assisi: 59, 111, 160, 168
St. Paul's Methodist Episcopal Church: 28, 33, 81
Swami Paramananda and His Work: 125, 143, 159, 160

Swami Ramakrishnananda, The Apostle of Sri Ramakrishna to the South: 88, 110
"Swami Ramakrishnananda, Sannyasin and Teacher": 163
Swami Vivekananda in the West, New Discoveries: 20

T

Tapasyananda, Swami: 88, 110
Temple of the Universal Spirit: 123, 145, *146*, *147*, 148, 167, 175
True Spirit of Religion Is Universal, The: 86
Thousand Island Park: VK teaching at, 17; 19, 84, 86

U

Udbodhan, India: home of Holy Mother, 100; 101, 102, 103

V

Vassar College: 42, *43*, *44*, 46, *47*, *48*, 49, 54, 58
Vedanta in Practice: 86
Vedanta Kesari: 9, 110, 160, 163, 168, 170
Vedanta Monthly Bulletin: 75, 78, 79
Vedanta Society: 15-17, 19-26, 66, 67, growth of NY, 69; 70, 71, 75-78, 80, 82, 83, 92, 98, 114, 115, 168
Vedanta Society of New York: 10, 26, 76
Vigil, The: poems of SP, 137
Vimala, Sister (Alice Afsprung): 125
Virajananda, Swami: 110, 142, 169
Vishwa Mandir: 148
Viswamandir, Temple of the Universal Spirit: 145
Vivekananda, Swami: 9, 10, 13, 15-26, *19*, in Chicago, 61; 66, 69–80, 82, 84, 86, 91, 92, 97, 103, 109, 110, 114, 115, 120, 142, 146, 163, 170, 176

W

Waldo, Sarah Ellen (Haridasa): 17, 21, 71, 82, 85, 103, 115, 169
Walton, Georgina Frances Jones (see Daya, Sister)
Way of Peace and Blessedness, The: 86
World's Parliament of Religions: 15, 61

Y

Yogin-ma: personal attendent to Holy Mother, 102-104; 163

www.ingramcontent.com/pod-product-compliance
Lightning Source LLC
Chambersburg PA
CBHW040551010526
44110CB00054B/2598